Life with Two Languages

Life with Two Languages

An Introduction to Bilingualism

François Grosjean

Harvard University Press

Cambridge, Massachusetts, and London, England

10   9   8   7   6   5   4

Library of Congress Cataloging in Publication Data

Grosjean, François.
    Life with two languages.

    Bibliography: p.
    Includes index.
    1. Bilingualism.   I. Title.
P115.G76   404'.2   81-23772
ISBN 0-674-53091-8   AACR2

*A ma femme Lysiane, pour ses encouragements
et son bilinguisme éclairant, and to my sons,
Marc and Eric, for their monolingualism,
so categorical and yet so natural*

Preface

This book is about people who use two or more languages in their everyday life. Contrary to general belief, bilinguals are rarely equally fluent in their languages; some speak one language better than another, others use one of their languages in specific situations, and others still can only read or write one of the languages they speak. And yet, what characterizes all of them is that they interact with the world around them in two or more languages. Bilingualism is present in practically every country of the world, in all classes of society, in all age groups; in fact, it has been estimated that half the world's population is bilingual. This book is about those people.

There are several aims to this book. The first is to present a general and comprehensive introduction to bilingualism. Literally hundreds of books have been written about this topic, and yet most are either too advanced for the general reader or too specialized, dealing with such specific topics as bilingual education, the neurolinguistics of bilingualism, interference and code-switching, or the simultaneous acquisition of two languages by children. In this book I attempt to survey the vast and complex field of bilingualism: bilingualism in the world and in the United States, bilingualism in society, the bilingual child and the bilingual adult, and finally, bilingual speech and language. My hope is that readers will turn to more specialized works to deepen their understanding of the particular areas that interest them.

A second aim of this book is to separate fact from fiction about bilinguals and bilingualism. Using two or more languages in one's everyday life is as natural to the bilingual as using only one language is to the monolingual. People rarely make a conscious decision to become bilingual; it happens because their interaction with the world around them requires the use of two languages. In this book I attempt to show how natural this really is. For me, both as a bilingual and as a psycholinguist, bilingualism is neither a problem nor an asset but quite simply a fact of life that should be dealt with in as unbiased a way as possible.

This leads to the third aim of this book: to allow bilinguals to speak about their bilingualism. Too much has been written by people who see the topic through the eyes of monolinguals. To avoid this, I have included boxes in the text in which bilinguals tell about their experiences: how they use their two (or more) languages, their attitudes toward bilingualism, their educational experiences, their feelings about code-switching and language borrowing, and the differences they feel exist (or do not exist) between themselves and monolinguals. These first-hand accounts play an important role in the general organization of this book.

Two more points need to be made. The first is that although I have put the stress in the book on *bi*lingualism—the regular use of two languages—much of what is written applies equally well to multilingualism (as it does, for that matter, to bidialectalism and multidialectalism). The second point is that I do not deal with second-language learning in the classroom. Although first and second language acquisition in the bilingual child is examined closely in Chapter 4, the stress throughout the book is on the *natural* acquisition and use of two or more languages. Formal language learning is not discussed.

Because of its scope, this work should be of interest to a wide audience. It can be used as primary reading material in courses on bilingualism, languages in contact, language borrowing, and minority languages. It can also be used as supplementary reading in courses on the psychology of language, the sociology of language, general linguistics, elementary and secondary education, special education, speech and hearing, and political science. The linguist may wish to consult Chapter 6, which surveys the literature on bilingual speech and language. The psychologist may want to read Chapters 4 and 5, which deal with how the bilingual acquires and processes two languages, as well as the apparent effects of bilingualism. The educator will find extensive discussion of bilingualism and education in

Chapters 1 and 4 and of bilingual education in the United States in Chapter 2. The sociologist may want to read the sections that deal with linguistic minorities (Chapter 1) and those that examine attitudes to languages and language groups, biculturalism, language choice, and code-switching (in Chapter 3). This book is also written for the lay person interested in languages in contact and in bilingualism. I have attempted to reduce to a minimum the linguistic terminology and have written the book in a nontechnical style. It is my hope that the general public—among them many bilinguals—will read this book to learn more about people who live with two languages.

To conclude, I wish to thank the many people who have helped me in preparing this book. First and foremost are those who believed in it and who gave me their much-needed support throughout the project: Eric Wanner of Harvard University Press, friends and colleagues at Northeastern University, as well as the members of my family, especially my wife, Lysiane. I also wish to acknowledge the very kind and constant support of Dr. Einar Haugen. His writings were a great source of inspiration to me, as were the many hours we spent together talking about bilingualism. In addition, Dr. Haugen read and gave me written comments on every chapter. I could not have had a better mentor. My warmest thanks also go to the four reviewers of the book whose comments I found very helpful. A number of colleagues very kindly took the time to read chapters and to give me comments on them. They are: Robbin Battison, Maria Brisk, Jim Gee, Fred Genesee, Kenji Hakuta, Judy Kegl, Harlan Lane, Joanne Miller, Michel Paradis, Shana Poplack, Carlos Soares, Richard Tucker, Calvin Veltman, and Dorothy Waggoner. To all of them I express my deep appreciation. I also wish to thank the many bilinguals who agreed to share with me their experiences: many of their first-hand accounts are included in this book, and these give it a dimension that I believe important. I am indebted to all those who have helped me put this book together: Marjorie Goldstein, who gathered the "raw material" for me; Janie Simmons de Garcia, who checked the quotes and references; Kristine Smith, who drew the figures in Chapter 2; Ivy Dodge, who coordinated the typing effort; and Sheila Duquette, Valerie Hawkes-Howat, and Theresa Massa, who typed and retyped the manuscript. To all my sincere thanks. And finally I wish to express my deep appreciation to Peg Anderson for her very thorough and very constructive copy editing of the book.

Contents

Life with Two Languages

1 Bilingualism in the World

To the average person in the United States or Europe bilingualism—the regular use of two or more languages—is a rather special language phenomenon restricted to a few countries such as Canada, Belgium, or Switzerland, where, presumably, every citizen is bilingual. This average person would say that very few people in the world are bilingual or multilingual; the majority is monolingual, that is, uses only one language on a regular basis. After all, isn't Russian the language of all Russians, English the language of all Americans and British, French the language of all the French, and so on?

But if we question a citizen of an African or Asian nation, Tanzania or Malaysia, for example, we would get a very different answer: bilingualism is the norm; most people speak two or more languages, and a large proportion of the world's population is bilingual.

This second point of view is in fact much nearer the truth: bilingualism is present in practically every country of the world, in all classes of society, and in all age groups. In fact it is difficult to find a society that is genuinely monolingual. Not only is bilingualism worldwide, it is a phenomenon that has existed since the beginning of language in human history. It is probably true that no language group has ever existed in isolation from other language groups, and the history of languages is replete with examples of language contact leading to some form of bilingualism.

In this chapter I will describe the wide-ranging characteristics of bilingualism in the world, first examining where bilingualism can be found: in countries that are supposedly monolingual, such as Germany, Japan, and France; in "bilingual" countries such as Canada, Belgium, and Finland; and in "multilingual" countries such as India and the Soviet Union. Secondly, I will show how certain nations support their linguistic minorities whereas others neglect or repress them, and I will enumerate the problems—social, cultural, and educational—these minorities face. I will then discuss the origins of bilingualism and study such factors as military conquest and colonization, nationalism and political federalism, education, urbanization, and intermarriage. And I will end by describing the two main outcomes: prolonged and stable bilingualism or, as often happens, a shift to monolingualism. Above all in this chapter, I will attempt to show the truth of a statement made by Lewis (1976): "Bilingualism has been and is nearer to the normal situation than most people are willing to believe" (p. 151).

The Extent of Bilingualism

It is an interesting fact that no really precise statistics exist concerning the number and distribution of speakers of two or more languages in the nations of the world. Although almost all current encyclopedias and survey books list the main languages of the world, the number of people that speak them, and where they are spoken, there are no comparable figures on the use of two or more languages. This can be accounted for partly by the fact that there is no widely accepted definition of the concept of bilingualism. As we will see in a later chapter, the term has often been paired with such modifiers as "early" and "late," "receptive" and "productive," "fluent" and "nonfluent," "balanced," "functional," and so on. Also, not all countries or world institutions are interested in bi- or multilingualism, even when it affects them directly.

And yet, to the inquisitive researcher, bilingualism offers a fascinating and varied set of patterns, as shown by Mackey (1967, 1976). In the border areas between two language groups—as between Spanish-speaking Mexico and English-speaking America—economic and commercial factors lead many people to use both languages on a regular basis. Bilingualism is also present in specific areas of some countries where linguistic minorities are concentrated. Thus in Brittany most speakers of Breton (a Celtic language) also speak French, and in Wales, most users of Welsh (also a Celtic language) speak English. Bilingualism in some countries is spread throughout a population, as in Paraguay, where Guarani-Spanish bilingualism is found in all areas. In some parts of the world bilingualism exists mainly in urban areas: in the town of Madina, Ghana, for instance, over eighty different languages are in contact, and most inhabitants speak at least three languages (Berry, 1971). In New Guinea, on the other hand, where the society is still mainly rural, many inhabitants speak two or more languages, and in the area straddling the Brazil–Colombia border, a mere 10,000 people speak some twenty-five languages, and most individuals are bi- or trilingual (Sorensen, 1967).

Bilingualism is also common in certain occupations. For example, most of the construction workers in Switzerland are immigrant workers from Italy and speak either French or Swiss German, depending on the area of Switzerland, in addition to their native language. Many diplomats know and use several languages on a regular basis. Bilingualism may also vary according to social class. For example, all members of the aristocracy in Czarist Russia were bilingual in Russian and French, as is clearly illustrated in Tolstoy's *War and Peace,* where the main characters often switch from Russian to French. Both age and sex may be factors in bilingualism; for example, the wives of immigrant workers from Turkey or Portugal living in Germany rarely learn German, whereas their husbands must have some knowledge of the language in order to work. Finally, bilingualism is affected by the degree of contact between two language groups; in Belgium, for example, there is everyday contact between Flemish and French speakers, whereas Lapps in Sweden know some Swedish but do not often have to use it (Mackey, 1967).

National Patterns of Bilingualism

These patterns could be expanded and others added, but I prefer to begin by examining the extent of bilingualism within the nations of the world. A first approach proposed by Mackey (1967) is to compare the number of languages in the world to the number of countries. If there are about as many languages as there are nations, it will indicate that bilingualism is not such an important phenomenon after all. But the more language groups there are, and the more concentrated they are in specific geographical or political areas, the more likely the spread of bilingualism. The reason is quite simply that different language groups living next to each other need to communicate. Either one group will learn the language of the other, or both groups will learn a third language for between-group communication, or lingua franca. The overall result will be a state of bilingualism.

As it happens, there are from 3,000 to 4,000 languages in the world today (without counting the many sign languages of the deaf) and only about 150 countries to house them in. Although I will qualify this statement below, it is a first indication of how widespread language contact within countries must be. Most countries house a number of different languages, which *de facto* leads to language contact and bilingualism. Mackey (1967) points out two factors that modify this statement somewhat, however. First, some languages are numerically more important that others: in fact, eleven languages are spoken by as many as 70 percent of the world's population. The most important numerically are Chinese, about 900 million speakers; English, about 400 million; Spanish, about 231 million; Hindi, about 154 million; and Russian, about 130 million. The great majority of languages are spoken by far fewer people. For example, Afrikaans, a South African language, is spoken by 7 million people; Aymara, a South American Indian language, is used by 1 million speakers in Bolivia and Peru; and Batak, an Indonesian language, is spoken by 2 million. And many other languages (the 300 or so American Indian languages, for example) are used by even smaller groups, in some cases less than a thousand.

The second factor qualifying the "many languages but few countries" statement is that some languages (English, Spanish, Portuguese, for example) are spoken natively in several countries, and others are restricted to very specific areas that correspond either to the political borders of a country (Icelandic is spoken only in Iceland), or to a particular geographical region (Basque is spoken in a small area divided between France and Spain).

However, even though not all languages have the same numerical importance or the same geographical distribution, most countries do house a number of different languages. Tiny Luxembourg has three languages: French, German, and Luxembourgian; Switzerland houses Swiss German, French, Italian, and Romansh; India has about 200 classified languages; Russia houses about 122; and other areas of the world are characterized by an even greater concentration of languages. On the island of New Guinea, for example, about 700 different languages—as different from one another as are French, English, and Russian—are spoken by not many more than three million inhabitants. This kind of language concentration cannot help but lead to bilingualism.

Bilingualism exists in three types of countries: "monolingual," "bilingual," and "multilingual." It is important to note that this progression in no way reflects the degree of bilingualism that really exists in these countries; as we will see, many so-called monolingual countries have a high percentage of speakers who use two or more languages on a regular basis, whereas many multilingual countries have rather few bilinguals. I have adopted this three-category approach to clarify the problem.

Monolingual Nations

It is practically impossible to locate a genuinely monolingual country, that is, one that does not contain one or several linguistic minorities whose members use, to some extent at least, both the majority and minority languages. Even in the countries of Europe or of North and South America, which we think of as monolingual, one is hard put to find a truly monolingual nation. France has a number of linguistic minorities: Bretons, Basques, Alsatians, Flemings, Catalans, Corsicans, Occitans, and North Africans. It has been estimated that approximately 6 percent of the present population of France uses two languages on a regular basis. In Great Britain, in addition to Welsh and Scottish Gaelic (the former used by about 800,000 speakers), one also finds Indo-Aryan and Dravidian languages, spoken by immigrant groups from India, Pakistan, and East Africa, as well as West Indian Creole. And in Spain one finds speakers not only of Castilian Spanish but also of Catalan, Galician, and Basque. It has been calculated that some 12 million people in Spain speak a minority language, out of a population of 38 million.

BASICALLY MONOLINGUAL NATIONS Two countries that at first appear to be totally monolingual are Japan and Germany. Although Japan is a highly monolingual and monocultural society, it does have three small minority groups—Ainu, Koreans, and Chinese—totalling about a million in number, or 0.7 percent of the population. The oldest group is the Ainu, an indigenous Caucasoid people who now live only on the northern island of Hokkaido. The older members of the Ainu group still lead a traditional life and speak Ainu with one another, but the younger generations have been totally assimilated into Japanese society. The Koreans are the most numerous minority, representing about 0.5 percent of the population. Both the Koreans and Chinese were brought to Japan, often by force, in the 1920s and the 1930s. They live in the industrial cities and lead an existence separate from that of the Japanese majority. They speak their respective languages (although most younger Koreans and Chinese also speak Japanese fluently), attend their own schools, and participate in their own community affairs. The Japanese make little effort to integrate them into the society, and there are numerous cases of discrimination against Koreans and Chinese in employment. Thus, although Japan is one of a very few countries with such a high proportion of people of one language and one culture (99.3 percent of the population is of Japanese origin), it is certain to retain its Chinese and Korean minorities, and hence bilingualism will continue for generations to come.

West Germany also appears to be totally monolingual. By the end of the two world wars, the country had lost its territories in the north and east that contained a number of linguistic minorities (Danish, Polish, and Czech, for example), and the current borders of East and West Germany pretty much reflect—without counting Austria and Switzerland—the borders of the German language. And yet, in addition to 62 million West Germans there are about 4 million immigrant workers who speak their native tongue as well as some German on an every day basis. Immigrant workers first started to arrive in 1955 when the rebuilt German economy needed cheap labor. It has been estimated that about 10 percent of the labor force is made up of immigrant workers—from Turkey (1 million), Yugoslavia (700,000), Italy (500,000), Greece (300,000), and smaller numbers from Spain, Portugal, Holland, Austria, France, and so on. They are concentrated in industrial areas such as Berlin, Frankfurt, Stuttgart, and the Ruhr.

As in other industrialized European nations, immigrant workers are brought in to fill the jobs that the country's own people do not want (those in heavy industry and textiles, and badly paid jobs such as construction work or garbage removal). But the "host" country does very little to help these immigrants and their families integrate themselves, at least temporarily, into the society. In fact, the official policy is to discourage them from settling down: they make up a temporary labor force that is hired or fired (and sent home) at the whim of the employers, and nothing is supposed to be done to alter this (Skutnabb-Kangas, 1981). The well-known saying clearly reflects the problem of these immigrant workers: "They called for labor but human beings arrived."

In a later section of this chapter we will examine the various problems faced by linguistic minorities that have lived in a country for generations. Immigrant workers face many similar problems, along with hostility from the native population, segregation, cultural shock, and lack of official support for cultural and language maintenance. There are few or no radio and TV programs in the group's language, few courses to help them learn the language of the "host" country, little if any bilingual education for their children, and so on. What is true in West Germany is also true in France, with its 2 million North Africans; Great Britain, with Indians, Pakistanis, and West Indians; Scandinavia, with Greeks, Turks, and others; and other industrialized nations. All these monolingual countries have growing linguistic minorities, most of whose members are bilingual. The tragic problem is that these countries do not want to face the human repercussions of bringing in cheap labor, which leads to tension, grief, and violence.

BASICALLY MULTILINGUAL NATIONS So far we have talked about monolingual countries in which the official language is the mother tongue of the great majority of the inhabitants—what Kloss (1967) would call a genuine nation state. Thus French is the language of the great majority in France, and Swedish that of most inhabitants in Sweden. However, almost all these countries do have linguistic minorities which have either been present for centuries or which have arrived rather recently. Other countries are officially monolingual in that there is only one official language, but they house many linguistic minorities. Numerically, this category is much more important than that of the nation states.

In all parts of the world there are countries with one official language but with numerous other languages, especially in Africa and Asia as a result of colonization. Their political boundaries rarely reflect linguistic boundaries. On becoming independent, these countries had the problem of choosing an official administrative language (it therefore had to have a written form and a varied and extensive vocabulary) that could serve as a means of communication with neighboring states and as a symbol of nationhood. It was important to choose a language that would not favor one ethnic group over another, thus creating unnecessary tensions and a potential cleavage within the young nation. Two basic types of solution were adopted. The first was to choose a language spoken by a linguistic group within the country, as in Tanzania with Swahili as the official language, the Philippines with Filipino (based on native Tagalog), Indonesia with Bahasa-Indonesia, and Malaysia with Malay. Kloss (1968), calls these nations "endoglossic." The second solution was to choose a language from outside the nation, as in Sierra Leone,

Zambia, and Ghana with English as the official language, and Chad, Gabon, Senegal, and Upper Volta with French. Kloss calls these "exoglossic" states.

We will examine both types of country, but it is important to note that many of these nations, although officially represented by just one language, are in fact highly multilingual. In Ghana, for example, there are some fifty different languages, and in Nigeria some four hundred. Lebanon has fifteen ethnic minorities and a number of languages, the more important being Arabic, the official language, and, French, English, Armenian, and Turkish. Practically half the population is bilingual in Arabic and French, others are bilingual in Arabic and English, and many are trilingual in Arabic, French, and English. One trilingual writes: "Bi- or trilingualism is very common in Lebanon. It is widely accepted, even expected of you. There are newspapers and radio and TV programs in all three languages, and many road signs, legal documents, telephone directories, and so on are in Arabic and French." In the Philippines one finds over a hundred indigenous languages and a high level of bilingualism in the local vernacular and Filipino, and in this language and the two ex-colonial languages, Spanish and English.

In addition to speaking their local language, the inhabitants of these countries often use a lingua franca to communicate with members of other language groups. This may be a natural language, such as Hausa in western Africa or Swahili in eastern Africa, or one that has developed from the contact of several languages—a pidgin, such as Fanagalo in South East Africa. In addition, a European language may be the medium of instruction in the schools, so that inhabitants of these countries are often trilingual.

Tanzania is an interesting case of a country that has adopted a native language as its official language. Swahili was chosen over others for a number of reasons, according to O'Barr (1976) and Myers Scotton (1978). First, it was spoken as a first language by very few inhabitants—about 10 percent of the population—which meant that giving it prominence did not favor one language group over another. Second, Swahili had long been a lingua franca in Kenya, Uganda, and Tanzania. Third, it had been the medium of primary schooling in Tanzania for some years, and fourth, it was linked to the movement for independence.

However, Swahili, the official language since 1967, coexists within each region with local languages and with English, the colonial language. Each language has its own domain of use, leading to extensive bi- or trilingualism. It has been reported that up to 90 percent of

---

BOX 1.1   **BILINGUALS SPEAK**

Attitudes Toward Bilingualism in Africa

An Akan-Fanti-English trilingual from Ghana: People take pride in being bilingual because they are generally looked upon with respect. Some of the languages are dominant, and being able to speak them is a great advantage. Ghana really encourages bilingualism. This is evident from the fact that the local languages are included in both the primary and high school curricula.

My experience as a bilingual is a great one. This is because I have been able to communicate freely and with ease with others who are not my kinsmen.

An Otetela-French-English trilingual from Zaire: In a country like Zaire where there are so many languages, everyone speaks at least two languages. Bilingualism is part of the Zairean's culture. My attitude toward my languages and bilingualism in Zaire is very positive since it gives one a different perspective when looking at things.

A Luganda-Swahili-English trilingual from Uganda: Everybody in my country is encouraged to speak as many languages as he or she can master. As a bilingual I find that I can relate to a wide range of people who come from different parts of Uganda.

---

the population is bilingual in a local language and Swahili. The local languages are used at home, in village activities, and in indigenous religious activities. Swahili is the language of the schools and hospitals, of government and political meetings, of posters and pamphlets, and of regional trade and commerce, while English retains its preponderance in certain government offices, in the universities, and in international business. Thus, although the official language is Swahili, and Tanzania could be placed among other monolingual countries, in fact it has one of the highest proportions of bilinguals. As in other African nations, bi- or trilingualism is considered quite natural, an everyday fact of life. In Box 1.1, trilinguals from three different African nations express their attitudes toward bilingualism. It is only when one turns to societies where bilingualism is rarer or where there is an open policy of assimilation toward minorities that such expressions as "the problems of bilingualism" or "the deficiencies of bilingual" appear.

One officially monolingual nation that has a high percentage of bilinguals is Paraguay. It is one of the few countries in South

America (Peru is another) where an Indian language—in this case Guarani—is given almost the same importance as the colonial language, Spanish. Spanish is the official language of government business, but Guarani is the national language, used on various public occasions, in the media, and so on. (Nations that do not want to be officially bilingual but wish to recognize the use of two languages in the country will often choose to make one the official language and the other the national language.) About 90 percent of the population in Paraguay use Guarani as a first language and about 60 percent speak Spanish, so the proportion of bilinguals in the country is about 55 percent.

As Rubin (1968) has reported, Guarani has remained an important language because during the initial period of contact between the native population and the Spanish settlers there was constant interaction and collaboration. A high proportion of Spanish-Guarani households were established at that time. In addition, the country remained isolated from other South American nations for a long period, thus allowing the nation to be built on both Guarani and Spanish cultures. The division of functions between Guarani and Spanish has maintained the high degree of bilingualism: Guarani is the language of the rural areas, of the home, emotions, and friendship, whereas Spanish is the language of public occasions, of the schools, the army, and official matters. The Paraguayans are extremely proud of their native language and realize that it is a unifying force in the country; in this sense Paraguay can be considered a nation devoid of any real linguistic problems—a very rare phenomenon in the world today.

I have already mentioned a number of factors that have led some countries—such as Zambia and Ghana—to choose an outside language (English) as the official language: the need for a written medium; its international character; the fear of internal cleavage when preeminence is given to a local language, and so on. However, in some cases the colonial language is chosen when a local language could serve just as well. Senegal is a good example of this; Wolof, a lingua franca in West Africa, is used by a large proportion (about 90 percent) of the Senegalese, and yet French, spoken by far fewer inhabitants, is the official language. One reason for this, according to Myers Scotton (1978) is that the colonial language is a means of access to the higher levels of the society; in a word, English and French are barriers between the elite (an extremely small minority, often educated in Britain and France) and the masses. Thus, in Senegal, French remains the key to social mobility. This is also the case in Niger; Hausa is spoken all over the country but French, spoken by a minority, is the official language.

This situation can only create resentment and antagonism, and hence the linguistic future of such nations is far from clear. Yet such rather unnatural situations have been known to last for generations. The elite, sometimes with the help of the ex-colonial power, instead of fostering a native language by giving it a writing system and developing its technical and scientific vocabulary, may even repress public use of a language. In this way the elite maintains its hold on public affairs through use of the outside language. A rather sad example of how far this can go is Haiti, where the official language is French but the actual language of the inhabitants is Creole. (French and Creole are mutually unintelligible; that is, a monolingual speaker of French cannot communicate with a speaker of Creole and vice versa.) Only about 10 to 15 percent of Haitians speak French, and only about 5 percent write it, whereas *all* Haitians speak Creole. In this sense Haiti is quite unlike African nations that house numerous languages and where an official language is chosen for administrative and economic reasons. Haiti is really monolingual, both officially and linguistically, as only a small proportion of the population is bilingual, but the language of the people is not the official language. This creates many problems and leads to such situations as political speeches being given in French and then explained and discussed in Creole!

To sum up, I want to stress that bilingualism is present in varying degrees in all countries that are officially monolingual: some, such as Japan, have few bilinguals; others, such as the Western European nations, have increasing numbers; and others still, such as many African nations, have very large proportions of bilinguals. As we will see, there is probably a larger proportion of bilinguals in monolingual nations than in bilingual and multilingual countries.

Bilingual Nations

A number of nations, such as Canada, Czechoslovakia, Cyprus, Israel, and Finland, have two official languages and are thus officially bilingual. Belgium is officially trilingual with Flemish, French, and German, but I will add it to this category as this is its best-known classification. The constitutions of these countries give full equality to the two languages, so governance is in essence bilingual: public administration, debates in parliament, and publication of laws all take place in two languages. But as Mackey (1967) has stressed, there is often a world of difference between the official, *de jure* bilingualism of a country and the actual, *de facto* bilingualism of its inhabitants. "In fact there are fewer bilingual people in the bilingual countries than there are in the so-called unilingual [monolingual] countries. For it is not always realized that bilingual countries were created not to promote bilingualism, but to guarantee the maintenance and use of two or more languages in the same nation" (p. 11). Concerning first the number of bilinguals in bilingual countries, a few examples will clarify Mackey's point. In Canada, where both French and English are official languages, only about 13 percent of the population speak both languages regularly, and in Belgium the proportion of speakers that use both Flemish and French on a daily basis is not much higher, only 15 percent. What a difference from some of the monolingual countries I have mentioned, such as Tanzania or Kenya!

That some countries are officially bilingual is due, as Mackey suggests, to a conscious effort by the central government to guarantee the use of two languages, of which one is used by a minority group. Thus, for example, Finland is officially bilingual although some 92 percent of its inhabitants speak Finnish. But as a gesture to the Swedish minority (about 7 percent of the population), and to protect and maintain Swedish, the country has been made officially bilingual. In Ireland, which is officially bilingual in English and Irish Gaelic, only about 2 percent speak Gaelic (the rest of the population is monolingual in English), but for historical and national reasons a great effort is being made to maintain and even revive Gaelic. In Canada we see again that a linguistic majority coexists with a linguistic minority: about 67 percent of the population speaks English as a first language, whereas only 26 percent are French speaking; the remainder of the population speak a Canadian Indian or Eskimo language or a European immigrant language.

When deciding on an official policy of bilingualism, countries often choose between the personality principle and the territorial principle. The personality principle states that bilingualism is the official policy throughout the country. Thus a speaker of language X can use that language to deal with the administration and can have his or her children educated in that language anywhere in the country. The whites in South Africa, the majority of whom are bilingual in Afrikaans and English, are governed by this principle, and their children are educated in their respective mother tongue. The territorial principle, on the other hand, states that the country is divided into different monolingual areas, each with its own official language used by the administration and in the schools, and individuals are required to use that language when dealing with the governing bodies of the area. The aim of this principle is to allow each language group to protect its own language and culture. Switzerland is a fine example: seventeen cantons are officially German speaking, three are French speaking, one is Italian speaking, and only four are bi- or trilingual.

Below we will examine the case of two bilingual countries, Belgium and Canada, that have opted for different principles: Belgium is now governed according to the territorial principle, and Canada has chosen the personality principle at the federal level. We will see that the linguistic minorities in both countries, although quite important numerically, have had a long history of struggle to obtain equal language rights. An official policy of bilingualism was instituted as a way of guaranteeing the linguistic rights of these minorities, but neither country has yet solved all of its linguistic problems.

BELGIUM   The 10 million inhabitants of Belgium are made up of two main language groups: the French-speaking Walloons represent 41 percent of the population, and the Flemings, who speak Flemish—a dialect of Dutch—represent 58 percent. (A German-speaking minority represents about 1 percent of the population.) Unlike countries where the language groups are dispersed throughout, in Belgium the north and west (Flanders) are Flemish speaking, and the south and east (Wallonia) are French speaking. The only exception is the capital city of Brussels, in Flemish-speaking Flanders, where 80 percent of the population speaks French.

As Lorwin (1972) writes, when Belgium became independent in 1830, the Flemish speakers were already more numerous than the French speakers, but the elite, whether Flemish or Walloon, were all French-speaking. French was spoken in the parlor, Flemish in the kitchen. This situation reflected in part the economic imbalance between rural, underdeveloped Flanders and booming, industrialized Wallonia and in part the fact that French was (and still is) a language of world status. Throughout the nineteenth century, French was the passport to upward social mobility: the language of instruction in secondary schools and colleges and the language of the church and administration. Under growing pressure from the Flemings, schools in Flanders started to use Flemish as the medium of instruction in 1883. In 1898 official texts started to be published in both languages, but it was only when equal manhood suffrage was instituted in 1919 that the numerical strength of the Flemish population began to produce any real gains in their struggle for equal linguistic rights. The first Flemish university was opened in Ghent in 1930, and just before World War II a series of laws finally put Flemish on a par with French in education, the law, the armed forces, and so on.

Since then the "Fleming problem" has been replaced by the "Walloon problem": the coal, steel, and textile industries that made the fortune of Wallonia have grown old and less competitive. The region no longer attracts new industries, and the Walloon businesses have lacked the necessary dynamism to escape the current slump. The Flemings, on the other hand, are not only more numerous and dynamic, but they control the newer industries—electronics, oil refineries—and they are now the richer group. The linguistic majority is now the economic majority, and this has created much resentment among French-speaking Belgians. An additional element of stress is that Brussels, largely a French-speaking city, is in Flemish territory. The Flemish speaker in Brussels sometimes must resort to French to make herself understood, and the French inhabitant is likely to have problems when he wants to live in the suburbs controlled by the Flemings.

This difficult linguistic situation is reflected in national politics, and great care is taken not to favor one linguistic group over another. In the last twenty years, disputes over language have led to general strikes and the toppling of numerous national governments. The federal solution that is being enforced at the moment is what Lorwin (1972) calls "territorial unilingualism." In 1970 the country was divided into four linguistic areas: a French area, a Dutch (Flemish) area, a German area, and a bilingual area that includes Brussels. Only in the bilingual area are both French and Flemish used in the public services and schools; in the Brussels post office, for instance, there are separate windows for French and Flemish speakers. In the other areas, the language of the schools and the administration is that of the area. The territorial principle and the long-standing mutual distrust between the Flemings and the Walloons explain why even with eight years of second-language learning (French for the Flemish-speaking children and Flemish for the French-speaking children), only 15 percent of Belgians are bilingual. In Box 1.2 a Belgian gives his own account of the linguistic situation in his country. It remains to be seen whether the new territorial policy of the government will allow "bilingual" Belgium to overcome, once and for all, 150 years of language strife.

BOX 1.2   BILINGUALS SPEAK

The Linguistic Situation in Belgium

Every child at school learns both languages starting in early primary school. Unfortunately, after so many years of learning that second language [six to eight years], only a small percentage of them can be called bilingual. Several factors seem to explain this rejection. One of these is that our early education is often biased by the fact that our parents transmit prejudices about the other group. Therefore it is sometimes hard to find the motivation for learning the other language. French-speaking people especially are very unwilling to learn Flemish, as the only places where they could use it are Belgium and Holland. Flemish-speaking people do learn and know French much better, because French is a much more useful and international language.

Many public services are supposedly bilingual, but very often employees that speak both languages are unwilling to speak the other language even if people address them in that language. Sometimes you may ask a question in French but the person will answer in Flemish and a conversation may go on like that without anyone being willing to speak the other language. Sometimes it is easier to ask for information in English because then you are sure you will get an answer!

CANADA   Canada is another officially bilingual country where the linguistic rights of the minority group, the French, have always been a subject of controversy. Of the 24 million Canadians, about 67 percent speak English as a first language and 26 percent speak French. The rest of the population—Native Americans and European immigrants—such as Germans and Italians in Ontario, Ukrainians in the western provinces—use their native languages on a regular basis. French Canadians are concentrated in Quebec (where they constitute 87 percent of the population) and New Brunswick (34 percent), but there are pockets of French speakers in Ontario and the other provinces.

The current linguistic situation in Canada can best be understood by scanning its history. In the early seventeenth century both the English and the French established settlements in Quebec and for awhile lived in relative peace. There was some intermarriage between the two groups, and hence some settlers were bilingual in English and French. The English came over in greater numbers, however, and by 1762, at the end of the Seven Years' War, there were 2 million English settlers in North America as compared to

80,000 French. In 1763, in the Treaty of Paris, France gave up its territories in Canada (and all those east of the Mississippi) to the British, and for two hundred years the French-speaking Canadians were left to their own fate, culturally and linguistically.

Although the 1774 Quebec Act guaranteed the French their religious rights and civil institutions, and the 1867 Confederation Act gave internal rule to the Canadian provinces, French Canadians had very little say in the running of the nation or of their own province, Quebec. They sought refuge in their rural-oriented, church-dominated society while the English dominated the economic and political life of the country. Thus, up to the 1960s the French were considered (and were led to consider themselves) second-class citizens. Speaking and writing English was the means of access to government service, higher education, and business. Even in Quebec the English Canadians ran the economy: they set up and managed the factories and department stores, and they chose their white-collar workers from among the English-speaking French. This explains why bilingualism in Canada is very much a one-way street; although the total number of bilinguals is only about 13 percent, it is the French Canadians who are bilingual, not the English. Only 8 percent of the English-speaking Canadians use both French and English on a regular basis, compared to 33 percent of French Canadians. And the farther away one goes from Quebec, the more the French minority is forced to be bilingual to meet everyday needs: 53 percent of the French in New Brunswick are bilingual and 81 percent in Ontario, for example.

In the 1960s, a "quiet revolution" took place among French Canadians: they secularized their schools, did away with the secular powers of the church, and became increasingly critical of English domination in all aspects of their lives. In 1963 a Royal Commission on Bilingualism and Biculturalism was set up by the federal government to study the status of English and French in the federal administration and to make recommendations on how to develop bilingualism at the federal level. The commission proposed using the personality principle, because it felt that the French minorities outside Quebec and the English minority inside Quebec would not be treated fairly by the territorial principle. Based on the work of the commission, the federal government passed the Official Languages Act in 1968–1969. English and French were declared official languages and were given equal status in all aspects of the federal administration. The Declaration of Status of Languages in the act reads: "The English and French languages are the official languages of Canada for all purposes of the Parliament and Government of Canada, and possess and enjoy equality of status and equal rights and privileges as to their use in all the institutions of the Parliament and Government of Canada."

The act underlined the government's intention of making the administration bilingual so that both English and French Canadians could address civil servants in their own language. Funds were allocated to second-language instruction, to minority students, and to the provincial governments to implement bilingual administrations. Bilingual school districts were to be set up in French-speaking areas where at least 10 percent of the population spoke English as a mother tongue, and in English-speaking areas where 10 percent spoke French, but this part of the act was never implemented. Its overall aim was to foster "institutional" bilingualism, not personal bilingualism. As the Royal Commission on Bilingualism and Biculturalism stressed, a bilingual country is not one where all the inhabitants have to speak two languages, but one where public and private institutions must provide services in two languages to citizens who may be monolingual.

Because each province in Canada is self-governing (like the states in the United States), the Official Languages Act has not had the impact it was expected to have. About one-third of French children outside Quebec still do not receive their schooling in French; many English-speaking civil servants are reticent to learn French; and the media do not offer as much air time in French as French Canadians would like. However, it is encouraging that many speakers of English, especially in Quebec, are agreeing to learn and to use French, and recent census reports suggest that bilingualism is growing among the school-age population, especially among those of English mother tongue. In every province or region except one, the proportion of students who are bilingual exceeds that of the general population.

When the Official Languages Act was passed, the people of Quebec were not as favorable to it as was the federal administration in Ottawa. This was because bilingualism in a minority group is often synonymous with assimilation of that group. If all Québecois became bilingual in French and English and used both languages in exactly the same situations, there would be no need to retain both languages, and the language that would be retained might well be the dominant language of the country, English. As Chaput, a Québecois, wrote in 1961: "The more bilingual our children become, the more they use English; the more they use English, the less they find French useful; the less they find French useful, the more they use English. The paradox of French-Canadian life is the following: the more we become bilingual, the less it is necessary to be bilingual" (in Saint-Jacques, 1976; p. 58, my translation).

In the early 1970s, the French language in Quebec was felt to be in danger: French Québecois were emigrating to other provinces in search of work; the birthrate had diminished considerably; immigrants to Quebec chose to learn English and not French, and English remained the dominant language in the domain of work. In a word, although French was the majority language of the province, one could live in Quebec without knowing any French (Saint-Jacques, 1976). To this must be added a change in attitude among Québecois: they no longer felt they were members of a Canadian minority; instead they saw themselves as a French-speaking majority in Quebec. This situation led the government of Quebec to run counter to the federal policy of bilingualism and to pass the Chartre de la Langue Française in 1977, which made French the sole official language of the province. Businesses were to adopt French as the working language (they were given a few years to do so); the children of immigrants were to be taught in French; all official documents were to be in French only; and so on. The members of the English minority retained the right to educate their children in English, but only if the parents could prove that they themselves had been educated in English in Quebec.

It is too early to see whether this monolingual policy, similar in fact to that of many of the English-speaking provinces, will allow French to be maintained, and even develop, in Quebec. It is difficult to see at this time how such a policy can coexist over time with the federal policy of bilingualism. Although much has been done in Canada, and especially in Quebec, to erase two hundred years of English domination, the situation is still far from being stable.

To conclude, it is important to stress that "bilingual" countries do not promote individual bilingualism and do not contain many bilinguals; their linguistic role is to guarantee the use of the languages spoken within their border and to help ease, when possible, tensions between the different linguistic groups.

Multilingual Nations

Kloss (1968) points out two types of "multilingual" countries. On the one hand, there are the countries, which he terms plurilingual, where the main national languages are recognized as official languages. For example, in Switzerland the three recognized languages are Swiss German, spoken by 65 percent of the population; French, used by 18 percent; and Italian, by 12 percent. Romansh, a language very similar to Latin, spoken by 1 percent of the population, has been given the status of a national language. Singapore has four official languages: Chinese, Malay, Tamil, and English. On the other hand, there are those countries that have a large number of national languages, of which for practical purposes only some are considered official. Thus in India fourteen national languages are listed in the constitution, but Hindi, and to a lesser degree English, is the official language.

These countries have chosen to be officially multilingual for very much the same reasons that other countries are bilingual. They wish to recognize the linguistic identity of the groups that make up the country, and they want to help certain linguistic minorities maintain and "defend" their language against the larger groups. To do this, almost all of these countries have adopted the territorial principle in preference to the personality principle. Yugoslavia is a good example. This multilingual and multiethnic nation of some 21 million inhabitants is composed of six republics and two autonomous regions, six ethnic groups (Serbs, Croats, Slovenes, Macedonians, Montenegrins, and Muslims) and nine national minorities, the most important being the Albanians, Hungarians, Turks, and Slovaks. Each republic has its own official language and laws respecting the linguistic and cultural rights of its minorities. Thus the Republic of Slovenia guarantees the rights of its two minorities, the Hungarians and the Italians. In addition, Article 33 of the Yugoslav Constitution states that all citizens have equal rights and duties without distinction as to nationality, race, religion, sex, language, education, and social condition.

As in the bilingual countries, the inhabitants of multilingual countries are not automatically bi- or multilingual. In India only about 10 percent of the population uses two languages regularly. And, although all the official languages have equal status, one or two languages usually predominate, either officially, as Hindi and English in India, and Russian in the Soviet Union, or *de facto*, as German and French in Switzerland. One way of determining the real status of a language in a multilingual country is to find out which language is learned and used by the people for whom it is not a native language. In Switzerland, for example, very few Swiss learn Romansh or Italian, but most speakers of Romansh and Italian learn and often use either German or French. The four languages of

Switzerland do not therefore share the same status. Inhabitants of a country are well aware of the unequal status of the country's languages, as can be seen in the jokes people tell one another. A Belgian joke goes:

> What do you call a person who speaks three languages?
> A trilingual.
> What do you call a person who speaks two languages?
> A bilingual.
> And what do you call a person who only speaks one language?
> A Walloon!

A second way to determine the status of the languages in bi- or multilingual countries is to find out which language borrows more from the others. The one that is the most influenced is the less prestigious. Thus Canadian French, which long remained a low-prestige, minority language in Canada, has borrowed extensively from English, whereas English, the language of the dominant group numerically, politically, and economically, has hardly borrowed from Canadian French.

Multilingualism can create certain problems, despite (or maybe because of) a lenient linguistic policy on the part of the central government. The Hapsburg Empire, which stretched from Vienna to the Black Sea and included a number of now independent nations, is a good example. German was the lingua franca throughout the empire, but each of the eleven nations retained its own language for its official business. However, as Simon (1969) suggests, the question of official recognition of different languages became an issue of national prestige with strong emotional undertones, and the unsettled linguistic issues not only disrupted the governance of the empire but were one of the factors that led to World War I. Simon gives an example of a railway station in a mixed language area that was not given a name because no agreement could be reached as to which language should come first on the sign. (The city was known as Goerz by the German-speaking inhabitants, Goricia by the Italian inhabitants, and Gorice by the Slovenian population.) This kind of problem often occurs in multilingual countries when the central government has no coherent linguistic policy, which is why many multilingual countries attempt to make one language "more official" than the others.

INDIA   A good example of a multilingual country is India. Of the 800 different vernaculars that were tabulated in the 1961 census, 200 can be classified as different languages and 33 have over a million speakers. According to Khubchandani (1978), the country is divided into four linguistic regions: the south is dominated by four Dravidian languages, Telugu, Tamil, Kannada, and Malayalam; the east, by three Indo-Aryan languages, Bengali, Oriya, and Assamese; the west has two main Indo-Aryan languages, Marathi and Gujarati; and the north center, where 46 percent of the inhabitants live has two main Indo-Aryan languages, Hindi-Urdu and Punjabi, and one Dardic language, Kashmiri. Hindi, spoken by 154 million, is the most widely used language in India; Urdu, which is very similar to Hindi but has a different writing system, has 29 million speakers. But a number of other languages are also used by large groups: Telugu, 45 million speakers; Bengali, 45 million; Marathi, 42 million; and Tamil, 38 million.

Fourteen languages are listed in the constitution as national languages; English is not one of these because it is the mother tongue of very few Indians, but it remains an important language for national and international communication and for higher education. The official language of the union is Hindi, with a provision to continue with English until it is no longer needed, but because there is major opposition to Hindi from the south (there is fear of political and economic domination from the Hindi-speaking north), the changeover from English to Hindi has been postponed indefinitely.

Thus India has a three-language formula (Apte, 1976): at the national level both English and Hindi are used for official communication (between states and the central government, for example), and each of the eighteen states in the union has an official state language. Hindi is the official language in five states; Marathi is the official language in Maharasthra, and Punjabi in Punjab. Three states use English as their official language. One should also mention that there are numerous languages in India that do not have official status; some have a written form and are used by millions of speakers, but many others do not have a written tradition and are used locally by a smaller number of inhabitants.

As Khubchandani (1978) notes, it is among speakers of these smaller languages that one finds the highest percentage of bilinguals, many of whom must learn one of the major languages in order to take part in the activities that are not wholly dependent on the monolingual community. However, although India is a multilingual country in that it houses numerous languages, it does not have a high percentage of bilinguals. In the 1961 census, only 42,-500,000 people—10 percent of the population—claimed they used a

---

BOX 1.3   **BILINGUALS SPEAK**

Bilingualism in India

A Marathi-Hindi-English trilingual: In India one must be at least bilingual—most people are; a large proportion are in fact trilingual. And it is quite common to come across people who know four or more languages well. Usually it is the native language of one's region, Hindi, and English. One may also learn the "neighbor" languages, particularly if living in a border region. Being bilingual in India is natural; it is expected, encouraged, approved, applauded. It is part of education.

---

subsidiary language on a regular basis. The two most-often claimed second languages are English (about 11 million) and Hindi (9 million). The intensity of bilingualism varies from one state to another, ranging from 2.5 percent of the population in Rajasthan to as much as 24 percent in New Delhi. The low percentages result from the fact that most Indians simply do not need to be bilingual—they manage very well in everyday life with only one language—along with the fact (pointed out by Khubchandani) that many speakers are quite unaware of their bilingual or multilingual behavior. For many, especially those in the Indo-Aryan group, switching from their native language to Hindi or Urdu is similar to switching styles (formal to colloquial, say) in English. When asked if they use a second language on a regular basis, many answer in the negative. In spite of the low degree of individual bilingualism, the general attitude toward speakers of other languages is usually very positive. As Pandit (1975) writes: "The Indian language speaker—whether it is Kannada or Punjabi—maintains his speech, no matter where [in India] he settles down or how long he has settled there. In order to settle down among other language speakers, an Indian does not have to give up his language. He is welcome despite his different language; speaking a different language does not make him an alien" (p. 81). In Box 1.3 an Indian student gives her impressions of what it means to be bilingual in India today.

THE SOVIET UNION   Lewis (1972) reports that there are about 122 languages in the Soviet Union, the most important in number being Russian (about 130 million speakers), Ukrainian (about 41 million), and Uzbek (9 million). The languages belong to five different groups, ranging from Indo-European (the group to which English,

French, and German belong) all the way to the Altaic group, which contains Manchurian and Mongolian. In the Russian Empire prior to 1917, the policy toward languages other than Russian was negative. Some were discouraged (printing in Ukrainian was forbidden, for example), and in general, the Czarist regime totally neglected other languages. Using Russian as one's main language was a prerequisite to social mobility.

After the 1917 revolution, regional languages were promoted: writing systems were devised for some sixty of them, and the "small" languages were enriched with cultural and technological terms often borrowed directly from Russian. Literacy programs were developed and books published in the regional languages. Although the authorities now encourage native languages, Russian is favored for a number of reasons. It is linked to a rich and varied cultural heritage and is the language of half the population and of the political leadership; mobility in the Communist party structure usually requires fluency in Russian. Also, because of the extensive multilingualism, there is need for a lingua franca, and Russian usually takes on that role. In addition, the authorities encourage learning Russian as a second language (in 1938 it was made a compulsory subject in all schools), and they exalt its vast vocabulary as a source of enrichment of minority languages.

However, a number of factors also favor the regional languages, as Lewis (1972) points out. Some languages, such as Ukrainian, are widely used; they have a written tradition and literature, an extensive technological and scientific vocabulary, and they play an important role in regional life. A second factor is cultural inertia; people maintain their language simply because it is there. A third factor is the usefulness of the regional language in facilitating the acquisition of Russian as a second language. And lastly, just as Russian has become a lingua franca in urban areas among immigrants with different language backgrounds, so too the regional language is adopted by immigrants to rural areas.

Bilingualism in Russia, although it is widespread, has never reached the levels of such countries as Paraguay (55 percent) or Tanzania (90 percent). The percentages in Russia range from 1 to 3 percent in the Russian, Abkhaz, and Estonian language groups to 30 and 40 percent for the Kurds and Slovaks. As with large language groups in other countries, the speakers of major languages are rarely bilingual (3 percent of Russian speakers, 6 percent of Ukrainians), whereas the small national groups within or next to larger linguistic communities are characterized by much higher levels of bilingualism. In addition, the more dispersed a language group is because of migration, the more bilingual it is. Internal migration has caused a marked increase in the number of language groups within each republic of the Soviet Union, so that at present most of the republics are starting to reflect the national multilingualism. Thus in the Russian Republic there are thirty-four different language groups; in the Ukraine, seventeen; in Latvia, fifteen. This situation is of course conducive to bilingualism, as members of different language groups in an area must adopt a lingua franca (very often Russian) to communicate with one another and with the local authorities.

To conclude, I stress once again that bilingualism is present throughout all nations in varying patterns of distribution. Such labels as monolingual, bilingual, and multilingual reflect more the linguistic policies of the individual countries toward their language groups than the degree of individual bi- or multilingualism that is found in those nations.

Language Policy and Linguistic Minorities

As we have seen, bilingualism is often a consequence of the contact between two linguistic groups that do not have the same numerical, political, and economic importance. When a country has large minority language groups, its multilingual aspect may be recognized and the linguistic rights of each group officially respected. This is the case, to some extent at least, in Belgium, Finland, Canada, the Soviet Union, and India. We also saw that in other countries that are officially monolingual but have numerous linguistic groups, a national language is promoted for social, political, and educational reasons, but local languages are considered very much a part of the social structure of the country (Tanzania, for example).

However, many countries contain linguistic minorities that are not officially recognized. Because these minorities are usually small, the countries that house them are considered monolingual; I mentioned Japan with its small Ainu, Korean, and Chinese minorities; Germany with its Turkish, Yugoslav, Italian, Greek, and Portuguese minorities; and France with its Basque, Breton, Alsatian, and North African minorities. These minorities have no official status, their languages are not recognized as national languages, and members of these groups must learn the majority language in order to interact with the majority linguistic group. In this sense, bilingualism is very much a social necessity: it opens the doors to education, jobs, the media, and public services. And what is more, little is done by the central government of these nation states to promote or maintain the minority languages. The policy of a country toward its minorities can range from open support and promotion of their languages and cultures, through neglect, to actual subjugation and repression. In what follows I first examine how a nation can support its minorities and then discuss the neglect and repression of linguistic groups.

Support of Linguistic Minorities

A nation that wishes to openly support and preserve its linguistic minorities can recognize minority languages in the national constitution and give them some official status in the regions where they are used. The government can also allow children of the minority group to be educated in that language (see Ferguson, Houghton, and Wells, 1977). Both Yugoslavia and the Soviet Union have minority schools where the medium of instruction is the children's mother tongue; at higher levels, schooling is often bilingual in the minority and regional or national languages, and in high school and college it is completely in the national language. The nation can also defend the minority culture and promote its literature, its music, its press, and its theater.

The country can help develop the minority language through language planning by standardizing the language, giving it an orthography if it does not have one, putting together a grammar and a dictionary, and extending its vocabulary by coining or borrowing new words. Many nations have official language planning bodies for their main languages: Israel has a Hebrew Language Academy, Tanzania has a Promoter of Swahili, India had a Central Hindi Directorate, and Ireland, Indonesia, and Malaysia have active language policies that have helped to develop Irish, Indonesian, and Malay, respectively. But it is not only the main languages that are developed in such a way. In the Soviet Union some sixty regional languages have been given an orthography since 1917, and work continues on standardization and vocabulary extension of many minority languages.

Of course, such policies are not applied to all languages: the status of the language, its numerical importance, its use and functions, people's attitudes toward it, the availability of trained teachers and materials in that language, not to mention the political militancy of its speakers, are all factors in how far the central or regional authorities will go in giving equal linguistic rights to a minority group. The true aim of the authorities is not always to give equal rights to the minority; in some cases this policy may be a first step to better assimilation of the group. Christian missionaries in Africa in the nineteenth and twentieth centuries converted many people by preaching in the local language instead of imposing their own. A similar approach can be used to impose one's politics, trade, and commerce.

It is important to note that active support of a linguistic minority does not always result in the group's continuing to be monolingual. Many members will also learn the regional or national language in school and use it in their work or outside their community. But they will have become bilingual in a less traumatic way than those who are refused basic linguistic rights.

Neglect and Repression of Linguistic Minorities

Policies supporting a country's linguistic minorities are still quite rare. A linguistic minority is often considered a threat to the nation, especially since nationalism has been equated with monolingualism. The "monolingual" nation often feels that language diversity will aggravate sectionalism and regionalism and create instability. It fears that the minority will have more loyalty toward its own language and culture than toward the nation. It feels that language, because it is such an important characteristic of group identity, may become a focus of discontent and may even lead to a request for independence or to annexation of the minority group by a neighboring state. For example, the Breton language has become an important factor in the struggle for independence being waged by a small minority of Breton speakers; most Bretons are satisfied in remaining French, however, if they can be given more cultural and linguistic rights. And the Corsican language is an important factor in a similar struggle, although again most Corsicans would probably prefer that their island remain a part of France.

As for using the minority and its language as a pretext for annexation by a neighboring state, there are numerous examples in recent history. When Czechoslovakia was established in 1918, a part of the country, Sudetenland was German speaking and later became a source of conflict between Czechoslovakia and Nazi Germany. After years of friction, Sudetenland was transferred to Germany in 1938, which was one of the factors that led to World War II. Alsace-Lorraine, a region with speakers of German, French, and Alsatian, has long been a source of dispute between Germany and France. It belonged to France in the nineteenth century, was annexed by Germany in 1871, and reacquired by France in 1919. During World War II Germany annexed the region once again but was forced to return it to France in 1945. Other regions containing linguistic minorities have also been sources of territorial disputes: Schleswig-Holstein on the border of Germany and Denmark; the Tyrol on the border of Italy and Austria; Macedonia on the borders of Greece, Yugoslavia, and Bulgaria, among others.

Until recently in the United States and Europe, as Comrie (1979) writes, the most enlightened policy toward minority languages was one of complete neglect. If a minority group wished to preserve its language and culture, it was free to do so, but it could not rely on the state to help. Neglect usually meant that the minority language had no official status: it could not be used as a medium of instruction in the public schools (often it couldn't even be learned as a second language), and all political, social, and economic, transactions were in the majority language. However, if the minority group wanted to print its own papers, publish its own books, and organize its own cultural events, it was free to do so. The United States, until very recently, followed this policy toward its linguistic minorities.

From neglect we go to the actual dissuasion of people from using minority languages, which can take many different forms. One very effective way of dissuading a people from using its language is to forbid its use in the schools. Many countries have had such a policy at one time or another. In France today, the children of the Bretons, Alsatians, Catalans, Basques, and North Africans are not taught in their respective languages, and until very recently they were punished for speaking it with one another in school. In Syria, children of the Kurdish minority are not taught in their mother tongue. A Kurdish-Arabic-English trilingual writes: "It is forbidden to teach Kurdish in Syria. I neither read nor write my mother tongue." In the United States, the official policy until very recently has been one of monolingual education in English. This has led to much insecurity, solitude, and resentment among minority children, as exemplified by the extract from the biography of Cesar Chavez, leader of the United Farm Workers, in Box 1.4. Chavez's experience as a child in a monolingual American school could be echoed by thousands of people who were refused the right to use their own mother tongue in school and were forced to learn in the majority language.

Speaking a minority language in public can also make an individual the object of public derogation; this has been reported for German and Yiddish in Israel. Thus as Van der Plank (1978) relates, quite loyal members of linguistic minorities in European nations

---

BOX 1.4 **BILINGUALS SPEAK**

Monolingual Education

Cesar Chavez: In class one of my biggest problems was the language. Of course, we bitterly resented not being able to speak Spanish, but they insisted that we had to learn English. They said that if we were American, then we should speak the language, and if we wanted to speak Spanish, we should go back to Mexico.

When we spoke Spanish, the teacher swooped down on us. I remember the ruler whistling through the air as its edge came down sharply across my knuckles. It really hurt. Even out in the playground, speaking Spanish brought punishment. The principal had a special paddle that looked like a two-by-four with a handle on it. The wood was smooth from a lot of use. He would grab us, even the girls, put our head between his legs, and give it to us. (In Levy, 1975, p. 24)

---

between the two world wars felt obliged to assimilate in order not to constitute a threat, so they were told, to their nation. After World War I, 50 million Europeans (a tenth of the total population) belonged to linguistic minorities, compared to only about 20 million at present. Many were forced to assimilate by first becoming bilingual (if they weren't already), then shifting over to the majority language. Van der Plank cites some figures that show this decline in minorities: in Austria there were a bit more than 100,000 speakers of Slovenian in 1880, but in 1961 only 25,000 remained; Germany had 52,-000 speakers of Frisian in 1890 but only 7,000 in 1925.

This policy of forced assimilation is very close to actual linguistic repression, and history in modern times is unfortunately rife with examples of actual suppression of linguistic minorities. One form of repression was to expel the minority from its homeland. For example, after the war between Greece and Turkey in 1921–1922, a massive exchange of minority populations took place between the two countries. As neither country wanted a potentially subversive minority in its territory, the Greek minority in Turkey and the Turkish minority in Greece were forced to return to their "homeland," which their families may have left generations before. In other examples, large numbers of Hungarians were moved out of Czechoslovakia and many Slovaks were moved from Hungary to Czechoslovakia in 1945–1946, and an estimated 3 million Sudeten Germans were transferred from Czechoslovakia to Germany just after the war.

Another repressive measure is to massively import speakers of the majority language into the minority region. Thus, after annexing part of the Austrian Tyrol in 1919, Italy tried to Italianize the region by importing laborers and civil servants into the towns and country. At present almost three-quarters of the urban population is Italian speaking, although very few Italians lived there before World War I.

Other measures may be directed at the language itself, as by making it illegal. Kloss (1977) mentions that during World War I, because of the strong anti-German feeling in the United States, a fine of $25 was levied on anyone speaking German in the streets of Findlay, Ohio, and that in 1918 the governor of Iowa prohibited the use of any language other than English in a public place (this proclamation was repealed very quickly).

Kloss (1967) reports that dominant language groups may attempt to do away with a minority language by replacing it with their own language or by dialectizing it. Replacement occurs when the two languages are linguistically very dissimilar, such as Basque and Spanish. Here the policy will be to ban the use of the minority language in the schools, in public life, in the media, and even, when possible, in the home, and to replace it with the dominant language. The focus of replacement of course is the children; they will be taught in the dominant language, admonished when caught using their mother tongue, and even separated from their own group in boarding schools so as to be assimilated more easily into the majority group. Sad examples of this are the replacement of American Indian languages by English in the nineteenth and twentieth centuries and of the sign language of the deaf by the surrounding spoken language in the United States and Europe.

The other manner of annihilating a language is to dialectize it, that is, to transform it in such a way that it is considered (and slowly becomes) a variety of the dominant language. This can be done only if the languages are related. Massive importation of words from the dominant language into the minority language and changes in the pronunciation and even the grammar of the minority language are routes followed in dialectizing it. But above all, speakers of the minority language are led to believe that their language is a "mere" dialect of the majority language and that consequently it is not worthy of being used as a national, cultural language. It is argued that the dominant language is more complete and more grammatically correct, which explains its national role.

Kloss (1967) writes that nearly all speakers of Low Saxon (Low German) in Germany and many Occitan (Provençal) speakers in

France are no longer aware of the linguistic identity of their languages, considering them as mere dialects of German and French, respectively. Catalan, a Romance language spoken by about 7 million persons in northeast Spain, has come very close to being dialectized by Castilian Spanish (this has already taken place in the Balearic Islands, writes Kloss). Catalan was the official and cultural language of Catalonia until it was annexed by Spain in 1714. Then, little by little, the government banned its use in schools and in public life. However, with the foundation of the Spanish Republic, Catalonia was given political autonomy in 1932, and once again Catalan was made the official language of the region. With the victory of Franco in 1939, Catalan was again banned, and dialectization was pursued for the next forty years or so. It is only since the recent liberalization of the Spanish regime that both Basque and Catalan have gained national status and are once again the official languages of the Basque country and of Catalonia.

In the last ten years, centralized monolingual states, especially in Europe, have been more liberal toward linguistic minorities. Many of them no longer repress the minority languages, and some have even started promoting these languages by allowing minority children to be educated in part or in full in their native languages and by having these languages used in some aspects of public life. However, there are still many cases of linguistic repression throughout the world, and members of most linguistic minorities still have to be bilingual to take part fully in the national community. It is still very rare that a minority group in a predominantly monolingual country can remain monolingual in its native language.

The Origins of Bilingualism

Groups of people may become bilingual for a number of different reasons; among these are the movement of the group for political, social, or economic reasons; political federalism and nationalism; and cultural and educational factors. We will discuss a number of the more important factors that have been uncovered by linguists such as Mackey (1967, 1976) to explain the origins of bilingualism.

Movement of Peoples

Although the reasons for group migration are numerous (military, economic, educational, political, religious, natural catastrophe), one usual outcome is that bilingualism develops when the group contacts the people who already live in the area of migration. Several patterns of bilingualism may develop: each group may learn the language of the other group, as in the case of Spanish settlers and Guarani Indians in Paraguay; the immigrant group may learn the language of the area, as immigrants to the United States have learned English; or the original population may learn the language of the settlers, as was the case of some of the Gauls in France and some of the Celts in Great Britain vis-à-vis Latin during the Roman Empire. Whatever the pattern, migration is one of the more important factors in the establishment of a bilingual community.

One type of movement that was especially important in past centuries was military invasion and subsequent colonization (Mackey, 1967). Latin, Greek, Arabic, Spanish, English, and French spread beyond their original borders in part because of military conquest: Alexander the Great and his armies spread Greek throughout the Middle East and all the way to the Indus River; the Roman Empire caused the spread of Latin from Britain to North Africa and the Middle East; Arabic was propagated by the Muslim invasions throughout the eastern Mediterranean, North Africa, and the Iberian Peninsula; the Spanish conquest of the New World led to the spread of Spanish in practically all countries of Central and South America; and in the nineteenth century both English and French were taken by colonizers into vast regions of Africa and Asia.

As Brosnahan (1963) and Cooper (1978) have pointed out, a language will spread and bilingualism will ensue from military invasion only if a number of conditions are present: the conquest must be followed by a long period of stability (the invasions of Attila and his Huns, and consequently the spread of their languages, was too short-lived to result in permanent bilingualism); the area of conquest should be multilingual so that the invader's language will be used as a lingua franca, especially in urban areas; and the use of the invader's language should enhance the inhabitants' social, political, educational, or commercial opportunities. It has been pointed out that the Turkish language did not spread throughout the Ottoman Empire because the non-Turkish members of the Empire obtained no benefits from using the language.

The Roman occupation of Great Britain is a good example. Lewis (1976) reports that when the Romans arrived in Britain, Celtic was the native language. It remained the first language of the population throughout the Roman occupation, but a number of Britons also learned and used Latin, which was used in the administration of the country, in the army (which recruited native Britons into its ranks), and in trade and commerce between the Romans and Britons and with other parts of the empire. Use of Latin enabled native Britons to profit from the many advantages of the Roman Empire, including its schools, markets, public baths, and amusement places. Latin was not imposed upon the peoples of the Roman Empire; learning it was a privilege that would allow the native Briton or Gaul to become fuller members of the empire (Mackey, 1967). It was mainly town dwellers, traders, and other people in contact with Romans who became bilingual; those who lived in the rural areas remained largely monolingual Celtic speakers.

Migration for social or economic reasons also leads to bilingualism. History is replete with cases of groups moving from their homeland to other regions or countries in search of food, work, and better living conditions. The potato famine in the nineteenth century in Ireland resulted in mass migration to the United States, where the Gaelic-speakers among the immigrants were forced to learn English to facilitate their entry into the English-speaking society. Similarly, Italians from poverty-stricken Calabria and Sicily immigrated to the United States in large numbers in the early part of this century. And in more recent times the immigrant workers in many countries of Western Europe have come from poorer nations such as Portugal, Turkey, Yugoslavia, and Algeria to obtain work. This type of migration will quickly lead to bilingualism; the immigrant will continue to use his native language in the home and with his friends, but will have to use the language of the country in his work and in his interactions with the monolingual society.

Trade and commerce are also reasons for bilingualism (Mackey, 1967), even when they are not linked to a mass movement of peoples. Traders and business people who travel to areas where another language is spoken often become fluent in a lingua franca as well as their native language. Thus it is through trade and commerce that Greek became a lingua franca in the Mediterranean in the third, fourth, and fifth centuries B.C. In more recent times Hausa and Swahili have been used as lingua francas in Africa, Russian is the language of trade in the U.S.S.R., and English has become the modern business language of the world.

Migration for political and religious reasons also leads to bilingualism (Mackey, 1967). In the twentieth century, we have witnessed the massive exodus of Russians to Europe and America after the 1917 revolution, and the departure of Cubans to the United States after the takeover of Fidel Castro. Many South Vietnamese left Vietnam after the 1975 reunification of the country and settled in France and the United States. As for religious factors leading to migration, I should mention the flight of about 250,000 Protestant Huguenots to Russia, England, Holland, and America after the revocation of the Edict of Nantes by King Louis XIV of France in 1685. And in more recent times Russian Jews, who are usually monolingual Russian speakers, have migrated to Israel and the United States. Here again migration will lead to bilingualism if the migrant group settles in a land that speaks a different language.

Thus the movement of peoples, no matter what the reason, is an important cause of bilingualism. Migration often leads to intermarriage (an immigrant marrying a member of another immigrant group or of the original native group), which in turn enhances bilingualism. Lewis (1979) reports that because of exogamy among the tribes of the northwest Amazon, a child's mother represents a different tribe and a different language group from that of the father. This ensures bilingualism in the family. Also, in many cities of the Soviet Union intermarriage among linguistic groups is quite common: in Ashkabad, 31 percent of the marriages in 1940 were contracted between different nationals (Lewis, 1979). Although an ultimate consequence of intermarriage may be a shift from one language to the other, its first effect will be bilingualism.

Nationalism and Political Federalism

Another main reason for bilingualism is nationalism and political federalism. Even though it is only since the nineteenth century that linguistic identity and national identity have been confounded, nationalism has had a great impact on the spread of national languages and hence on the degree of bilingualism in many countries. Fishman (1972b), in his book *Language and Nationalism,* quotes a number of writers who defend the idea of a national language for each nation. Among these is Davies (Fishman, 1972b), who writes, "A people without a language of its own is only half a nation. A nation should guard its language more than its territories—'tis a surer barrier, a more important frontier than fortress or river" (p. 49). This nationalistic attitude toward language often leads to the spread of a national language in preference to regional languages, and this in turn leads to bilingualism if some inhabitants speak a native language as well as the national language. As we saw in the previous section, if government policy forbids the use of the regional language in schools and in public life (as was the case for Breton in

France, for example), then bilingualism will be short-lived, and most inhabitants will slowly become monolingual in the national language. However, if the policy is more moderate and is one of political federalism, a permanent state of bilingualism may be maintained. Mackey (1967) mentions Malaysia, Yugoslavia, and the U.S.S.R. as nations in which minorities are accepted and recognized within the national boundaries and bilingualism is maintained by the central government. Modern African nations are good examples of political federalism where bilingualism is the norm. Almost no African state is made up of only one ethnic group and one language, and the inhabitants of such countries as Tanzania, Kenya, and Senegal are usually bilingual in their local language and in a lingua franca. It is interesting to note here that a small linguistic group may not be contained within a single country, as are the Bretons in France, the Navajos in the United States, and the Ainu in Japan. There are many cases where a linguistic group's geographical region has been divided among several countries and, as a consequence, the different segments of the group are bilingual in their native language and in the national language of the country that has control over them. The Kurds, for example, are divided among Turkey, Iraq, Iran, Syria, and the Soviet Union. Among this linguistic group one finds Kurdish-Turkish bilinguals, Kurdish-Arabic bilinguals, and so on. The Kurds have long fought for independence—or at least some form of autonomy—but this has always been refused, often violently, as in the case of the uprising in Iran in 1979.

Education and Culture

A further cause of bilingualism is educational and cultural (Mackey, 1967). Throughout history, particular languages and cultures have dominated the life of peoples across the world. In the Roman Empire, for instance, Greek was the language of education and culture. Almost all educated Romans were bilingual in Latin and in Greek, which was the language of philosophy, medicine, rhetoric, and much of the literature; wealthy Roman families made sure their sons were educated in Greek (Kahane and Kahane, 1979). Some were even sent to Athens to pursue their studies, and Lewis (1976) reports that Greek was not just a subject in the curriculum but was regarded as the foundation of a child's education. With the spread of Christianity, Latin became the dominant language of culture.

In the period of the Crusades and again during the period of

Louis XIV and his successors, French dominated the cultural life of Europe. Under the influence of the Huguenot émigrés, French took over a quasi-official status in Prussia during the reign of Frederick the Great (Kahane and Kahane, 1979). Voltaire wrote from Berlin in 1750: "It is as if I were in France. Everyone speaks our language." Italian was prominent during the Renaissance, and today English is the usual international language of science and technology. Thus, in all these periods, many educated people have been bilingual in their native language and in the language that was culturally prominent at the time.

Today many students are educated in a language that is not their native language: in English, for example, in India, Pakistan, and many African states, and in French in countries that once belonged to the French colonial empire. Many students travel to other countries to pursue their studies, so that the Soviet Union, France, Great Britain, and America have large numbers of foreign students in their colleges and universities. This educational bilingualism is further enhanced by the fact that books and other written and audiovisual materials are produced in a limited number of world languages, which forces students to be proficient in one of these languages. Mackey (1967) writes that in many countries, to be educated means to be bilingual.

Other Reasons

The industrialization of a multilingual nation such as the Soviet Union often leads to bilingualism because workers of different linguistic backgrounds must use a lingua franca that may not be their native language. Urbanization, often linked to industrialization, also enhances bilingualism. Again a lingua franca has to be used at work, with the administration, and with other linguistic groups, and consequently bilingualism develops. Or a religion may be tied to a specific language, and the spread of the religion will result in bilingualism. For example, the spread of Christianity made Latin an important lingua franca, and Arabic was carried with the spread of Islam. And bilingualism will develop in a border zone between two static linguistic groups. If these groups are in essence monolingual, then it is the bilinguals who will enable communication, trade, and commerce between the two groups. Such "border bilingualism" is in existence throughout the world.

The causes of bilingualism are extremely numerous; in Box 1.5, a few bilinguals report how they or their parents became bilingual.

BOX 1.5   **BILINGUALS SPEAK**

Origins of Bilingualism

MOVEMENT OF PEOPLES

A Chinese-Thai-English trilingual: The origin of my family is Chinese. My parents moved down from the South of China to Bangkok about thirty years ago. My father is a businessman and I grew up in a large Chinese community. Our house is located in the large business section of Bangkok. Most of the business firms in Thailand are owned by Chinese, and both Chinese and Thai are spoken in the business community.

INTERMARRIAGE

An English-Spanish bilingual: I was born and grew up in Colombia, South America. In the type of family environment I was brought up in, hearing and speaking two languages [Spanish and English] was a normal thing. My mother is Canadian and my father Colombian, and each would speak to us in their respective native language.

EDUCATION

A Farsi-English bilingual: I did not know how to speak English until I was ten years old, when I went to an English-speaking school in Teheran.

A Marathi-Hindi-English trilingual: When I first went to school I did not know English, but I started English as a subject in secondary school and then English was the medium of instruction at college.

A Greek-English bilingual: I came to the U.S. in order to go to college. I have now reached the point where I have no problems in communicating in English.

An Arabic-French-English trilingual: I learned English and Arabic at home but French at school, starting in the earliest grades. It took several years before I felt comfortable speaking French.

And yet the bilingualism that ensues from the movement of peoples, political federalism, education, industrialization, urbanization, and other factors is rarely permanent, as we will see in the next section.

The Outcome of Bilingualism

Just as the factors that lead a group to become bilingual are numerous and complex, so too the possible consequences of bilingualism are many and not easily classified. I will concentrate here on two possible consequences: bilingualism maintained within the group for a lengthy period of time or the group returning to a state of monolingualism. This latter path is the more common, with many nations going through long periods of monolingualism interspersed with shorter periods of bilingualism. Great Britain is a good example of this: before the Roman invasion, Britain was a Celtic-speaking nation. When the Romans occupied the lowlands, a number of Britons became bilingual in Celtic and Latin. Then, when the Teutonic Angles, Saxons, and Jutes invaded Britain, they pushed the Celts back to the west and north, and although they did not attempt to preserve or absorb the Roman-Celtic culture, there must have been some contact between the invaders and the Celts, leading to some bilingualism. Apart from Wales, the north, and the southwest, the country remained predominantly Anglo-Saxon until the Scandinavians invaded and settled in north and northeast Britain in the eighth and ninth centuries. This led to a new period of bilingualism among the Anglo-Saxons, who spoke Old English, and the invaders, who spoke Old Norse. The Norman invasion in 1066 triggered two centuries of contact and Anglo-Saxon–French bilingualism; French was the language of the court and the ruling nobility, and English the language of the people. English eventually prevailed, and in 1362 it became the official language. Aside from Welsh and Scottish Gaelic, Great Britain remained monolingual until recent times, when a large immigration of foreign workers from Kenya, India, Pakistan, and the European Common Market countries has brought back, admittedly on a smaller level, some degree of bilingualism.

Prolonged Bilingualism

There are numerous instances of prolonged bilingualism, but as Mackey (1968) argues, there must be good reasons for a group to remain bilingual. He writes: "A self-sufficient bilingual community has no reason to remain bilingual, since a closed community in which everyone is fluent in two languages could get along just as well with one language. As long as there are different monolingual communities, however, there is likelihood of contact between them; this contact results in bilingualism" (p. 555). Some of the bilingual or multilingual countries already mentioned, such as Belgium, Canada, and Switzerland, are destined to have long-term bilingualism, even though only a small percentage of the population is in fact bilingual. These countries are made up of separate monolingual communities with a small portion of the population serving as bilingual contact between groups. The bilingualism of Canadians and Belgians, for example, does not lead to loss of one of the languages in the next generation, as is often the case in immigration countries.

The next generation is at first monolingual (in Flemish or French in Belgium, or in English or French in Canada), then some members of this generation learn the other language in order to continue the contact between the two groups. And the language of contact is usually the dominant or prestige language. It is usually the French-speaking Canadians who learn English (and not the English Canadians who learn French), and the Flemish-speaking Belgians are still more likely to learn French than are the French-speakers to learn Flemish.

Between-group communication and interaction also explains the permanence of bilingualism in younger nations that are the result of recent colonization, such as those in Africa. But here again, children learn their local language first and only later become fluent in the lingua franca, thus ensuring the perpetuation of bilingualism from generation to generation.

Another instance of prolonged bilingualism occurs when a group uses two languages for its own internal needs. This is the case in Paraguay, where Spanish is the language of government, schools, cities, and much of the media, whereas Guarani is the language of the country, of informality, of popular and folk culture. This type of situation, also found in Switzerland, with Swiss German and High German; in Greece, with Dhimotiki and Katharevousa, and in many Arab-speaking countries, with dialectal and classical Arabic, guarantees a prolonged state of bilingualism.

Finally, prolonged bilingualism is associated with most Deaf people who, in addition to sign language, have some knowledge of the written form of the dominant oral language, which they use to write to each other and to interact with the hearing world.

Return to Monolingualism

The usual outcome of bilingualism, however, is a return to monolingualism: this may take the form of maintenance of the group's original language and the disappearance of the second language; a shift to the group's second language and the disappearance of the first language (often referred to as mother-tongue displacement or language shift); or the evolution to a new language through processes of pidginization and creolization.

LANGUAGE MAINTENANCE   In a number of instances a group that has become bilingual through military invasion and colonization reverts to its original monolingualism when the foreign influence diminishes or is removed. This was the case in many nations that belonged to the Hapsburg and Ottoman empires, whose official languages were German and Turkish, respectively. Because of the rather short duration of contact, the monolingualism of the groups involved, and the few opportunities given to the colonized groups by the colonizer, German and Turkish never implanted themselves in these empires in the same way that Latin spread throughout the Roman Empire or Spanish invaded South America. Admittedly, some inhabitants of Hungary, Romania, and other Hapsburg Empire countries learned and used German in addition to their own mother tongues (and the same is true of members of the Ottoman Empire vis-à-vis Turkish), but the official language never resulted in prolonged bilingualism or displaced the mother tongue after the dismembering of the empire.

Lewis (1976) reports another instance, further back in time, of a group reverting to being monolingual after a period of bilingualism. This concerns the Latin-speaking inhabitants of Italy after their bilingual contact with the Germanic invaders from the north. Although we have no information about the extensiveness of this bilingualism, probably some of the German invaders learned Latin and some of the native population in Italy learned the Germanic languages that were brought in. However, because of the lack of reinforcement necessary for the maintenance of the Germanic languages and the pressure of Latin (both social and cultural), not only did the Latins return to their former monolingualism, but the Germanic invaders themselves, after a few generations, shifted over to Latin. Lewis reports a similar evolution in Gaul, where the Germanic conquerors, the Franks, were obliged, after a period of time, to use Latin, the language of the vanquished.

LANGUAGE SHIFT   Instead of maintenance of the group's original language and the disappearance of the second language, bilingualism may lead to a language shift to the group's second language, as in the case of the Germanic invaders in Italy and Gaul in the sixth and seventh centuries. This mother-tongue displacement frequently occurs when a nation is established or when a group of people migrates to another land. In Chapter 2 we will examine in detail the numerous sociolinguistic factors that lead a group to maintain its native language or shift to another language.

Van der Plank (1978) gives a clear example of a shift from bilingualism to monolingualism triggered by nationalistic reasons. In 1867 Hungary was made an autonomous kingdom within the Hapsburg Empire, and Hungarian was promoted as the national language of the kingdom. The German-speaking population of Budapest shifted over to Hungarian, passing through a state of German-Hungarian bilingualism. In 1880, 33 percent of the city's population was German-speaking and of these, 41 percent were bilingual, whereas in 1900 only 14 percent were still German-speaking but 71 percent were now bilingual. Thus in a twenty-year time span, there was a considerable reduction in the German-speaking group, while the number of German-Hungarian bilinguals increased. This was a transition stage in the shift from German to Hungarian as a first language.

The migration of peoples, as we saw earlier, usually leads to bilingualism, which in turn often results in mother-tongue displacement, either in the native group or in the migration group (Fishman, 1980). Language shift in the native population occurred with the Egyptian language, which disappeared from Egypt after several periods of transitional bilingualism (Mackey, 1967). The Persians, the Greeks, the Romans, and finally the Arabs occupied part or all of Egypt at various times, and their rule created periods of bilingualism, the longest and last being Arabic-Egyptian. The native population shifted away, little by little, from Egyptian, and finally, sometime in the eighteenth century, the language died out. A similar trend may be taking place in Wales. Lewis (1978b) reports that for centuries Welsh was the mother tongue of most Welsh people, despite the fact that English was the official—and hence, prestigious—language of the United Kingdom. In 1840, two-thirds of the population still spoke Welsh, and half were monolingual in that language. But the massive industrialization of South Wales in the nineteenth century brought in a flow of English immigrants to the coal mines and iron works, and English slowly began to replace Welsh. Today only 1 percent of the population is monolingual in Welsh, 20 percent are bilingual in Welsh and English, and 79 percent are monolingual in English. The outlook for Welsh is not encouraging: there are no daily Welsh newspapers, only 4 percent of radio and TV broadcasting is in Welsh, and even in thoroughly Welsh areas there is considerable doubt about the usefulness of retaining the language. Thus, a period of Welsh-English bilingualism may well be followed by English monolingualism. Other languages that have ceased to be used after similar stages of bilingualism are Cornish, a Gaelic language spoken in Cornwall, England, and numerous Indian languages in South America, where Indians shifted over to Spanish, and in North America, where they shifted to English.

The bilingualism resulting from migration may also result in the migration group adopting the native language of the country. This was the case of the Germanic invaders in Italy and Gaul and of the Norman French in England in the fourteenth century, and this is generally the case in so-called immigration countries like Australia, New Zealand, Brazil, Canada, and the United States. For example, millions of monolingual immigrants have come to the United States in the last two hundred years from such diverse countries as Norway, Germany, France, Portugal, Russia, Vietnam, and Japan, and although some members of these groups have maintained their native languages, most have first become bilingual and then shifted over to English. This shift was often very rapid and there are many cases of members of the second generation being totally monolingual in English.

PIDGINIZATION AND CREOLIZATION   Bilingualism can also lead to a monolingualism in which the language spoken is a new language that has characteristics of both of the languages in contact. This occurs when one or more language groups start using as a lingua franca a simplified form of another group's language and inserting in that language some features of their own language; this is called pidginization. When this "new" language becomes more developed lexically and grammatically and is passed on to children as their mother tongue, the stage is called creolization. Haitian Creole, Jamaican Creole, and Neo-Melanesian (Tok Pisin) are the result of pidginization and creolization. Haitian Creole evolved from contact of different dialects of French, of Spanish, of native Indian languages, and of African languages. It was first a pidgin and was used as a between-group means of communication, but little by little it became the mother tongue of the Haitians, and is now the language of 85 percent of the population of Haiti, most of whom are monolingual in this language.

We have seen therefore that bilingualism can be prolonged for a long time, as in the case of certain bilingual or multilingual countries made up of separate monolingual groups or of new nations where a lingua franca is necessary for between-group communication. On the other hand and more commonly, bilingualism will lead to one of the two languages in contact becoming the sole language of the group or to the evolution of a new, creolized language from the two (or more) languages in contact.

2 *Bilingualism in the United States*

For any person interested in languages in contact and bilingualism, the United States is a nation to study. To illustrate this I will describe a little trip a friend and I took. My French friend had been brought up with the erroneous idea that the United States was a monolingual English-speaking country with few, fast-disappearing linguistic minorities. One day I took him to work with me by a roundabout route to show him the great linguistic diversity that can be found in an American city—in this case, Boston.

As we walked to the bus stop, we passed a group of Haitian children playing ball and shouting at each other in Haitian Creole. On the bus to Cambridge we sat next to an Armenian American from Waltham reading one of the two daily Armenian newspapers published in the Boston area. Walking down Cambridge Street, we found ourselves for a short while in a little Portugal—the people around us spoke Portuguese, the stores sold Portuguese goods, the restaurants offered Portuguese specialities, and the children in the area were off to their bilingual programs in school. We continued on our tour and went to Boston's North End for breakfast. Now we were in Italy. A procession in honor of a saint was getting under way, a group of elderly Italian-speaking people was playing cards in the shade of a tree, and storekeepers were setting up their displays of Italian cold cuts and cheeses. Notices posted on the walls were in

Italian, and as we entered a pastry shop the customers were all speaking Italian to one another. From the North End we walked a few blocks to Chinatown, with its Chinese-speaking inhabitants, street signs in Chinese and English, bilingual school, and Chinese stores, clubs, and temples. Because time was getting short we decided not to visit Dorchester with its large Creole-speaking Haitian population, and we quickly passed through South Boston, where many Hispanic Americans live. We did have time, however, to buy the local bilingual Spanish-English paper and check the times at the local cinema that shows only Spanish films. We then arrived at my university, which welcomes, in addition to its American student population, students from thirty foreign countries. In the laboratory we set about our day's work on a research project concerning yet one more language actively used in the United States, American Sign Language, the manual-visual language of many deaf Americans.

This little trip within an American city clearly shows the diversity and vitality of minority languages and bilingualism in the United States. Einar Haugen, a long-time researcher on bilingualism in America, stresses this very point in Box 2.1. The contact between the languages of native Americans, colonists, and later immigrants to this country has created extensive language contact and enduring bilingualism.

In this chapter we will first examine the numerical importance and geographical locations of the different linguistic minorities in

---

BOX 2.1

The Extent of Bilingualism in the United States

The United States has probably been the home of more bilingual speakers than any other country in the world. Ever since the beginning of the great Atlantic migration, wave upon wave of non-English speakers has inundated the American shore. A vivid appreciation of the need for survival caused most of the immigrants to learn as much English as was necessary to make their way in the new environment. But at the same time most of them continued to use their old language whenever occasion offered. More than that: many of them passed their language on to their descendants, thereby making them also bilingual. So it has come about that millions of Americans have been predestined by birth to a more or less pronounced bilingualism. (Haugen, 1969, p. 1) the United States, review how they have come to be here, and give some indication of the extent and type of bilingualism in the country. This will be followed by a study of the linguistic minorities: how they are organized, what their rights are, how they have been discriminated against, and what the general attitude of the Anglo-American majority is toward minorities and their languages. A third part of the chapter will examine bilingual education in the United States: why it was reinstated in 1968 after a long absence and how it has evolved since then. I will then describe the Native Americans, the American Deaf, the German Americans, the Franco-Americans, and the Hispanic Americans, sketching their history, their problems, and how they have coexisted with the Anglo-American majority. Finally we will examine the complex topic of language maintenance and language shift: why certain linguistic minorities have practically disappeared—their members have become monolingual English speakers—whereas others are maintaining their native languages. These topics will all point to a recurring theme: bilingualism in the United States is basically short-lived and transitional, in that it links monolingualism in one language—usually an immigrant language—to monolingualism in the majority language, English.

Language Diversity and Bilingualism

Unlike Canada and Belgium, which have precise statistics on bilingualism within their borders, the United States has little data on the subject. Although everyone recognizes that bilingualism is extensive in this country, no absolute figures have ever been published by the Bureau of Census on the number and types of bilinguals in the fifty states. Most statistics that do exist concern people's mother tongue. For example, the 1970 census asked, "What language other than English was spoken in this person's home when he was a child?" The answers to this question have often been used as a basis for figures on bilingualism in the United States, but this approach has its drawbacks. The fact that a language other than English was spoken in the home when a person was a child does not mean that the person actually used that language and if he or she did, that person may no longer be using that language on a regular basis as an adult. Also, a person can be an active bilingual without having been in contact with a language other than English as a child.

Despite these reservations, the mother tongue data are nevertheless extremely interesting in the information they do give concerning linguistic minorities in the United States: their importance, their location, and their age distribution.

Persons with a Non-English Language Background

In the spring of 1976 the Survey of Income and Education, conducted by the Bureau of the Census, included a number of questions on language background and current usage that were developed and later analyzed by the National Center for Education Statistics. The data below are derived from this survey (National Center for Education Statistics 1978a, 1978b, 1979; Waggoner, 1980).

According to the survey there were in 1976 as many as 27,985,000 persons in the United States with a non-English language background, that is, persons living in a household in which a language

FIGURE 2.1   Estimated number of persons with a non-English language background in sixteen minority language groups. (Based on the 1976 Survey of Income and Education, *National Center for Education Statistics Bulletin 78 B-5.* The estimate for American Sign Language was obtained from unpublished sources.)

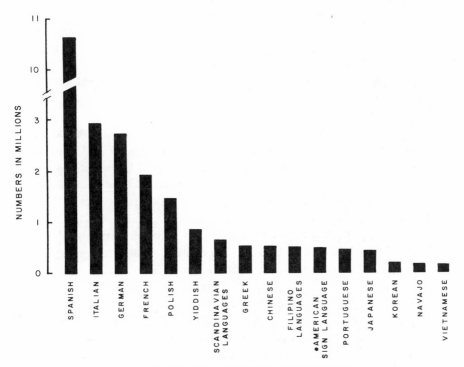

NON-ENGLISH LANGUAGE BACKGROUND

other than English was spoken or who lived in such a household when they were children. This represented about one person in eight or 13 percent of the total population. Figure 2.1 shows the numerical strength of the most important of these linguistic minorities. We see that people with a Spanish language background are by far the most numerous (10.6 million), followed a long way behind by Italian (2.9 million), German (2.7 million), French (1.9 million), and Polish (1.5 million). Other language backgrounds fall below the million mark, for example, Yiddish (0.8 million), Greek, Chinese, and Filipino (each 0.5 million). I have added an estimate for American Sign Language (about 0.5 million), although there are no precise statistics. Unfortunately, the published data do not mention the many other languages that can be found in the United States; missing are the three hundred or so Native American languages (with the exception of Navajo) and the many other European, Asian, and African languages.

Figure 2.2 shows where linguistic minorities are found in the country. Thirty-two states have 100,000 or more persons with a non-English language background (NELB), and in twenty-three (outlined in thick black lines on the map) 10 percent or more of the population have an NELB. The states with the largest NELB proportions are New Mexico (44 percent), Hawaii (35 percent), California, Texas, and New York (each 25 percent), and Arizona (23 percent). It is interesting to note that most people with an NELB live in the Southwest, the Northeast, and the North Central states; few are found in the South (with the exception of Louisiana and Florida), the mountain states, and the Northwest.

As for the location of specific linguistic minorities, distinct patterns can be seen on the map. Although Spanish is present in all regions and states, three out of five persons with a Spanish language background are in Arizona, California, Colorado, New Mexico, and Texas. Other important concentrations of Spanish speakers are in Florida, New York, and New Jersey. Persons with a German language background are also spread throughout the country (more than 100,000 live in each of ten different states), but the largest numbers are found in New York, Pennsylvania, California, Illinois, and the North Central region. Louisiana has 25 percent of those with a French language background, and the northeastern states (Maine, Massachusetts, and New York) have 40 percent of the group. Other minority groups are also located in specific regions: persons with an Italian language background are found in New York, the northeastern states, Illinois, and California; and Polish-Americans are found

FIGURE 2.2   Estimated proportion of persons with a non-English language background in each of the fifty states and the distribution of some of the minority languages in these states. States whose proportion is 10 percent or more are etched in thicker lines. (Based on the 1976 Survey of Income and Education, *National Center for Education Statistics Bulletin* 78 B-5.)

	LANGUAGES				
A	APACHE	H	HAWAIIAN	P	POLISH
Ar	ARABIC	HC	HAITIAN CREOLE	Po	PORTUGUESE
C	CHINESE	I	ITALIAN	S	SPANISH
Ch	CHEROKEE	In	INUPIAT	Sl	SLOVAK
Cz	CZECH	J	JAPANESE	Sw	SWEDISH
Cr	CROW	K	KOREAN	T	TEWA
F	FRENCH	L	LAKOTA	V	VIETNAMESE
Fi	FILIPINO	M	MOHAWK	Y	YIDDISH
G	GERMAN	N	NORWEGIAN	Yu	YUP'IK
Gr	GREEK	Na	NAVAJO		

in the northeastern and north central states, especially Illinois and Michigan. More than half of those with a Yiddish language background live in New York, and the largest number of persons with a Scandinavian language background are found in Minnesota, Iowa, and the Dakotas. People speaking Far Eastern languages live mainly on the two coasts: Chinese, Japanese, Korean, and Vietnamese in California; Chinese in New York and Massachusetts; Vietnamese and Korean in Maryland, for example.

The map also shows smaller language groups: Arabic speakers in Michigan; Haitian Creole speakers in New York, Florida, and Massachusetts; Slovak speakers in Pennsylvania; Czech speakers in Nebraska. In addition, a number of Native American languages are shown on the map: Navajo in Arizona and New Mexico, Cherokee in Oklahoma and North Carolina, Yup'ik and Inupiat in Alaska, Tewa in New Mexico, Mohawk in New York, and Lakota in South Dakota.

The 1976 survey gives us the additional information that contrary to the popular belief that speakers of a language other than English are born outside the United States, the majority of NELB persons (two out of three, or 18.5 million) were in fact born in one of the fifty states, Puerto Rico, or a United States territory. Among the French and Polish groups, nearly three out of five are native born, and the proportion for the Spanish group is three out of four. Among the Asian group, only the Japanese have a majority of native born: nearly three-fourths of Chinese, Filipino, Korean, and Vietnamese language background persons are immigrants.

The data on age distribution of NELB persons show that overall, they are older than the general population. This is especially true of people with a European language background—Italian, French, German and Polish, for example. However, persons with a Spanish language background are younger than the general population: two out of five are under nineteen.

Finally, the 1976 survey found that as many as 2.4 million persons in the United States aged four or over do not know English, 90 percent of these being adults. Most (61 percent) are Spanish speaking, but the figure includes speakers of French, Chinese, and Italian, among others.

The Evolution of Minority Languages

To understand better the data of the 1976 survey, we must quickly return to the past. Before the first Europeans arrived, what is now the United States was already highly multilingual. It has been estimated that there were between 500 and 1,000 Native American languages in fifteenth-century North America. And as we will see later in this chapter, language contact and bilingualism were already quite widespread among the Indian nations. With the arrival of Europeans, seven languages (also known as the colonial languages; see Haugen, 1956) implanted themselves in the continental United States: English along the Eastern seaboard; Spanish in the South from Florida to California; French in Louisiana and northern Maine (because of the large French settlement in Quebec); German in Pennsylvania; Dutch in New Amsterdam (New York); Swedish in Delaware; and Russian in Alaska. Dutch, Swedish, and Russian did not survive for very long, but the other four are still present in the United States today. English was constantly reinforced by the arrival of new settlers in the seventeenth and eighteenth centuries, and by 1776 the United States was predominantly English-speaking. In the 1790 census, 60 percent of the population were of English descent and 18 percent of Scottish and Irish descent. The largest linguistic minority at the time was the Germans, representing 9 percent of the population.

From that time on the United States acquired its current multilingual character in two ways: on the one hand through purchase, acquisition, and annexation of territories that housed peoples of different mother tongues, and on the other hand through the immigration of non-English-speaking groups. In the first category, Louisiana, with its majority of French speakers, was purchased from Napoleon in 1803, and Alaska, with its Russian, Eskimo, Aleut, and Indian population, was purchased from Russia in 1867. In the Mexican-American War of 1846–1848, the United States invaded and occupied the northern part of Mexico. The territory, which comprised a large part of California, Arizona, New Mexico, Colorado, and Texas, was transferred by Mexico to the United States in the Treaty of Guadalupe Hidalgo in 1848. Along with a large number of Indian nations, notably the Pueblos and the Navajos, the territory was populated by some 75,000 Mexicans. To this series of territorial gains we should add the transfer of Spanish-speaking Puerto Rico to the United States in 1898 and the slow invasion and annexation of Native American nations throughout the nineteenth century as "the West was won."

The second and probably more important reason for the fact that America now has close to 28 million persons with a non-English language background is immigration. Until about 1880 most of the immigrants came from a small number of western and northern European countries—Great Britain, Ireland, the Scandinavian countries, Germany, Austria-Hungary, and France. They came for many of the reasons mentioned in Chapter 1: flight from economic and social disadvantages; escape from religious and political discrimination; the appeal of land to farm and of gold to find; the attraction of adventure and the need to cut social ties.

From 1880 until the immigration laws of 1924, immigrants arrived in very large numbers; about 28 million people came to the United States in that period. Most came from the southern and eastern European countries: the Balkan states, Italy, Poland (divided before World War I among Russia, Austria-Hungary, and Prussia), Austria-Hungary (including Bohemia, Hungary, Slovakia), Russia, and Armenia. On the West Coast numerous Chinese and Japanese came to work in the mines, on railroads, and on the new agricultural estates. Unlike their British, German, and Scandinavian predecessors, few immigrants in this period became farmers; most settled and worked in the industrial centers of the northeastern and north central states: in the steel plants of Indiana, the textile mills of the Northeast, and the coal mines of Pennsylvania. Many French Canadians also came across the border from Quebec to work in the mill towns of New England.

Since 1930, another 5 million immigrants have come to these shores, and once again their origins have been extremely diverse. The nation has seen the arrival of German Jews before World War II and political refugees from Europe after the war; the migration of Puerto Ricans to the mainland in the 1950s and 1960s; the arrival of Hungarians after the 1956 revolution, of Cubans after the takeover by Fidel Castro, and of Vietnamese after the fall of South Vietnam. And it has seen the regular flow of immigrants from such diverse countries as Mexico, Greece, Portugal, Korea, the Philippines, Taiwan, Laos, and the West Indies, notably the Dominican Republic, Jamaica, and Haiti.

This short description of immigration and annexation patterns not only gives us a better understanding of the linguistic makeup of the United States today, it also allows us to comprehend better why some minority languages are on the decline while others are showing sharp gains. Figure 2.3 presents mother-tongue data for ten languages for 1940 and 1960 and non-English language background data for 1976. Although mother-tongue data are not the same as non-English language background data, and the 1960 figures were extrapolated by Fishman and Hofman, these data present an interesting trend. We can see, for instance, that many European languages are declining in importance: German, the most important minority language in 1940 with about 5 million claimants, is now in third position with 2.7 million persons; Italian, which about 4 million persons claimed as their mother tongue in 1940, now has only 3 million claimants; Polish, with 2.5 million claimants in 1940, is now at the 1.5 million mark; and Yiddish has passed from 1.7 million to 0.8 million claimants.

FIGURE 2.3 The evolution of ten minority languages between 1940 and 1976. (The 1940 and 1960 figures are based on mother tongue data presented by Fishman and Hofman, 1966, and the 1976 figures are based on non-English language data obtained in the 1976 Survey of Income and Education, *National Center for Education Statistics Bulletin, 78 B-5.*)

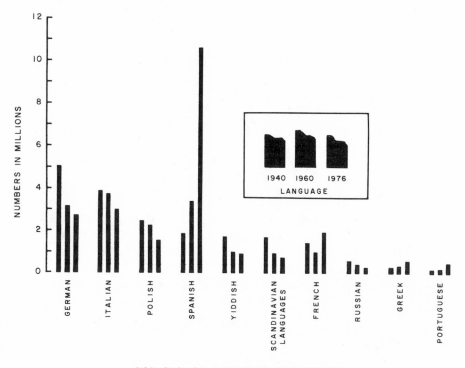

The factors that lead to language maintenance and language shift are discussed in the last part of this chapter, but we can see that the cessation of massive immigration in the 1920s, the return of a number of immigrants to their homelands during the depression in the 1930s, the closing of the Iron Curtain in the fifties, and the natural assimilation of minorities into the Anglo-American majority are all factors in this decline. Of the "big six" minority languages—German, Italian, Polish, Yiddish, Spanish, and French (Fishman and Hofman, 1966)—only the latter two show any gain since 1940. French has been able to maintain its position because it is well implanted and its use now encouraged in Louisiana, and because Franco-Americans in the Northeast were until quite recently extremely active in maintaining their language and culture. As for

Spanish, Figure 2.3 shows its incredible gains since 1940: from 2 million persons in 1940 it is now the language of close to 11 million, and this 1976 figure probably does not include the many undocumented workers who speak Spanish. This sharp gain is mainly due to a strong immigration flow from Mexico, Cuba, and Central and South America since the 1950s.

Thus, in a span of forty years, the picture of linguistic minorities in the United States has changed substantially: the languages that were important in the first half of the century are now on a rather sharp decline, and other, less important, languages at that time, such as Swedish, Norwegian, Danish, Czech, Slovak, and Slovenian, are showing severe losses. On the other hand Spanish, from being in fourth position in 1940, is now first, while Greek, Portuguese, and some Asian languages have shown sharp gains.

The Use of Minority Languages

Mother tongue or language background data are useful in obtaining a general picture of the identity and location of linguistic minorities in the United States, but they do not tell us which languages are actively being used. Because the United States is a country of immigrants, many inhabitants report that a language other than English was spoken in their home when they were children, but it is not clear how many of these people use this language in their everyday life. To obtain a better feeling for the minority languages that are actively being used, the 1976 Survey of Income and Education asked a question about daily language use of those born outside the United States and those who reported that a language other than English was spoken in the household, either at present or when they were children. Some of the results from this question are presented in Figure 2.4.

Spanish is not only the most important minority language in the United States, it is also used as an everyday language in the households of most people reporting a Spanish language background. It is interesting to note, however, that Spanish is not the usual everyday language for all—English is claimed by slightly more respondents (49 percent) than is Spanish (46 percent). Figure 2.4 also indicates that (mainly because of the arrival of recent immigrants), Chinese, Greek, and Portuguese are used in the household by more than 70 percent of the persons claiming those language backgrounds and that Chinese and Portuguese are reported as the usual language more often than English, a clear indication of the vitality of these

FIGURE 2.4 The use of minority languages by persons with a non-English language background. For each language, the first bar represents the proportion of persons with a non-English language background who actually live in a household where the language is used. The second and third bars are breakdowns of the first: the second represents those whose usual language is not English, and the third those whose usual language is English. (Data based on the 1976 Survey of Income and Education, *National Center for Education Statistics Bulletin* 78 B-6, 79 B-12, and Waggoner, 1980.)

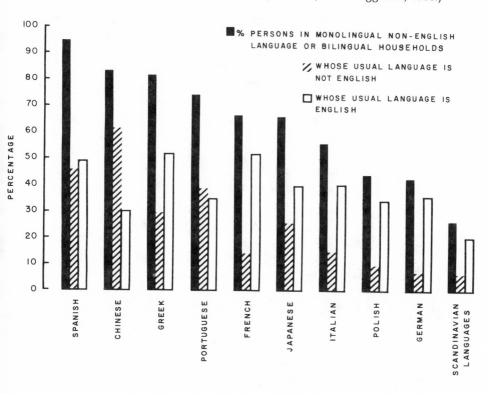

languages in the United States today. Both Korean and Vietnamese, which are not shown in the figure, show the same trend. They are used in the majority of Korean and Vietnamese households and are the usual language of those claiming these language backgrounds.

Especially interesting are the data pertaining to the other big six languages. German is used in the household by only 43 percent of those reporting a German language background (the other 57 percent are probably no longer in contact with German) and of those 43 percent, a mere 7 percent report is as their usual language. Thus, although German may still be an important mother tongue, in that it was once spoken in the household of many German Americans, it is no longer a very active language in the United States. The same trend is true for Italian (only 15 percent of claimants use it as their usual language), Polish (10 percent), and Yiddish (8 percent). The Scandinavian languages show a sharp decline; only 27 percent of those who claim Norwegian, Swedish, Danish, Finnish, or Icelandic as their language background are actually in contact with the language in the home, and only 6 percent of those still claim it as their usual language.

Thus, there is not always a relationship between mother tongue data and the daily use of a minority language. The really active languages today in the United States are not German, Polish, Yiddish, or Italian, as one might conclude from mother tongue data, but Spanish, Chinese, Greek, Portuguese, Korean, Vietnamese, a number of Filipino languages, and some Native American languages (Navajo, Inupiat, Yup'ik, Cherokee, and Lakota). This is also clearly illustrated in the languages used in bilingual education: very few programs exist for children of German, Polish, or Italian language background, and programs for Spanish, Portuguese, Asian, and Native American languages abound.

The Extent of Bilingualism

By careful analysis of the 1976 Survey of Income and Education language data, it is possible to obtain some indication of the extent of bilingualism in the United States. Although the language questions ("What language does X usually speak? What other language does X speak?") were not asked of people who reported that only English was spoken in the household, some of whom—businessmen, teachers, diplomats—could very well be bilingual, and was not asked of children under four, the unpublished data obtained by the National Center for Education Statistics are extremely interesting. It is important to note that I am comparing language usage figures with total non-English language background figures. This procedure has been questioned by some, but I feel the trends that emerge are probably very close to reality. In 1976 there were approximately 12,-762,000 persons who reported speaking both English and a minority language on a regular basis. This means that about 6 percent of the total population is bilingual. Of these, the great majority (8,799,000) say that their usual language is English and can therefore be termed "English dominant"; the other 3,963,000 claim that the minority language is their usual language; I will refer to these as "non-English dominant." If we add an estimated 2,426,000 persons who do not speak English at all (approximately 1 percent of the population), 7 percent of the American population speaks a language other than English on a regular basis. On the one hand, this percentage confirms the large dichotomy between the language background data and the language use data; about 13 percent of the population reports a non-English language background, but only 7 percent actually use a minority language regularly. And on the other hand, these results clearly show how monolingual the United States really is—a full 93 percent of the population speaks only English.

The language groups that have the most bilinguals are Spanish Americans (about 6.2 million), Italian Americans (about 1 million), German Americans (about 800,000), Franco-Americans (about 777,-000) and Polish Americans (about 493,000). What is perhaps more interesting, however, is the way each language group is broken down into monolingual English speakers, bilinguals, and monolingual non-English speakers, as shown in Figure 2.5. As expected, the older language groups (Scandinavian languages, German, Yiddish, Polish, Italian, and French) have larger proportions of monolingual English speakers than of either bilingual or non-English speakers, while newer language groups (Portuguese, Greek, Korean, Vietnamese) still have many more bilinguals and non-English speakers. It is interesting to note that Spanish, an "old" language, really behaves like a newer immigration language because of the recent arrival of Mexican and Cuban Americans and because of the maintenance of Spanish in Texas. Navajo also shows an interesting configuration: Navajo Indians are the language minority group with the second largest proportion of bilinguals (61 percent), which shows extremely strong language maintenance after generations of English influence.

Two comments follow from Figure 2.5. The first is that bilingualism in the United States is extremely diverse, in that many different languages—Native American languages, older colonial languages, recent immigration languages—are paired off with English. In Switzerland, in contrast, only four main languages are spoken, and as the two prestige languages are French and Swiss German, bilingualism is usually French-German, Romansh-German, Italian-German, or Italian-French. Second, American bilingualism on the whole is transitional in nature; it stretches across one or several generations, linking monolingualism in the original minority language to English monolingualism. Unlike the bilingualism found in Belgium, Switzerland, or Canada, where the contact of rather stable monolingual groups creates permanent bilingualism, in the United States—and again with many exceptions—bilingualism has merely

FIGURE 2.5 The proportion of persons who are monolingual in a non-English language, bilingual in that language and English, and monolingual in English in the total population and in each of seventeen minority language groups. Each language group comprises all those persons reporting a background in that language. (Based on the 1976 Survey of Income and Education, *National Center for Education Statistics Bulletin* 78 B-6, 79 B-12; Waggoner, 1980; and unpublished data.)

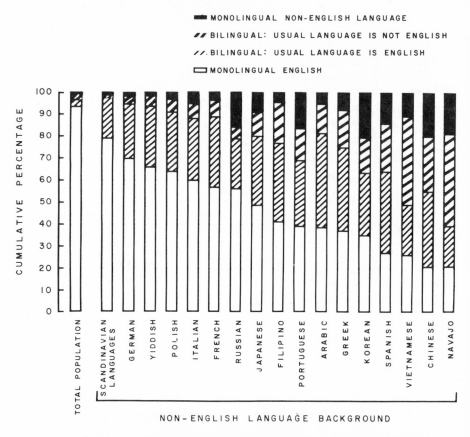

been a transitional stage in the linguistic integration of language minorities. (The exceptions include Mexican Americans in Texas, Puerto Ricans on the island, and the Navajo.) This appears in a rather striking way in Figure 2.5; if we take a recent minority group like the Vietnamese, we find that 11 percent are monolingual in Vietnamese, 63 percent are already bilingual (40 percent are still dominant in Vietnamese, while 23 percent have become dominant in English), and 26 percent are already monolingual English speakers. If we compare this to an older immigration group, the German Americans, we find a very different picture. A mere 1 percent are monolingual in German, only 29 percent are still bilingual (and of these most are English dominant) and 70 percent have now become monolingual English speakers.

In an interesting study on the 1976 Survey of Income and Education, Veltman (1979) shows how rapid the anglicization (or linguistic assimilation) of minority groups in the United States really is. More than half of foreign-born immigrants shift over to English as their usual language within a short period of time, retaining their mother tongue essentially as a second language; the exceptions are Chinese Americans and Hispanic Americans. According to Veltman, there is no danger of the United States becoming "Balkanized": even among Hispanic Americans in Texas (the most retentive minority group in the country along with the Navajo), the anglicization rate of new Spanish immigrants is ten times higher than that of the French in Quebec, the one non-English speaking group in North America that is maintaining its language. And the anglicization of native-born Hispanic Americans is nearly twenty-five times higher. Of course, many factors can speed up, slow down, or even prevent this passage from one monolingualism to the other, as will be discussed in the last section of the chapter.

To summarize, the United States is linguistically extremely diverse: it houses millions of persons spread throughout the country who speak Native American, European, Asian, and African languages. Census figures, based on mother tongue claimants, reflect only grossly the regular use of these minority languages. And finally, bilingualism in this country is extremely diverse and is usually a transitional stage between monolingualism in the minority language and monolingualism in English.

Aspects of the Life of Linguistic Minorities

The history and life of the linguistic minorities in the United States have been the subjects of innumerable studies, essays, histories, and novels. Reference books list hundreds of pages of titles of such works, and numerous courses in universities and colleges are dedicated to this aspect of American history. In this section I will only highlight the main aspects of the life of linguistic minorities in the United States, mentioning examples of discrimination they have encountered and evoking the general attitude of the Anglo-American majority toward linguistic minorities and toward bilingualism in general.

Almost all linguistic minorities, whether of Native American or of foreign origin, have organized themselves to maintain their language and culture, at first in a quite basic geographical regrouping. A Greek immigrant, for example, usually stays with friends or relatives upon arrival in the United States and from that base looks for work in areas recommended by Greek relations—maybe where other Greeks already work. This natural regrouping (which has been forced upon Native Americans by the creation of reservations) has led to whole geographical areas becoming dominated by particular linguistic minorities: the Norwegian farming "islands" in Minnesota and the Dakotas; the French Canadian areas (often called Le Petit Canada) in the New England mill towns; the Puerto Rican barrios in New York City and Jersey City; the Chinatowns in San Francisco and New York, for instance.

These geographical regroupings, whose first and main motivation was survival in a foreign land, slowly evolved into well-organized communities with all the amenities required by its members—stores selling ethnic foods and products, churches and temples to look after their spiritual needs, schools, clubs, societies and ethnic organizations, newspapers and, more recently, radio or television programs.

Box 2.2 presents two extracts illustrating how linguistic minorities organize themselves in the United States. And what is true of Franco-Americans fifty years ago in New England and of Russian Americans today is in part true of other minority groups such as Hispanic, Vietnamese, or Portuguese Americans. Of course, not all members of linguistic minorities live in ethnic areas: many have assimilated themselves into the general American society, and others, such as foreign students or persons belonging to small, dispersed minority groups, are not surrounded by a community sharing their language and culture. It remains true, however, that most larger minority groups have organized themselves at one time or another into ethnic communities. See, for instance, Haugen's (1969) very informative account of the experiences and lifestyles of Norwegian Americans in the Middle West in the nineteenth and early twentieth centuries.

How have linguistic minorities fared in the United States? In *The American Bilingual Tradition* (1977), Kloss studies the history of immigrant communities and concludes that this country has generally been tolerant toward its linguistic minorities, a situation that is far from common in the world (see Chapter 1), especially in countries that contain many immigrants. Kloss enumerates the many rights minorities have enjoyed in this country—rights that are in no way different from those of the Anglo-American majority. In general, the

---

BOX 2.2   **BILINGUALS SPEAK**

Aspects of the Life of Linguistic Minorities in the United States

A Russian American: Russian children and teenagers take an active part in the church, which gives them a chance to meet other Russian young people and maintain their heritage at the same time. We live in an ethnic community whose stove burns on Russian literature, Russian classical music, the old traditions of the church, folk dancing and folk music, Russian cooking, and our new "immigration" history. Russian cultural organizations, choruses, summer camps, gym clubs, and theater groups also help maintain the Russian language. An average evening for a group of Russian teenagers can include stopping for a six-pack of beer, sitting in the car and harmonizing on monastic hymns, going to McDonalds and then to someone's house to listen to a new balalaika folk record.

A Franco-American: A stranger could have easily recognized this [French-Canadian] neighborhood by its very distinct inward characteristics. The church was usually the nucleus of the area, reflecting the geographical structure of Quebec's rural villages. In the immediate vicinity of the church one would find the school, the rectory, and the convent. Not too far away there might be a grocery store, a drugstore, and perhaps a hardware store, all owned and operated by French Canadians. These businesses, whose customers all knew one another, often served as social gathering places. There, men and women could chat about the daily occurrences in the neighborhood. Also in this area, one would find the French-Canadian club, which offered a variety of diversions . . . Little children played in the yards, on the sidewalks or in the street, always speaking French amongst themselves. *Le Petit Canada* was generally located near the textile factories, this meaning that for all practical purposes one could go to work, to school, to church, to buy provisions, and to socialize, all within walking distance of the home. (Robert B. Perreault, 1976, p. 20)

---

human, civil, and political rights protected by the first ten amendments to the Constitution—including freedom of speech, religion, assembly; freedom from unwarranted search and seizure; the right to a speedy and fair trial—have been respected, although there have been many cases in which people belonging to a linguistic minority have been deprived of basic rights.

Kloss cites three examples of such discrimination in this century. During World War I, anti-German feeling—often hysteria—led to the physical maltreatment of many German Americans. Some were attacked and beaten, others were tarred and feathered, even though

---

BOX 2.3   **BILINGUALS SPEAK**

The Effects of Pearl Harbor in School

A Japanese American: Of course, it was worst the first day, the Monday after Pearl Harbor, 'cause every class you went to discussed it and kids acted just like it was your fault. It wasn't inferred. It was, "Those damn Japs!" It was all of this, and you were part of it. There were those who included you, that you were responsible, too, because you're of Japanese descent, was the feeling we got. It was, "Oh God, I'm going through the floor." And there were those that said, "I'm not speaking to you any more." You know, I began to feel so guilty—that I had to take the blame too because it was Japan and my parents are from Japan. (Namias, 1978, p. 131)

---

most were American citizens and their families had been in the United States for several generations. Similarly, during World War II more than 110,000 people of Japanese descent were interned, without formal hearings and without protests from the general public, in camps in the deserts of California, Arizona, Utah, and Wyoming. Of these, 70,000 were American born and hence citizens of the United States. Families were forced to leave and sell their houses and store their belongings. As can be seen from the extract in Box 2.3, this sad episode marked the lives of many Japanese Americans. This minority group had to wait until 1976 for President Ford to apologize publicly and rescind the executive order that had initiated the deportation proceedings.

The third example of discrimination mentioned by Kloss concerns Hispanic (especially Mexican) Americans, now the largest linguistic minority group in the country, who have been the object of numerous discriminatory acts. Its members have time and time again been prevented from exercising their civil and political rights, such as voting. After the annexation of the greater part of the southwestern states in 1848, many Mexican Americans lost their land through extortion, bribery, and physical violence. And during the depression about half a million Mexican Americans were deported to Mexico, even though many had been born in the United States and were American citizens.

To these examples should be added the immigration policies enacted by the United States at the turn of the century, which affected the lives of legal immigrants. For instance, in 1884 Chinese wives of all but merchants and American-born Chinese were forbidden to enter the country, and in 1924 the Immigration Act forbade the entry of any Chinese women who wanted to settle permanently. These acts meant that the Chinese Americans, who had already undergone great discrimination during the anti-Chinese agitations of the 1880s in California, had to remain for a long time a single-sex society, creating terrible hardships. And today the plight of undocumented workers is ever present, especially in the southwestern states. Some maintain that undocumented workers, who number between 5 and 12 million, are taking jobs away from American citizens. Others reply that these jobs are so badly paid and so strenuous that Americans would not fill them anyway. What is sure, however, is that undocumented workers—be they Mexican, Haitian, or Dominican—are exploited and underpaid and do not have the civil or political guarantees of their legal counterparts.

These cases of discrimination, to which we must add the negative policies that have been adopted toward native Americans until recently, must not conceal the fact that on the whole the policy of the United States has been to respect the human, civil, and political rights of linguistic minorities. And when one compares the fate of linguistic minorities in this country to that of minorities in certain European, African, and Asian countries, the general picture is far from bleak.

Kloss (1977) also mentions that linguistic minorities have had the right to use their mother tongue not only at home, but also in the street, in meetings, in church, and so on. Although no language other than English has official status (with the exception of French in Louisiana in the early nineteenth century and of Spanish, semiofficially, in New Mexico at the beginning of this century), the citizens of the United States have been allowed to use their mother tongue in everyday life. Again, exceptions exist, but they are not numerous. Kloss mentions that during World War I several attempts were made to prevent the use of German: in Findlay, Ohio, a $25 fine was imposed for speaking German in public and in 1918, the governor of Iowa prohibited the use of languages other than English in public places and on the telephone, but these policies were very quickly repealed.

A third right of linguistic minorities mentioned by Kloss is the freedom to assemble and organize, to establish clubs and societies, found churches, publish newspapers, and broadcast on radio and television. Linguistic minorities have been extremely active in this domain. Fishman (1965b, 1981) reports that in 1960 there were some 1,800 ethnic cultural organizations in the United States and that 1,600 radio stations were broadcasting more than 6,000 hours of non-English language programs per week. (In 1980 the number of radio and TV stations was up to 2,500.) Hispanic Americans are the biggest users of ethnic broadcasting and, in 1980 they broadcast over some 430 radio stations and 34 television stations, some of which were completely monolingual in Spanish.

The minority press has been extremely active. Fishman (1965b) reports that in 1960 there were over 500 periodic publications, with a combined circulation of approximately 5½ million, ranging from totally monolingual through bilingual to English language publications. (In 1980 there were 750 publications.) Figure 2.6 reproduces the titles of some monolingual dailies and weeklies published by linguistic minorities. The *Ayer Directory of Publications* (1979) lists some thirty dailies published in a minority language: five are in Chinese (of which one is the *Chinese Times*), six are in Spanish (for example, *La Opinion* and *El Diario-La Prensa*), three are in German, and three in Polish (for example, the Chicago *Dziennik Zwiazkowy*). Figure 2.7 reproduces the title of some newspapers written in both the minority language and in English. Some are dailies (the Chinese American *East-West*), some weeklies (the Hispanic American *La Semana*), and some monthlies (the Franco-American *Louisiane* and *Le F.A.R.O.G. Forum*). There are also some 13,000 movie theaters (Kloss, 1977) that show movies in minority languages, 550 of these almost exclusively.

There have been violations of these rights. Kloss mentions that in 1917 a federal law was passed that forbade the publication of articles in the non-English language press concerning the war and foreign policy unless an English translation was first submitted to the nearest post office. In addition, minority labor unions, such as the United Farm Workers of Cesar Chavez, have encountered many difficulties, as have private militias, but again these are exceptions to the rule. A final right mentioned by Kloss, the right to private nationality schools, is discussed in the next section.

Although the official policy toward linguistic minorities has been neither one of encouragement nor one of repression but more a policy of toleration, the general attitude of the nation (as compared to its laws) and of the Anglo-American majority has been that members of linguistic minorities should integrate themselves into the English-speaking society as quickly as possible. This attitude has not changed much since the beginning of this century. In 1917 Theodore Roosevelt wrote that any person who comes to the United States must adopt the institutions of the country and therefore its

Matan Mujer Dice Comifatdmizd con 500 Polinas

EL DIARIO
La Prensa.

35c

CAMPEON DE LOS HISPANOS

Edición Metropolitana De Fin de Semana

NUEVA YORK - Domingo 6 de Mayo de 1979

Pescaria transforma-se em tragédia na Califórnia

Cinco mortos num naufrágio

AT comunidade
Azorean Times

126

ANO IV / ABRIL 4, 1979 / 25c

EL MUNDO

El Periódico de la Comunidad

Massachusetts • Rhode Island • Connecticut • New York • New Jersey • Florida

Boston ....15¢
New York ......15¢
New Jersey ....25¢

Miami ....35¢
Otras ciudades .....35¢
estados de Nueva
Inglaterra ....25¢

PRIMERA SEMANA DE MAYO DE 1980   EDICION NO. 407

SENADOR EDMUND S. MUSKIE, NUEVO SECRETARIO DE ESTADO

PAGINA 10

ΕΘΝΙΚΟΣ ΚΗΡΥΞ

NATIONAL HERALD greek american daily newspaper

TUESDAY, JANUARY 22, 1980   ΑΝΕΞΑΡΤΗΤΗ ΗΜΕΡΗΣΙΑ ΕΦΗΜΕΡΙΔΑ   ΤΡΙΤΗ 22 ΙΑΝΟΥΑΡΙΟΥ 1980

65 χρονια
στην υπηρεσια
του Ελληνισμου
της Αμερικης

(212) 477-2550   **25 CENTS**

Μέ ἀναλογία 2 πρός 1

ΕΝΤΥΠΩΣΙΑΚΗ Η ΝΙΚΗ ΤΟΥ κ. ΚΑΡΤΕΡ ΣΤΙΣ ΠΡΟΚΡΙΜΑΤΙΚΕΣ ΤΗΣ Α·Ι·ΟΒΑ

Η ΚΥΠΡΙΑΚΗ ΚΥΒΕΡΝΗΣΗ ΑΠΟΡΡΙΠΤΕΙ ΤΟ ΑΜΕΡΙΚΑΝΙΚΟ ΣΧΕΔΙΟ

THE YOUNG CHINA

THE YOUNG CHINA

49-51 Hang An St., San Francisco, Calif. 94108, U.S.A.
Tel. (415) 982-0685

Tuesday APR. 22, 1993 Vol. 71 No. 96

Chinese Times
(usps 105-980)

Friday April 18, 1980

THE ONLY CHINESE DAILY OWNED, EDITED AND PUBLISHED BY CITIZENS OF THE UNITED STATES

THE CHINESE TIMES PUBLISHING COMPANY   SAN FRANCISCO, CALIF. 9011

FIGURE 2.6 Titles of some non-English newspapers published in the United States.

LA SEMANA — NEW ENGLAND
Hispanic News Journal

First Bilingual Newspaper In New England

25¢ En Massachusetts
35¢ Fuera Del Estado
475 C Street, Boston Ma 02210
Tel: (617) 482-2879

Año 18 — No 80

Presidente Carter...
Ordena La Marina Cooperar Con Refugiados
"Nadie Será Devuelto A Cuba!"... PAGE 9

President Carter...
Orders Navy Cooperate With Refugees
"Nobody Will Be Returned To Cuba!"... PAGE 9

Alcalde White...
Pondrá Hispanos A Cargo Organismos De La Alcaldía! PAG.2

Mayor White...
Hispanics Will Be Appointed To City Posts! PAG.9

LOUISIANE

Mensuel publié par la Fondation Louisianaise des Mass-Media
Lafayette, LA

PRIX: 25¢

NO. 33, AVRIL 1980

Nix Reaffirms Support For Bilingual Education

LE F.A.R.O.G. FORUM
Vol. 6 - No. 6 — JOURNAL BILINGUE — mars 1980

"Religion et Nationalité": Une voix d'autrefois

Le Messager of 1880 - The Message was Loud and Clear

By Paul Paré

EAST WEST
THE CHINESE AMERICAN JOURNAL

PUBLISHED WEDNESDAYS • VOLUME 14, NUMBER 18 • APRIL 30, 1980 • 25 CENTS

東西報

市參議選舉
雙語要案
欲和控解

NORDISK TIDENDE
NORWEGIAN NEWS — Norske Nyheter

Published by Norse News Inc.
8104 5th Avenue, Brooklyn, N.Y. 11209

TORSDAG DEN 12. APRIL 1979

35 cents per copy

Lekkasje ved kjernereaktor i Sverige
Heftig politisk debatt fører til folkeavstemning

News in Brief From Norway

BOX 2.4

Attitudes toward Foreign Languages and Bilingualism
in the United States

Bilingualism has been treated as a necessary evil, a rash on the body politic, which time might be expected to cure without the need of calling in the doctors. . . . Very little prestige has been attached to the having of bilingual capacities. (Haugen, 1969, p. 2)

In the United States monolingualism traditionally has been the norm. Bilingualism was regarded as a social stigma and a liability . . . This hostility toward bilingualism has nothing to do with language as such. The hostility is directed not at language but at culture. The bilingual represents an alien way of thinking and alien values. (McLaughlin, 1978, pp. 2, 3)

The more locally irrelevant an ethnic language and culture is, the higher its social status, and the more viable it is locally, the lower its social status. (Kjolseth, 1972, p. 98)

American speakers of non-English languages have, of late, become objects of more positive attention than has previously been their common lot in most American communities . . . [but] they continue to be objects of curiosity in that their atypicality is obvious even if it is no longer considered shameful. (Fishman, 1965b, p. 150)

---

language. Americans believe that the use of ethnic languages and the maintenance of ethnic culture are to be tolerated, but in no way should they slow down the acquisition of English and the rapid assimilation of the "foreigner" into American life. Thus, as Haugen writes (see Box 2.4), bilingualism has been treated as a "necessary evil," a transition from monolingualism in a foreign language to monolingualism in English. And the "foreigner," until he or she is integrated into the community both linguistically and culturally, is treated as an alien and an object of curiosity (see the extracts from McLaughlin and Fishman in Box 2.4).

This negative attitude toward different lifestyles and languages has probably created more hardship and discrimination than any legal repression. As can be seen in Box. 2.5, many a member of a linguistic minority has a tale of mistreatment and hostility. Some minority groups have not met hostility and resentment (for example, Franco-Americans from France are respected and welcomed), but when such factors as low socioeconomic status, strong foreign ac-

---

BOX 2.5   BILINGUALS SPEAK

Hostility toward Members of Linguistic Minorities

A Franco-American: Once I heard a brother (an Irishman) explain the meaning of the word 'redundant' by stating that "a stupid frog" (meaning a stupid Franco-American) was a redundant statement. I never witnessed any rock throwing or any other violence against Franco-Americans during my high school years (as was the case in past generations, as told to me by my older relatives), but I must say that psychologically, I suffered tremendous pain because I was Franco-American.

A Cuban-American: The first day they left us the doughnuts and a metal case to carry them. We went out with this stuff and walked around. Finally we found this guy out mowing his lawn. He thought we were just kids selling stuff so he called us over. He said he wanted one. We gave him the bag. As he gave us the money, he must have realized we were Cubans, not American kids. He took the package he'd bought and threw it in the garbage. (Namias, 1978, p. 10)

A Portuguese-American: We bought a big house there. We had some trouble with some American kids over there. They burned six garages that were part of the house. In that neighborhood, these American kids, they see strangers, they don't like 'em. I don't think they like foreign people. They see foreign people, start in to call us names and everything . . . I was coming from school with my brother and they were asking me for money. I told 'em I didn't have any money. If I had it, I wouldn't give it to them. This kid slapped me. They slapped me, spit at me. (Namias, 1978, p. 172)

---

cent, and color of skin are combined, the society is at best indifferent and at worst openly hostile.

From the above we can better understand why bilingualism is treated as a stigma and a liability in the United States, whereas in many European and African countries it is considered a great asset. Those who are bilingual in this country are usually poorer than the average, and because they still use their minority language, they are seen as not having fully integrated themselves into American society. This pressure to Americanize and to become monolingual in English has led the country into a bizarre paradox: most Americans, many of whose families are originally of a foreign language background, prove to be extremely incompetent in learning and speaking foreign languages. According to *Strength Through Wisdom*, a report from the President's Commission on Foreign Language and International Studies (1979), the incompetence of Americans in foreign languages is nothing short of scandalous and is becoming worse.

The report adds that this gross national inadequacy has become a serious and growing liability. The paradox, of course, is that there *are* many speakers of foreign languages in the United States, but most are not in the positions of power, political or economic, in which foreign language skills are needed. Had the linguistic skills of minorities been reinforced instead of denigrated, the United States would now be rich in bilinguals and would not be spending millions of dollars in foreign language instruction.

It is difficult to end this section on a totally optimistic note. Admittedly, the needs of linguistic minorities have received more attention both from the government and from the English-speaking majority in the last twenty years. Bilingual education has been reinstated and even extended to undocumented workers in Texas; federal laws, such as the Voting Rights Acts of 1965 and 1975, which provide voting materials in minority languages, have enhanced the civil rights of minorities; and state and local administrations have shown more concern for their linguistic minorities by giving certain state examinations for accreditation in minority languages. But on the other hand there are clear signs that the country is not prepared to give up its monolingual and monocultural policies: in the 1980 election, for instance, the voters of Dade County, Florida, repealed the 1973 statute that made the county officially bilingual in English and Spanish; in that same year a federal court in Texas sustained an earlier decision that allowed an employer to forbid the use of a minority language among employees in the work place, and President Reagan's Republican administration has made substantial cuts in the services offered to minorities, such as in bilingual education. Hence it is difficult to forecast at this time whether this country will one day accept its cultural and linguistic diversity and whether the monolingual majority will finally realize that being bilingual and bicultural in the United States does not mean being "un-American."

Bilingual Education

A very important aspect of the life of a community is the education it gives to its children. Instruction in most countries has usually been in the majority language (although numerous exceptions exist, as we saw in Chapter 1). In the United States, English has generally been the language of instruction. In fact, school has long played an important role in the Americanization of the varied population; for many a minority child it has been the first step toward integration and assimilation into the Anglo-American society.

Many members of minority groups have from the first resisted this approach to assimilation by insisting on having their children educated in their minority language, either instead of or along with English, and on having access to their ethnic culture in the school. The type of education that has been devised in answer to this need has been termed "bilingual education." As we will see in Chapter 4, this term has many meanings, but for our current purposes it usually involves two languages; in the United States these are English and a minority language. Bilingual education is introduced in the following way by Pifer (1979):

> While the particular approaches used vary widely, the term usually refers to programs that employ a child's native tongue as a medium of instruction while he or she is being helped to learn English. The theory is that, by enabling students to master cognitive skills in the language they know best before making the transition to English, bilingual classes will prevent academic retardation. Often, a secondary aim is to enhance and maintain a child's proficiency in the home language. Classes also frequently draw on a child's heritage and culture as a means of building self-esteem and increasing comprehension and motivation to learn. (p. 3)

The following section reviews the history of bilingual education in the United States since the nineteenth century, concentrating first on private schools and then moving on to public schools. (Chapter 4 will describe and assess different types of bilingual education programs in the United States and in other countries.)

Private Schools

Among the rights that linguistic minorities have enjoyed in the United States, Kloss (1977) mentions the right to found and run private nationality schools. Linguistic minorities have made extensive use of this right, and in the nineteenth century there were many private, often religiously sponsored, schools. There were German schools in Ohio, Pennsylvania, Indiana, and other states with strong German minorities; French schools in Louisiana and later in New England, usually run by Catholic priests, brothers, and nuns; Spanish schools in New Mexico and in other Spanish-speaking areas. Most of these schools were at first monolingual, with the minority language as the medium of instruction. The legislation of the different states in no way opposed this practice, and Kloss reports that before 1889 only three states prescribed that private schools should use English exclusively as the language of instruction.

Little by little, and under pressure from state legislation and from parents who wanted to help their children assimilate, these private schools became bilingual; children were taught in both the minority language and in English. A typical Franco-American school in New England would teach basic subjects in English in the morning, and the history of Canada, religion, and the French language in French in the afternoon.

By the turn of the century a number of states had passed laws limiting the use of native languages as the medium of instruction, and the advent of World War I led to even greater restrictions on the use and teaching of foreign languages in private schools. Many states not only prohibited minority languages for instruction but even prohibited teaching them as subjects. But a Supreme Court decision in 1923 reaffirmed the right of minorities to cultivate their languages as subject matters in private elementary schools and allowed instruction in the mother tongue. Thus throughout the first half of the century, bilingual education was organized by a number of minorities, the most fervent being Franco-Americans, Polish Americans, and Italian Americans.

The depression, World War II, and the ensuing Americanization of minorities created hard times for private minority schools. A survey of these schools by Fishman and Nahirny in 1966 found them on the decline. Although the authors estimated that there were still about 2,000 ethnic schools in the United States (Fishman, 1981, reports 5,500 ethnic community schools in 1980), they also found that almost all used English as the sole medium of instruction and that the minority language had become merely a subject matter. In addition, most parents were either indifferent or opposed to the teaching of the mother tongue, and the teachers estimated that on the whole their students had only minimal fluency in their minority language. Thus, private ethnic schools had slowly evolved from being active defenders of minority language and culture to being rather passive defenders of minority culture and ethnicity but no longer of language. It is rather paradoxical that the public schools were to take up the relay from private schools.

Public Schools

Contrary to what one might expect, the public schools in the United States have not always been the primary champions of assimilation of linguistic minorities. In the nineteenth century, a number of public schools in Ohio, Minnesota, Maryland, and Indiana, used German either alone or with English for instruction. Some public schools in New England used French, and a number of schools in the Southwest used Spanish. A few bilingual public schools even survived up to the time of America's entry into World War I in Cincinnati, Baltimore, and Indianapolis. In addition, until 1868 French was allowed as the medium of instruction in the public schools of Louisiana.

But on the whole, most public schools used only English, and by 1917 bilingual instruction had disappeared. In fact, many states in the late nineteenth and early twentieth century passed legislation requiring that English be the language of instruction and imposing fines on teachers who used any other language. Children were punished for talking to one another in their mother tongue, and the non-English-speaking child was forced to "sink or swim" in a totally Anglo-American environment. Numerous stories have been told by members of minority groups about their first months at school: their isolation and frustration, discrimination by teachers and fellow students, the effort to slowly integrate themselves into the system. Courses in English as a second language (ESL) were organized for them, but the type of English taught was academic and did not relate to their everyday lives, and being pulled out of class to attend these sessions only emphasized the differences between them and other children. Box 2.6 presents a very vivid description of what a child from a minority language background had to go through at that time.

The 1960s brought many changes to American life. Minority groups, encouraged by the Black civil rights movement, started reacting against the assimilation process of American society. They wanted to express their ethnic identity and demanded that their languages and cultures be respected and maintained. With this revival of ethnicity, school officials and education experts finally accepted the fact that the Anglo-American English-speaking public school was not meeting the needs of children from minority language backgrounds. These children were disadvantaged from the start, and the school system only maintained, if not increased, their disadvantage. Mackey and Beebe (1977) report that in 1960, 87 percent of all Puerto Ricans aged twenty-five or older had not graduated from high school; Padilla (1977) reports that in 1971, 40 percent of Mexican Americans entering first grade never finished high school, and Waggoner (1980) reports that in the 1976 Survey of Income and Education, 24 percent of all people claiming a Spanish language background never completed twelfth grade, as compared to 13 percent of people with a French language background and only 10 percent of those with an English language background. In addition, in

BOX 2.6

A Minority-Language Child in Elementary School Before Bilingual Education

A child from a Japanese-speaking home usually starts his first-grade education as a tiny minority in the class. He does not understand English well enough to follow the activities of the others, nor does he know how to ask for help. Often he is the only one in the class who looks physically different and who cannot communicate in English. He is immediately labeled as inferior, is pushed into a corner, and is neglected. The child develops a shy, insecure personality. Unless he is exceptionally bright, he will not have a chance to overcome this initial handicap . . . Concerned parents of Japanese-American children are advised by the school to abandon everything Japanese at home in order to attain the goal of becoming American. Sometimes Japanese does cease to be spoken at home and eventually the family gives up everything Japanese. In spite of this effort, the child soon discovers that his parents are incapable of fulfilling their role in helping the child with his school problems. The parents have even greater language problems than he does. They cannot help him with homework assignments, nor, in many cases, can they comply with directives from school to allow them to take part in activities and organizations set up by the school. The child lacks the background and the help that are readily available in some English speaking homes and that are taken for granted by many of his teachers. During his entire academic career the child must solve his problems by himself or not at all. (Han, 1978, pp. 199–200)

---

many states such as California and Texas, Mexican American children were put into classes for the mentally retarded.

To these two factors—the rise of ethnicity and the inability of schools to give equal educational opportunities to children of linguistic minorities—must be added the fact that many educators finally accepted the notion that the home language should, at least at first, be the child's language of instruction and that bilingualism is not detrimental to cognitive growth. Thus the stage was set for a renaissance of bilingual education in public schools, and in 1963 a federally funded bilingual program was set up for exiled Cuban children in grades one to three in the Coral Way School in Dade County, Florida. The next year, schools in Webb County, Texas, and in San Antonio also started bilingual programs. What was now needed was a federal law allowing and encouraging bilingual education, and this came in 1968.

The Bilingual Education Act, or Title VII of the 1965 Elementary and Secondary Education Act, was signed into law on January 2, 1968, by President Johnson. The declaration of policy states:

In recognition of the *special educational needs of the large numbers of children of limited English speaking ability* in the United States, Congress hereby declares it to be the policy of the United States to provide *financial assistance to local educational agencies to develop and carry out new and imaginative elementary and secondary school programs* designed to meet these special educational needs. (Italics added)

The law authorized grants for bilingual demonstration projects for children with limited English-speaking ability from homes in which the annual income was $3,000 or less. The act did not establish bilingual education for all children in need of it; instead it funded model programs that would develop curriculum, train teachers, and encourage state and local authorities to follow suit (Schneider, 1976). In the first fiscal year, [1969], $7.5 million was used to fund seventy-six programs, most of them in California, Texas, New Mexico, Arizona, and Colorado, and the great majority in English and Spanish.

As Schneider reports, the Bilingual Education Act was ambiguous enough to allow the programs to have different goals and to follow differing approaches. Four aspects remained unspecified: (1) whether the programs should help maintain the language and culture of the minority group or should be a transition into an English-speaking classroom; (2) when each language should be used in the classroom and for how long; (3) how much community involvement was necessary; and (4) what were the criteria for selecting participants.

Nevertheless, the mere existence of federally funded bilingual education was extremely significant, and as Box 2.7 points out, many minorities found renewed hope in this. In addition, the act did encourage state and local authorities to initiate their own programs, and in 1971 Massachusetts became the first state to mandate bilingual education with its Transitional Bilingual Education Act. Under the measure, every school district with twenty or more children of one language group with limited English-speaking ability had to provide a bilingual program. Parent involvement was made mandatory, bilingual teacher certification was required, and a Bureau of Transitional Bilingual Education was set up. It is important to note that the Massachusetts law explicitly states that bilingual education should be transitional, and children stay in the program only for three years. During that time they develop basic skills in both English and their native language and receive instruction in the his-

---

BOX 2.7   **BILINGUALS SPEAK**

Bilingual Education

Governor Robert Lewis in an address to the National Indian Bilingual Education Conference: It does my heart good to see all of you here, so many in number, and to have the opportunity to talk to you about a subject so important to the American Indian: bilingual education . . . I am quite positive that you know in your hearts that we are getting into an area that is very important for young people: being able to speak two languages . . . It makes me feel sad when I come across some young Indian people who never learned to speak their language, because, as I said, it is very valuable to be able to speak and think in two languages. When we consider today's attitudes, we find that many of the young people do not try to communicate with the older people. As a result they are sometimes losing sight of some of the valuable things that only the old people still have. I have talked with our young people, even in high school, and I have tried to teach them our language. But you find that after a while they lose interest and revert to English. I think that this is very sad, because when a people loses *its* language, then it loses practically everything.

As far as the Indian is concerned, we have been misunderstood for so many years. I remember the time when I was going to boarding school. When we wanted to speak our language we had to sneak off somewhere and get together as a group and talk to our heart's content . . . I forgot my language because I went to boarding school when I was six. I mean the way of speaking it. I understood clearly whatever was spoken to me. When my parents or grandparents would come to meet me, I would understand them and be able to greet them, but since I could not speak I would get embarrassed and run away . . . I had to relearn the language. (Lewis, 1974, pp. 12–18)

---

tory and culture of their own country and of the United States. In the first year the native language is used about 95 percent of the time; in the second year the two languages are used equally, and in the third year the native language is used only about 5 to 10 percent of the time.

Public bilingual education might very well have been as short lived as some of the other social reforms that came out of the tumultuous sixties and early seventies, had not the U.S. Supreme Court handed down a decision on the *Lau* v. *Nichols* case in 1974. The action originated in 1970 in San Francisco, where a group of Chinese-speaking students alleged that they were being denied an equal education because they could not understand the language in which they were being taught. In its decision the Supreme Court declared that "the failure of the San Francisco school system to provide English language instruction to approximately 1,800 students of Chinese ancestry who do not speak English, or to provide them with other adequate instructional procedures, denies them a meaningful opportunity to participate in the public educational programs" and thus violated the Civil Rights Act of 1964. The court did not specify how to remedy the problem: "Teaching English to the students of Chinese ancestry who do not speak the language is one choice. Giving instructions to this group in Chinese is another. There may be others." But in the Department of Health, Education and Welfare guidelines informing school authorities on how to interpret and enforce the *Lau* decision (which of course concerns all minority groups and not just the Chinese Americans in San Francisco), transitional bilingual education, including instruction in English as a second language, is proposed as a minimum requirement at the primary school level, and English as a second language at the secondary school level. As Troike and Perez (1978) state, the thrust of the *Lau* decision is that if a school district has twenty or more students from the same language background with limited English proficiency, it must offer bilingual education, at least on a compensatory basis, whether or not state funds are available. They continue: "More than any other single development, then, the *Lau* decision may result in the institutionalization of bilingual education as a basic part of American education" (p. 68). In addition, for the first time in the United States, language rights were recognized as a civil right.

The *Lau v. Nichols* decision played a large role in the 1974 amendments to the 1968 Bilingual Education Act, marking yet another stage in the history of public bilingual education in the United States. As Schneider (1976) reports, although the federal government would continue funding a number of purely demonstration projects, the amendments also set up more long-term provisions. The government would assist state and local authorities to establish bilingual educational programs; provide resources for teacher training, technical assistance, and research on bilingual education; and create an Office of Bilingual Education and a National Advisory Council on Bilingual Education. In addition, as Schneider states, although bilingual education was still considered transitional (but stress was put on both the bilingual *and* the bicultural components of the programs), the possibility of programs that would maintain the native language and culture throughout the school years was not excluded. And lastly, English-speaking children were encouraged to enroll in bilingual programs to acquire a better understanding of the cultural heritage of ethnic minorities. Thus, with the 1968 act and its 1974 amendments, bilingual education was slowly being established as an important component of public education.

In 1978 a second set of amendments to the Bilingual Education Act was voted into law. They did not modify the fundamental nature of the act as amended in 1974 but did bring the following main changes: the communities, especially parents, were to be involved in applications for federal funds; each local program was to have an evaluation plan to study the effects of bilingual education; a research program was to be carried out by the National Institute of Education; native speakers of English were allowed to participate in bilingual programs (up to 40 percent of the class), and each project was to show how federal funds would help it become a regularly funded program. Perhaps the most significant aspect of the 1978 amendments, however, was that the Secretary of Education was to investigate and offer a plan for transforming the federally funded bilingual education program into a formula grant program: that is, instead of certain projects being funded while others are not, demonstration of need would automatically result in funding. If this is approved (it will be taken up by Congress in 1984), public bilingual education will indeed have reached full recognition in the country. Part of the Bilingual Education Act, containing the 1974 and 1978 amendments, is presented in Box 2.8.

By 1980 bilingual education, whether funded by the federal government or by the states, had made great progress. In the federal program, Title VII, there were 575 projects in forty-two states and five territories. The states with the most projects were California (140), New York (92), and Texas (69), but even states long thought to be totally English speaking, such as Georgia, Tennessee, Mississippi, and Kentucky, had bilingual programs. These Title VII programs involved seventy-nine minority languages in addition to English; by far the most important language was Spanish (about 80 percent of the programs), but other languages included French, Navajo, Apache, Italian, Japanese, Algonquin, Ilocano, Vietnamese, Haitian-Creole, Greek, Yiddish, Armenian, Ojibwa, Chinese, and Oneida.

About 315,000 children (77 percent of them having limited English proficiency) were enrolled in these programs, and the overall budget for fiscal 1980 was $167 million (in 1969, $7.5 million had

---

BOX 2.8

Extracts from the Federal Bilingual Education Act, as Amended in 1974 and 1978

POLICY; APPROPRIATIONS

Sec. 702. (a) Recognizing—

1. that there are large numbers of children of limited English proficiency;

2. that many of such children have a cultural heritage which differs from that of English-speaking persons;

3. that a primary means by which a child learns is through the use of such child's language and cultural heritage;

4. that, therefore, large numbers of children of limited English proficiency have educational needs which can be met by the use of bilingual educational methods and techniques;

5. that, in addition, children of limited English proficiency and children whose primary language is English benefit through the fullest utilization of multiple language and cultural resources;

6. children of limited English proficiency have a high dropout rate and low median years of education; and

7. research and evaluation capabilities in the field of bilingual education need to be strengthened,

the Congress declares it to be the policy of the United States, in order to establish equal educational opportunity for all children (A) to encourage the establishment and operation, where appropriate, of educational programs using bilingual educational practices, techniques, and methods, and (B) for that purpose, to provide financial assistance to local educational agencies, and to State educational agencies for certain purposes, in order to enable such local educational agencies to develop and carry out such programs in elementary and secondary schools, including activities at the preschool level, which are designed to meet the educational needs of such children, with particular attention to children having the greatest need for such programs; and to demonstrate effective ways of providing, for children of limited English proficiency, instruction designed to enable them, while using their native language, to achieve competence in the English language . . .

---

been appropriated). The administrative structure needed to coordinate and implement the Title VII programs was already quite large: an Office of Bilingual Education and Minority Languages Affairs within the Department of Education coordinated the programs under the supervision of a National Advisory Council on Bilingual

BOX 2.8 continued

DEFINITIONS; REGULATIONS

4 A. The term "program of bilingual education" means a program of instruction, designed for children of limited English proficiency in elementary or secondary schools, in which, with respect to the years of study to which such program is applicable—

i. there is instruction given in, and study of, English and, to the extent necessary to allow a child to achieve competence in the English language, the native language of the children of limited English proficiency, and such instruction is given with appreciation for the cultural heritage of such children, and of other children in American society, and, with respect to elementary and secondary school instruction, such instruction shall, to the extent necessary, be in all courses or subjects of study which will allow a child to progress effectively through the educational system; and

ii. the requirements in subparagraphs (B) through (F) of this paragraph and established pursuant to subsection (b) of this section are met.

B. In order to prevent the segregation of children on the basis of national origin in programs assisted under this title, and in order to broaden the understanding of children about languages and cultural heritages other than their own, a program of bilingual instruction may include the participation of children whose language is English, but in no event shall the percentage of such children exceed 40 per centum. The objective of the program shall be to assist children of limited English proficiency to improve their English language skills, and the participation of other children in the program must be for the principal purpose of contributing to the achievement of that objective. The program may provide for centralization of teacher training and curriculum development, but it shall serve such children in the schools which they normally attend.

Education; a National Clearinghouse for Bilingual Education, created in 1977, collected, analyzed, and disseminated information about bilingual education and programs; Bilingual Education Support Centers and National Evaluation, Dissemination and Assessment Centers helped to train bilingual teachers and to prepare and disseminate bilingual teaching materials; and finally, a National Center for Bilingual Research in Los Alamitos, California, was involved in three broad areas of research: language acquisition in a first and second language; language functioning in two languages, and bilingual education.

At the state level, and here the information dates back to 1976

(Development Associates, 1977), forty states either mandated or permitted bilingual education: ten, including Alaska, Massachusetts, California, and Texas, actually required it; sixteen states permitted it (including Arizona, Florida, Maine, New York), and fourteen tacitly permitted this type of education in that their laws were not explicit. Only ten states, as compared to twenty in 1968, prohibited bilingual education (for examle, Alabama, Arkansas, West Virginia, Nebraska) but four of these had Title VII programs and thus were not enforcing the prohibition. The great majority of the states had transitional bilingual education programs as opposed to maintenance programs and in that sense closely followed Title VII programs, which are officially transitional in nature. Only eleven states in 1976 had adopted comprehensive bilingual education laws that not only implemented the programs but also stipulated the qualifications required of bilingual education teachers, mandated a cultural component, established a regular census of children of limited English proficiency, and so on. In this sense, state legislation lagged behind the federal laws by a few years, but enormous progress had nevertheless been made in a short time.

Because bilingual education is still in its infancy in the United States, it is quite naturally accompanied by a number of problems, which are slowly being dealt with. An important one is the discrepancy between the need for this type of education and the number of children who are actually enrolled in programs. A 1979 issue of *Forum,* the newsletter published by the National Clearinghouse for Bilingual Education, reports on a study by the National Institute of Education which estimates that about 3.6 million school-age children in the United States are limited in English proficiency and hence require some form of bilingual education. Most are Hispanic Americans and live primarily in Texas, California, and New York. Although no exact figures exist concerning the number of children enrolled in federal and state-funded bilingual programs, it has been estimated that less than 40 percent of those who need such programs actually receive them. States with mandatory bilingual education naturally have a much higher percentage: in Massachusetts 92 percent of those children who are entitled to bilingual education received it in 1977–1978.

In the whole country, not only are the majority of children with limited English proficiency not enrolled in bilingual programs, but the prospect that they ever will be is not very bright. First, these children are in many cases scattered among the English-speaking population and thus do not meet the minimum number of twenty that many school authorities require in order to offer bilingual education. Some states, however, have made provisions for such children in their legislation; the California Bilingual-Bicultural Education Act of 1976 includes a Bilingual Individual Learning Program for any child with limited or no English proficiency for whom no regular bilingual-bicultural program existed. Second, some states have not yet passed legislation permitting bilingual education, and third, perhaps more important, many states that do allow bilingual education are not appropriating enough funds to offer the necessary number of programs. For example, in 1975–1976, only four states were reported to have allocated more state funds for bilingual education than they received from the federal government during that year (Development Associates, 1977).

Other problem areas affecting bilingual education, which are being addressed and solved little by little, concern teacher training, materials development, community involvement, and research on bilingual education. Until recently it was difficult to find qualified teachers who were both bilingual in English and a minority language and also bicultural, so that children from the minority background could easily identify with them. This problem, although less acute, is still present, especially in states such as California that have programs for all children with limited English-speaking ability either in regular bilingual instruction or in individual programs. Another problem has been the lack of quality instructional materials and good curriculum models. Also, community involvement has often been lacking, and many uninformed members of minorities were at first actually opposed to their children being taught in their minority language. But opposition has usually turned to encouragement when parents have become directly involved in the program. Finally, substantive research on bilingual education has been lacking; little is known about its long-term effects, how it should be implemented, the best curriculum, and so on. But all of these problems are being addressed at both the state and federal levels and with time they will be solved.

Two aspects of bilingual education have been extremely controversial from the onset. The first concerns its effectiveness, and the second pertains to its role: should it be compensatory and transitional or should it maintain the minority language and culture? Although the Bilingual Education Act was signed into law in the late sixties, its opponents have not disarmed, and their opposition can be summarized by remarks such as: "I didn't get bilingual education when I went to school, why should my child?" "Bilingual education will stop my child from learning English," "Bilingual education promotes the maintenance of minority groups when the schools should be helping to assimilate them," "Bilingual education is expensive and in these hard times the society cannot affort it," "Bilingual education will lead to the Balkanization of the U.S.," "Immigrants choose to come to the United States; they should therefore accept its language and education," and so on.

People who make comments of this type—from the senator in Congress to the passerby in the street—are reinforced in their position by the fact that evaluation of the effectiveness of bilingual education has been lagging. Unfortunately there are no agreed-upon evaluation standards and criteria, so the studies that report on the effectiveness of bilingual education come to different conclusions. Some show that it is extremely effective: it reduces the educational gap between Anglo-American and minority language children, cuts the dropout rate considerably, improves the self-concept of minority children, and helps them maintain their language and culture; see, for example, Schneider (1976), Blanco (1978), Troike (1978), and Dulay and Burt (1979). Other studies, however, show that bilingual education is not effective. For instance, a much-publicized report issued by the American Institute for Research (A.I.R.) in 1978 (Danoff, 1978) stated that teachers believed that of the 11,500 Hispanic students evaluated, less than a third were in bilingual education because of their need for English instruction (that is, they were not considered to have limited English proficiency) and that relative to national norms, these students were performing generally at about the twentieth percentile in English reading. In addition, participation in the bilingual program did not bring about a more positive student attitude toward school and school-related activities. Since its publication, this report has come under heavy criticism. Gray (1978), for example, enumerated a number of flaws in the study, including the makeup of the experimental and control groups, the inappropriate use of evaluation tests, and the unreliability of teacher assessment of students' language ability. Concerning this last point, it seemed surprising to Gray that less than a third of the students were judged by their teachers to be in need of English instruction when they were performing at a 20–30 percentile level on a test of basic skills. (Also see Dulay and Burt, 1979, for additional criticism of the A.I.R. study.) From the above we can conclude that the evaluation of bilingual education needs much improvement, and until programs have clearly set their goals (educational, cultural, linguistic, attitudinal) and have used appropriate instruments to measure whether these goals have been achieved, it will be difficult to come to any unbiased conclusion on the effectiveness of the programs. What is sure is that the general public still does not understand the goals and the many positive aspects of bilingual education: whereas 96 percent of those polled by *Newsweek* (April 20, 1981), approved of special education programs for gifted children and slow learners (2 percent disapproved), 64 percent approved of bilingual education and 32 percent disapproved.

The second controversial aspect of bilingual education, which is linked to the first, concerns its ultimate role. Should it be compensatory and transitional, helping the linguistic minority child ease into the Anglo-American educational system, or should it help maintain the minority language and culture so that the child will become both bilingual and bicultural? (Some people even propose that the child remain monolingual and monocultural in the minority language and culture.) Today almost all of the state bilingual programs and all Title VII projects are officially transitional (although many stress the importance of integrating the minority culture in daily instruction), but certain minority groups have demanded that the programs become more pluralistic in nature so that the majority language and culture does not replace those of the minority, however "well" this is done. The argument is that minority children should have the right to learn about their own culture in addition to the majority culture; the United States is a land of many cultures and many languages, and allowing minority groups to identify with both the minority and the majority cultures will make the country all the more cohesive and strong. Bilingual education is one approach to achieve this goal.

At the present time, the trend is for the government to support state and local options and not to impose federal policy. The directions taken by local bodies—transitional bilingual education by some, ESL programs by others (as in Fairfax County, Virginia)—will be respected. As the Secretary of Education said in February, 1981, the administration will protect the rights of children who do not speak English well, but it will do so by permitting school districts to use any method that has proven to be successful. We are therefore still far from a mandatory federal policy guaranteeing bilingual education for all who need it; state and local initiatives will be critical in the years to come.

Some Linguistic Minorities

This section will give a very brief overview of five groups: Native Americans, Deaf Americans, German Americans, Franco-Americans, and Hispanic Americans. Two reasons have led to the choice of these minorities: on the one hand, I want to draw attention to two groups, Native Americans and Deaf Americans, that have been oppressed for many years. On the other hand I want to show how European language groups have fared in the struggle to maintain their language and culture: the German Americans were once the strongest and most active linguistic minority in the United States, yet today practically all have been assimilated into American society; the Franco-Americans, also very active in their fight for language maintenance, are now going through a difficult period, with impending assimilation in both New England and Louisiana; finally, Hispanic Americans are the largest linguistic minority in the United States, and are in no apparent danger of rapid assimilation. Readers interested in these and other minority groups can consult the *Harvard Encyclopedia of American Ethnic Groups* (1980).

Native Americans

Indians, Aleuts, and Eskimos, unlike the majority of Americans, do not have their origin in overseas immigration—at least not in the last 4,000 years. They were here when the first Europeans arrived, and it was their land that was conquered and annexed by the white men. It is estimated that there were approximately a million Native Americans at the time of Christopher Columbus; they were geographically dispersed, culturally diverse, and spoke an estimated 500 to 1,000 languages. Some of these languages were common to several tribes (the Algonquin language in New England, for example), while others were spoken by just one group. Certain areas were heavily populated; for example, the Pacific Northwest had seven language families, each with several distinct languages. This led to much language contact and bilingualism, especially because many Indians in that region were traders and sold goods all the way to the Great Plains (Bright, 1973; Bright and Sherzer, 1976). A number of pidgin languages developed for intergroup communication: Mobilian Jargon in the Southeast; Chinook Jargon in the Northwest, Sign Language in the Great Plains.

When the Europeans first arrived, it was usually the Indians who learned the European languages when contact took place: Spanish in the Southwest, Russian in Alaska, French in Quebec and Louisiana, English in the East. But a few Europeans also learned the Indian languages; many French fur hunters and traders lived among the Indians and learned their languages, and later some missionaries did likewise.

More than four hundred years of war, deportation, annexation, and general oppression have left Native Americans in a difficult state. Rosen and Gorwitz (1980) report that according to the 1970 census, there were an estimated 764,000 Native Americans in the United States, belonging to more than 150 culturally distinct nations and tribes. The most important groups were the Navajo (97,000), the Cherokee (66,000), the Sioux (48,000), and the Chippewa (42,000). Most Native Americans live in the West: Oklahoma, Arizona, New Mexico, and California, but there are also many in Alaska, North Carolina, and New York. Almost half live in cities and towns, and many others live on the two hundred or so Indian reservations. Native Americans are characterized by a high birthrate and a short lifespan; 40 percent fall below the poverty level; and they have one of the highest school dropout rates: only a third complete high school as compared to more than half of the general population.

In the 1970 census, 34 percent of Native Americans reported an Indian or Eskimo language as a mother tongue; thus the majority are native English speakers, although about 25,000 reported Spanish as their mother tongue and 8,000 reported French. It is estimated that about three hundred Native American languages are still in use today, the most important being Navajo, Sioux, Algonquin, Pueblo, Muskhogean, and Iroquois. However, most of the languages are used by very few Native Americans, and most of these are elderly. The number of Native Americans who are mother tongue speakers of the nation's or tribe's language varies a great deal: Spolsky (1977) reports that in Alaska many Indians, Aleuts, and Eskimos have been able to maintain their languages (Aleut, Yup'ik, Inupiaq) and that in Montana 82 percent of Crow children speak Crow as a first language, but only a third of the 30,000 Cherokee in Oklahoma and the 3,000 in North Carolina in 1960 were believed to speak their language fluently. Seminole is still used by adults speaking to each other, but most parents speak to their children in English. The factors that explain the better maintenance of some Native American languages over others include geographical isolation (Alaskan languages), religiosocial isolation (Pueblo languages, Crow, Keresan), size of the nation (Navajo), and the attitude of the group toward maintenance (Spolsky reports that maintenance of the Crow language is considered a task of the home). In recent years there has been renewed interest and pride in Native American cultures and languages, and some fast-disappearing languages (Bright, 1973 cites Luiseño, Cupeño, and Dieguño in southern California) have been the object of revival through teaching and use.

The education of Native American children has clearly reflected the fluctuations in federal Indian policy; as Spolsky (1978) writes, the policy has evolved from virtual genocide to moderate acceptance and from assimilation or relocation to the support of some degree of maintenance of culture and language. Until the 1930s, the policy was to separate Native American children from their parents and their natural cultural environment to better assimilate them into the majority culture. Many were put into white foster homes, and many others were sent to military-style boarding schools. All ties with the nation or tribe were broken: children were forbidden to speak their native language among themselves, and parents were discouraged from visiting them (see Box 2.7).

But in recent years, bilingual education has been introduced for many Native Americans. In 1979 Title VII money provided bilingual education for 14,000 Native Americans in fourteen states. Twenty-eight different languages in addition to English were used in the programs. Spolsky reports that programs range all the way from bilingual-bicultural projects to maintain the native language and culture (as for the Navajo, Crow, and Yup'ik) to revival programs in which the children are taught their Indian language as a second language (such projects exist for Passamaquoddy, Seminole, and Tewa). Spolsky adds that opposition to bilingual education comes from parents who are worried that their children will not learn English and will thus remain second-class citizens, as well as from the educational establishment, where bilingual education is seen as a rejection of past programs and practices and a threat to the monolingual English-speaking staff. But the future for Native American children is hopefully reflected in such bilingual-bicultural programs as those at the Pine Hill School on the Ramah Navajo Reservation in northwestern New Mexico and the Rough Rock Demonstration School Bilingual-Bicultural Project in Arizona. At Pine Hill, Hale (1978) reports that Navajo parents teach the children about their traditions and culture. Children do rug and belt weaving, sand painting, and beading, and follow courses in Navajo science, math, history, law and government, economy, and religion. This form of bilingual education will certainly play an important role in the revival and maintenance of Native American ethnicity and language.

Deaf Americans

If one defines deafness as the inability to hear or understand speech with or without a hearing aid, then there are about 2 million Deaf people in the United States today. Some 1.5 million have become

Deaf after the age of nineteen through sickness, accident, or old age; the other half million were born Deaf or became Deaf in early infancy or in childhood. (Only about 10 percent of Deaf children have Deaf parents.) An estimated additional 6 million Americans have significant hearing impairment; this group is often called hard of hearing.

It would be an error to think that the level of hearing impairment or audiometric deafness is the main criterion for becoming a member of the Deaf community. In fact, the Deaf community includes people who are profoundly Deaf, those who are hard of hearing and even some hearing people, such as interpreters and children of Deaf parents. The two important criteria that make one a member of the community are a common culture and a common language: American Sign Language (Woodward, 1980). (Other criteria are hearing impairment and political interest or influence in the Deaf community.) The Deaf share a number of social and cultural traits that have evolved from common experiences and social isolation. Their special education creates lifelong social ties, and such interests as legal rights, education, sports, and the welfare of the community are shared by all. The Deaf have national, state, and local organizations (the National Association of the Deaf at the national level), publications (*The Deaf American*, for instance), and theater groups (the National Theater of the Deaf is well known). In addition, the Deaf have a rich folklore and a long social history, all of which reinforce group cohesiveness and cultural identity.

The second criterion is knowledge and use of American Sign Language (ASL). For many years a number of myths have surrounded ASL: that it is universal, word-based, pantomimic, concrete, ungrammatical, and pictorial. In fact, recent research (Stokoe, 1978; Wilbur, 1979; Klima and Bellugi, 1979; Lane and Grosjean, 1980) has clearly shown that ASL is a rule-governed language with the systematicity and breadth of any oral language, and with its own complex phonology, morphology, syntax, and discourse structure. What is especially interesting is that as a gestural-visual language ASL makes important use of the space in which the signs are presented and of the signer's body (eye gaze, head tilt, facial and body movement).

Thus, like other linguistic minorities in the United States, the Deaf are characterized by a language and a culture of their own. Similarly, but often to a greater degree, the Deaf have suffered from the prejudice and discrimination that befall linguistic minorities. As can be seen in Box 2.9, the hearing majority still sees Deaf people as less intelligent and less cultured—in a word, as marginal members

---

BOX 2.9   **BILINGUALS SPEAK**

Discrimination against the Deaf

A hearing child of Deaf parents, bilingual in ASL and English: One time I was in a restaurant in Boston. I was meeting my father there but [as] he didn't seem to be coming . . . I ordered for both of us . . . Then my father joined me. The person in the restaurant came over and tried to shoo him away, saying, "Get out of here, get out of here." I said, "What are you doing?" and the person said, "Well, he's just bothering you." I replied, "He's not bothering me, he's my father, he's talking sign language, he's Deaf." And she replied, "Oh, yeah, I bet he's blind too."

I can remember my uncle saying to me, "When you grow up, you'll go away with the hearing people and you'll never pay attention to us again."

My father is a union carpenter. Although a master carpenter, he's never been promoted to foreman even though he's worked fifty years in the trade. He said to me, "You know, I'll never be a foreman because I'm not hearing."

---

of the society. Some researchers have used the results of IQ tests to show that the Deaf are less intelligent and incapable of abstract thought. However, when such factors as socioeconomic status and language of the test are controlled for, any differences between the hearing and the Deaf tend to disappear.

Discrimination against the Deaf is found at all levels of society. In employment, 80 percent of the Deaf are in blue-collar jobs (as opposed to 50 percent of the general population), and their earnings are only 70 percent of those of hearing people. And in education, one domain that should be at the service of the Deaf, one finds many examples of prejudice and ostracism. Although bilingual education was introduced into U.S. public schools in 1968, it still appears very far away in the case of ASL and English: ASL is not a medium of instruction in any school for the Deaf and is, in fact, still prohibited in many schools. ASL is not recognized by the U.S. Office of Bilingual Education and Minority Languages Affairs as a language to be used with English in bilingual programs, and bilingual education for Deaf children was ranked almost last as an important issue in a recent survey of educators of the Deaf (Lane, 1980). The absence of bilingual education and the long history of monolingual English education has led to the same kind of underachievement that has marked other minorities: about 30 percent of

Deaf adults are functionally illiterate, only half of Deaf adolescents complete high school, and a mere handful go on to college.

Finally, the sign language of the Deaf has come under constant attack over the last hundred years: there have been endless efforts to suppress it, mainly by forbidding its use in schools and by ridiculing it outside the schools, or to dialectize it by making it more English-like (Lane, 1980). The negative attitudes of hearing people toward ASL have been adopted by many of the Deaf themselves, who until recently were embarrassed to use their language in public (Covington, 1980). They looked upon it as a mere system of gestures used by lower-class, uneducated people, and one often heard remarks like, "My mother and father are not smart! They use ASL" (Berke, 1980).

In contrast to other linguistic minorities, for most Deaf people enculturation into the community and acquisition of the minority language does not take place in the home because only about 10 percent of Deaf children have Deaf parents, and thus very few are native users of ASL. For the majority of Deaf children, enculturation and the acquisition of ASL take place in residential or day schools for the Deaf, where their peers and a few Deaf adults serve as teachers and models. The children who go to totally oral schools, where sign language is strictly prohibited, even outside class, do not at first come into contact with the Deaf community and ASL. Many go through a long period of social isolation among hearing people but ultimately seek out other Deaf people, learn their language and, despite the opposition of some parents and educators, do become full members of the Deaf community. It is interesting that in the end—however difficult the route—most prevocational Deaf (those who have become Deaf before age nineteen) are acculturated into the Deaf community, as shown by the fact that 95 percent of the married Deaf are married to another Deaf person.

Two types of bilingualism have evolved in the Deaf community: a sign-sign bilingualism, involving ASL and an English form of signing, and a sign-English bilingualism, involving ASL and spoken or written English. ASL, the natural language of the Deaf, is used in the family, with friends, and with other members of the community. It serves as a powerful cohesive force, a sort of buffer between the hearing and Deaf worlds, and this is no doubt one reason why it is rarely used with hearing outsiders. With hearing people, the Deaf tend to use an English form of signing, often referred to as Sign English of Pidgin Sign English. It is characterized by ASL signs used in English word order, more finger-spelling, and very little use of such ASL grammatical mechanisms as use of space, inflections, and facial and body movements. Sign English is used in schools and to communicate with hearing people who have learned some signs. Many Deaf people who know ASL are also fluent in some kind of Sign English.

Sign-English bilingualism is far less widespread because very few Deaf have native competence in English. Only 12 percent of young Deaf adults can read or write above a fourth-grade level, only 15 percent of Deaf children are completely intelligible in spoken English (more than half are unintelligible), and very few Deaf can lipread satisfactorily. Because speaking English is a slow and tedious process for many Deaf persons, and understanding spoken English is even more difficult, many prefer to write when communicating with a hearing person. But in general, contact with hearing people is limited unless an interpreter is present or the hearing person knows some sign language. The people who are truly bilingual in ASL and English are the hearing children of Deaf parents, who often serve as interpreters for members of the Deaf community.

In sum, Deaf Americans share many characteristics of other linguistic minorities in the United States: they have a language and a culture of their own; they have suffered much discrimination and prejudice in such domains as education and employment; they have adopted many of the majority's negative attitudes toward their language and culture; and many of them are—to some extent at least—bilingual. However, Deaf Americans also have certain unique characteristics. First, they are not recognized as a linguistic and cultural minority by the hearing majority, mainly because the audiological aspect of deafness (the "impairment" or "handicap") has prevented the hearing from considering their culture and language. Second, ASL is usually learned at school from peers rather than at home. Third, their hearing impairment is a strong factor in the maintenance of ASL as a minority language, but it also means that not all Deaf people will become fully bilingual in ASL and spoken English. And last, unlike other minorities, the Deaf are not concentrated in any one area of the country, although there is a greater proportion of Deaf people in urban than in rural areas.

German Americans

If a person studying linguistic minorities in the United States could go back a mere eighty years in time, he or she would be struck by the dominance of one linguistic minority group over others—the German Americans.

Just as today Hispanic Americans are the largest and most active minority group, so then German Americans were playing the leading role. In this section I will review how German Americans came to be the most active and influential minority group at the turn of the century and how they have since become almost completely assimilated into the Anglo-American society.

The first permanent German settlement was founded in 1683 in Germantown, Pennsylvania, by a group of religious refugees. By the beginning of the Revolution, Germans numbered about 225,000—by far the largest non-English immigrant group. Most settled in Pennsylvania, and in 1775 about a third of that state's population was German. Mainly farmers, they organized themselves in a semi-independent manner: they founded schools (regular teaching in German was recorded as early as 1694), published newspapers, held town meetings, all in German, of course. Throughout the nineteenth and early twentieth centuries, German immigrants arrived in large numbers. Kloss (1966) reports that between 1820 and 1962, as many as 6 million German-speaking people left Germany, Austria, Switzerland, and Russia to settle in this country.

Some of these people were farmers and traders, some were teachers and lawyers. Some belonged to religious sects such as the Mennonites, Amish, and Moravians, others were political liberals who had participated in the 1848 revolution in Prussia. They settled in Pennsylvania and in "German islands" in Illinois, Ohio, Missouri, Wisconsin, and Texas.

What is particularly striking about German Americans in the nineteenth century is their constant efforts to maintain their language, culture, and heritage. They set up monolingual and bilingual private schools in most of the states where they settled, and they opened bilingual public schools in Ohio, Maryland, and Indiana. They lobbied state legislatures for more linguistic and cultural rights; Kloss (1966) mentions that a law passed in Pennsylvania in 1863 made it mandatory to have official notices appear in German-language newspapers in eight counties. In addition, German-American intellectuals were extremely active in the arts and sciences and published articles and books in German. Thus in the 1850s, in addition to a flourishing press, one finds German-language works in philosophy, poetry, zoology, archaeology, history, and theology.

Kloss (1966) reports that toward the end of the nineteenth century a certain opposition to the extensive use of German and the maintenance of German culture was making itself felt. Wisconsin and Illinois passed laws making English the only medium of instruction in public schools, and the Catholic hierarchy, dominated by the Irish, put pressure on the German Catholic schools and clergy to use English. But because of their numerical strength, their language islands, their schools, and their maintenance efforts, the German Americans reached a high point at the beginning of the twentieth century. Kloss reports that in 1910 about 9 million German Americans spoke German natively. Gaarder (1977) adds that in 1900 close to 4 million persons attended church services in German, and in 1904 the German press had a circulation of nearly 800,000. More than 4,100 public and private schools used German as the language of instruction, and in 1914 there were 10,000 German clubs.

What has happened in the last eighty years to change this picture, so that it is now difficult to find a single school where German is the medium of instruction or a single church where the service is in German? The main answer is World War I. When the United States entered the war, extreme anti-German feeling led to two series of events. On the one hand, laws were passed forbidding the use of German in the schools, in the press, even in public. And on the other hand, extreme pressure was put on German Americans to assimilate—in a sense to choose to be either German or American but not both. Those who had been active in German language and culture maintenance, but also ordinary German-speaking people, were persecuted and humiliated, and many cases of beatings and tarring and feathering were reported. German American children were humiliated in school, and many reacted by rejecting their background and refusing to speak German in public or even with their parents.

Although between the two world wars restrictions on the press and on the teaching of German were lifted, the assimilation of German Americans was progressing rapidly, and World War II, although less hurtful to German Americans, only speeded up the process. Even the Orthodox Lutheran Church, which had been a pillar in maintaining the language, now discouraged its use in church, and the continuing exodus from farms in the German-language islands to the cities only hastened the assimilation.

Today 2.7 million people report a German language background, but even though immigration from Germany has continued since World War II, only 43 percent of these report that German is spoken in the household, and only 7 percent say it is their usual language. There are still a few German islands in Ohio, Pennsylvania, Texas, and Indiana where the language is used on a daily basis (in many cases by ecclesiastic groups such as the Amish, Mennonites, and Hutterites), but were it not for new immigrants, German would have practically disappeared as a minority language in the United States. As Kloss (1966) writes, "The assimilation of 9 million German Americans is the most striking event of its kind in the annals of modern history. No other nationality group of equal numerical strength and living in one country has ever been so wellnigh completely assimilated" (p. 249).

Franco-Americans

In the 1976 Survey of Income and Education, 1.9 million Americans reported a French language background, making the Franco-Americans the fourth largest minority group after the Hispanic, Italian, and German Americans. Of these 1.9 million, about 43 percent use French in their everyday life, either as monolingual speakers (3 percent) or as bilinguals (40 percent). Who are these people and where are they found?

Although there are Franco-Americans in most states, and quite large groups in California, Texas, and Mississippi, the largest numbers live in Louisiana and in the Northeast. To understand why, we must go back to the time of the early explorers of the New World. In 1534 Jacques Cartier sailed to America, explored the New England coast, and ventured up the Saint Lawrence Valley, which he claimed for the king of France. Some years later Samuel de Champlain established a colony in Quebec, which marked the beginning of French immigration to the New World. The French came to what is now Quebec and the Atlantic provinces but also traveled farther inland to the Great Lakes and the Ohio and Missouri valleys. (Antoine de la Mothe Cadillac established a settlement in Detroit in 1701.) At the same time the French were exploring the southern part of the United States; in 1682 La Salle claimed Louisiana for France, and subsequently French settlers established themselves in that state.

When compared to the numbers of British settlers who arrived in the New World in the seventeenth and eighteenth centuries, the French were never very numerous, and throughout the eighteenth century they gave up or lost territories to their long-time foes. In the 1713 Treaty of Utrecht, France ceded to the British the Hudson Bay Territories, Newfoundland, and Acadia (which included New Brunswick, Nova Scotia, Prince Edward Island, and parts of Maine and Quebec). In 1762 Louisiana was ceded to Spain, and in 1763 France gave up its remaining North American territories to the British. The French settlers thus came under British rule in the North and under Spanish rule in Louisiana, with all the negative consequences that subservience could mean at the time. For example, in 1755 some 16,000 Acadians were expelled from their homeland, because they were considered a threat to British rule in that part of the New World. Many of them made their way to southern Louisiana, where they resettled and became known as Cajuns (from [A]*cadians*). In 1800 France reclaimed Louisiana from Spain, but in 1803 the territory was sold to the United States. Thus, at the beginning of the nineteenth century the French were mainly concentrated in Louisiana and in Quebec, although a few thousand could also be found along the Ohio and Missouri valleys. Only in the middle of the nineteenth century did French Canadians start to immigrate to the northeastern states in search of work and economic and social betterment. And throughout the nineteenth and twentieth centuries French immigrants from France have continued to come to the United States, but never in very large numbers. Thus, this discussion of Franco-Americans will concentrate on two large groups: the French in Louisiana and the New England Franco-Americans.

THE FRENCH IN LOUISIANA   Some 500,000 persons in Louisiana report a French language background, most of whom live in the southern part of the state. Some are descendants of the original French settlers, the Creoles, who lived in such areas as New Orleans and Baton Rouge; others are descendants of the Acadians,—called Cajuns; and still others are French-speaking Blacks. When Louisiana was purchased by the United States, the territory was ruled by the Creoles, who furnished the political leaders, writers, clergy, and so on. And from the time the territory became a state, in 1812, to the middle of that century, all the governors were descendants of Creoles. During this time Louisiana was very much a bilingual and bicultural state, and in the 1845 constitution French and English were given the same importance in official matters (Kloss, 1977). This was confirmed in 1847 when a law stipulated that the medium of instruction in schools could be English or French.

The 1861 secession of the southern states and the subsequent defeat of the South had drastic consequences for the rights of the French population in Louisiana. The 1864 constitution made English the only official language and the only language of instruction in schools, and although in 1879 French regained certain privileges (Kloss, 1977), the French-speaking population now had to struggle to maintain their linguistic and cultural heritage. By the middle of the twentieth century, French was fast disappearing: it was taught in school only as a subject, fewer and fewer children spoke the language natively, and of the adults who did speak French, very few could read and write it.

However, since 1968 there has been an attempt to revive French in Louisiana. In that year a Council for the Development of the French Language in Louisiana (CODOFIL) was created; its aim was to collaborate with the government of France to revive and maintain French language and culture in Louisiana. (In 1973 Quebec and Belgium joined the Council.) In 1968 also the state legislature passed a law mandating all public elementary schools to offer at least five years of French instruction, starting with oral French in first grade. And in 1975 the new constitution confirmed the right of inhabitants to "preserve, foster and promote their respective historic, linguistic and cultural origins" (Kloss, 1977).

Today language maintenance efforts are everywhere present: CODOFIL organizes summer study programs in Quebec, France, and Belgium; the governments of these countries send French-speaking teachers to Louisiana; some 45,000 children are enrolled in bilingual programs; radio and television stations broadcast in French at least part of the time; French language papers such as *Louisiane* publish information concerning the French community as well as stories, poems, and letters; Acadian music festivals are organized, and Cajun films are shown. It now remains to be seen whether such efforts will be able to keep French alive in Louisiana and whether the young will choose to use both French and English in their everyday life instead of English only, as most now tend to do.

THE FRENCH IN NEW ENGLAND   About 40 percent of those who report a French language background live in the Northeast—New York, Massachusetts, Rhode Island, Connecticut, Maine, and New Hampshire. Most of them are descendants of French Canadians who started immigrating to the United States in the 1840s pushed by lack of work in Quebec at the time (in part because of a strong population increase) and drawn by the new mill towns in New England that needed manpower. They found jobs in textile and paper mills, on the railroads, on potato farms in Maine, and in lumber industries throughout New England. At first, like most across-the-border workers, they planned to go back as soon as they had put aside enough money; but when they realized that their stay might be longer, they began organizing themselves into an expatriate community. Priests were brought over from Quebec to establish parishes (the first French Canadian church was established in Burlington,

Vermont, in 1850); schools were founded and were run by nuns; clubs and societies, such as L'Association Canado-Américaine and L'Union St. Jean Baptiste d'Amérique, were started, and newspapers were published.

As we saw in Box 2.1, the French Canadians lived in French neighborhoods (Le Petit Canada) and were extremely good at keeping themselves a tight-knit linguistic and cultural minority (Perreault, 1976). For a long time they were considered the most unassimilable of all immigrant groups, and this created constant friction between them and the Anglo-American majority. Their close attachment to their faith and to their French parishes led them to be even more conservative about their language. The Irish religious hierarchy did not want to name French Canadian priests to French-speaking parishes and was strongly opposed to French Canadians running their parishes, as they did in Quebec. But over the years the French held firm; as Lemaire (1966) writes, "Loss of language meant loss of faith, and loss of faith meant loss of eternity" (p. 264).

It was only at the turn of the century that many French Canadians, realizing that they were here to stay, began to ask for naturalization and hence became Franco-Americans (Perreault, 1976). When World War I brought strong anti-minority feelings, the French started to assimilate. Some changed their names and moved out of the French areas, but for most others assimilation took place more slowly: the children started speaking less French at home and among themselves; they married out of their ethnic group and thus spoke English with their spouses and children; newspapers lost some of their circulation as more people switched over to the English press; and even in church, a French stronghold, English was used more and more. As for the parochial schools, under the combined pressure of state laws, the Irish hierarchy, and the parents themselves, French became a medium of instruction in the afternoon only and then, little by little, only a subject.

It is difficult to assess the status of French in New England today. Of the estimated 800,000 who report a French language background, many still use the language regularly and many others are in contact with French in their everyday life. A visitor to Lewiston or Biddeford, Maine, Woonsocket, Rhode Island, or Manchester, New Hampshire, will realize that French is alive and doing quite well in the Northeast. But is this only the older generations, or are the younger people also using French? Some, like the Franco-American who speaks in Box 2.10, feel that the young are not as bi-

BOX 2.10	BILINGUALS SPEAK

A Franco-American in New England: We have had our share of being called names, having stones thrown at us (as children), being laughed at in school (non Franco-American schools, that is), being overworked and underpaid by Yankee bosses. But today, in the 1980s, I personally feel that the Franco-Americans have come a long way since being called "the Chinese of the East" in the 1880s . . . Some would say that Franco-Americans are discriminated against even today, and that it is society's fault, while others would say that in this day of equal opportunity, anyone, Franco-Americans included, can "make it" if they really want to, and if we don't succeed, it's not society's fault, it's our own. I personally have taken the attitude "I'll go ahead and do as I wish, I'll speak French when and where I feel that it's appropriate to do so, I'll speak English when and where I feel that it's appropriate to do so, I'll be myself, a Franco-American, unafraid to say who and what I am, and if someone doesn't like it, that's *their* problem, not mine."

The Prospects

Most young Franco-Americans no longer speak French (we have no parochial schools left, and parents rarely speak French in the home to their children, a phenomenon that has gradually come about since the Great Depression of the 1930s and World War II) . . . I think that my generation, that is, Franco-Americans born between the end of World War II and up to about 1955 are the last generation of *la vieille école* type of Franco-Americans. We were the last to be brought up in French and English at home, to receive a truly bilingual education at school. Of this last generation, very few still speak French today, and their children are often growing up with no ethnic identity whatsoever.

lingual as their parents were and that they are growing up without a linguistic and ethnic identity. But the editors, writers, and readers of the *F.A.R.O.G. Forum,* a monthly paper published by Franco-American students at the University of Maine at Orono, would probably not agree with this. This paper is full of stories, studies, tales, plays, and poems about and by Franco-Americans, written both in French and English. And the fact that the New England states have numerous bilingual programs for French-speaking children shows that the French language is still a mother tongue in the region. How long this will continue, and whether French in New England will someday take the road of German and the Scandinavian languages in other parts of the country, remain to be seen.

Hispanic Americans

According to the 1976 Survey of Income and Education, 11.2 million persons in the continental United States identified themselves as being of Hispanic origin. If we add to these the recent immigrants from Cuba and Mexico and an estimated 7 million Spanish-speaking undocumented workers, we arrive at a figure of about 20 million Hispanic Americans—by far the largest linguistic minority group in this country. Interestingly enough, this makes the United States the fifth largest Hispanic country in the world, after Mexico, Spain, Argentina, and Colombia. Of the 11.2 million Hispanic Americans identified by the 1976 survey, three out of four are native born, 8.9 million live in Spanish-speaking households, and the majority (about 59 percent) are bilingual in Spanish and English. An estimated 1.5 million are monolingual in Spanish.

It is important to distinguish among the subgroups that make up the Hispanic-American population, as their origins are very diverse: an estimated 61 percent are Mexican American, 14 percent are mainland Puerto Ricans, 7 percent are originally from Central and South America, 6 percent are Cuban Americans, and the remaining are of varied origins. Mexican Americans are found mainly in the Southwest, especially Texas and California, and also in the Midwest. Mainland Puerto Ricans live in New York and other parts of the Northeast but also in north central states such as Illinois; Cuban Americans live mainly in Florida and New Jersey. Cities with more than half a million Hispanic Americans are New York (mostly Puerto Ricans), Los Angeles, San Francisco, and San Antonio (Mexican Americans), and Miami (Cuban Americans).

It is well-nigh impossible to present a rapid survey of such a diverse linguistic minority (see Box 2.11), but in the following pages I will say a few words about Puerto Ricans, Cuban Americans, and Mexican Americans. It is important to note, first, that although numerically powerful, Hispanic Americans have not had the political and social impact they have merited. In 1980, only six Hispanic Americans were members of the House of Representatives, none were in the Senate, and there were no Hispanic state governors. In addition, although about 30 percent of Roman Catholics in the United States are Hispanic Americans, no Spanish-speaking cardinal represents them. However, Hispanic Americans have begun organizing at all levels and are now playing a larger role in their communities. For example, the United Neighborhoods Organization in Los Angeles and the Communities Organized for Public Ser-

---

BOX 2.11   BILINGUALS SPEAK

A Hispanic American: We are people of all colors and hues. Ethnic mixture is our salient characteristic . . . Indian American is part of our heritage as well as the Iberian, Mediterranean strain, and the complex West African tradition . . . the Hispanic element is the common denominator. In spite of its many contradictions, its pride of castes, and its claims to domination, the Spanish influence provides a meeting ground where Chicanos, Cubans, and Puerto Ricans, as well as other Hispanic elements, find a common link in their common ancestry. (Morales-Carrión, 1980, pp. 28, 30)

---

vice in San Antonio are playing an increasingly important role in local politics. In addition, Hispanic Americans have had an increasing impact on labor unions (for example, the United Farm Workers, led by Cesar Chavez), and they have been very active in the development of bilingual education at both the federal and local levels. It has been said that the 1980s will see the political and social emergence of Hispanic Americans: if this is so, it will be an important step for linguistic minorities in this country; with the exception of German Americans at the turn of the century, these minorities have rarely played a role in national politics.

MAINLAND PUERTO RICANS   The first Spaniards landed on Puerto Rico in 1493, and until 1898 the island remained under the control of Spain. In that year the Treaty of Paris put an end to the Spanish-American War, and Puerto Rico was ceded to the United States, which has retained political and economic control of the island. In 1946 the island became a commonwealth, but the ultimate status of Puerto Rico—independence or statehood—has yet to be decided.

Until World War II, few Puerto Ricans migrated to the mainland, but such factors as an exploding population, rising unemployment, the attraction of better economic opportunities on the mainland, and the low cost of air travel led many Puerto Ricans to come to the mainland after the war. Between 1945 and 1965 over a million arrived on the continent; settling first in New York City, then spreading out to Newark, Jersey City, Chicago, Boston, and Philadelphia. Today there are between 1.6 and 2 million Puerto Ricans on the mainland and approximately 3 million on the island. Of those in the continental United States, about 40 percent were born on the mainland. Puerto Rican migration is unusual in that it is a two-way movement; many Puerto Ricans return to the island to visit or to re-settle, and it has been estimated that in the 1970s about 1½ million Puerto Ricans traveled in each direction each year.

About 60 percent of the mainland Puerto Ricans live in New York City, mainly in East Harlem (El Barrio), the lower East Side, the South Bronx, Brooklyn, and Queens. New York has become in many ways a bilingual city: there are Spanish-language television and radio stations, monolingual Spanish newspapers, official no-tices, publications, and ads in Spanish, and so on. But the life of Puerto Ricans, in New York or any other city, has always been dif-ficult. About three out of five are blue-collar workers, many of whom work in the service sectors (cleaning, hauling, delivering), and most are very badly paid. The median family income for Puerto Ricans in 1978 was about $8,000—the lowest income of all Spanish-speaking groups and a long way from the average family income of the United States (about $18,000 at that time).

A number of problems have accompanied Puerto Ricans in their migration to the mainland. First is the language barrier; although many have become bilingual in English and Spanish, many are monolingual Spanish-speakers, especially among the older genera-tions and the young children. Until the advent of bilingual educa-tion, children had great difficulties in English schools and hence often dropped out before finishing high school. Second, many Puerto Ricans are regarded as nonwhite by large segments of the population (a third are Black), and the discrimination that accom-panies poverty and speaking a "foreign" language is enhanced by the race barrier. And third, although they are officially American citizens, Puerto Ricans have not found their expectations as citizens upheld on the mainland: instead they have found discrimination in jobs, housing, and education. This is clearly reflected in the writings of Piri Thomas and Oscar Lewis and in the poems of Victor Her-nandez Cruz. Recently, however, mainland Puerto Ricans have begun organizing, and such groups as the National Puerto Rican Task Force on Educational Policy, the National Puerto Rican Forum, and the more localized East Harlem Council for Human Services have been instrumental in obtaining better jobs, education, and housing. And Puerto Ricans are now actively working with other Hispanic Americans to obtain the rights and opportunities that are open to Anglo-Americans.

CUBAN AMERICANS   Unlike Puerto Ricans, who have come to the mainland for economic reasons, Cuban Americans are political refugees and would not be in this country today in such large numbers (about 900,000) if Cuba's history had not taken the turn it did some twenty years ago. Before 1960 very few Cubans immigrated to the United States, and those who did—some 124,000, according to the 1960 census—were slowly assimilating themselves into the American linguistic and cultural mainstream. The takeover by Castro in 1959 led to an almost constant flow of refugees into the United States (125,000 came in 1980 alone) and today Cubans make up the largest group of political refugees that has ever come to the United States. The federal government has tried to relocate Cuban refugees in nearly all of the states, and now there are large numbers in New York, New Jersey, California, and Illinois. Many, however, have stayed in or returned to what Cubans consider their mainland home: Miami and the rest of Dade County. Here we find between a third and a half of all Cuban Americans; about 400,000.

Although some 77 percent of Cuban Americans are foreign born and hence originally monolingual speakers of Spanish, they have not had the problems that Puerto Ricans have had in finding employment. Many of the refugees were businessmen, teachers, lawyers, nurses, and skilled workers who set up their own businesses or rapidly went through remedial training to enter the job market. And although recent immigration has included more blue-collar workers, the median family income for Cuban Americans in 1978 was still the highest among Hispanic Americans—around $15,000, as compared to $13,000 for Mexican Americans and $8,000 for Puerto Ricans.

Because Cubans were at first intent on going back home and believed that their stay in the United States was only temporary, they organized themselves to maintain their language and culture. In the Dade County area they were instrumental in developing bilingual education, in starting Spanish-language TV and radio stations, in encouraging the publication of Spanish papers and periodicals (the daily *Miami Herald* has a Spanish supplement), and in sponsoring Cuban theaters, clubs, and cinemas. Whole sections of Miami are entirely Spanish speaking: businesses are owned and run by Cuban Americans, and the whole rhythm and style of life are definitely Cuban.

But like every other immigrant group, Cuban Americans have their difficulties. The more successful they appear to be and the more permanent their stay, the more prejudice there is against them as the local Anglo-Americans fear for their jobs and other minorities fear for their hard-gained rights. In addition to problems from outside, Cuban Americans have in-group problems that are typical of minorities that considered themselves temporary immigrants but are remaining permanently (like the French Canadians). Elderly Cuban Americans who have retained their traditional values and Cuban-oriented way of life are now finding themselves more and more separated, both physically and mentally, from the younger generations. The latter feel they are both Cuban and American, but they do not have the same feeling of attachment to Cuba as their parents. However, the young are not totally assimilated into American society either (despite bilingual education, there is a high dropout rate for Cuban Americans in the Dade County schools), and many will continue to suffer from the side effects of being bicultural in a society that tends to reject anything that is not Anglo-American.

MEXICAN AMERICANS Unlike most mainland Puerto Ricans and Cuban Americans, who have been in the United States for only one or two generations, Mexican Americans have been here since the middle of the sixteenth century, when Ponce de Leon, Coronado, and Cabeza de Vaca explored what is now Florida and the Southwest. In 1548 the first permanent Spanish settlement was founded in Arizona, and in 1609 Santa Fe was permanently settled. For some 250 years the area from California to Texas was under Spanish and then Mexican rule; the towns, rivers, and mountains were given Spanish names (San Diego, San Jose, San Antonio, Rio Grande, Sierra Nevada); the settlers spoke Spanish, and the houses and churches were of Spanish and Mexican design. It was only in 1845, when Texas was annexed by the United States, that the Mexicans first came under American rule. Three years later the Treaty of Guadalupe Hidalgo put an end to the Mexican-American War, and Mexico ceded to the United States a third of its northwest territory, comprising Arizona, California, Nevada, New Mexico, parts of Colorado, and parts of Texas. By this treaty some 75,000 Mexicans came under American rule, and although they were guaranteed civil and religious rights, they were treated as a conquered people— strangers in their own land. Apart from New Mexico, where they retained much of their influence, Mexican Americans in the Southwest suffered great prejudice and discrimination. They lost their land through bribery, extortion, and violence; they met with unequal justice; they were discouraged and often prevented from voting; their children were segregated in schools; and in general they were faced with strong racial prejudice, which at times culminated in lynchings. America was certainly not the land of equal opportunity for Mexican Americans in the hundred years that followed the Treaty of Guadalupe Hidalgo.

Until the beginning of this century, few Mexicans immigrated to the United States, but between 1910 and 1930 there was a sudden large influx of immigrants—about a million between 1910 and 1920. Some fled the disruptions of the Mexican Revolution; others were attracted by the agricultural jobs in Texas, Arizona, and California, still others came to work in the mines and the railroads. But more often than not they were exploited and discriminated against. And in the depression of the 1930s, when unemployment was extensive, about a half million Mexican Americans, many of whom were citizens of the United States, were deported to Mexico. However, in the last forty years, with increased economic opportunities in the Southwest and the demographic explosion in Mexico, millions of Mexicans have come into the United States. Many have come as legal immigrants or contract seasonal workers to help harvest crops or work in canning and packing plants, but many others have slipped across the 1,952-mile border, and these undocumented workers have been exploited in low-paid jobs in restaurants, hotels, small factories, and the garment industries.

Today there are some 7 to 8 million Mexican Americans in the United States and an unknown number (some estimates say 5 to 7 million) of undocumented workers. Nine out of ten Mexican Americans live in the Southwest, primarily in California, where one in five inhabitants is Mexican American), and in Texas, where one in four is Mexican American. Contrary to what one might expect, most live in cities: in Los Angeles (2 million) and San Antonio, where half the population is Mexican American, but also in San Francisco, Malibu, and Calexico, California; Tucson and Phoenix, Arizona; El Paso and Santa Fe, New Mexico; and Redford and Crystal City, Texas—to name but a few.

Mexican Americans are extremely attached to their language and culture and have no problems in retaining them. The region they live in once belonged to them, as the Spanish place names remind them; they often return to Mexico to visit relatives, newcomers to the States arrive almost daily, many TV and radio stations broadcast in Spanish, and they live in Spanish-speaking areas, where life is imbued with Mexican customs and traditions. Although they still face police brutality, insecurity, the language barrier, badly paid jobs, and general prejudice, they have in recent years found renewed pride in their Chicano culture and heritage. The murals one finds in many cities of the Southwest are vivid reflections of their past and present: they represent the Aztecs, the Conquistadores, Zapata and the Mexican Revolution, Cesar Chavez and the United Farm Workers. In addition, Mexican Americans are becoming much more militant in the social and political realm. COPS (Communities Organization for Public Service) in San Antonio has pressed the city to build schools and work on drainage, TELASCU (the East Los Angeles Community Union) has founded several banks and is building an industrial park that will create jobs for Mexican Americans, and individuals are making their mark in business, education, and entertainment. It will be interesting to see how this dynamic minority that is largely bicultural and bilingual will evolve in the years to come.

Language Maintenance and Language Shift

In previous sections of this chapter, we have seen that some minority groups in the United States have practically lost the use of their native language. Others are still using their languages, although less and less, such as Polish Americans, Franco-Americans, and Yiddish-speakers, while the languages of other groups—Navajos, Chinese, Korean and Hispanic Americans—are actively used in all domains of life.

Why do some minority groups lose their language while others retain theirs? This question has been the object of much study by researchers, including Fishman (1965, 1966, 1972), Glazer (1966), Gaarder (1977), Kloss (1966), and Haugen (1969, 1973). In 1966 Fishman edited a whole volume on the subject entitled *Language Loyalty in the United States*. Inspired by his work and that of his colleagues, I will attempt to explain why certain linguistic groups manage to maintain their native language either as monolingual speakers or, usually, as bilinguals, and others shift little by little into English monolingualism. The phenomenon of language shift has existed for as long as languages have come into contact—the Egyptians shifted from Egyptian to Arabic, and the people of Cornwall shifted from Cornish to English—but it is especially striking in immigration countries like the United States, where the shift from one language to another is usually very rapid.

Glazer (1966) poses this question:

How can we explain why, in the country which was most open to immigration, and most undisturbed when it came to the maintenance of immigrant cultures, there was also the most rapid flight from and abandonment of key aspects of immigrant cultures on the part of the children and grandchildren of immigrants as well as on the part of immigrants themselves? . . . Just why America produced *without* laws that which other countries, desiring a culturally unified population, were not able to produce *with* laws—is not an easy question. (pp. 359, 360)

In this discussion we will consider linguistic groups that have immigrated to the United States in the last 200 years, as opposed to Native American language groups, examining first, language maintenance and language shift in the immigrant family, then the sociological factors that explain this phenomenon.

The Immigrant Family

Figure 2.8 is a very simplified flow chart of the general language evolution of immigrant families in which, to simplify the picture, the parents (the first-generation Americans) have immigrated to the United States, and the children (the second-generation Americans) have been born in this country.

On arrival in the United States, the parents are generally monolingual in their native language (L1), and they may either remain

FIGURE 2.8 Language evolution in an immigrant family.

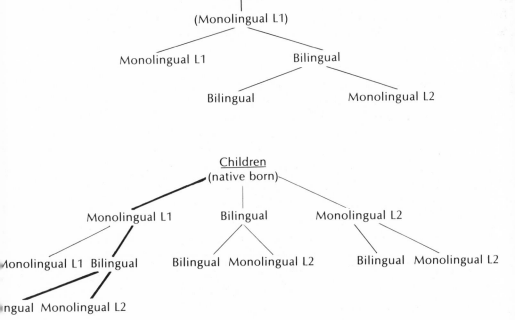

monolingual or become bilingual in their native language and English (L2). To remain monolingual, that is, to use no English, the parents must live in a close-knit ethnic community where they can work, shop, converse with friends and relatives in their own language. This was often possible at the turn of the century in the areas where such groups as Franco-Americans and German Americans lived, and it is still possible today among groups of Hispanic, Chinese, and Portuguese Americans, for instance. However, most first-generation Americans, especially if they are young, come into contact with the English-speaking majority and become bilingual. Most remain bilingual for the rest of their lives, but a few who have no way of maintaining their first language, who desire to assimilate quickly, or who actually reject their native language (Russian Jews, for example) will become monolingual speakers of English.

The language patterns of children born to first-generation Americans may be more complex. Some are bilingual from the beginning, and some are monolingual in English if, for instance, the parents want them to assimilate as rapidly as possible. Most, however, follow the rather straightforward route marked in Figure 2.8 in thick black. Their early language input will be the native language of their parents provided that they are the first born and that their parents speak the native language at home. Thus, an Italian couple who have a child a few years after their arrival will speak to him or her in Italian, and the child's first words will be in that language. In this sense, the child will be monolingual in the minority language (L1). However, quite quickly, English will enter the child's life, through the playground, television, English-speaking friends of the family, or in day care. Some minority children living in close-knit non-English-speaking communities may hear less English and may retain their monolingualism for some years, but this usually ends when the child goes to school. Although some bilingual education programs may postpone the learning of English for some time, by the age of eight or nine the child is usually bilingual in the home language and in English.

The question now becomes whether the child will remain bilingual or will shift entirely to English. If the parents are themselves bilingual and the social pressure to use English is very strong (peer pressure or negative attitudes of the English majority toward the minority) then the child will slowly shift over to English. In Box 2.12 Haugen gives a very vivid description of the route taken by children in many immigrant families.

BOX 2.12   BILINGUALS SPEAK

Language Shift in the Norwegian Family
Early in the Twentieth Century

Only by the establishment of iron-clad rules by which English was banned from the home could the parents resist this invasion. This counterpressure by the parents had to be stronger than the social pressure of the environment towards English . . . Whenever the point was reached that the community as such grew sufficiently Americanized . . . instead of a full competence, the children acquired only a partial competence. Writing fell away first, then reading. The effort required to impose these skills became too great for the parents. Similarly, the children succeeded in limiting the sphere within which Norwegian was spoken. They spoke it only to one or a few older members of the family, usually a grandparent, while they spoke English to all others. If their position was exceptionally strong, they succeeded in evading the speaking entirely, even to their parents. This bilingual situation was highly typical, with parents speaking Norwegian and children answering in English. Eventually the parents might also succumb to the pressure exerted by this uncomfortable situation and go over to English themselves. (Haugen, 1969, pp. 234, 235)

However, if communication in the home, with the family, and with friends can take place only in the minority language and there are enough psychosocial factors encouraging this language, such as the concentration and size of the group, its religion, and its cultural activism (see the next section), then the child will remain bilingual and will grow up proficient in both the minority language and English.

The above description is of course quite general, and many different patterns and fluctuations do occur. Fishman (1965), for example, reports that older children are more retentive of the native language than younger children, that first children retain it more than later-born children, and that children speak the language better than grandchildren. But as Haugen (1969) writes about Norwegian children shifting from bilingualism to English monolingualism: "The development here sketched is so typical that one encounters it again and again in discussing these matters with immigrant children. Both children and parents seem almost like pawns in a game which they do not themselves understand" (p. 235).

In Box 2.13 a French couple describe how English was brought into the home by their oldest child and how now, after six years in

BOX 2.13   BILINGUALS SPEAK

Language Shift in a Bilingual Family

When we first arrived in the United States six years ago the only language we used in the family was French. Cyril, our eldest and then only son was almost two and was making fine progress in learning French. For some time after our arrival, French remained the only language of interaction in the home, but English did start making inroads—through American friends and through children's television programs—"Mr. Rogers," "Sesame Street," "Captain Kangaroo." Cyril started to attend day care and hence began to learn English, and it wasn't long before he began speaking it along with French at home. We would, of course, only speak to him in French and insist that he answer back in French, but enforcing this became difficult when friends of his would come home to play. In addition, speaking one language and being answered back in the other became tiring, and little by little we started answering back in English. With time, Cyril used less and less French with us, and he slowly became monolingual in English. Of course he maintained a good comprehension of French; not only was it (and still is) our household language, but it was important for him to know what was being said in his presence. In this sense, Cyril has become a totally passive bilingual—he can hardly utter three words of French and yet he understands it quite well.

Four years after our arrival in the States, Pierre, our second son was born. We hoped that with him we would do things right and make a real bilingual of him. We made sure to speak French to him and we read him stories in French. However, from birth, he was also in contact with English—through his brother, his brother's friends, his brother's TV programs and finally at day care. For the first few months of language learning, Pierre spoke both French and English, but he quickly realized (like his brother four years before) that he really only needed to use one language and that, for reasons related to school and to life outside the home, it had to be English. So he too slowly became monolingual in English.

We have now been in the States for six years, and from being a monolingual French-speaking family we have become a bilingual family in that two languages are spoken in the home—English and French. However, only we, the parents, are in fact bilingual; the two children are monolingual in English although their comprehension of French is quite good. The language we use as a couple is French, but we do find ourselves at times speaking to one another in English, for example, when the four of us are together and we want to make sure that the children understand what we have to say. Our French is beginning to be riddled with English words, and despite our efforts, we do at times shift into English to report things that were told to us by friends outside the home. We hope to keep French as our everyday language at home, but as years go by we feel English closing in on us. Could it be that one day the whole family will only communicate in English?

the United States, they are using English more and more in their everyday lives. Their testimony is similar to that of many other immigrant families that have no reason to use English when adults are speaking to one another at home but that are often forced into using English by the children.

Factors in Language Maintenance and Language Shift

In this section I will discuss a few of the factors that explain why a particular minority group maintains its language while another group shifts over to English. These factors underlie the language evolution of the type of immigrant family discussed above.

Box 2.14 lists some of the factors proposed by such researchers as Gaarder, Kloss, Fishman, and Haugen. It is important to note that some of these factors are ambivalent, in that they may favor either

---

BOX 2.14

Factors Affecting Language Maintenance and Language Shift

Social aspects

Size of group
Birthrate of group
Time of immigration
Continued immigration
Permanent immigration
Geographic concentration
Urbanization
Isolation from other minority
    groups
Isolation from majority groups
Isolation from home country
Intermarriage
Social configuration of group
Social mobility
Religion
Activism (political, cultural, linguistic)
Mobility within the family
Occupations
Educational policy of the group

Attitudes

Of the minority group
    Toward their language
    Toward the majority language
    Toward cultural pluralism
    Toward bilingualism
    Toward linguistic "purity"
Of the majority group
    Toward the minority group

Use of languages

Where used (domain)
For what (function, topic)
With whom (interlocutor)

Government policy

Laws pertaining to languages
Educational policies

Other factors

Periods of nationalism
Assimilative power of majority
    group
Cultural support by foreign state

maintenance or shift. For example, if a minority group is small, it is easier for the leaders of the group to control it and hence to favor language maintenance, but at the same time fewer people and funds will be available for maintenance institutions such as the ethnic press, schools, clubs, and so on. In this discussion I will point out some of the factors that are ambivalent in this way.

The immigration pattern of a minority—When did it start immigrating? Is it still immigrating? Does it consider its immigration permanent—plays a large role in determining whether the group will maintain its language for a long time or rapidly shift over to English. A group that arrived a long time ago and is not at present being renewed by new arrivals from the home country, such as the Polish Americans, is more likely to shift to English than are recent immigration groups that are being reinforced by new monolingual speakers (Portuguese or Korean Americans, for example). In addition, a group that believes it will stay only a short while in this country, such as the French Canadians in the late nineteenth century and the Cubans in the 1960s, has a natural tendency to retain its language and culture and to make sure that the children can speak and write the home language. Political and religious refugees fall into this category if they hope to return to their homeland. Some Russian Americans believe that Communism in the Soviet Union is only a temporary phenomenon and that one day they will be able to return home, a belief that is a very powerful factor in helping them maintain and pass on their Russian language and culture. On the other hand, German Jews in the 1930s did not believe they would ever return to Germany, and thus they assimilated very quickly into American society.

The geographic concentration of a group, especially if it is large, is an important factor in language maintenance; the German language islands in Ohio and Texas, the urban concentrations of Chinese in New York and San Francisco and of Franco Americans in the New England mill towns were a great help in the maintenance of their languages. And today the concentrations of Mexican Americans in Los Angeles and San Antonio and of Puerto Ricans in New York are preventing a rapid shift to English. We should note here that if the family presented in Box 2.13 had lived in a French neighborhood, the children would probably have retained their French, because they would have interacted with people speaking French outside the home. Throughout the history of immigrant groups in the United States, there is evidence that the breakup of ethnic concentrations has led to rapid language shift; this was the case when German and Norwegian Americans left their rural islands to find work in the cities and when French Canadians moved out of Le Petit Canada to the suburbs.

Isolation may favor either maintenance or shift. It favors maintenance if the members of the group, because of geographic concentration, for example, do not have to interact with other minority groups (for which they would need English) or with the English-speaking majority. But it favors shift when the group is isolated from the home country. Thus, the Albanian community in the United States is isolated both politically and geographically from Albania, and young Albanian Americans are not receiving the strong reinforcement they would if native speakers were continually arriving or if they themselves could travel to Albania. On the other hand, the continual two-way flow of people between Puerto Rico and the Puerto Rican communities on the mainland and between Mexico and the Mexican American communities in the United States greatly enhances the maintenance of Spanish.

The group's degree of cultural mobilization and organization also affects language maintenance or language shift. German Americans in the nineteenth century were not only numerous but also extremely well organized in their language and cultural maintenance efforts. This massive mobilization led to strong maintenance of the language until World War I. Italian-Americans, on the other hand, were much less active in their maintenance efforts and English encroached little by little on their daily lives.

A factor that has often been mentioned as powerful, either as a tool of maintenance or as an instrument of shift, is religion. When a religion is closely linked to a particular national group and to its language, it is an extremely powerful force for language maintenance. Thus the only remaining German language islands in the United States are mainly those of the Mennonites, the Amish, and the Hutterites, for whom religion and language are strongly linked. But when a national church decides to abandon the minority language for English, as the Orthodox German Lutherans did after 1945, then a strong factor for maintenance disappears all at once. The fact that the Catholic Church has until very recently not defended the minority languages of its members has often been seen as one of the stronger de-ethnicizing phenomena in the country, almost as strong as the public school system.

The attitude of a group toward its native language is also an important factor. If the group is emotionally attached to the language and has pride in its literary and cultural heritage, it will make efforts to maintain it and pass it on to the children. This was the case of German-Americans in the nineteenth century who, as we saw, represented all levels of society: intellectuals, priests, and professionals, as well as workers, farmers, and so on. But many immigrant groups do not share this explicit valuation of their mother tongue and are not prepared to struggle for its maintenance. This is often the case of immigrants who have come to the United States mainly for economic reasons and are not accompanied by teachers, social leaders, journalists, and writers. In addition, many immigrants want their children to assimilate as quickly as possible, and hence either do not reinforce the language or actually forbid its use. As Kegl (1975) writes: "At the time when I was acquiring language, speaking a second language such as Slovene was looked down upon as detrimental to one's ability to speak either language well and as an indication of one's immigrant background ... [Now] I seriously regret having been deprived of the unique opportunity of being raised both bilingual and bicultural" (p. 31).

Although many other factors play a role, such as the group's social configuration, its social mobility, its ethnic origins, and its size, I will end this section with three factors that have played a major role in language shift in the United States. These are educational policy, periods of American nationalism, and the assimilative power of American society. As we saw earlier in this chapter, the educational policy has been to employ English as the medium of instruction. Aside from the private minority schools and the instances of public school bilingual education in the nineteenth century, the aim has been—and remains in large part—linguistic and cultural assimilation of minority children. Public education is thus an important factor in language shift: minority children are taught in the majority language in an Anglo-American environment, and very quickly many of them begin to identify with the English language and its accompanying culture. When the home language and culture are strong enough, stable bilingualism and biculturalism may result, but most often it leads to English monolingualism. Whether the recent comeback to bilingual education will slow down this trend or even stop it is an open question; many believe that this change will only postpone language shift, not reverse it.

Periods of nationalism in the United States linked to wars and to economic difficulties have played a large role in language shift. As we have seen, the strong nationalistic feelings fostered by World

---

BOX 2.15

The Assimilative Power of American Society

The rapidly developing, manpower-hungry, industrial-commercial metropoli in which the majority of immigrants settled weakened the traditional social relationships and pre-established role structures in which the use of their mother tongues was customarily involved. In addition, American nationalism was primarily non-ethnic or supra-ethnic in comparison with the nationalisms of most of Europe. Consisting primarily of commitment to the ideals of American democracy, rationality in human affairs, political and social equality, unlimited individual and collective progress, it did not obviously clash with or demand the betrayal of immigrant *ethnic* values or patterns. (Fishman, 1965b, p. 149)

There was no apparent logical opposition between the ethnicity of incoming immigrants and the ideology of America. Individually and collectively, immigrants could accept the latter without consciously denying the former. However, once they accepted the goals and values of Americans the immigrants were already on the road to accepting their life-styles, their customs, and their language.

Similar observations may be made concerning the role of the English language in American nationalism. Just as there is hardly any ethnic foundation to American nationalism, so there is no special language awareness in the use of English. (Fishman, 1966, pp. 29, 30)

War I played a primary role in the language shift of German Americans and also of other language groups, such as Franco-Americans. Although surrounded by less xenophobic feelings, World War II also encouraged the linguistic assimilation of minority groups.

A final factor that has led many millions of immigrants to give up their native languages for English is quite simply the assimilative power of American society. The extracts in Box 2.15 stress the primarily nonethnic character of the society. This nonethnic factor does not threaten the cultural and linguistic aspects of the minority groups and hence does not foster the kind of linguistic and cultural opposition that is characteristic of many minority groups in Europe. According to Fishman and Glazer, the American society stresses democracy, equality, progress, and opportunity, rather than American nationalism or the importance of English. Thus, minority groups do not feel threatened and do not react by overdefending their language and culture. This lack of opposition leads to easier assimilation. As Glazer writes, the languages of minorities "shrivelled in the air of freedom while they had apparently flourished under adversity in Europe" (p. 361.)

To conclude, it is important to stress that no one factor accounts for a group's maintenance of its native language or its shift over to English. The many factors affecting maintenance and shift interact in complex ways so that shift may be enhanced, neutralized, or even opposed. What is sure, however, is that until now all immigrant minority groups have taken the road of assimilation; some are only starting on this road, others are well along, and others have reached the end. It remains to be seen whether the renewed interest in ethnicity and bilingual education will slow down or even suspend the process which leads, on the language level, from monolingualism in the native language to monolingualism in English through a transitional period of bilingualism. It will also be interesting to see how Hispanic Americans, the largest and most active minority group in the country today, will maintain and enhance their language in the years to come. Will they continue to transmit their culture through Spanish, or will they do so more and more through English as has happened with many other minority groups? As things stand, the linguistic future looks a bit brighter today, both for Hispanic Americans and for some other minority groups, than it did some years ago.

3 *Bilingualism in Society*

Nicole was born in France and lived in the Paris region until she was twenty-five. She then moved to the United States with her husband, Roger, and their one-year-old child, Marc, and they have lived in this country for eight years. Nicole is now a registered nurse in the cardiovascular unit of a large urban hospital. Both Nicole and Roger are bilingual in French and English, but Marc, now nine, speaks only English.

On the day that interests us, Roger is the first up and is preparing breakfast. When Nicole comes into the kitchen, he turns to her and asks:

> Tu veux du café ou du thé?
> (Do you want coffee or tea?)

> Du café mais dans un *mug*, s'il te plaît.
> (Coffee, but in a mug please.)

(Note that I have italicized the switch into English.) While Roger continues to prepare breakfast, Nicole goes into Marc's room and says:

> Marc, you'd better get up; your bus is coming by in half an hour.

Having made sure that Marc is awake, Nicole goes back to the kitchen. During breakfast she tells Roger about the cardiac catheterization that took place in her unit the day before. Her French sentences are replete with English technical terms pronounced in English, such as blood flow, pacemaker, anticoagulants, blood pressure, and heart transplant.

Realizing suddenly that Marc is still not out of bed, she says to Roger:

> Va chercher Marc (go fetch Marc) *and bribe him* avec un chocolat chaud (with a hot chocolate) *with cream on top.*

This mixture of French and English makes Roger laugh, and he remarks:

> Tu aurais pu dire tout ça en français.
> (You could have said all that in French.)

Roger goes into Marc's room and says:

> Now it's really time to get up. *Lève-toi* (get up).

Marc gets out of bed and comes yawning into the kitchen. After greeting her son, Nicole says:

> Now eat quickly, you've got to go soon.

and in the same breath but with a slight turn of her head:

> Tu me donnes encore un peu de café?
> (Can you give me some more coffee?)

Naturally this is meant for Roger, who gives her another mug of coffee.

Half an hour later we find Nicole on the bus to the hospital, quietly reading a French novel. Suddenly the bus brakes, and she bumps into a lady next to her. After mutual apologies, in English, of course, the lady asks Nicole if she is French. When Nicole answers in the affirmative, the lady remarks:

> Oh, I love French; in fact, I took four years of French in school. When my husband and I went to Quebec last year, I tried speaking it, but I just couldn't understand them. Do they speak *good* French?

Nicole spends the remainder of the trip explaining the difference between Parisian French and Canadian French, and why one is just as "good" as the other.

When she arrives in her unit at the hospital, her two colleagues and friends, Ann, an American, and Martine, who is French, are already there. She says "Hi" to Ann and kisses Martine on the cheeks, asking the latter:

Tu étais malade hier?
(Were you out sick yesterday?)

She exchanges a few more words with Martine in French while Ann is busy in a corner of the room, but when Ann comes toward them, Martine and Nicole switch over to English, and the three continue to chat for a while. Throughout the morning Nicole works with Martine, and their conversation switches back and forth between French and English: French with some English words when they are alone, English when a doctor is in the room or when the topic is highly technical. At one point they are asking a patient some questions about his recent heart attack. Toward the end of the interview, Nicole switches quickly into French without turning away from the patient and says softly:

Ça me paraît grave.
(It seems to be serious.)

She then asks a few more questions in English.

Nicole leaves the hospital early that day to take Marc to his baseball cookout. When she arrives home, she finds her son rather distraught. She asks him what is wrong, and he tells her that a group of older kids in the street have called him a "dirty frog." She tries to cheer him up by telling him that he is in no way different from other American kids and that they only tease him because they know his parents are French. Nicole and Marc then drive to the cookout, where Marc goes off with his friends, and Nicole chats with the other parents about the cost of sports equipment, school busing, the next school play, and so on.

Nicole then rushes back home to prepare dinner because Roger's parents are coming over that evening. They are in the States for a month and have been staying in a nearby hotel for the last few days. Roger has come home from work early to help, and Nicole tells him about Marc's misadventure:

J'ai trouvé Marc tout triste quand je suis revenue.
(I found Marc all upset when I came back.)

Il m'a dit (he said to me), *"The big kids down the road called me a dirty frog."*

Roger and Nicole talk about the incident while they prepare the meal, which will consist of pâté de campagne, boeuf bourguignon with string beans, camembert and fromage de chèvre and finally a homemade tarte aux pommes. When Roger's parents arrive at eight, the table has been set, and both Roger and Nicole have dressed up for the occasion. And until ten o'clock, when Marc comes home from his friend's house, one might think that the dinner were taking place in France. Not a word of English is heard during this whole time, and the dinner conversation turns around a favorite theme in France at that time—the upcoming presidential elections. Would Giscard-d'Estaing be reelected and would Rocard represent the Socialist party, or would it be Mitterand once again?

The events and conversations of this day in Nicole's life illustrate quite well the content of this chapter. The first topic will be the attitudes toward languages and language groups in countries where different language groups coexist. This will help us understand why, for example, the woman on the bus considered the French spoken in Canada not as "good" as Parisian French, and why Marc was called a "dirty frog" by some of the kids in his neighborhood. We will also consider the consequence of negative attitudes on language learning, language maintenance, and language use.

Our second topic is language choice—"who speaks what language to whom and when"—to take the title of an article by Fishman (1965). This is one of the most interesting questions in the study of bilingualism, and I will attempt to explain why Nicole spoke French at home with her husband but English with her son (often making the switch in the same breath), French with Martine for some topics but English for others. We will also examine why Nicole spoke French to Martine while Ann was busy in another part of the room, then switched over to English when Ann joined them.

This will lead us quite naturally to language switching, better known as code-switching—the alternate use of two or more languages in the same utterance or conversation. We will examine Nicole's various switches when speaking to Roger about catheterization or when quoting from her conversation with Marc. We will see why Roger switched from English to French when he told Marc to get out of bed and why Nicole switched momentarily into French when questioning the hospital patient with Martine. And we will examine Roger's attitude toward Nicole's mixture of English and French when she told him to bribe Marc with hot chocolate.

Our last topic is bilingualism and biculturalism: what it means to be bicultural and to what extent the two phenomena coexist. We will see that Nicole has attained a rather high degree of biculturalism: she says "Hi" to Ann but kisses Martine on the cheeks, although both are equally good friends; she interacts quite naturally with the other parents at the cookout, then dresses up for a French meal with her in-laws, where one theme of conversation is French politics. This degree of biculturalism is not always the norm; in fact, many bilinguals are monocultural.

Attitudes toward Language Groups and Languages

It is a well-accepted notion among sociolinguists that language is not just an instrument of communication. It is also a symbol of social or group identity, an emblem of group membership and solidarity. Haugen (1956) writes that language "is at once a social *institution*, like the laws, the religion, or the economy of the community, and a social *instrument* which accompanies and makes possible all other institutions. As an institution it may become *a symbol of the community group*" (p. 87).

Both as an instrument of communication and as a symbol of group identity, language is accompanied by attitudes and values held by its users and also by persons who do not know the language. For example, although few readers of this book know American Sign Language, most hold some value judgment about this manual-visual language, which they may have seen on TV. What is important to realize, however, is that attitudes toward a language—whether it is beautiful, efficient, rich and so on—are often confounded with attitudes toward the users of that language. In the case of American Sign Language, it is difficult to separate people's attitudes toward the language from attitudes toward its users, the Deaf.

This confounding of attitudes is illustrated in a joke told by a French professor to his students in a Sorbonne auditorium one day. He was explaining how certain languages sound "harsher" than others. Languages with many consonant clusters and palatal consonants such as /g/,/k/,/j/ sound "harsher" or "harder" than languages characterized by open syllables and vowel-consonant sequences. To exemplify this, the professor placed three European languages along the harsh–soft continuum: German on the harsh end, French on the soft end, and English in the middle. He continued, "That is why you should speak German to your horse, English to your husband or wife, and French to your lover," a clear reference to common stereotypes of the English, the German, and the French people.

In a community where different language groups coexist, language attitudes play an important role in the lives of users of these languages. Haugen (1956) writes: "Wherever languages are in contact, one is likely to find certain prevalent attitudes of *favor* or *disfavor* towards the languages involved. These can have profound effects on the psychology of the individuals and on their use of the languages. In the final analysis these attitudes are directed at the people who use the languages and are therefore inter-group judgments and stereotypes" (pp. 95, 96).

Attitudes toward Language Groups

One of the tasks of the social psychologist and the sociolinguist is to account for the attitudes of language groups toward themselves and toward other groups. The approaches that can be used are quite diverse. For instance, the researcher can simply question members of a group about their attitudes, but the danger with this approach is that certain negative opinions may be withheld. One way to circumvent this is to use the matched-guise approach of Lambert and his colleagues (1960). In this method, perfectly bilingual speakers tape record a passage first in one of their languages and then in the other. The voices and the languages on the tapes are randomized and are then presented to judges who are asked to use the voice cues of the speakers to evaluate their personality characteristics: leadership, intelligence, character, kindness, and so on. The results show that the judges do not realize that the speakers are bilingual. In addition, they do *not* give equal ratings to the two readings, one in each language, by the same speaker. What the judges are evaluating in fact, is the group that the speaker represents, although throughout the experiment they believe they are evaluating a person's personality.

In a first study of this kind, Lambert and colleagues (1960) studied group attitudes in Montreal, Quebec, which has a long history of tension between English- and French-speaking Canadians. They asked two groups of students—one English-speaking and one French-speaking—to evaluate the personality characteristics of English and French speakers reading a two-and-a-half-minute passage of prose. The speakers were six male bilinguals who recorded the passage in both English and French and two male monolinguals. The fourteen traits to be evaluated were accompanied by a 6-point scale with "very little" at one end and "very much" at the other.

As expected, the results showed that English judges were more favorable toward the English guise (or voice) than the French guise. They evaluated the English guise more favorably on seven traits, including intelligence, dependability, kindness, ambition, and character. Other traits, including leadership, self-confidence, sociability, and likeability were judged to be equal in the English and French guises. On only one trait did the English judges give the French guise a better rating: sense of humor. These results were considered normal in that one expects a group to be more positive toward its own members than toward those of another group.

The surprise came when the responses of the French judges were tabulated. Lambert and his colleagues found that they evaluated the English guises significantly *more* favorably than the French guises on ten of the fourteen traits. The French judges considered the English speakers taller, better looking, more intelligent, more likeable, more dependable, more ambitious, to have more leadership, self-confidence and character, and to be more sociable than the French speakers. French guises were rated better on only two traits: religiousness and kindness. Furthermore, and again this came as a surprise, on nine traits the French judges evaluated the French speakers less favorably than did the English judges; in other words, the English judges found the French better looking, more intelligent, more ambitious, and so on, than did the French themselves.

These results, although surprising at first, clearly illustrate the types of attitudes that exist within and between two language groups when one is dominant politically, economically, culturally, and, in the Canadian case, also numerically. The negative attitudes of the majority group toward the group without power and prestige are adopted in part or in whole by this group, and are often amplified to such an extent that members of the minority group downgrade themselves even more than they are downgraded by the dominant group. The consequence, paradoxical as it may seem, is that members of the majority group are sometimes more positive about the minority group than are members of that very group.

Anisfeld and Lambert (1964), again studying the situation in bilingual Montreal, found that ten-year-old French Canadians did not show the negative attitudes of their adult counterparts. French-speaking children rated the French guises significantly more favorably on all traits except height, showing that ten-year-olds do not have a negative bias against their own group. In an attempt to study when the bias starts after the age of ten, Lambert, Frankel, and Tucker (1966) studied the responses of French Canadian girls ranging in age from nine to eighteen listening to passages read in the two languages by girls their own age and by adult men and women. They found that a definite preference for the English guise appeared at about age twelve and that upper-middle-class girls were especially biased after that age, whereas working-class girls had a less pronounced and less durable bias. These extensions of the earlier study show that language attitudes are likely to be affected by age, socioeconomic status, and sex. Other studies of this type in the United States, Peru, Singapore, Switzerland, and Israel have produced very similar results.

What is interesting in most of these studies is that bilingual judges often react differently from monolinguals, in that their attitudes toward the two groups differ less. Peal and Lambert (1962) found that French-English bilingual children attending French schools in Montreal were more favorable toward the English language group than were the monolingual French-speaking children, and Anisfeld and Lambert (1964) reported that bilingual ten-year-olds in the same setting showed very little difference in response to the English and French guises. On nearly all personality traits, their ratings of the French Canadian guises were essentially the same as their ratings of the English Canadian guises. It would be erroneous to conclude from this that bilingualism always reduces the difference in attitudes between the majority and minority groups. There are in fact many examples, as in strongly nationalistic countries where minorities are repressed, of bilinguals reflecting the attitudes of the two groups in question, that is, being negative toward the minority group and positive toward the majority group. Lambert (1977) calls this a subtractive form of bilingualism because the dominant group is putting pressure on the minority to assimilate as quickly as possible. However, it is true that bilinguals are often less negative about the minority group and less positive about the majority group than are monolingual members of the minority group.

Attitudes toward Languages

Although, as I have said, attitudes toward languages often reflect attitudes toward the users of those languages, it is of interest to review some of the studies that have specifically examined language attitudes. Whenever two languages are in contact, one is usually considered more prestigious than the other. In this section I use the term "majority language" or "dominant language" for the language spoken by the group that holds the political, cultural, and economic power in the country. As we saw in Chapter 1, this group is not necessarily the largest group numerically. The term "minority language" refers to the language spoken by the group that has less power and prestige. In almost every country of the world one can find examples of languages that do not share equal prestige. In Haiti the prestigious language is French, and the language of the uneducated and poor—the vast majority of the population—is Creole. In Peru, Spanish is the language of the educated and urbanized middle class, and Quechua is the language of the rural Indian poor.

It is interesting to note that in a few communities, attitudes toward the two or more languages in contact may be equally positive, especially when they are both "world" languages, such as English and French or Spanish and German. Heye (1975) examined the canton of Ticino, Switzerland, where a number of languages are in contact: Standard German, Swiss German, Standard Italian, and Ticinese, an Italian dialect. He found that the German speakers and the Italian speakers held each other's standard language in very high esteem. Neither of the two considered its language the most beautiful (the Italian group selected French, and the German group Italian), and both groups considered the dialects (Swiss German and Ticinese) useful and important means of communication. Heye concludes from this that the lack of social friction between the two groups has created a rather unique situation in which all languages are held in high esteem.

However, in most contact situations one language is usually considered more prestigious. In Paraguay, Rubin (1968) reports that although positive attitudes are associated with both Spanish and Guarani, Spanish tends to be revered, whereas Guarani is frequently belittled. Those who reject Guarani—usually the upper classes, whose first language is Spanish—say that Guarani has no world value, is not productive, has no written grammar, and does not lend itself to the expression of abstract concepts. They consider the use of Guarani to be doomed, and the person who is monolingual in Guarani to be ill-bred, less intelligent, and less cultured. For those who defend Guarani, however, the language has special linguistic qualities: an extensive vocabulary and a musical and a poetic quality all of its own. These people consider it perfectly adequate for the discussion of philosophical, theological, scientific, and other abstract ideas, although they do recognize the importance of Spanish in economic, political, and intellectual exchange with the outside world.

Attitudes such as these can be quite extreme. The prestige language is often considered more beautiful, more expressive, more logical, and better able to express abstract thoughts, and the other language is felt to be ungrammatical, concrete, and coarse. This is the attitude toward classical Arabic as opposed to dialectal Arabic in most Arab countries (Ferguson, 1959).

The sign languages of the Deaf have long been associated with negative attitudes. Jean-Marc Itard, the instructor of the Wild Boy of Aveyron, refers to signs as a "barbaric language" with incomplete sentences without verb tense, without pronouns, without articles indicating case. For example, instead of the sentence 'Would you like us to water your garden this evening?' the signs say only this: 'We, this evening, to water garden you' " (Itard, 1826, cited in Lane, 1976, p. 228). Itard was unfortunately only a precursor of those, both hearing and Deaf, who have maintained that the sign languages of the world are ungrammatical, concrete, iconic, and pantomimic—in a word, glorified gestures—when in fact they have been shown to be full-fledged inflected languages that are rule-governed and morphologically complex (see Lane and Grosjean, 1980).

Although attitudes do not usually reach this level of negativity, the languages of minorities in bilingual or multilingual countries have often been the object of attack by the dominant group. One very common approach is to call the language a dialect or a patois, and to heap on it the negative connotations associated with dialects by nonlinguists—that they are less rich than the standard languages, less grammatical, and are spoken in a coarser, less refined way. This is the way the Walloons consider Flemish, the French-speaking Swiss view Swiss German, and the English-speaking Canadians talk about Canadian French. These attitudes originate within the dominant language group but are slowly adopted by the minority group, so that in the end its members feel they are speaking an "impoverished" language.

It is interesting that attitudes evolve and that a once-stigmatized language can become accepted and respected. (The reverse is unfortunately also true.) For example, Rhodes (1980) found that after Guarani was recognized officially as a national language in Paraguay, attitudes toward it changed considerably. Whereas twenty years ago (Rubin, 1968), Guarani was thought of as a low-prestige language that should not be used by educated people and not be taught in the classroom, today 78 percent of informants in Rhodes's survey think it should be used as a language of instruction; 82 percent state that it is important for their great-grandchildren to know Guarani; and 63 percent say that a person must speak Guarani to be considered a true Paraguayan.

A change in the attitude toward a language, from negative to positive, can be caused by the official recognition of a language by the government (Guarani in Paraguay, Quechua in Peru), a nation's independence (Swahili in Tanzania), or by increased autonomy (Canadian French in Quebec, Catalan in Spain), as well as by civil rights movements (native and immigrant languages in the United States) or even the work of social scientists and linguists (the sign language of the deaf in the United States and France). But because of our inherent ethnocentrism, many minority languages in the world will continue to be stigmatized.

Consequences of Language Attitudes

Negative or positive attitudes toward a language can have profound effects on the users of the language. One effect concerns learning the language. As we saw in Chapter 2, the dominance of a language in a situation of contact is often determined by who learns that language. The majority or dominant language is learned by the majority group as well as by members of the minority group, but the minority language is learned only by members of that minority. Few French persons learn Breton or Alsatian, but most Breton and Alsatian native speakers also speak French. Pap (1979) reports that in the secondary schools of German-speaking Switzerland, French is taught widely, and many youths from the German-speaking part spend some months or a year in the French area for the sole purpose of learning French. However, few French-speaking Swiss do the same with Swiss German. An identical situation is found in Belgium, where the Flemish-speaking population has a higher percentage of Flemish-French bilinguals than does the French-speaking group.

Language attitudes also influence the learning of a first language. In her book on German-Hungarian bilingualism in Oberwart, Austria, Gal (1979) reports that because German is the national language and symbolizes the urban, future-oriented society, it is preferred over Hungarian—the language of the old way of life and of the peasant community. Hence children of monolingual German speakers or bilingual German-Hungarian speakers virtually never learn Hungarian, and bilingual parents make sure their children speak faultless German so that they can pass as monolinguals and dissociate themselves from the stigmatized Hungarian peasant identity.

The phenomenon of parents helping their children learn the "correct" language, so as not to be stigmatized later in life and so as to advance socially, is widespread. Rubin (1968) reports that twenty years ago parents in Paraguay attempted to speak only Spanish to

---

BOX 3.1   BILINGUALS SPEAK
_____

Losing One's Mother Tongue

As a child my life seemed strange and confusing. At home, which meant
brothers, parents, an aunt and uncle (at different times) and grandparents,
the language was mainly Spanish and the culture distinctly Mexican. At
school, the language was only English, and the culture was a cold and
distant way of being treated—like the re-molding process of an Army
boot camp . . . When my parents first told me that I had to learn English in
order to survive in this country, the impact of that statement had little immediate effect. But later, as a young person, I began to associate my feelings of alienation with the need to identify with a group, a cultural group.
My capacity to use Spanish had dwindled to nothing. Identification with
the dominant culture was no longer possible, but recreating my group
sense seemed equally impossible without the help of Spanish, the language of my Chicano culture. I felt alone and lonely . . . My parents were
not at fault; from them English was a gift of love—a gift they had never
received. They were sure that I would not endure the suffering that accompanies such labels as *foreigner* or, in my case, *wetback* and *spic* . . .
My years without Spanish now appear tragic. How can I ever make up that
loss? I barely communicated with my own grandparents! They died, in
fact, before I re-learned Spanish. (Castro, 1976, pp. 4, 5, 8)

---

their children so that they would become fluent in it. And in the
United States, there are innumerable examples of immigrant parents encouraging, if not forcing, their children to learn English, with
the potential consequence that some may become rootless and
alienated from their native language group. Box 3.1 gives Ray Castro's firsthand account of this process.

Stigmatization of a language also has a profound effect on the
knowledge that people *feel* they have of the language. Gal (1979)
reports that Oberwarters, even those who can approximate both
standard languages, feel unsure and insecure about both their Hungarian and German when talking to monolinguals or outsiders.
When asked to rank their knowledge of each language, only half
scored themselves in the highest capacity for Hungarian and only a
fifth in the highest rating for German. And in Norrbotten, a province in northern Sweden with a small proportion of Finnish speakers, Haugen (1973b) reports that the latter consider themselves inadequate in both Finnish and Swedish.

Negative attitudes toward a language can also effect its everyday
use. For instance, speakers of the language may refuse to speak it in

BOX 3.2 — BILINGUALS SPEAK

Consequences of Negative Language Attitudes

An English-French bilingual: The attitudes of people to bilingualism vary so much according to the social prestige of the languages spoken. This was brought home to me very vividly once when I was in a hospital in Corsica. I shared a room for two days with an old Corsican lady who, one afternoon, received the visit of several other old ladies, neighbors and relatives from her village. For an hour they chattered in Corsican, occasionally turning to me to smile or say a word or two in French. When they had left, my roommate turned to me and apologized for having spoken in Corsican but, she said, her friends were old and found it difficult to converse fluently in French since they always spoke Corsican at home. I replied that on the contrary it was I who should apologize, if anyone, for not having so far made the effort to learn Corsican, and I added, what's more, I was a foreigner, not even French. Oh, no, she said, no one should be expected to learn Corsican since it was only a "patois." She found it more acceptable that I should speak English than she Corsican in her own country. We talked for a long time about languages and their importance, and she at last confided that when she was a young girl and worked on the continent (in France), the moment she longed for was when she would get on the boat to come home for the holidays, and the minute she and her friends set foot on the boat they would start speaking Corsican, "it was so much more friendly."

public. Gumperz (1976a) reports that in an Austrian village on the Austrian-Yugoslav border where both Slovene and German are spoken, it is considered impolite to speak Slovene in the presence of German speakers, whether they are from within or outside the village. He adds, "In fact, so strong is the injunction against speaking Slovenian in mixed company, that tourists can live in the village for weeks without noticing that any language except German is spoken" (p. 7). This refusal to speak a stigmatized language in public may also occur in the presence of an outsider who is perfectly bilingual and who wishes to use the minority language. Barker (1975) reports that in Tucson, Arizona, even if a Mexican American knows that the Anglo he is addressing speaks Spanish, he will almost always use English. Similar examples have been found with other languages such as dialectal Arabic, American Sign Language, Haitian Creole, and so on. In Box 3.2, an English-French bilingual tells about her experience in Corsica, where an elderly Corsican lady apologized to her for speaking Corsican. This phenomenon is espe-

BOX 3.3   BILINGUALS SPEAK

The Effect of Negative Language Attitudes on Children

I would say that between the ages of fourteen and eighteen, I had temporarily cast my Franco-American identity aside. I identified with rock music, the cinema, dances, generally having a good time, always in English, whether with Franco-Americans or non-Franco-Americans. At this time, my parents would speak to me in French (though not always) and I would reply in English . . . When I returned from France, I felt as if my friends and relatives who spoke Franco-American French were inferior and so I refused to speak any French, to them, not wishing to speak "their" French and not feeling comfortable speaking "Parisian" French to them. After graduation, I obtained a job as an oral history interviewer, doing interviews with old Franco-American mill workers. It was by doing some 120 such interviews that I began to acquire a taste for my Franco-American heritage, that I began to realize that the Franco-Americans had as valid a language and culture as anyone in France.

cially alarming when a child or adolescent turns away from the native language and refuses to speak it with his or her parents. Box 3.3 presents the testimony of an American child of immigrants concerning the consequence of negative language attitudes. In the long run, negative attitudes can lead to language shift; the minority language is used less and less, and fewer children learn it as a first language.

Another consequence of negative attitude is pointed out by Weinreich (1968) in his analysis of the role and status of Romansh in Switzerland. He relates how the Romansh-German bilingual who is speaking German must guard himself from borrowing words from Romansh (or switching into that language), as this might give away his Romansh origin at an inopportune moment or be taken as an index of incomplete acculturation into the Swiss German society.

However, the stigmatization of a minority language can also have the opposite effect: that of reinforcing the loyalty and solidarity of a group toward their language and people (see Giles, Bourhis, and Taylor, 1977). Even though use of a stigmatized language may be associated with a less prestigious group—at least in the eyes of the majority group—it may reinforce the group's positive values and symbolize solidarity for them. This has been found by Gal (1979) concerning Hungarian in Oberwart, Austria, by Gumperz (1976b) concerning Spanish in the Southwest, and by Barber (1973) for Yaqui by the Yaqui Indians of Pascua, Arizona. Gumperz writes that with the recent awakening of ethnic consciousness, urban professionals and intellectuals of Mexican American origin now deliberately adopt Mexican American speech along with English and literary Spanish to symbolize solidarity with their ethnic group. And in the trilingual (Yaqui, Spanish, and English) society of the Yaqui Indians in Pascua, Barber reports that failure to use Yaqui in the appropriate circumstances can be enough to isolate one from the society. Barber quotes a Yaqui Indian who denounces those who are ashamed to be Yaqui and try to deny their origins: "If I'm with Mexicans and a Yaqui comes up and talks to me in Spanish, I always answer in Yaqui. They say it's a good thing to do if you're Yaqui to speak it. Like the Chinese—they don't hide their language" (p. 314). Barber adds that the public denial of being Yaqui by refusing to use the language calls forth the real scorn of other Yaquis.

Giles, Bourhis, and Taylor (1977) also report that because of the renewed pride of French Canadians toward their culture and language, some refuse to use English with English Canadians in Quebec, even though many are perfectly bilingual. And some French Canadians who speak fluent English with no trace of a French accent are treated with caution by other French Canadians; their accentless English could be a sign that they are more English Canadian than French Canadian.

Throughout this book we will continue to see the profound effect that language attitudes can have on the life and the languages of bilinguals. In the end, language attitude is always one of the major factors in accounting for which languages are learned, which are used, and which are preferred by bilinguals.

Language Choice

In our daily interactions with others, we are constantly changing the variety of the language we use. There are many ways to express the need to drink some water: I want a drink of water; Give me some water; I'm thirsty; Water, please; Could I please have a drink of water; Would it be possible to have a drink of water; It's really hot in here; and so on.

Ervin-Tripp (1968) writes: "A speaker in any language community who enters diverse social situations normally has a repertoire of speech alternatives which shift with situation" (p. 197). She presents four main factors that account for change in code or variety: first, the setting (time and place) and the situation, such as a family breakfast, a party, a lecture, or a date; second, the participants in the interaction: their age, sex, occupation, socioeconomic status, origin, ethnicity, and their roles in relation to one another, such as employer–employee, husband–wife; third, the topic (work, sports, national events); and fourth, the function of the interaction: request; offering information or interpretation; routines, such as greetings, thanks, apologies; and so on. These factors help explain why you might say, "Could I please have a drink of water?" in your employer's office, but "Give me some water" to your roommate. Current sociolinguistic research by Labov, Fasold, Wolfram, and Gumperz, among others, has been aimed at describing and predicting changes in language varieties. Based on their results, they propose variable rules in phonology and syntax that take into account the social and psychosocial factors in language interaction.

In a bilingual setting involving two or more languages, we find a similar but more complex situation. Not only can bilingual speakers, like their monolingual counterparts, choose among different varieties of a language but, when speaking to other bilinguals, they can also choose between two languages. Whereas a monolingual can only switch from one variety to another (colloquial to formal, for instance) in one language, a bilingual may change varieties in one language, change languages, or do both. Because of this complex situation, most sociolinguists have concentrated on language choice in bilingual interactions, and few studies have examined both the switch in variety and the switch in language (see Ma and Herasimchuk, 1971, for an exception).

As we saw when we followed Nicole through her daily interactions, the choice of language and the switches from one to another followed a very complex pattern. She spoke mostly French with her husband but included many English lexical items; she spoke both English and French to Martine, using one or the other language (with a lot of code-switching) depending on the topic and situation. She spoke English, with no switches, to her neighbors, and French, again with no switches to her in-laws.

To show that such patterns are far from rare in bilingual interactions, we can examine the language patterns in any bilingual community. Kegl (1975) studied the Slovene-English bilingual community in Chicago and described some of its prominent language patterns. At meetings of the Slovene National Club, only Slovene is used. In the ethnic neighborhood among first-generation Ameri-

FIGURE 3.1   Language choice and code-switching.

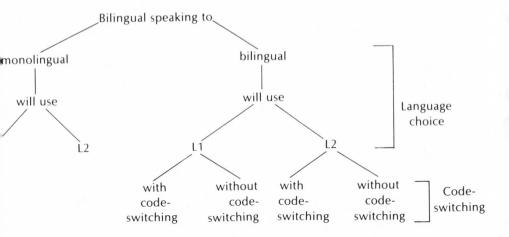

cans, Slovene is used with some English lexical items (supermarket, bingo game). Between two English-Slovene bilinguals who are intimately related, both languages are used with a lot of switching from one to the other. Between an English-Slovene bilingual and an intimate acquaintance who is monolingual in English, English is normally used with some Slovene word order and inflections. And finally, between a bilingual and a nonintimate monolingual, English is the dominant language, but with some word-order deviations.

In the following section I will attempt to put some order into what may appear at first to be a random pattern of two languages with a lot of code-switching. We will first study the factors that account for language choice (also called "language use" or "language usage" by researchers), and in the next section we will examine when it is that code-switching takes place. Figure 3.1 presents a two-stage approach in which the bilingual first decides on the base language to use and then, if the interlocutor is also bilingual, whether or not to code-switch. The bilingual may also borrow words from the other language and integrate them phonologically and morphologically into the base language. Such borrowing, as well as the influence of grammatical or phonological patterns of one language on another, will be studied in some detail in Chapter 6.

When studying language choice in bilinguals ("Who speaks what language to whom and when?" Fishman, 1965), we should differentiate between a bilingual speaking to a monolingual and to another bilingual. In the former case, the bilingual will quite naturally choose the language of his interlocutor, and the interaction will be like that of two monolinguals. Some bilinguals find themselves in monolingual settings more often than others. Thus, if Nicole did not have a French friend at the hospital, she would be speaking English from the moment she left home in the morning to the time she came back from work. Others live and work with bilinguals, and hence are less often in a totally monolingual situation. There is little to say about bilinguals in a monolingual environment except to note that their language behavior is rarely different from that of other monolinguals. They rarely switch to their other language, which would be of no help and might even set them apart. What is interesting for a monolingual is to discover that a person he or she has known for months or even years is in fact bilingual, and in the appropriate circumstances will switch back and forth between the two languages.

The language choice of bilinguals speaking to other bilinguals is of much greater interest. The appropriate language is usually chosen unconsciously with no extra time or effort. Hence a researcher's questions about language choice seem rather uninteresting to bilinguals. As Barber (1973) writes about her study of language choice among the Yaqui Indians in Pascua, Arizona:

> The men often find questions about their use of their languages rather ridiculous; naturally they speak Yaqui to Yaquis, Spanish to Mexicans, and English to Anglos. As one of them said, "I could talk to you in Yaqui—you wouldn't understand me." The problem does not seem so simple, however, when it is realized that in many of their social relationships they are dealing with people who speak at least two of their languages. Why then do they choose to speak one language at one time and another at some other time? (p. 305)

Diglossia or Restricted Language Choice

Diglossia is a situation in which two languages or two varieties of a language have very precise and distinct functions, so the bilingual speaker has little leeway in deciding which to use. Ferguson (1971) defines the term in the following way:

> Diglossia is a relatively stable language situation in which, in addition to the primary dialects (which may include a standard or regional standards), there is a very divergent, highly codified (often grammatically more complex) superposed variety, the vehicle of a large and respected body of written literature, either of an earlier period or in another speech community, which is learned largely by formal education and is used for most written and formal spoken purposes but is not used by any sector of the community for ordinary conversation. (p. 16)

Ferguson studies four cases of diglossia in which a high (H) language or variety coexists with a low (L) language or variety: Classical and dialectal Arabic in most Arab countries, French and Creole in Haiti, standard and Swiss German in Switzerland, and Katharévusa and Dhimotiki in Greece. Ferguson reports that the H language is considered more beautiful, more logical, and better able to express important thoughts. Speakers regard H as so superior to L that at times L is reported not even to exist. Thus educated Arabs will maintain that they never use dialectal Arabic, even though they employ it regularly in ordinary conversation. Similarly, some speakers of Haitian Creole deny its existence and assert that they always speak French. There is a large body of written literature in H, whereas L may not even have a written form, and when H has a long history it is considered normal to borrow words, phrases, and constructions from it. Children learn L from their parents and H at school. Ferguson notes also that H has grammatical categories not present in L (French has gender and number in the noun, but Creole does not) and although H and L share many lexical items, there are many paired items (one H, one L) where the use of one or the other will mark the utterance as H or L. Ferguson gives the example of menus in Greece having the word *inos* on them (H "wine"), but the diner will ask the waiter for *krasi* (L "wine").

What is particularly interesting about diglossia is the specialization of functions for H and L. H is used for sermons, letters, political speeches, university lectures, news broadcasts, newspaper editorials, and in poetry; L is used to give instructions to servants, waiters, and workmen, to converse in the family, to talk with friends and colleagues, and in folk literature and radio soap operas. Ferguson reports that typically someone reads aloud from a newspaper written in H and then discusses the contents in L; in the Arab world, formal university lectures are given in classical Arabic, but drills, explanations, and section meetings are mostly in dialectal Arabic. Ferguson is careful to stress that diglossia differs significantly from the familiar situation of a standard language with regional dialects. In diglossia H is never used in regular conversation, and any attempt to do so is considered artificial, pedantic, and in some sense disloyal to the community. Thus a Greek person speaking Katharévusa in the street would be considered pedantic, because Dhimotiki is the language of everyday communication.

Despite Ferguson's rather strict definition of diglossia, the concept has been extended to situations where any two languages are in contact and even to cases where two or more varieties of the same language are used in different social settings. As Timm (1980) writes: "Since Fishman's extension in 1967 of the term diglossia, . . . it has come to mean little more than the functional distribution of two or more languages or language varieties within a speech community" (p. 33). The concept now extends to the coexistence of all forms of speech in a society, whether the forms are different languages, different dialects, or different social varieties of the same language.

In this discussion, however, we will retain Ferguson's restricted definition of diglossia and stress the fact that the H variety is *not used by any sector of the community for ordinary conversation,* that it is learned largely at school and is used for most kinds of writing. In addition, H and L play very specialized functions or roles in the community and little choice is left to the bilingual as to which language to use with whom and when. In most bilingual situations the two languages in contact tend toward diglossia but do not reach the point attained, for instance, by classical and dialectal Arabic. The bilingual speaker has greater choice as to which language to use in a given situation, and either may often be used for writing. Thus, although a Mexican American will speak Spanish in certain circumstances (in the family, with friends, in the neighborhood) and English in others (at work, with the authorities), he or she can usually have an ordinary conversation in either language, depending on the interlocutor. In a word, the roles of English and Spanish in the Southwest are not as specialized and as static as are classical and dialectal Arabic.

The Complexity of Language Choice

Language choice in bilingual communities has been a favorite topic in recent sociolinguistic work; it has been studied in such areas as Oberwart, Austria (German-Hungarian bilingualism, Gal, 1979); Paraguay (Spanish-Guarani bilingualism, Rubin, 1968); Kenya, Tanzania, and Uganda (vernacular-Swahili-English trilingualism, Muthiani, 1979; Mkilifi, 1978; Scotton, 1979); Tucson, Arizona (Spanish-English bilingualism, Barker, 1975); the Gail Valley, Austria (German-Slovene bilingualism, Gumperz, 1976a), and the Philippines (Filipino-English bilingualism, Pascasio and Hidalgo, 1979). Below are summarized three such studies.

Fishman, Cooper, and Ma (1971) undertook an extensive study of the Spanish-English bilingualism of a Puerto Rican neighborhood in Jersey City, New Jersey. The Puerto Ricans they surveyed were mostly young (70 percent were twenty-five or under), mostly of low occupational status, and many had received little formal education. Almost half had been born on the mainland. Through questionnaires and interviews the researchers, principally Hoffman (1971), studied language use in a number of domains: the home, the neighborhood, the school, the church, and the working place. In the home, although Spanish was used the most frequently, its choice over English depended on the participants and topics. The mother usually spoke Spanish to other members of the family; the father spoke Spanish to his wife and usually to his children—reprimanding and disciplining were done in Spanish, but education and work were sometimes discussed in English. The children used Spanish with their grandparents, both English and Spanish with their parents, and mostly English among themselves. However, they would use Spanish to tease and joke, to create emotional and intimate bonds, to keep out non-Puerto Ricans, and when visiting a date's parents.

In the neighborhood, the survey found that Spanish was usually spoken in the small shops (bodegas) owned by Puerto Ricans, but English was used in the American-run stores. For chatting on the sidewalk, older Puerto Ricans spoke Spanish, but both English and Spanish were used by younger members of the group. At school both languages were used for instruction. All official matters involving the bureaucracy (health, welfare, banking) usually took place in English. What is surprising is that this was also true in check-cashing services with Spanish-speaking clerks. Hoffman (1971) explains this by the fact that the English utterances used are simple and rather automatic. For church services, 55 percent of the respondents said that Spanish was the language used, 21 percent said that it was English, and 24 percent reported both languages. If the church offered both Spanish and English services, the parents usually attended the former and the children the latter. At work, most persons used English because their jobs required them to communicate with monolingual English speakers and also because of specialized terminology, as in government and union regulations. Hoffman adds that many non-Spanish employers did not allow Puerto Ricans to speak Spanish on the job; others appointed Puerto Rican foremen who would speak English during work to maintain their authority but Spanish during lunch to interact with members of their own group.

A second study that illustrates the complexity of language choice takes us to Pomerode, a small town in the state of Santa Catarina, Brazil. Heye (1979) reports that Pomerode was founded in 1870 by German immigrants from upper and lower Pomerania in Germany.

The population today is 13,000, a large segment of which works the fields and raises vegetable crops and cattle. Of the sixty-nine informants in Heye's study, only four were born in Germany; the remainder were born in Pomerode or elsewhere in Santa Catarina. Most (80 percent) reported that their mother tongue was German, and most had learned Portuguese when they started to go to school. In self-evaluations of their language proficiency, 30 percent reported that they spoke German better than Portuguese, 23 percent reported better Portuguese, and 47 percent reported that they spoke the two languages equally well. In understanding, 75 percent reported equality of the two languages, but the majority felt that they read and wrote Portuguese better than German.

The pattern of language use in Pomerode is rather complex. German dominates in church, Portuguese in clubs and sports, and both languages are used equally at work and in stores. At home, German is used to a greater extent at mealtimes, when putting the children to bed, for prayers, and for scolding, but Portuguese is employed more for songs and storytelling. Heye reports that German is used more in the family and with neighbors, Portuguese and German are used equally with friends, and Portuguese is definitely the language for speaking to authorities and to strangers. Heye concludes that the functional value of German in Pomerode is comparable to that of Portuguese.

A third study of language choice takes us to Pascua in northwest Tucson, Arizona. There Barber (1973) studied the language usage of the Yaqui Indians, who learn Yaqui at home, Spanish in the home and the community (Tucson has a large group of Mexican Americans), and English at school, at work, and in the army. The twelve young men studied were all trilingual. In their families, these men spoke Yaqui with the older people, Spanish with the children, and both Yaqui and Spanish with people their own age. Barber mentions a man in his early twenties who spoke Yaqui to his mother, both Yaqui and Spanish to his father and oldest sister, and Yaqui to his younger brothers. Another man spoke Yaqui to his parents, wife, and children, but Yaqui and Spanish to his younger brothers.

Yaqui is the principal ceremonial language, although at times some Latin and Spanish are also used. At work the language most used depends on the type of work, the people in the group, and where the person works. For example, Barber reports that Yaquis generally do agricultural work together—often in family groups during the cotton-picking season—or with Mexican Americans. Either Yaqui or Spanish is spoken depending on the group and on whether Mexican Americans are to be included or left out of the conversation. English is usually the language of communication with the employer, be it for agricultural or railroad work. For jobs in town, Yaqui is hardly ever used; English and Spanish are used most, because the other workers are mainly Anglos and Mexican Americans. When spending money, the Yaquis speak English or Spanish, but usually Spanish. Stores have Spanish-speaking clerks, and bars, dance halls, and restaurants are predominantly Spanish speaking. With friends, they speak Spanish and Yaqui about equally; with an Anglo friend, they speak English, but if the friend knows Spanish, that language is preferred. The language of the law is English; although a man may be arrested in either English or Spanish, legal procedures beyond this are conducted in English.

These three studies of language usage are highly typical of other such studies: the patterns of usage are so complex that it is difficult to determine at first how bilinguals choose the appropriate language with a particular person in a specific situation. In the next section we will examine some of the main factors that account for language choice and why, depending on the bilingual community, some factors are more important than others.

Factors in Language Choice

Box 3.4 lists some of the factors that account for language choice in bilingual settings. Any one factor may account for choosing one language over another, but usually it is the combination of several factors that explains language choice.

PARTICIPANTS   The language proficiency of the speaker and of the interlocutor is very important. Rubin (1968) reports that in Luque, Paraguay, the head doctor speaks Guarani or Spanish with his patients, depending on which language they know better and feel more comfortable in. And in general, Rubin states that people often consider the ability of the addressee in choosing between languages. Thus, when asked which language they would use with a "barefoot woman," almost all respondents answered Guarani, whereas with an "unfamiliar well-dressed person," most said Spanish. In northern Maine, Schweda (1980) reports that a fair number of the English-French bilinguals she interviewed greeted everyone in English and used cues such as the interlocutor's French accent, broken English, or a confused look to decide whether they should continue in English or switch to French. To the question, "Why did you speak

---

BOX 3.4

Factors Influencing Language Choice

Participants	*Situation*
Language proficiency	Location/Setting
Language preference	Presence of monolinguals
Socioeconomic status	Degree of formality
Age	Degree of intimacy
Sex	
Occupation	*Content of discourse*
Education	Topic
Ethnic background	Type of vocabulary
History of speakers' linguistic	
interaction	*Function of interaction*
Kinship relation	To raise status
Intimacy	To create social distance
Power relation	To exclude someone
Attitude toward languages	To request or command
Outside pressure	

---

language X to this person instead of language Y?" one will often receive answers of the type: "I speak language X better," "He is more proficient in X," "I believe she is more proficient in X."

The history of linguistic interaction between the two participants also plays a large role. In many instances two people speak a particular language to one another simply because they always have, even if one or both have become more proficient in the other language. This is especially true of the children of immigrant families, who as youngsters spoke the minority language to their grandparents or parents and continue to do so as adults, even though they now know the majority language much better than their other language. It is indeed rare to find bilingual friends or relatives who do not have an "agreed-upon" language of interaction when the situation or topic do not impose a particular language. Violation of this "agreement" is likely to create an unnatural or even embarrassing situation, which may end with the question, "Why are you speaking language X to me?" As an English-French bilingual writes: "I never speak English to French friends, even if they are fluent in English. I find it unnatural, and I hate it when close friends suggest I speak to them in English to help them." Of course, if a third person enters the room, or if the location of the interaction changes, or the particpants want to exclude someone, speaking the other language is considered perfectly natural. But as soon as the situation permits it, the participants will revert to their customary language of interaction.

Age plays a role in language choice. Gal (1979), for example, reports that in the German-Hungarian community of Oberwart, the younger people speak mainly German (except in church-related activities or with their grandparents), whereas older people mostly speak Hungarian. She writes: "Among the various attributes of speakers it is neither their status as peasants nor the nature of their social networks that correlates most closely with language use. It is their ages" (p. 136). Schweda (1980) found a similar situation in northern Maine. The respondents in her study report that older people prefer to speak French, whereas those under thirty, approximately, prefer to speak English. Wald (1974) reports that in coastal Kenya the young use both Swahili and the local language when speaking to one another, but never use Swahili when talking to the elders, who would consider it an affront, even though they, too, are bilingual.

The socioeconomic status of the participants—real or apparent—is also an important factor. Muthiani (1979) reports that in Kenya, an African of high socioeconomic status will speak Swahili to an African of lower status (unless they both share the same vernacular), but in English to an African of his own socioeconomic status. This is also true for an African speaking to an Indian. Scotton (1979) reports that in Uganda a well-dressed African stranger will be addressed in English. If a European in Kenya uses Swahili with an African who knows English, then the African will answer in English right away to show that he does not belong to a lower class (Muthiani, 1979).

The degree of intimacy between the speakers is also important. Rubin (1968) reports that Guarani-Spanish bilinguals use Spanish with strangers or mere acquaintances, whereas with friends (drinking tea, being angry, saying something intimate, joking) they switch to Guarani. It is interesting to note that when young Paraguayans start courting and the relationship is still formal, Spanish is the language of interaction, but as they become more intimate, Guarani is used more and more.

Rubin also clearly illustrates how outside pressure can lead to the use of one language over another. At the time of her study, parents in Paraguay were urged to use Spanish with their children at home to give them more practice in the language. Thus, in Luque, the parents spoke Guarani or both Guarani and Spanish to one another when they were by themselves, but mainly Spanish when the children were present, and almost always Spanish with the children by themselves.

As we saw in the previous section, the participants' attitude toward a language (and therefore toward the group that speaks it) plays a role in language choice. For example, the children of a stigmatized minority may decide not to use their native language with their parents and relatives so as not to be differentiated from the children of the majority group. And recently, when a Russian Jew who had just emigrated from the Soviet Union, was greeted at the New York airport in Russian, he was heard to say in Hebrew, "Never speak that language to me again."

The many factors we have examined so far interact in such a way that if we put aside such other factors as situation, topic, and intent, bilinguals will choose a particular language easily and almost automatically. Di Pietro (1977) reports that in Italian stores in Washington, D.C., the clerks are guided by a number of cues, including nonverbal ones such as stance, dress, and facial expression, in deciding whether to address a customer in English or Italian. He adds that they are rarely wrong in their choice. And Barber (1973) writes, concerning language choice in Pascua:

A bartender in a Mexican bar will say to his customers "Qué quieres?" or "What'll you have?" without conscious thought, and similarly a Yaqui at the ticket window of a theater will say either "Quiero un boleto" or "I'd like a ticket." In such cases the person judges the linguistic background of the person he is talking to and accommodates his own usage to this. (p. 310)

SITUATION   For Rubin (1968), the most important variable to be considered in predicting language usage in Paraguay is the location of the interaction. When asked which language they would use out in the country, respondents in Luque overwhelmingly replied Guarani. Most people in the rural areas speak Guarani as a first language, and almost all activities in the country are conducted in that language. Schweda (1980) reports an interesting trend in northern Maine, where the inhabitants of the St. John Valley cross the border between New Brunswick and Maine quite freely. When asked which language they would speak at a party, some said that at a party on the American side of the border they would speak English, but at a party in Canada, they would speak French. Others said it would depend on the particular town on the American side: French in Frenchville, English in Fort Kent, and both languages in Madawaska.

In other contexts, bilinguals speaking among themselves may

choose a particular language so as not to stand out from the people around them. This is especially true in communities that have negative attitudes toward a minority group language. I have witnessed North African students in Paris speaking French to one another on the boulevards of the Latin Quarter, but switching back to Arabic, their usual language, in their apartment. It is interesting to note that the location of interaction does not have as much importance in some bilingual communities. Gal (1979), for example, reports that in Oberwart the setting does not affect language choice. An informant told her that whatever the context, "If it is my mother, I talk to her in Hungarian."

The formality of the situation has been reported by a number of researchers to play a role in language choice. In Paraguay, Rubin observed that bilinguals would choose Spanish when speaking to a doctor, a teacher, or to someone in authority in Asuncion, but in less formal situations they would speak Guarani. Rubin adds that at a dance where the floor is packed earth (and therefore the atmosphere is not formal), the informants reported using both Spanish and Guarani, but at a dance where the floor is brick, Spanish is the usual language. Barker (1975), in his study of Spanish-English bilingualism, reports similar findings. In intimate or familial relations, Spanish is almost universally dominant in Tucson's Mexican American community. However, in economic and formal social relations, English is widely used. Heye (1975) finds similar trends in Ticino, Switzerland: the two dialects, Swiss German and Ticinese, are limited to informal situations and are almost never used in the courtroom, the church, or even in a business meeting. However, one can imagine asides between two friends taking place in one of the dialects.

The presence of monolinguals in the interaction is a most interesting variable in language choice. Concerning Kenya, Muthiani (1979) writes:

Swahili is used as a lingua franca intensively between Africans and Asians but if an African and an Asian meet a European, it will be highly probable that they will switch to English if they intend to include him in the discussion. The reverse is also predictable—an African and a European will switch from English to Swahili if they want to include an Indian in their discussion. Here the two parties are assuming that the third party does not understand English. Should their assumption be wrong, they will then switch back to English. (p. 384)

Gal (1979) reports that in Oberwart, bilinguals speaking Hungarian to one another will always switch over to German when a monolingual German speaker comes toward them. This is done out of politeness, as is the switch from Slovene to German in the Gail Valley, when a German monolingual comes within hearing distance of bilinguals speaking Slovene (Gumperz, 1976a). Similarly, Nicole and Martine, in the example at the beginning of the chapter, spoke French while Ann, their American colleague, was busy in another part of the room. However, as Ann came toward them, Martine and Nicole naturally switched over to English to include her in the conversation. When a doctor enters the room during the day, the two again switch to English, even though the doctor may not necessarily interact with them.

Choosing a language because of the presence of monolinguals can lead to strange situations, such as a group of friends speaking the monolingual's language although they usually use the other language with each other. They will continue to speak the monolingual's language throughout a meal or even for a whole evening, using their customary language of interaction only when the monolingual is engaged in a side conversation or has left the room. But as soon as the monolingual returns, everyone will revert to that language. Bilinguals have endless stories to tell concerning similar—and at times frustrating—episodes, often with deviations of the type: "There were two monolinguals with us, a language X speaker and a language Y speaker, and we had a hard time including the language X speaker," or "Some friends arrived halfway through the meal and we all switched to language Y for about five minutes, but then we suddenly realized that A [the monolingual] had been left out."

CONTENT OF DISCOURSE   The content of the discourse has often been invoked as a factor in language choice. Fishman (1965a) writes that some topics are better handled in one language than another, either because the bilingual has learned to deal with a topic in a particular language, the other language lacks specialized terms for a topic, or because it would be considered strange or inappropriate to discuss a topic in that language. In Box 3.5, three bilinguals discuss the effect of topic on language choice—the first has problems talking about her work in her first language; the second talks in her sleep about her work in the language spoken at work; and the third either changes languages when explaining his professional activities or code switches extensively.

In Paraguay, Rubin (1968) found that school, legal, and business affairs were usually discussed in Spanish; in Jersey City, Hoffman (1971) reports that for in-depth discussions concerning school, English was found more appropriate than Spanish by students and

---

BOX 3.5   **BILINGUALS SPEAK**

Language Choice

When I speak about my job, I have difficulties expressing myself in my native language [French] since all my formal schooling [college and graduate school] was undertaken in the United States and I therefore learned all the "jargon" in English.

I always speak English (exclusively) in the laboratory. One night my husband heard me talking in my sleep. I was referring to an experiment of mine and the whole description was done in English, obviously.

Whenever I have to explain in French anything about my professional activities or my former school experience in the U.S., I find it very hard not to use English words, because these experiences belong to my "English-related background." I have learned the business language in the U.S. and find it difficult to express the same ideas in French. Luckily this occurs most of the time with bilingual friends and therefore it doesn't bother anyone to switch from one language to another or to mix both in the same conversation.

---

parents alike. Barber (1973) reports that Yaqui Indians prefer to swear and insult in Spanish, although they probably could also do so in Yaqui and English.

FUNCTION OF INTERACTION   The function or intent of the interaction is the last major category of factors influencing language choice. One function, status raising, has been found to play an important role in a number of different situations. Rubin (1968) reports that in Paraguay some upwardly mobile individuals in Luque insist on using Spanish in situations where Guarani would be expected. Hoffman (1971) mentions the Puerto Rican foremen who change language when they change roles: they speak Spanish to other Puerto Ricans at lunchtime but employ English during work. Scotton (1979) writes that respondents in her Kampala, Uganda, survey reported in overwhelming numbers that they would use only English in a number of situations where status raising was at stake.

Just as bilinguals change languages to include a monolingual, they may choose a language to exclude someone. In a crowded bus, at a store, or on the beach, this is not very serious, but it can have profound effects if the third person (a monolingual) is supposedly part of the conversation. Of course, excluding someone in this way can sometimes backfire. For example, two Greek-American students in a crowded student cafeteria, thinking that if they spoke Greek they would not be understood by anyone, started commenting on the people around them. After five minutes of this, one of the people whom they had commented on extensively folded his newspaper, turned toward them, and with a large grin on his face said "Goodbye" in Greek!

Finally, different languages may be used in different modes. Thus, on the Navajo reservation, Navajo is spoken almost exclusively—in the home, at the store, on the radio, and at council meetings—but almost all writing is done in English. The minutes of meetings are kept in English, although the meetings are conducted in Navajo; the texts of radio broadcasts are in English, but they are read in Navajo, and court records are kept in English but the cases are heard in Navajo. Such a situation occurs when one of the languages (such as American Sign Language) does not have a writing system or has a system that has not been learned by everyone and is not used very much, such as Navajo.

When a bilingual chooses a language, the underlying choice is made rapidly and automatically. If someone initiates a conversation in a particular language, others usually answer in that language. However, there are cases of nonreciprocity, that is, speaker A starts with language X and speaker B answers in language Y. Usually, a rapid adjustment follows, with one of the two languages predominating, but at times the conversation may continue in both languages. Barber (1973) cites a Yaqui Indian who speaks Spanish to his wife and receives replies in Yaqui, with neither ever changing to the other's language. This is quite rare, however, as nonreciprocity usually leads to embarrassment and even anger, because choosing a particular language can signal status raising or lack of group solidarity. Gal (1979) writes: "An old man, preparing to play cards, recounted to his friends how insolent a young bilingual salesman at the local grocery store had been to him . . . 'The little creep answered me in German' " (p. 142). The young man should have replied in Hungarian, the language he had been addressed in, but for some reason he broke the "reciprocity rule."

In such a situation, friends can discuss why one of them refused to speak language X (he had not seen that a third person was present, for instance), but when the two are merely acquaintances, there may be no explanation offered, and once the (usually shortened) interaction is over, one of them will probably walk away wondering why the other did not reply in the appropriate language. The adjustment to the other person's language, also known as language accommodation, has been the object of some recent research (see, for instance, Giles, Taylor, and Bourhis, 1973; Genesee and Bourhis, 1981) and has been linked to social status, language attitudes, prestige of the language, and other psychosocial factors.

A breakdown in a person's language choice may occur if a multilingual person is in a multilingual environment, as illustrated by this example from Epstein (1915):

Young R. is fluent in all the languages used in Mrs. R's boarding house: Hebrew, French, Russian, Polish, and German. One evening in the middle of a conversation in Hebrew, he decided to address himself to an Alsatian guest: he first murmured a few words of Hebrew; interrupted himself; then said a few words of Russian; interrupted himself again; remained silent for a few seconds and then finally began to speak German. (p. 63, my translation)

However, this is an extreme example; usually language choice is made rapidly and automatically.

The Weighting of Factors

Rarely does a single factor account for a bilingual's choice of one language over another. As Gal (1979) writes: "A few weeks of observation in Oberwart made it clear that no single rule would account for all choices between languages. Statements to the effect that one language is used at home and another in school—work—street, would be too simplistic" (p. 99). Usually some factors are more important—have more weight—than others and thus play a greater role when combined with other factors. Gal found that in Oberwart certain characteristics of the speaker and of the listener allowed one to predict language choice in a majority of cases. Age was an important component in that situation; topic and setting had less weight than the factors related to the participants.

Rubin (1968), in her study of Guarani-Spanish bilinguals in Paraguay, states that in three areas usage is fairly rigidly defined: the country (Guarani), school (Spanish), and public functions in Asunción, (Spanish). Usage in all other situations, she reports, is defined by social dimensions, social pressures, and individual considerations. Rubin has attempted to order the factors in language choice according to their importance in Paraguay. Figure 3.2 presents her decision tree, which bilinguals theoretically work through to decide which language to speak.

The location of the interaction is the most important factor: out-

FIGURE 3.2   Deciding which language to use in Paraguay. (From Rubin, 1968, p. 109.)

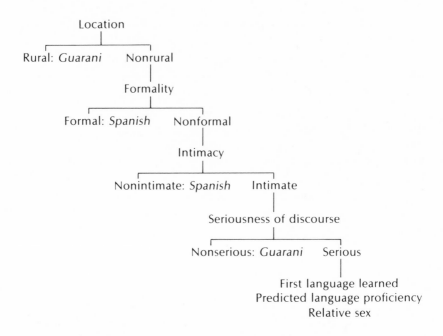

side of rural areas, where Guarani is the norm, there are no clear rules, except in school and at public functions in Asunción, so the bilingual has to take into account the formality of the situation. In formal settings Spanish is the rule. If the situation is informal, the bilingual has to take into account the degree of intimacy. If the interlocutor is a stranger or a mere acquaintance, Spanish will be the rule, but if he or she is an intimate friend or parent, a further decision has to be made on the seriousness of the discourse. For casual banter or jokes, Guarani will be used, but in a serious interaction other factors may influence the choice: the language first learned (most informants use their first language with intimates), the addressee's apparent language proficiency, and the sex of both participants (men tend to use Guarani more with other men than with women, and women tend to use Spanish more with both sexes).

Other bilingual communities could probably be characterized by their own decision trees, with factors ordered according to their importance or left out entirely if not applicable. A diagram for Oberwart would not include the location of the interaction, whereas a diagram for East Africa would include the socioeconomic status of the participants. Not only does the weighting of factors change for different bilingual communities, it probably changes under certain circumstances, such as unexpected events or stress. It can thus become extremely difficult to predict which language will be used in a particular situation; and hence language choice in a normal bilingual community can be quite different from the typical diglossic situation, in which usage is strictly delimited.

I will end this section by stressing again how rapid and automatic language choice really is. A bilingual rarely asks the conscious question, "Which language should I be using?" Language choice, like the act of speaking itself, is a well-learned and complex behavior whose extreme complexity only becomes apparent when it breaks down. In everyday life, the bilingual will go through his or her daily activities quite unaware of the many psychological and sociolinguistic factors that interact in what are probably complex weighted formulas to help choose one language over another.

Code-Switching

Figure 3.1 presented a two-stage decision process underlying language choice. In the first stage the bilingual decides which base language to use, and in the second stage he or she determines whether to code-switch. This second stage occurs only when the bilingual is addressing another bilingual, and even then the decision may be delayed for some time. What is sure is that this stage does exist, because a bilingual will code-switch in certain situations but not in others.

Code-switching is a very important aspect of bilingualism, and only of late has it received the unbiased attention of researchers. Di Pietro (1977) defines it as "the use of more than one language by communicants in the execution of a speech act." Valdes Fallis (1976) refers to it simply as "the alternation of two languages," and Scotton and Ury (1977) propose that "code-switching [is] the use of two or more linguistic varieties in the same conversation or interaction." For our purposes I will define code-switching as the alternate use of two or more languages in the same utterance or conversation, as in these three examples:

1) A French-English bilingual speaking French and switching (words in italics) to English:

Va chercher Marc (go fetch Marc) *and bribe him* avec un chocolat chaud (with a hot chocolate) *with cream on top.*

2) A Tanzanian speaking Swahili and switching to English (from Mkilifi, 1978):

Ile (the) *accident* Ilitokea alipolose (occurred when he lost) *control* Na (and) Aka*overturn and landed in a ditch.*

3) A Mexican American speaking Spanish and switching to English (from Valdes Fallis, 1976):

No me fijé hasta que ya no me dijo (I didn't notice until he told me): *Oh, I didn't think he'd be there.*

From these three examples, we see that code-switching can involve a word (*accident* in example 2), a phrase (*and bribe him* in example 1), or a sentence (*Oh, I didn't think he'd be there,* in example 3). It can also involve several sentences. What is important is that switching is different from borrowing a word from the other language and integrating it phonologically and morphologically into the base language. In code-switching the switched element is not integrated; instead there is a total shift to the other language. Here I will discuss only code-switching, but in the last chapter we will compare borrowing and code-switching in some depth.

Code-switching is an extremely common characteristic of bilingual speech, and some bilingual writers and poets reflect this in their works. The poem in Box 3.6, by Pedro Ortiz Vasquez, a Mexican American poet, presents code-switching as a common phenomenon in Mexican American speech, which is also used to enhance the content of the verse.

In the following section we will study attitudes toward code-switching and the reasons for it. In later chapters we will investigate the syntactic rules that govern code-switching and the psycholinguistic operation that underlies the switch from one language to another.

Attitudes toward Code-Switching

Monolinguals have long had a very negative attitude toward code-switching, which they see as a grammarless mixture of two languages, a jargon or gibberish that is an insult to the monolingual's own rule-governed language. Code-switching is given pejorative names such as Franglais, the "mixture" of French and English or the use of too many English loan words in French, and Tex-Mex, the "mixture" of English and Spanish in the Southwest. Those who

BOX 3.6   BILINGUALS SPEAK

Quienes Somos

it's so strange in here
todo lo que pasa
is so strange
y nadie puede entender
que lo que pasa aquí
isn't any different
de lo que pasa allá
where everybody is trying
to get out
move into a better place
al lugar where we can hide
where we don't have to know
quienes somos
strange people of the sun

lost in our own awareness
of where we are
and where we want to be
and wondering why
it's so strange in here

—Pedro Ortiz Vasquez,
in *The Bilingual Review/
La Revista Bilingüe* 2
(1975): 293–294

code-switch extensively are often said to know neither language well enough to converse in either one alone and they are termed "semi-lingual" or "nonlingual."

As can be seen in Box 3.7, this negative attitude toward code-switching has been adopted, at least overtly, by many bilinguals. Most of the bilinguals I have questioned made remarks such as: "Switching is done mostly out of laziness," "It is embarrassing," "It might be dangerous if it becomes too common," "I try not to code-switch," "Code-switching is not very pure." One consequence of this attitude is that some bilinguals never switch, while most others restrict it to situations in which they will not be stigmatized for doing so. As can be seen in Box 3.8, bilinguals avoid code-switching with those who have very strict norms concerning language use, such as parents and teachers, reserving it for close acquaintances and those who also code-switch.

It is important to note that despite the strong negative attitudes toward code-switching, little if any evidence has been found that it leads to "semilingualism." Haugen (1969) writes about Norwegian Americans: "Reports are sometimes heard of individuals who 'speak

---

BOX 3.7   **BILINGUALS SPEAK**

Attitudes toward Code-Switching

A Swiss German-French-English trilingual: In principle I reject switching because I feel it destroys the ethnicity of a language. In practice, however, I often code-switch without knowing it.

A French-English bilingual: This whole process of code-switching is done mostly out of laziness, for if I searched long enough for the correct word, I would eventually find it . . . I try to avoid code-switching . . . one would quickly end up speaking a language of its own.

A Kurdish-Arabic bilingual: When I switch (inadvertently), I usually realize soon afterward and correct myself, but it is still embarrassing.

A Russian-English bilingual: I have a very positive attitude toward code-switching because it helps me to express myself more precisely. However, I feel it might be dangerous if it becomes too common—where you have to code-switch in order to speak.

A Portuguese-English bilingual: Although I try not to code-switch, it inevitably happens, especially when I try to explain to other Portuguese what my research is about.

A Hebrew-Arabic-English trilingual: Code-switching is not very pure.

A French-English bilingual: My attitude toward code-switching is a very relaxed one.

---

no language whatever' and confuse the two to such an extent that it is impossible to tell which language they speak. No such cases have occurred in the writer's experience, in spite of many years of listening to American-Norwegian speech" (p. 70). And Mkilifi (1978) writes about Swahili-English code-switching in Tanzania: "There is a school of thought which believes that in a situation like that obtained in Tanzania the multilinguals concerned fail to master perfectly one of the languages they operate in . . . [However] most of the bilinguals seem to be able to maintain well either English or Swahili where the setting demands the use of one or the other" (pp. 144–145).

Code-switching not only fills a momentary linguistic need, it is also a very useful communication resource, as we will see below. It takes place quite unconsciously; speakers (including those who condemn code-switching, like Roger at the beginning of this chapter)

BOX 3.8   **BILINGUALS SPEAK**

With Whom Do You Code-Switch?

A Greek-English bilingual: I find myself code-switching with my friends who are all Greek ... they know English so well and nobody gets offended with code-switching ... I don't switch with my parents as I do with my friends.

A Russian-English bilingual: When I am with my Russian-American friends our conversation is usually basically in English with many, many instances of code-switching. In fact, sometimes all the nouns and adjectives are in Russian ... I don't know why we don't just speak Russian, perhaps just to infuriate our parents who hate this "verbal salad."

A Persian-English bilingual: When I am speaking with my Persian friends, sometimes I have difficulties saying a word in Persian and so I say it in English.

A Hebrew-Arabic-English trilingual: I find that I switch only with friends and people close to me. I think familiarity and intimacy are the motivations of code-switching.

A French-English bilingual: I tend to use both English and French within the same conversation, within the same sentence, when I'm with Francos who are obviously bilingual, but also with Francos with whom I am at ease.

---

are often quite unaware that they are switching from one language to another. Their main concern is with communicating a message or intent, and they know that the other person will understand them whether they use one or two languages. In some bilingual or multilingual communities, code switching is the norm rather than the exception (see Chapter 6). As an Arabic-French-English trilingual from Lebanon writes: "Code-switching between Arabic, English and French is one of the most distinctive features of Lebanese culture, and I have never seen it practiced to such an extent in any other culture." He adds that French monolinguals who overhear trilingual code-switching of this type ask, "Which language are you speaking? It often sounds like French, but it isn't!"

Reasons for Code-Switching

Bilinguals usually explain that the reason they code-switch is that they lack facility in one language when talking about a particular

---

BOX 3.9   **BILINGUALS SPEAK**

Reasons for Code-Switching

A French-English bilingual: I tend to use both languages when I feel tired or lazy as an "easy way out" when I cannot find a word in the language I am speaking.

A Kurdish-Arabic bilingual: I find that when I'm speaking about politics, science, or other specialized topics, I will mix languages, especially the nouns.

An Alsatian-French bilingual: Sometimes I switch from Alsatian into French when I do not find the appropriate word after a long absence from Alsace.

A Russian-English bilingual: When I speak to another Russian-English bilingual, I don't speak as carefully and often the languages blend. This also happens when I am tired or excited or angry.

A French-English bilingual: The reason why I use so many words in English when I speak with French-speaking people is because I find it very hard to convey certain ideas or information about my daily life in this country [the U.S.] in a language other than English. Notions such as "day care center," "finger food," "window shopping," and "pot-luck dinners," need a few sentences to explain in French.

A Swiss German-French-English trilingual: I may purposely switch within a conversation in order to confuse people who are eavesdropping.

A Spanish-English bilingual: I was speaking to a Puerto Rican student in English about giving her a ride to New York. After a while she switched to Spanish to ask me how much it would cost her. I felt this was an attempt to get the cheapest price, since I too was Puerto Rican. Later that day she came up to me and said in English that fifteen dollars round trip was too expensive.

---

topic. They report that they switch when they cannot find an appropriate word or expression or when the language being used does not have the items or appropriate translations for the vocabulary needed; see Box 3.9. Some notions are just better expressed in one language than another. Thus for a French person in the United States, "day care" does not have the same meaning as its French translation, "crèche," and "playground" does not have the same connotations as "parc." At other times, however, the bilingual simply has not learned or is not equally familiar with the terms in both languages. For instance, Scotton (1979) describes how a Kikuyu university student in Nairobi, Kenya, switched constantly from Kikuyu to English to discuss geometry with his younger brother:

Atīrīrī *angle* niati *has* ina *degree eighty;* nayo *this one* ina mirongo itatu."

These brothers probably learned geometry in English and did not know the corresponding terms in Kikuyu. Similarly, a French computer technician trained in the United States can talk about his job only in English, or in French with a lot of code-switching. Very often a bilingual knows a word in both language X and language Y, but the language Y word is more available at that moment when speaking language X. He or she may switch to language Y to say the word but later on in the conversation will use the equivalent word in language X. This phenomenon of "the most available word" is extremely frequent in bilingual speech and occurs, according to many bilinguals, when they are tired, lazy, or angry. They know that with more effort and time they could find the appropriate word or expression in the base language.

In some instances, members of a community are reported to code-switch regularly when a particular topic is discussed. Both Valdes Fallis (1976) and Lance (1979) have noticed that Mexican Americans in the Southwest often switch from Spanish to English when talking about money. For instance:

La consulta era (the visit cost) *eight dollars.*
(Valdes Fallis, 1976)

This is probably because most buying and selling is done in English.

In addition, switches may involve fixed phrases of greeting or parting and discourse markers such as: oyes (listen), fijate que (look), you know, pero (however). (See Hasselmo, 1970, for a detailed study of discourse markers in Swedish-English bilinguals.)

In his study of code-switching by Australians of German origin, Clyne (1967) found that a single word switch often triggered a continuation in the language of the switch. Valdes Fallis (1976) found many examples of this in Spanish-English bilingual speech. Thus:

No yo sí brincaba en el (no, I really did jump on the) *trampoline. When I was a senior . . .* *(Valdes Fallis, 1976)*

In this case, the switch to English for "trampoline" triggered a continuation in English. The same happens in the following example:

Porque allí hay (because here are some) *cashews. You don't like them?* *(Valdes Fallis, 1976)*

BOX 3.10

Some Reasons for Code-Switching

- Fill a linguistic need for lexical item, set phrase, discourse marker, or sentence filler
- Continue the last language used (triggering)
- Quote someone
- Specify addressee
- Qualify message: amplify or emphasize ("topper" in argument)
- Specify speaker involvement (personalize message)

- Mark and emphasize group identity (solidarity)
- Convey confidentiality, anger, annoyance
- Exclude someone from conversation
- Change role of speaker: raise status, add authority, show expertise

---

Although many instances of code-switching can be explained by the lack of appropriate terminology in one language, the "most available word" phenomenon, habit, or triggering, many others involve particular verbal or communicative strategies. Gumperz (1970, 1976a, b; Gumperz and Hernandez-Chavez, 1978) has stressed that switching at a particular moment conveys semantically significant information. According to him, code-switching is a communicative resource that builds on the participants' perception of two contrasting languages. He writes that code-switching is meaningful in much the same way that lexical choice is meaningful: it is a verbal strategy, used in much the same way that a skillful writer might switch styles in a short story. Gal (1979) reinforces this view stating that listeners interpret code-switching as an indicator of the speaker's momentary attitudes, communicative intents, and emotions. According to this school of thought, code-switching is an important means of conveying linguistic and social information.

Box 3.10 lists some uses of code-switching. As Gumperz (1970) notes, switching may emphasize varying degrees of speaker involvement. He reports on a conversation between E, a faculty member and M, a social worker, who is talking about giving up smoking:

An' . . . an' . . . an' they tell me, "How did you quit, Mary?" I di'n' quit. I . . . I just stopped. I just stopped. I mean it wasn't an effort that I made. *Que voy a dejar de fumar porque me hace daño?* (That I'm going to stop smoking because it's harmful to me?) this or tha', uh-uh.   (*Gumperz, 1970*)

The passage continues for some time, and Gumperz writes:

What someone studying the passage sentence by sentence might regard as almost random alternation between the two languages is highly meaningful in terms of the conversational context. M is quite ambivalent about her smoking and she conveys this through her language use. Her choice of speech forms symbolizes her alternation between embarrassment and clinical detachment about her own condition. Spanish sentences reflect personal involvement . . . while English marks more general or detached statements. (p. 135)

This interpretation is generalized by Gumperz (1976b) to other code-switching situations: the majority language, the "they code," is associated with more formal, stiffer, and less personal out-group relations, whereas the minority language, the "we code," becomes associated with in-group and informal activities.

Closely related to this is that switching into the minority language can signal group solidarity. Gumperz and Hernandez-Chavez (1978) give examples of ethnic identity markers, consisting largely of exclamations and sentence connectors whose role is to emphasize group identity. They report the end of an exchange between M and a woman visitor:

Woman: Well, I'm glad that I met you. O.K.?
M: *Andale, pues* (OK, swell), and do come again. Mm?

The authors comment: "The speakers, both Mexican-Americans, are strangers who have met for the first time. The *andale pues* is given in response to the woman's okay as if to say: 'Although we are strangers, we have the same background and should get to know each other better' " (p. 280).

Di Pietro (1977) reports that among Italian immigrants at the turn of the century, code-switching from standard Italian to a dialect served to consolidate those Italians who felt alienated from their homeland and unwelcome in the new country. In other instances, Italian immigrants would tell a joke in English and give the punch line in Italian, not only because it was better said in that language, but also to stress the fact that they all belonged to the same minority group, with shared values and experiences.

Switching can also help to amplify or emphasize a point. Gal (1979) reports several instances in which a switch at the end of an argument helps to terminate the interaction. In one incident a child is at home in Oberwart, Austria, with her mother and grandparents. The little girl has apparently misbehaved all day and is tired and whiny. As the child continues to whine, her grandfather expresses his sympathy for her. But the two women do not agree: the grand-mother orders her to stop fooling around and the mother recommends a good slap. The grandfather comments indirectly on that suggestion, which the mother takes as disapproval of her methods of discipline. She proceeds to support her view by giving a principled reason for her methods. What is interesting is that she says this in German, while the language up until then had been Hungarian. The comment marks the end of the exchange between the mother and grandfather, who drops the subject. Gal interprets this switch to German as a means of adding more force to the statement and thereby ending the argument.

In our example at the beginning of this chapter, Roger tells Marc to get up in English, then switches to French to repeat and underline his request:

Now it's really time to get up. *Lève-toi.*

And Hoffman (1971) reports that in Puerto Rican homes in Jersey City, the mothers give short commands to their children in English, such as "Stop that," "Don't do that." The rest of the mother's speech is in Spanish, and switching to English signals the child that the mother is getting angry.

Another use of code-switching is to exclude someone from a portion of the conversation. In our example at the beginning of the chapter, Nicole switched momentarily to French during her questioning of a patient with cardiovascular problems. She wanted to let Martine know that she felt the case was serious, but she did not want the patient to understand. She could have waited to be alone with Martine to tell her this, but she probably knew that the patient did not know French, so she slipped among her questions a rapid

Ça me paraît grave.

However the switch could backfire if the patient realized that a switch to French could only mean that the situation was serious.

Scotton and Ury (1977) give a good example of exclusion in their account of code-switching in West Kenya. Five Luyia men are talking about setting up a business. The first speaker, the informal chairman of the group, speaks first in Kikuyu. He tells the others that 2,000 shillings are needed to start the business, and since they are five it means that each one will pay 400 shillings. One of the members of the group says that is too much, and the chairman replies:

Mumanye khwenya mapesa manyisi. (You know we need a lot of money.) *Two thousand shillings should be a minimum. Anyone who can't contribute four hundred shillings shouldn't be part of this group. He should get out.*

The member who thinks that 400 shillings is too much asks in Kikuyu what has been said (he does not understand English), but he is ignored, and a supporter of the chairman intervenes to say, in English, that the specified amount is correct. He then repeats himself with less force in Kikuyu. Scotton (1979) explains that the chairman wanted to gain the support of the English-speaking, and wealthier, members of the group and let them know his attitude toward those who could not invest a large sum of money. By switching to English he did not insult them directly.

Code-switching to exclude someone is used extensively by bilingual parents with their monolingual children. Di Pietro (1977) reports that Italian American parents switch to Italian to discuss topics that they wish to keep from their young, supposedly monolingual, English-speaking children. To counter this strategy, children often develop a receptive competence in Italian, which parents usually learn about after awhile. Then their only strategies are either not to talk in front of the children or to spell words out in their native language!

Of course, switching to another language to exclude someone can backfire and lead to embarrassment, as in these two real-life examples related by a Russian-English bilingual. Two adolescents were seated in a bus in New York when a rather stout woman climbed aboard. Switching from English to Russian, one said, "We'd better make room for the fat cow," and moved over to free up a seat. The stout woman settled down in the seat, took a few deep breaths, and said in Russian, "The fat cow thanks you!" On another occasion, these adolescents were seated in a park when a very fat little man sat down on the bench opposite them. Switching over to Russian, one said to the other, "He's like a balloon, he's going to blow up!" They then continued their conversation in English but were startled when, some time later, the little man walked past them and said, in Russian, "You see, I didn't blow up!"

Code-switching can also be used for many other reasons, such as quoting what someone has said (and thereby emphasizing one's group identity), specifying the addressee (switching to the usual language of a particular person in a group will show that one is addressing that person), qualifying what has been said, or talking about past events. I will concentrate, however, on one other use:

code-switching to raise one's status and give one added authority or expertise. Scotton and Ury (1977) give two very clear examples of this in Kenya. In the first, a passenger on a bus in Nairobi and a conductor (fare collector) are conversing in Swahili. The passenger says he wants to go to the post office, and the conductor replies that the fare is fifty cents. The passenger gives him a shilling and the conductor tells him to wait for his change (fifty cents). As the bus nears the post office, the passenger becomes worried that he will not get his change and addresses the conductor again.

> *Passenger:* Nataka change yangu.
> (I want my change.)
> *Conductor:* Change utapata, Bwana.
> (You'll get your change, mister.)
> *Passenger: I am nearing my destination.*
> *Conductor: Do you think I could run away with your change?*

Scotton and Ury (1977) explain the passenger's switch to English as a bid for authority, changing his role from one of equal status with the conductor to a higher status (English is the language of the educated elite in Kenya) to make sure he will obtain his change before he gets off. Interestingly, the conductor counters this attempted shift in status by replying in English, thereby reestablishing equality. Scotton and Ury report that 90 percent of the Kenyans who listened to a recorded version of this interaction explained the switch to English as an attempt by the passenger to change status.

A second example given by Scotton and Ury takes place in Luyialand in west Kenya. A Luyia shopowner is exchanging greetings with his sister in their own Luyia dialect while other customers are present in the store. Then quite suddenly the brother switches to Swahili and says:

> Dada, sasa leo unahitaji nini?
> (Sister, now today what do you need?)

The sister replies *in the Luyia dialect* that she wants some salt, and for the rest of their interaction the brother speaks Swahili and the sister Luyia. Scotton and Ury interpret the brother's switch to Swahili, the business language of Kenya, as a way of increasing the social distance between himself and his sister and thus decreasing the distance between himself and the other customers. By switching languages, the brother switches roles: from brother to shopkeeper. The sister now becomes, in his eyes and those of the customers, a customer like the others and should not expect to be privileged in any way, such as obtaining something for free.

Thus code-switching in bilingual speech is far from being a "grammarless language mixture or gibberish" by "semilingual" speakers. We have seen that code-switching is often used as a communicative strategy to convey linguistic and social information. In a later chapter I will show that it is governed by very strict linguistic constraints.

Bilingualism and Biculturalism

Anthropologists commonly agree that culture consists of a number of components: the human's way of maintaining life and perpetuating the species, along with habits, customs, ideas, sentiments, social arrangements, and objects. Culture is the way of life of a people or society, including its rules of behavior; its economic, social, and political systems; its language; its religious beliefs; its laws; and so on. Culture is acquired, socially transmitted, and communicated in large part by language. Biculturalism—the coexistence and/or combination of two distinct cultures—is a highly complex subject that extends far beyond the scope of this book. Although it has been studied by relatively few researchers, especially when linked to bilingualism, many bilinguals are aware that in some sense or other they are also bicultural and that biculturalism or its lack has affected their lives.

Rare are the cases of a person being brought up outside of a culture: Victor, the Wild Boy of Aveyron (Lane, 1976) and Genie, a modern "wild" child (Curtiss, 1977) are such exceptions. However, if all monolinguals belong to a culture, do bilinguals automatically belong to two cultures? Are they *de facto* bicultural in that they combine two distinct cultures? The answer is no: as Haugen (1956) writes, bilingualism and biculturalism are not necessarily coextensive. Some people who use two languages on a regular basis are really monocultural. In countries with a lingua franca, such as Tanzania, Kenya, and other African nations, one could argue that a bilingual really has only one culture: that of his or her ethnic group. A similar argument could be made for functional bilingualism in Luxembourg or Switzerland: people may be bi- or trilingual but monocultural.

On the other hand, a monolingual person may be bicultural. Some French-speaking Bretons or English-speaking Scots would argue that they are bicultural, in that they share the beliefs, attitudes, and habits of two (at times overlapping) cultures. In the United States, where language shift takes place extremely quickly, one finds many English-speaking Native Americans and second- or third-generation immigrants who share two overlapping cultures. This is the case for many English-speaking Italian, Japanese, and Polish Americans, for example, as well as for many American Jews.

In this section we will consider those who are both bilingual and, to some extent at least, bicultural. First we will consider persons who move to a new country and adjust, or fail to adjust, to the new culture, and then we will examine their children.

Adjusting to a New Culture

Cultures, like languages, come into contact in many different ways. One of the most common is when people move from one country to another and overnight are confronted with the task of surviving in what seems to be a very different world. Blum and Steptoe (1980) describe the adjustment that confronted two families who had recently arrived in the United States: the Azvolinskys from the Soviet Union and the Nguyens from Vietnam, both of whom suffered from "culture shock." Mrs. Azvolinsky expected clean, prosperous cities in the United States but was met by graffiti, crime, and decay. Blum and Steptoe write:

An urbanite planted in a suburb, she desperately missed the bustle of the city streets. She still feels culturally deprived, finding nothing here to compare with Moscow's ballet, symphony, and stage. And she was isolated almost completely by her lack of English. "For the first two years here, I cried every day," she says, weeping again at the remembrance. (p. 22)

As for the Nguyens, Blum and Steptoe relate the difficulties they had in finding a job and in confronting the cost of living. It took them months to find someone who would rent them a house, as no real estate agent would believe that the whole family could fit into a three-bedroom house, whereas the Nguyens found the house rather large. They were shocked by retirement homes. Mr. Nguyen says: "In Vietnam, when parents grow old, they live with their children, and their children take care of them . . . children like their parents; they don't separate" (p. 22).

When the difference between two cultures is very large (as between the Japanese and American cultures), the adjustment is much harder than when two cultures are similar or even overlap (such as the British and American cultures). But some degree of "culture shock" is inevitable, created by the combination of differences, large and small: eating habits, courting behavior, child rearing, family organization, religious beliefs, the level and nature of education, the

BOX 3.11   BILINGUALS SPEAK

Adapting to a Different Culture

An English-French bilingual: I once shocked my friends at a small dinner party by using the familiar "tu" form of address to one of the guests, a girl roughly my own age. She was introduced to me as a friend by my host, who was a good friend of mine, and so I thought I should treat her as a potential friend. I was quite unaware of the embarrassment my behavior was causing the other guests; it was only when she left that the others asked me why I had been so insulting to her. Hadn't I noticed that everyone else said "vous" to her? I realized that the relationships covered by their term "amie" and my unconscious translation "friend" were not equivalent. For me a friend is someone to be friendly with, whereas one may not necessarily be "amical" with an "amie."

urban or rural nature of the community, and so on. In Box 3.11, an English person in France relates the problems she had with what at first seems to be a very minor matter—the *tu/vous* distinction in French. In general, adapting to cultural differences is usually very trying and can result in loneliness, hostility, self-pity, disorientation, and fear of ridicule.

Immigrants adjust in different ways to the new culture. Some never adjust, either because they choose not to or because the surrounding society does not allow them to do so. Elderly immigrants living in minority communities often attempt to continue, as best they can, the lives they led in the home country. They make little attempt to learn the majority language, interact only with members of their own group, and follow the customs and traditions of their people. To this group we should add the people who have come to a country for a short time and who intend to return to their home country, many of whom, especially if they have children, adjusting as little as possible so as to make the return less difficult. Such is the case of Japanese business people and university researchers who live in the United States for a year or two. They make every effort to retain their way of life and educational principles and not let themselves be Americanized.

Also in this category are the members of a culture that has been invaded by another people or culture. For them, adjusting to the culture of the invader—becoming bicultural—is the first stage of acculturation and should therefore be avoided. (Similarly, a group's bilingualism can be the first stage of language shift, ultimately leading to monolingualism in the majority language.) A Kurd in Syria writes:

Whenever there were national holidays at school where attendance was obligatory, we would go for roll call and then sneak out when they would start singing nationalist songs. Although there are certain aspects that are common to the two cultures because of the [Muslim] religion, I follow the customs of my own people—the Kurds.

Among those who fail to adjust to a new culture are those who are rejected by the majority group. This is the case of immigrant workers in countries that need cheap labor, such as Germany, France, Norway, Saudi Arabia, and Kuwait. Many of these workers are unmarried and live together in segregated housing. They are often deterred from mixing with the local population, and after several years they may still speak the language of the "host" country very badly and may not have adopted many of its cultural traits.

At the other extreme we find persons who overadjust to the host culture and do everything they can to assimilate themselves into that culture. Going back to the Azvolinsky family, Blum and Steptoe (1980) relate that Mr. Azvolinsky is now very American in his attitudes: he decided not to buy a house in a neighborhood dominated by other Russian immigrants, and he sent his son Eric to a public school rather than a Jewish school so he would learn English quickly. Such overadjustment, which can be due to a total rejection of the native culture or to a strong wish to be accepted as a member of the new culture, often goes hand in hand with rapid abandonment of many traits of the original culture, so that once again one can not really talk of biculturalism.

Between these two extremes, however, we find people adjusting to a certain level of biculturalism. The level attained by each person depends on a number of factors, many of which are similar to those affecting language maintenance and language shift, such as the size of the minority group, its immigration pattern, geographic concentration, intermarriage, language use, and so on. (See Chapter 2, as well as Schumann, 1978). Unlike bilingualism, where the two languages can be kept separate, biculturalism does not usually involve keeping two cultures and two individual behaviors separate. A true bicultural person, for instance, someone who is *fully* French in France and *fully* American in the United States, is probably not very common. Little is known about such people in whom two cultures coexist but do not blend, and yet behavior shifts and behavior interferences (like language shifts and interferences) would be fascinating subjects to study.

More common is the person who combines traits of the two different cultures. Lambert, Hamers, and Frasure-Smith (1979), comparing the child-rearing values of Portuguese immigrants in the United States with those of Portuguese in Portugal and Americans in the United States, found evidence of the combination of cultural traits. The immigrants adopted certain American traits, such as being less lenient about insolence and being more restrictive on guest privileges, but they also retained many Portuguese traits: they did not encourage gestures of autonomy, and fathers were more vigilant than mothers with respect to sex-role differences.

This trend toward integration of traits from two cultures may lead some people to feel that they do not belong to either culture. As a forty-four-year-old North African woman in Marseilles once said: "I don't have a country . . . I am not an Arab and yet I am not French . . . although I now speak Arabic less well, I do not feel that I am French." A German-English bilingual writes:

I can't deny that I am American, yet because of my German upbringing I have different beliefs and ways of living and doing things. There are strong elements of my character which are undoubtedly German, but there are times when I might react totally "American." I have been told that this mixture makes me complex and makes my reactions difficult to predict. As far as the German aspect goes, I am not liable to fit in very easily in Germany either . . . I am too much used to the so-called "American way of life," with its conveniences . . . I am essentially in limbo and I sometimes become very distraught because I cannot seem to reconcile these cultural forces and differences within myself.

The term "marginal person" has been used to label such people, and some believe that all members of immigrant or minority groups are marginal in this way. However, as McLaughlin (1978) writes:

The characterization of the bilingual as a "marginal man," lacking a sense of self- and group identity has been criticized as overdrawn (Goldberg, 1941). If bilinguals are members of a community of other bilingual individuals as, for example, most Chicano and Puerto Rican Americans are, it is misleading to think of them as marginal . . . it is their culture that is marginal, which is psychologically a quite different experience. Within that culture the individual can develop a strong sense of identification and personal worth. (p. 179)

Many people in contact with two cultures may at first seek to belong solely to one or the other, but with time they realize that they are most at ease with people who share their bicultural experience. As an Arab American writes:

At home in the Middle East, I am seen as the Americanized Arab . . . and in America, I am seen as an Americanized Arab by people that have come to realize that they are Americanized Arabs also. Therefore, almost anywhere I go I make sure my world is full of Americanized Arabs.

The worst experience for such a person is to be without roots, not to feel at home in any cultural group. This, fortunately, is not too frequent: many feel quite at home in both cultures, and many others feel at ease with people who, like them combining the traits of two cultures, make up a new cultural group.

Children and Biculturalism

Adjustment to two cultures can be especially difficult for the children of immigrants. Vulnerable to peer and outside influences, they may find themselves in the difficult situation of not being able to assume the two cultures. The need for absolute identity with peers in such domains as values, attitudes, language, clothes, and leisure, along with the fear of ridicule, may lead to a state of conflict between the home and the outside society. Although the parents of these children are, to some extent at least, slowly becoming bicultural, they are still very different from the parents of the majority group: they speak the majority language less well, and they are less familiar with the children's school and cultural environment. In addition, their values and customs may be completely at odds with those of the majority group.

A number of social psychologists have studied the conflict that arises between immigrant parents and their children. Child (1943), for instance, investigated second-generation Italians in New England to determine whether they were more Italian or American. He had observed that relations with other American youngsters could be strained if the Italian American adolescents were "too Italian." On the other hand, if they rejected their background completely, there was the danger of being cut off from the comfort and refuge given by the family and the community. Child found that the Italian American adolescents could be subdivided into three groups: the first group rebelled against their Italian background, making themselves as American as possible; the second group rejected the American culture and fully adopted their Italian heritage; and those in the third group were withdrawn and unsure, refusing to think of themselves in ethnic terms at all.

Gardner and Lambert (1972) found similar trends among Franco-Americans in New England and Louisiana. Some oriented themselves toward their French background and tried to ignore their American roots; others were tugged more toward the American pole, negating the value of knowing French and in general rejecting their French background; and still others apparently tried not to think in ethnic terms at all: they were ambivalent about their identity and seemed to face a conflict of cultural allegiance. (We will discuss a fourth group a bit later.)

Researchers have been especially interested in the child who rejects his or her parents, their values, and their language. Bossard (1945) cites two adults who remember their past:

I remember I used to cross the street to avoid meeting up with my father or mother. Neither had good eyesight, and I would be on the alert whenever I got anywhere near to places where I might see them.

Another thing I remember . . . is that I brought none of my school friends to my home, because the few times I did, my parents seemed to go out of their way to display their native speech and mannerisms to my friends. (pp. 702, 703)

In Box 3.12 two bilinguals relate how they rebelled as children against the language and culture of their parents.

Lambert (1977) summarizes the adolescents' different reactions to the contact of two cultures in the following way: "To me these ways of coping characterize the anguish of members of ethnic groups when caught up in a subtractive form of biculturalism, that is, where social pressures are exerted on them to give up one aspect of their

---

BOX 3.12   **BILINGUALS SPEAK**

Children Rejecting the Home Language and Culture

An Arabic-English bilingual: As an adolescent I pretended I did not know Arabic, and I tried very hard to lose my foreign accent. I did this because I wanted very badly not to be any different from the rest of my friends. As I got older, though, I started to learn and appreciate my native language and culture much more.

A German-English bilingual: As for my own experience, I felt a bitterness somewhat because I was "different," not only in language but also in culture *and* dress, from my primary school peers. I used to cry when the children called me "Little Hitler" and this prompted my own rebellion against the German forces within our family . . . My "rebellion" resulted in my mother addressing me in German and me constantly replying in English.

dual identity for the sake of blending into a national scene" (p. 31). This process, often forced upon a minority group, of shifting from one culture to another has been termed acculturation and has affected the children of minority groups throughout the world. In the United States forced acculturation was especially evident in the government's efforts to assimilate American Indians at the turn of the century. Indian children were taken from their parents and put into boarding schools where speaking any other language than English was forbidden, and parental visits were strongly discouraged. The consequences were often painful: under the pressure of the school, the children would reject at first the language and culture of their own ethnic group and then, as they grew up and understood what had taken place, many turned against the culture that had been imposed on them. These people often were without definite cultural roots, ill at ease both in their Indian group and in the American culture.

What happened in the United States with the American Indians happened (and in some cases is still happening) in other countries: in France with the Bretons and the Basques, in Turkey with the Armenians, in Syria and Iran with the Kurds, and so on. Second-generation North Africans in France, for instance, feel they are rejected by both the country of their parents' origin and by the country where they were born (France). When they return to Algeria or Tunisia they are treated like foreigners with radical ideas and Western morals, and yet in France they are often discriminated against: their identification papers are checked constantly, they are mistreated by the police and are often threatened with deportation. Thus they see themselves as "neither French nor Algerian," as "people from nowhere."

Children of parents who travel from one country to another for business or other reasons, never staying in a community long enough to allow the family to adjust to the new environment can also have problems adjusting. The children are often sent to boarding schools, and as Box 3.13 shows, this can lead to a feeling of not belonging to any cultural group.

It is important to note that not all bilingual-bicultural children are withdrawn and rootless persons who face a conflict of cultural allegiance. Gardner and Lambert (1972) found a fourth group of Franco-Americans: they were skilled in both languages, felt they were members of both cultural groups, and were comfortable with their bicultural identity. Box 3.14 presents an extract by a Franco-American who reports being perfectly comfortable and at ease in both French and English settings.

BOX 3.13	BILINGUALS SPEAK

Belonging to Neither Culture

I was taken from my French environment at the age of eight and put into an English boarding school. Overnight I switched from being a primary school boy in a little village on the outskirts of Paris to being a boarder in a century-old school in the English countryside. I stayed in that school for ten years, and only left it at age eighteen to enter the Sorbonne. My adjustment to the life in France was extremely painful. I suddenly realized that I belonged to neither culture—I was (and had always been) a stranger in England, but I was also definitely a stranger in France. I didn't know the simplest everyday facts: who had won the National Football Championship, who Leon Zitrone was, why there was a problem with the "pieds noirs" . . . I found "my" people extremely distant, unfriendly, uninviting, and I suffered from the fact that they did not know how to deal with my case. I wasn't a foreigner to whom you have to explain everything from A to Z, and whose mistakes and errors in adjustment you tolerate; and yet I wasn't like everyone else who had lived in France all of their lives: I knew little about French customs and habits and I spoke with a slight accent. I was, in a word, a rare bird, and most of my peers just did not know how to interact with me.

Realizing that I was neither English nor French, I came to the conclusion that I had to choose one country and one culture. As I was living in France, I decided to reject my English background and consciously strove to become French.

The shift to one culture took a number of years to accomplish and probably came to an end when I married a French person and thus had for the first time direct access to a completely French family. My friends know that I am still a bit English (how can you eradicate ten years of boarding school in England?) but I have now assumed that difference, as it is slight: most strangers and mere acquaintances think that I am completely French. For a long time I felt that it was impossible to be bicultural—that it was too painful—and I therefore strove hard to adopt one culture and reject the other. Now that this is done, and with the years gone by, I realize that had the circumstances been different and had I been helped more by my family and friends when I first came back to France, life would have been easier and I could perhaps have retained both cultures.

Aellen and Lambert (1969) report on how adolescent children in Montreal, of English-French mixed marriages adjust to their biculturalism. They compared them with adolescents of a homogeneous background (English or French) and controlled for such factors as age, socioeconomic class, intelligence, and number of siblings. The researchers report that the profile of the children with mixed ethnic parentage is a healthy one: they identify with their parents as well as

---

BOX 3.14   **BILINGUALS SPEAK**

A Franco-American's View of His Biculturalism

To me, being bilingual in the U.S. and, more specifically, being Franco-American in our pluralistic society, means that I have two languages, two heritages, two ways of thinking and viewing the world. At times these two elements may be separate and distinct within me, whereas at other times they are fused together. When I'm with Anglophone [English-speaking] Americans, I can speak English with them and identify with their American values just as easily as I can speak French with Franco-Americans and identify with their values. In certain instances, such as with family and close friends who are Franco-Americans, I feel both Franco and American, yet neither of these . . . more like a mixture of the two. In any case, I feel comfortable in either setting.

---

the comparison groups; they identify with both ethnic groups; they show no signs of personalilty disturbances, social alienation, or anxiety; their self-concepts and general attitudinal orientations are normal. In a word, instead of rejecting one or both cultures, they are truly bicultural in that they identify with both cultural groups.

Lambert and Tucker (1972) report similar findings for English Canadian children who have taken the majority of their elementary schooling in French (in "immersion programs") and who by grade five or six are functionally bilingual in English and French. By grade five these children think of themselves as being both French Canadian and English Canadian, and they feel at ease in both social settings.

It is important to note that the languages and cultures in these studies were of international stature and were prestigious. In addition, in the Aellen and Lambert study the parents were more or less bicultural, and in the immersion program the parents were very supportive of their children's efforts. Although these situations are quite far from the norm, they do point to ways that the society can help children adjust to two cultures. If the two cultures are valued equally in the home, in the school, and in the society at large, and if biculturalism is judged to be as valuable as monoculturalism, then children and adolescents who are in contact with two cultures will accept both instead of rejecting or being rejected by one or the other or by both.

The Bilingual Child

Ingrid and Dieudonné, who live in the same American city, are both in third grade. Both are bilingual—Ingrid in Swedish and English, and Dieudonné in Haitian Creole and English. Although they are both bright and happy children, many factors differentiate them, not the least being how they became bilingual.

Ingrid's father is a researcher in organic chemistry at a large research institute, and her Swedish mother is a lecturer in Scandinavian languages at a nearby college. They met when Ingrid's father was visiting the University of Stockholm, and after two years in Sweden, they came back to the East Coast to settle down. When Ingrid was born, her parents decided that they would bring her up as a bilingual, using a one person–one language policy: Ingrid's father would speak to her in English and her mother would use Swedish at all times. Swedish friends would be invited over as often as possible so that Swedish would be heard in the house and, when financially possible, Ingrid would go and visit her Swedish grandparents.

Although at first Ingrid's language output was mixed—part English, part Swedish—by the age of three her two languages were well separated, and visitors marveled at her ability to switch from one language to the other when addressing her parents. As English was the language of the environment, it became her stronger language, but the strict policy maintained by her parents and her trips to Sweden also made her fluent in Swedish. When she entered kindergarten at age five, nothing distinguished her from her other classmates: she was bright, happy, and mischievous and in no way behind in her language skills. In fact, Ingrid was one of the first in the class to learn how to read, and her teacher once remarked to her mother that maybe Ingrid's bilingualism was an asset to her cognitive development. At present, Ingrid is in third grade and doing very well. She continues to speak Swedish to her mother, to her parents' Swedish friends, and even to her baby brother. Her Swedish grandparents have come to visit a few times, she has traveled to see them twice, and all of this has made her functionally bilingual. Her mother is now teaching her to read and write in Swedish.

Dieudonné's background is very different. He was born in Haiti, the third of five children in his family. Before coming to the United States, he spoke Haitian Creole in his everyday life. His parents immigrated when he was five and settled down in a largely Haitian neighborhood. Dieudonné's father found a night job in a local factory and worked part time during the day to maintain his family in the United States and send money back to his parents in Haiti. Dieudonné's mother also took on a part-time job in the local parish and, as a consequence, the children looked after each other during the day. They watched TV and played in the street and at the playground, interacting with Puerto Rican and Black American children, but mainly with other Haitian children. Thus, Dieudonné picked up some English but not nearly enough to converse freely with English-speaking children.

A few months after their arrival, Dieudonné's mother enrolled him in first grade at a local school. The school did not offer a bilingual education program in Haitian Creole and English, so Dieudonné was put into a mainstream program with other minority language children, to whom English as a second language was taught on a regular basis. Despite the efforts and good will of the teacher, Dieudonné was completely lost in the program: he had great problems understanding what was being said to him, he was teased by some of the children, and above all, he was homesick. After three months in school, Dieudonné had made almost no progress in English, and he had become withdrawn and very unsure of himself. His mother talked to the parish priest about him, who told her about a bilingual education program in another city school. At first she was quite opposed to sending Dieudonné there, stating that her children had to learn English and that they would not do so if they were taught in Creole (Creole wasn't even a language, was it?), but with a little persuading she agreed to let the priest find out if there was an open slot.

Such a slot did exist, and Dieudonné was transferred into the program. His first day was a revelation to him: he was greeted in Creole by the teacher (an American who had worked in Haiti for two years), the other kids spoke Creole to him, and the whole classroom had something of Haiti, including bright colorful posters of the island. Dieudonné spent two years in the program, at first learning in Creole, then doing more and more of his school work in English until he was transferred into a mainstream program in third grade. He recovered his self-assurance and gaiety and became quite fluent in English, which he learned both in and out of school. At present Dieudonné is doing very well in his third-grade program and is functionally bilingual: he speaks Creole at home and with friends, and English at school, with school friends, and when he goes shopping for his mother.

These two bilingual children differ on a number of points: Ingrid learned her two languages simultaneously and in a nontraumatic way; Dieudonné acquired English as a second language and at first under stress. Ingrid's bilingualism was very much a "planned affair," whereas Dieudonné's was a consequence of immigration. Ingrid's schooling was a success from the start, whereas Dieudonné's began as a disaster. Despite their many differences, Ingrid and Dieudonné are similar in many ways: at the age of eight, both are quite fluent in their two languages and, like other bilingual children, they choose which language to use according to the situation; they code-switch quite freely, and, above all, they do not give a second thought to being bilingual; it is as natural to them as walking, sleeping, or playing.

In this chapter we will study the bilingualism of children such as Ingrid and Dieudonné, first listing the factors that lead a child to be bilingual and describing how they can apparently forget languages just as quickly as they can learn them. Second, we will examine the differences between simultaneous acquisition of two languages, by children like Ingrid, and successive acquisition, by children like Dieudonné. Third, we will cover various aspects of childhood bilingualism, such as the person–language bond, language choice, and code-switching. We will then examine two types of educational programs: those that lead to linguistic and cultural assimilation and those that lead to bilingualism and biculturalism. And finally, we will review the studies of the effects of bilingualism on the child's cognitive development, from those that claim that bilingualism has a negative impact on intelligence and cognition to those claiming that bilingual children are brighter, more creative, and have a higher level of concept formation than their monolingual counterparts. This chapter concerns only those children who *acquire* and *use* two languages in a natural environment, at home, with friends and family, and in the community. It does not deal with the formal learning of a second language by children in a classroom, as this rarely leads to the regular use of two languages.

Becoming Bilingual

Although childhood bilingualism is a worldwide phenomenon and much of adult bilingualism results from it, few studies have examined why some children become bilingual while others remain monolingual. Most children become bilingual in a "natural" way, in the sense that their parents, unlike Ingrid's parents, did not actively plan their bilingualism. As we saw in Chapter 1, such factors as movement of peoples, nationalism and political federalism, intermarriage, the plurality of linguistic groups within a region, urbanization and education inevitably lead to bilingualism in children as well as in adults.

Lewis (1972) reports that in the U.S.S.R. people move from one to another republic quite extensively, and hence interethnic marriages are common. For example, in Ashkabad 29 percent of marriages between 1951 and 1965 involved men and women of different nationalities, resulting in the children acquiring two languages. This happens not only if both languages are used in the home but also if only one language—the father's, for instance—is the family language, because family members on the mother's side will communicate with the children in their native language. Another example of bilingualism in the family comes from South Africa: Malherbe (1969) reports that some 43 percent of white South African families are bilingual at home in Afrikaans and English to varying degrees.

The proximity of other linguistic groups also leads to bilingualism in the home. For example, Mkilifi (1978) reports that ten out of the fifteen Tanzanians he studied spoke the local language along with Swahili before going to school. They learned the local language first, but because both parents, especially the father, knew and used Swahili at home, they acquired that language as a second home language and as a medium of communication in the community. Mkilifi reports that this took place quite naturally, and none of the respondents realized that he or she was already speaking two distinct languages before entering primary school.

BOX 4.1   BILINGUALS SPEAK

Becoming Bilingual

An Arabic-Hebrew-English trilingual: The very first language I spoke was Arabic, as my parents are Israeli Arabs. I first came into contact with Hebrew by watching programs on TV, and I began using it around four or five when we had to help our mother buy things from the store or when we met Jewish children at the beach or in the parks.

A Russian-English bilingual: I didn't speak a word of English when I first went to school. There was another little boy entering kindergarten with me, but our mothers separated us so that we wouldn't speak Russian between ourselves. I can't specifically remember learning English; I seem to have picked it up very quickly.

A Greek-English bilingual: I came to the United States when I was twelve years old, and I was put into an all-American class. I did not know any English then and it was a little hard in the beginning since I did not understand what the other children or the teacher were saying to me.

Even when the other language (the majority language or the lingua franca) is not spoken in the home by the parents themselves, it nevertheless makes its way into the house and the children are exposed to it. The language may be spoken by the parents' friends and acquaintances, older siblings and their friends, neighbors, nurses, and caretakers, not to mention television. And as the children venture outside to play or go shopping with their parents, their exposure to the other language increases. In Box 4.1 an Israeli Arab reports how she started to acquire Hebrew by being exposed to it inside and outside the home.

One of the main factors in childhood bilingualism is of course the school. Unless the linguistic group to which the child belongs has its own schools or has public education conducted in its own language, the children's medium of instruction in school will be some other language, such as the regional or national language. This is the case for countless minority groups throughout the world: the Bretons, Basques, and Alsatians in France, most minority groups in the United States, the Greeks in Turkey, the Kurds in Iran, and so on. And if the ethnic composition of the school is quite varied, as in numerous African and Asian nations, children adopt the school language as a medium of communication among themselves. Thus, Mkilifi (1978) reports that in Tanzania, Swahili is the language of learning in the primary schools and that in most cases it alternates with the vernacular as the playground language. The position of Swahili is reinforced in the secondary schools, which are often outside the vernacular area. In these schools, meeting places of children from diverse linguistic and cultural backgrounds, Swahili becomes the primary language of communication in and out of school and is the basis of acculturation into the wider sociocultural norms and values of the country.

In the United States, an unknown number of minority Americans have become bilingual in the public school system. From the turn of the century on, children were put directly into mainstream classes and forced to sink or swim. This caused much stress and hardship and resulted in high dropout rates, but those who survived became bilingual in their home language and in English. In Box 4.1 two bilinguals talk about their experiences in American schools. It is important to note that such an ethnocentric approach often leads to a form of transitional bilingualism: because of the permanent pressure on the minority child to assimilate, he or she often stops using the minority language and becomes either a "covert" bilingual, concealing his or her knowledge of the minority language (Sawyer, 1978) or a monolingual in the majority language. Like many other monolingual countries, the United States is replete with members of minorities who no longer speak their minority language.

Children may also become bilingual because there is a policy in the community or in the family to make them bilingual. At the community level, different types of bilingual education programs teach the majority language but also maintain and develop the minority language. Such programs exist in the public schools of the U.S.S.R., Wales, Singapore, India, Hong Kong, Lebanon, and to some extent, Canada and the United States, and in private bilingual or international schools throughout the world. One interesting case of community-planned bilingualism, reported by Gal (1979), occurred in Oberwart, Austria, at the turn of the century. The wealthier Hungarian peasants would send their sons to live in a German-speaking village for a year and would welcome in exchange a German-speaking boy from that village for the same amount of time. This practice continued as long as the region was part of Hungary and knowledge of Hungarian was considered an asset. In fact, sending children to other regions or other countries to make them bilingual has gone on throughout history. Roman families, for example, sent their children to Greece to be educated and to learn Greek, and today, numerous exchange programs exist between schools in different countries.

BOX 4.2   BILINGUALS SPEAK

Planned Bilingualism in the Family

A French-English bilingual: When I was a child, my parents spoke mainly French to me from birth to age four, so as not to offend my maternal grandparents who spoke only French . . . Later on, they gradually spoke English to me as well, while still maintaining French, so that I wouldn't have any trouble getting by in school in either language. They were successful, because I had no trouble at all in either language.

At the family level, parents may decide on a particular strategy to make their child bilingual, as was the case for Ingrid in the introduction to this chapter. Their reasons range from preparing the child to go to school in the majority language (see Box 4.2) to enabling him or her to communicate with other family members, such as grandparents, all the way to making the child fluent in a prestigious world language, as was the case of Russian aristocrats acquiring French in Czarist Russia. The strategies used are quite diverse (Schmidt-Mackey, 1977; Arnberg, 1979). One of the earliest to be written about was the "une personne, une langue" (one person, one language) formula proposed by the French linguist Grammont to Jules Ronjat at the turn of the century. Ronjat was French and his wife German, and they decided to bring up their child as a bilingual. They agreed that Ronjat would speak only French to the boy, Louis, while his wife would speak only German to him. This strategy was highly successful, and Ronjat (1913) reports that after an initial period of mixed language, Louis quickly learned to use each language just as any native-speaking child would have done. Numerous other case studies of bilingual children report the use of this learning strategy, the most famous being that of Hildegard Leopold, who learned to address her father in German and her mother in English (see the next section). Arnberg (1979) reports that a number of English-Swedish families she interviewed in Sweden had adopted this same strategy. It allowed each parent to communicate with the child in his or her native language, thereby ensuring naturalness in communication while making the child bilingual. (See Bain and Yu, 1981, for a longitudinal study of this strategy.)

Another strategy adopted by parents is to use one language in the home, usually the minority language, and the other outside the home, the rule being that everyone must speak the home language at all times at home. This strategy leads to the pattern found among numerous minorities throughout the world, where the minority language is used in the home and the neighborhood, and the majority language is used at school, at work, and in the larger community. The only difference is that in this case the family has decided to enforce the home–outside the home dichotomy, whereas in general it is not enforced.

A third strategy consists of using one language with the child initially and then, at a specific age (between three and five, for instance) introducing the other language. Zierer (1977) reports on a German-Peruvian child whose parents decided that the child should become bilingual in German and Spanish before entering school. They decided that the best way to do this was to start with German, the weaker language in Peru, and to delay the learning of Spanish for at least two years. To make this approach as successful as possible, they spoke German to each other and to the child, found him some German-speaking playmates, and went so far as to ask the child's Peruvian grandmother *not* to speak to him in Spanish. At age two years and ten months, when the child's German was firmly established, they allowed him to play with Spanish-speaking children, and within four months he had learned Spanish.

A fourth strategy is to use the two languages interchangeably in and out of the family, letting such factors as topic, situation, person, and place dictate which language should be used. Finally, Schmidt-Mackey (1977) reports that some families have chosen to use a "language time" approach: one language in the morning and the other in the afternoon, or one language during the week and the other during the weekend.

How successful are these different strategies? There are no clear answers, but observers stress that the most unnatural tend to break down. For example, the "language time" approach is not very successful, because it is based on a very arbitrary factor: the time of day or the day of the week. On the other hand, the free alternation of languages is by far the most natural approach, but it suffers from the fact that the majority language may slowly become dominant as the child brings home school friends and spends more time at school and in the majority language community. As for starting with only one language and bringing in the other at the age of three or four, it can succeed only if parents take the kind of measures reported by Zierer or if the family is surrounded by a well-organized and quite large ethnic community, so that the child is exposed to the minority language in and out of the home. These same factors lead to the success of the home–outside the home language strategy; it is only when the home language is heard on radio and television, used by siblings, their friends, and the various visitors to the home that such a strategy will work.

Finally, the one person–one language approach, despite its reported success, also has potential problems. The majority language, spoken by either the father or the mother, may become dominant when the child goes to school and starts interacting with the outside community. In addition, the parent speaking the minority language may be in a difficult position when conversing with the child outside the home, especially if that language is looked down upon by the majority group. Such a situation may occur when the child is with playmates and does not wish to be singled out; in these cases, the parent often switches over to the majority language in order not to embarrass the child.

What is essential in the maintenance of the "weaker" (often the minority) language and hence in the development of bilingualism is that the child feels the *need* to use two languages in everyday life. In Box 2.13 (Chapter 2) a family relates how the home–outside the home language strategy broke down: when Cyril, a little French boy in the States, started going to an English-language day care center, he brought home English-speaking friends, he watched television, and American friends of his parents quite often came to dinner. Above all, Cyril realized that his parents spoke quite good English, and as there was no other reason for speaking French (no French-speaking grandmother or playmate, no French-speaking social activities outside the home), Cyril probably decided that the price to maintain both languages, English and French, was too high. Little by little he started speaking English to his parents and ceased to be an active bilingual, although he retained the ability to understand his first language (a very frequent phenomenon in the children of immigrants). Cyril's parents could have isolated him from the English environment, just as Zierer's family did with their child, but they either did not think it was natural or did not have the time and energy to do so. Frequent trips back to France or even the presence of a monolingual French-speaking family member probably would have been enough to maintain Cyril's bilingualism.

Arnberg (1979) concludes her study of strategies in Swedish-English families:

The most important finding of the study was that, regardless of strategy, it is probably difficult for a child to become a true bilingual while living in a country in which one of the languages is dominant, even when the minority language is a high-status language. Most of the children who were bilingual . . . had either lived in an English-speaking country for several years, were attending a school in which English was the medium of instruction, or were still young enough for the English of the home to balance the dominant Swedish environment. (p. 110)

The only exception to this is if the child belongs to a cohesive linguistic minority with monolingual speakers and if the minority language is used in various social activities. If the family does not have this kind of support and cannot afford trips back to the homeland, the task of bringing up a child as a bilingual becomes quite considerable.

In and Out of Bilingualism

Whatever the factors that lead to childhood bilingualism—societal or personal, planned or not—most observers agree that children have great facility in becoming bilingual or even multilingual. McLaughlin (1978) reports that Geissler, a German teacher in Belgrade, observed children who had mastered as many as four languages without mixing them. Barber (1973) recounts how Yaqui Indian children, whose first language is Yaqui, acquire their second and third languages at about age five or six: Spanish through contact with Mexican American children in and out of school and English in school, where it is the medium of instruction. Mkilifi (1978) reports that many Tanzanian youngsters acquire at least three languages: the local language in the home and immediate surroundings, Swahili in the community and at school, and English at school.

Box 4.3 presents an extract by a person who lived in India at the turn of the century and whose children learned to converse in Bengali, Hindustani, and Santali with the nurses, servants, and groundsmen, as well as in English with their parents. In the second extract, a bilingual tells how she spoke four different languages as a child. Outside the home she spoke Swahili and Portuguese, and within the family she spoke English to her older sister, Portuguese to her younger sister, and French to her parents. Such multilingual behavior is possible only if the child realizes that in order to communicate with a particular person, he or she must acquire that person's language. Had the bilingual in the extract been able to use French with all the members of her family, instead of using three different languages, she would never have become multilingual. Today, as an

BOX 4.3	BILINGUALS SPEAK

Pluralingual Abilities of Children

It is a common experience in the district of Bengal [India] in which the writer resided to hear English children three or four years old who have been born in the country conversing freely at different times with their parents in English, with their *ayahs* (nurses) in Bengali, with the [groundsmen] in Santali, and with the house servants in Hindustani, while their parents have learned with the aid of a *munshi* (teacher) and much laborious effort just sufficient Hindustani to comprehend what the house servants are saying (provided they do not speak too quickly) and to issue simple orders to them connected with domestic affairs. It is even not unusual to see English parents in India unable to understand what their servants are saying to them in Hindustani and being driven in consequence to bring along an English child of four or five years old, if available, to act as interpreter. (Tomb, 1925, reprinted in Andersson, 1977, p. 209)

A French-English bilingual: As a French-speaking child I spoke different languages at different times. First of all, Swahili when I was very young (up to the age of seven). Then Portuguese, followed by English. French was spoken at home, English at school, and Portuguese at home and in the community. With my older sister I always tended to use English, whereas with my younger sister I spoke Portuguese. My two sisters would communicate mostly in Portuguese, but the three of us always spoke French with our parents.

adult, she has retained fluency in only two languages, French and English; she now communicates in French (instead of Portuguese) with her younger sister, and she no longer needs Swahili for communicating outside the home.

Most case studies of bilingual children emphasize the acquisition of languages; very few examine the reverse trend: how a child returns to monolingualism or becomes monolingual (if bilingual in infancy) when the psychosocial factors that caused bilingualism disappear. One case study that does examine the acquisition and the loss of a second language is reported by Burling (1978). He and his wife and their son Stephen spent almost two years in the Garo Hill district of Assam, India. Stephen was sixteen months old when they arrived and just starting to speak. He began using Garo words within a few weeks of their arrival, but his English was clearly dominant at first. Little by little, however, as he interacted with his Garo nurse and with other Garo speakers, Garo took over. Five months after their arrival, Stephen's mother was hospitalized for two months, and as Burling writes, this "removed him from close contact with his most important single English model." Stephen was thus forced into greater use of Garo, especially as his father often spoke to him in that language. Nine months after their arrival, when Stephen was just over two years old, the family spent two months in another region of India where Stephen came into contact with several English speakers. He quickly learned which people did not speak Garo and rarely attempted to speak to them in that language. On his return to the Garo hills, he became more fluent in English (he had more contact with his mother now) and used it with native English speakers and with his father. When the family left that region, Stephen, who was a bit more than three, was truly bilingual in Garo and English. He translated and switched from one language to the other with much ease, but there was still no doubt that Garo was his stronger language (when he spoke in his sleep, Burling reports, it was in Garo).

What is especially interesting is Stephen's loss of Garo. As the family traveled across India, he attempted to speak Garo with every Indian he met, but after a month he realized that it was to no avail. The last time he ever used Garo extensively was on the plane home. He sat next to a Malayan youth whom he mistook for a Garo, and as Burling writes, "A torrent of Garo tumbled forth as if all the pent-up speech of those weeks had been suddenly let loose." Although his father would speak to him in Garo from time to time, Stephen would use only an occasional Garo word in response, and after a few months he did not seem to be understanding his father's Garo, though, as Burling writes, "It was frequently difficult to know just how much was really lack of understanding and how much was deliberate refusal to cooperate." Within six months of their departure, Stephen was having trouble with even the simplest Garo words.

Burling finishes his report:

In the fall of 1958, at the age of five and a half, Stephen is attending kindergarten in the United States. He speaks English perhaps a bit more fluently and certainly more continuously than most of his contemporaries. The only Garo words he now uses are the few that have become family property, but I hope that some day it will be possible to take him back to the Garo Hills and to discover whether hidden deep in his unconscious he may not still retain a remnant of his former fluency in Garo that might be reawakened if he again came in contact with the language. (p. 74)

Stephen is a fine example of how children will become bilingual when psychosocial factors create a need for communication in two languages (in this case, English-speaking parents but a Garo environment), and how they will revert back to monolingualism just as quickly when such factors disappear or are no longer considered important. On his return to the United States, Stephen realized that he no longer needed Garo, and his father's reasons for speaking it to him were not important enough to encourage him to retain that language. Hence he forgot Garo as quickly as he had learned it. The interesting question that Burling alludes to in his last sentence is whether somewhere in Stephen's unconscious, in some part of his brain, Garo is stored to some extent, and whether it can be regained. Many people believe that having known and used a language in childhood is a great asset when relearning it later in life, if that language has been forgotten in the meanwhile. People report that the language "sounds familiar" and that they have no problems with certain sounds, but unfortunately, no systematic study has substantiated these reports (see Eisenstein, 1980, however).

In conclusion, bilingualism in childhood usually occurs because of the need to communicate with those who play an important role in the child's life—parents, siblings, other family members, peers, and teachers. As long as these factors are important to the child, he or she will remain bilingual; when they lose their importance or are removed altogether, the child will just as naturally revert to monolingualism.

The Acquisition of Two Languages

In this section we will study the processes underlying two main types of language acquisition by bilingual children: simultaneous and successive. We will use McLaughlin's (1978) age criterion to differentiate between the two types: a child who acquires two languages before the age of three is regarded as doing so simultaneously, whereas a child who acquires one language in infancy and the second after age three is considered to be doing so successively. It should be noted that the degree of bilingualism attained is not related to whether the languages are acquired simultaneously or successively. It is psychosocial factors, such as the use of the language in the family or in the school, that will condition when, to what extent, and for how long a child will be bilingual, not the age of acquisition of the two languages.

Simultaneous Acquisition

Much of the information we have about simultaneous acquisition comes from diaries kept by parents who brought up their child bilingually, most often with the one person–one language strategy. The parents have either published the diaries themselves or have given them to linguists to analyze and write up. As McLaughlin (1978) observes, such case studies are extremely informative, but they vary in quality and reliability: direct observation by parents may well lead to errors in transcription or to the misperception of ill-formed utterances. But despite these failings, they are useful documents, and much of what we know about infant bilingualism is based on them.

One of the best-known and best-documented case studies is that by Leopold (1970) concerning his daughter Hildegard. She was brought up according to the one person–one language strategy, speaking German to her father and English to her mother. Leopold (1978) reports that during her first two years, Hildegard combined her two languages into one system and was therefore not really bilingual. Her speech sounds belonged to a unified set, undifferentiated by language. She mixed English and German words and failed to separate the two languages when speaking to monolingual English or German speakers. It was only at the end of her second year that Hildegard showed the "first flicker of the later unfolding of two separate language systems," and from then on she slowly began to distinguish between them. Her knowledge of the existence of two languages was revealed in various ways: for instance, she would ask her father, "How does Mama say it?", a sly contrivance, Leopold notes, to get her dad to say an English word. When she was four, she asked: "Mother, do all fathers speak German?"—a clear indication that she was conscious of the one person–one language dichotomy. Four weeks later she asked her father: "Papa, why do you speak German?"

From the age of two to the age of five, Hildegard was dominant in English, because her exposure to that language through her mother and the surrounding English environment greatly exceeded her contacts with German. Whereas her English pronunciation was similar to that of English monolingual children, in German she had problems with rounded front vowels and with certain consonants. In addition, she gave German nouns English plural endings, and her German grammatical constructions were very simple, often following English word order. Hildegard realized that she did not master

German fully, and she refrained from saying certain things in German to avoid casting them in an English word order. By the end of her fifth year, German was by far her weaker language and was in danger of being lost. At that time, however, Hildegard spent half a year in Germany, with dramatic consequences. She became quite fluent in German, while her English receded. After four weeks in a totally German environment, she was unable to say more than a few very simple utterances in English (the parallel between Hildegard and Burling's son Stephen is striking here), and she had a pronounced German accent in English. She progressed in German very quickly and learned to invert the subject and the verb after an introductory word or clause, but certain idioms and structural aspects did remain influenced by English.

When she returned to the States, Hildegard quickly recovered her English. After two weeks she was quite fluent again, and after four weeks she was starting to have difficulties with German. The last features of German that she had acquired, such as the uvular *r* and the verb placement, were the first to be forgotten. However, after six months, Leopold noted that the reaction to English was overcome, and from then on she was really bilingual, although dominant in English. This latter language continued to influence her choice of words and idioms in German, and to a lesser degree her grammatical structures, but not her German pronunciation and morphology.

Hildegard's case is interesting because certain aspects of her development of the two languages are found repeatedly in bilingual children: the initial mixed language stage; the slow separation of the two language systems and increasing awareness of bilingualism; the influence of one language on the other when the linguistic environment favors one language; the avoidance of difficult words and constructions in the weaker language; the rapid shift from one language dominance to the other when the environment changes; the final separation of the sound and grammatical systems but the enduring influence of the dominant language on the other in the domain of vocabulary and idioms. Each of these aspects will be studied in the next section.

Before continuing, however, I should note that whether a child acquires only one language and becomes monolingual or acquires two languages and becomes bilingual, the rate and pattern of language development are the same. The first words are spoken at the same time in both monolingual and bilingual children: Doyle, Champagne, and Segalowitz (1978) report that the average age of the first word, as recalled by mothers, is 11.2 months for bilinguals and 11.6 for monolinguals. In addition, language develops similarly in both monolinguals and bilinguals: sounds easier to produce appear sooner than sounds such as fricatives (/f/, /s/, /z/, for instance) or consonant clusters (/fr/, /st/); meanings of words are overextended, so that "doggie," for example, will be used for horses and other four-legged animals as well as for dogs; utterances slowly increase in length; and simpler grammatical constructions are used before more complex ones, such as relative clauses.

Padilla and Liebman (1975) conclude their study of the language development of three English-Spanish bilingual children in the following way: "In spite of the linguistic 'load' forced on to them due to their bilingual environments, [the children] were acquiring their two languages at a rate comparable to that of monolingual-speaking children" (p. 51), and McLaughlin (1978) writes: "In short, it seems that the language acquisition process is the same in its basic features and in its developmental sequence for the bilingual child and the monolingual child. The bilingual child has the additional task of distinguishing the two language systems, but there is no evidence that this requires special language processing devices" (p. 91–92).

FROM ONE TO TWO LANGUAGE SYSTEMS   Researchers do not fully agree on whether infant bilinguals go through an initial mixed stage that consists of a single language system containing elements from each language (as did Hildegard) or whether they are able to keep the two languages separate from the onset of language development. Proponents of the latter view, such as Bergman (1976) and Padilla and Liebman (1975), point to the fact that the children they have studied produced very few if any mixed utterances of the type:

Baila (dance) Mommy.
That *papel* (paper).
Está (it is) *raining.*   (*Padilla and Liebman, 1975*)

Also, their sound systems appeared to be differentiated from the onset of language. Support for this latter claim comes from two case studies: Pavlovitch (1920) reported that his son mastered the French and Serbian phonological systems at about the same time and without confusion, and Ronjat (1913) said his son Louis did the same with French and German. Bergman (1976) reports that her daughter Mary, acquiring Spanish and English simultaneously, showed that she clearly differentiated her two languages at a very early age (fifteen months), responding in Spanish to her babysitter and in English to her mother. Bergman thus proposes an independent development hypothesis, which states:

As it is being acquired, each language is able to develop independently of the other with the same pattern of acquisition as is found in monolingual children learning that language. (p. 88)

It is only if the child receives mixed language input that he or she will produce mixed utterances. Thus the cause of mixed language in children can be traced to the input itself and not the child's inability to keep the two languages separate, Bergman proposes.

However, this position is not supported by many other researchers. Most believe that initially the child has a single system that combines elements of the two languages. Swain (1972) went so far as to entitle her Ph.D. dissertation, "Bilingualism as a first language." She proposes that infant bilinguals begin with a single set of rules, from which rules are later tagged to a particular language. She shows that English-French bilingual children at first use devices common to both languages when asking a yes/no question, that is, a rising intonation (he's coming?) or adding "eh" at the end of a sentence (he's coming, *eh*?). Then, as their languages develop, they acquire other devices specific to each language such as tags in English (he's coming, *isn't he*?) or the permutation of the pronoun and noun in French (vient-il?).

Volterra and Taeschner (1978) propose a three-stage model of language development in the bilingual child: in the first stage, the child has one lexical system that includes words from both languages; in the second stage the child has two different lexical systems (or lexicons) but only one grammar (or syntax); and in the third stage the child has not only two lexicons but also two grammars. We will examine each of these stages in relation to the evidence proposed by Volterra and Taeschner as well as by other case studies.

What is especially interesting about the first stage, when the child has one lexicon with words from both languages, is that there is rarely any overlap in the words taken from each one; that is, if the child uses the word for "table" in one language, he or she will not use the corresponding word in the other. For example, a Georgian-Russian bilingual child (Imedadze and Uznadze, 1978) used the Russian word for flowers (tsiti) and the Georgian word for ball (buti) but never used their corresponding words in the other language. In their study of two Italian-German bilingual girls, Volterra and Taeschner only found three corresponding words out of a vocabulary of eighty-seven words in the first girl, Lisa, and six corresponding words out of eighty-three words in the second, Giulia. And the children did not give those few words the same meaning: Lisa used Italian *la* with things that were not visible at the time and German *da* (there) for things that were present. In addition, the girls did not use these few corresponding words with equal frequency. These results are similar to those reported by Prinz and Prinz (1979), who brought up their little girl, Anya, bilingual in American Sign Language and English. Anya's spoken vocabulary complemented her sign vocabulary, and less than 16 percent of the words had sign counterparts. Thus she labeled a basic concept or object or event in one or the other language but rarely in both.

An interesting aspect of this stage is the use of blends and compounds. Juliette, a two-year-old English-French bilingual, blended the French word "chaud" and its English equivalent "hot" into "shot." She also blended the English word "pickle" and its French equivalent "cornichon" to give "pinichon." Both blends remained in her vocabulary for some time. Eric, another young French-English bilingual, would tell people to sit down with "assit," from the French "assis" and the English "sit." In addition to blends, young bilingual children will compound corresponding words in the two languages into one word. Thus, Juliette would point to the moon and say, "lune-moon." She also said "pour-for" instead of either "pour" or "for." Hildegard said "Bitte-please," and Eric produced "papa-daddy" and "chaud-hot." Both blends and compounds illustrate further the one-word-for-one-concept aspect of this first stage, even though these "words" are constructed from the two languages. In this first stage the few two- or three-word constructions appear as a mixture of both languages, thus reflecting a single language system.

In the second stage the child distinguishes two different lexicons but applies the same syntactic rules to both languages. For almost any word, the child has a corresponding word in the other language. However, the transition between the first and second stages takes place over time and is quite complex. For instance, Celce-Murcia (1978) describes the vocabulary of her daughter, Caroline, an English-French bilingual, at two years and four months. She knows and uses some words in both languages: "horse" and "cheval," "bird" and "oiseau," for example. Words that sound similar in the two languages create confusion; these she will use together but in a hesitant way. For instance, she will point to a bus and say:

bus (English) . . . bus (French) . . . bus (English).

The child knows a third set of words in only one or the other language, thus, "milk," "dog," "car," "book" in English but not their counterparts in French, and "dodo," "nounou," and "barbu" in French but not their English equivalents. Finally, she knows some words in both languages but avoids them in one, as they are too difficult to pronounce (Celce-Murcia terms this phonological avoidance). Thus she will say "couteau" but not its English equivalent, "knife," which is harder to pronounce; she will use "spoon" but not "cuiller," "home" but not "maison," "citron" but not "lemon," "boy" but not "garçon." This avoidance of words that are difficult to pronounce has also been reported by Leopold concerning Hildegard.

The complex picture that results from Caroline's slow transition from one to two lexicons explains why Volterra and Taeschner note that during this second stage, children continue to mix words in their two languages. This is the case with Lisa, who speaks Italian to her mother but inserts German words into her utterances, as in:

Mami vuole *Stickzeug,* vuole *Arbeit* si?
(Mommy wants knitting, wants work, yes?)

Once the child has accomplished the transition leading from one to two lexicons, he or she is able to translate from one language to the other. Volterra and Taeschner (1978) quote a little dialogue between father and daughter taken from Leopold's report:

Hildegard: Nose.
    Father: Wie heisst das auf Deutsch?
        (What is the name in German?)
Hildegard: Nase.

They also report how Lisa asks the same question in two languages. She says to an Italian friend:

Dov'è Kitty?
(Where is Kitty?)

and immediately afterward, without waiting for an answer, asks her mother in German:

Wo ist Kitty?
(Where is Kitty?)

An interesting aspect of this stage, according to Volterra and Taeschner, is that the child still has only one grammar, or syntax. Thus, to show possession, Lisa uses the same strategy in German:

Lisa Hose.
(Lisa pants.)

as in Italian:

Lisa bisicletta.
(Lisa bicycle.)

This strategy makes use of both the German construction:

Maria's Haare.
(Mary's hair.)

and the Italian counterpart:

I capelli di Maria.

In the third stage, the child's two languages are differentiated both in lexicon and in syntax. To help differentiate the two languages, the child rigidly associates the languages with different persons. As the authors write: "The act of labelling a person with one of the two languages makes the choice of words and rules a kind of automatic process, thus reducing the effort she has to make" (p. 325). The rigid association of a person with a language is well illustrated by Redlinger and Park (1980), who report on a three-way dialogue between Danny, an English-German bilingual child; his mother, who always speaks English to him; and the investigator, who speaks German. Danny is looking at a book and telling the investigator about a cat in the picture. The mother asks a question about a bird in German:

Was macht der Vogel?
(What's the bird doing?)

Danny is startled and says to his mother:

Nicht Vogel.
(Not bird.)

He points to the investigator and says:

Du Vogel.
(You bird.)

and then points to his mother and says:

Du sag *birdie.*
(You say birdie.)

Volterra and Taeschner continue by stating that the tendency to label people with definite languages decreases as the syntactic differences between the languages become more apparent. After a while the child accepts the possibility of speaking either language with the same person, although the person–language link continues to remain strong (see next section).

Interference, that is, the involuntary influence of one language on the other, still occurs, especially when the child needs to switch rapidly from one language to another or when he or she has to express something that is usually said in the other language, but on the whole, it is reduced. Volterra and Taeschner conclude their study: "At the end of this [third] stage, the child is able to speak both languages fluently, that is, with the same linguistic competence as a monolingual child, with any person. It is only at this point that one can say a child is truly bilingual" (p. 326).

The very complex process of separation of languages that Volterra and Taeschner report on is still poorly understood. Most case studies report that the child does pass through a period in which he or she starts to show an awareness of two different languages. The child may ask questions of the type: How do you say this in Italian? (for example) or by testing out a new word in one language and in the other before assigning it to the appropriate one. As an aid to language differentiation, the child relies heavily on the context in which the language is used and on feedback from adults, as when they fail to answer when addressed in the wrong language. It also appears that the phonological configuration of the word helps in assigning it to one language or the other.

Additional evidence for language separation is proposed by Redlinger and Park (1980). They observed the language mixing of four bilingual children for periods ranging from five to nine months and noted that as time went on, each child produced fewer mixed utterances. At the beginning, 30 percent of the utterances produced by Marcus, a Spanish-German bilingual, were mixed, but by the end only 21 percent were mixed. Danny, an English-German bilingual, went from 21 percent to 4 percent, and Henrik, a French-German bilingual who was older than the first two, went from 12 percent mixed utterances to 3 percent. The most frequently mixed elements were nouns (also reported by other researchers), as in:

> *Danny:* From up in *Himmel* (sky).
> *Henrik:* Wo ist die *livre*?
> (Where is the book?)

Adverbs were also quite frequently mixed, for instance:

> *Danny: Da* (there) big truck.

Vihman (1980), studying an Estonian-English bilingual child, also reports a decrease in mixed utterances as the languages were separated: 34 percent of utterances were mixed at twenty months, 11 percent at twenty-three months, and only 4 percent at twenty-four months.

It seems that bilingual children slowly become aware of the words and grammatical rules of a particular language and realize that communication in that language will break down if elements from the other language are used. This is illustrated in a short dialogue reported by Swain (1974), between Michael (M), a French-English bilingual child, and an English-speaking investigator (I), who has never shown that she understands French:

> *M:* Marcel's going to be ... *Marcel va être le payeur* (Marcel will be the teller).
> *I:* What?
> *M:* Marcel's go ... *Marcel va être le payeur.*
> *I:* What?
> *M:* Marcel's going to be the *payeur*. Let's wait.
> *I:* Why?
> *M:* Because Marcel's going to be the man who ... who pay.

Swain comments that at the beginning of the dialogue, Michael switched over to French rather than insert a French word, "payeur," into his English. However, because of the investigator's apparent lack of understanding, he finally did use "payeur," but was immediately dissatisfied with this, thinking that maybe a French word would only extend the period of misunderstanding. Thus, he provided a definition of the word (the man who pay), and to do this, he used a rather complex construction, a relative clause. Had Michael known that the investigator understood French, he probably would not have gone to so much trouble. In fact, it has been noted that mixing in the speech of bilingual children may continue for some time if the child lives in an environment where a lot of code-switching takes place, but even then mixing will be reduced in time.

DOMINANCE IN ONE LANGUAGE   There are two reasons for a bilingual child to show dominance in one of the two languages. The first, and relatively minor one, is that certain linguistic constructs are harder to internalize and produce in one of the languages. The second is that the child may be exposed to and may need one language more than the other. Concerning the complexity of constructs in the bilingual's languages, Mikeš (1967) reports how two Hungarian-

Serbo-Croatian bilingual children encoded the locative relation in Hungarian earlier than in Serbo-Croatian. The reason proposed is that Hungarian only needs an inflection on the noun to express location, whereas Serbo-Croatian requires an inflection on the noun and a locative preposition. Before age two, the children were already marking location in Hungarian, but when they spoke Serbo-Croatian, they failed to do so either with a preposition or an inflection. Imedadze and Uznadze (1978) report a similar finding in their Russian-Georgian bilingual child. The subject-to-object relation in Georgian was expressed first by analogy with the Russian form, which adds an accusative ending; it was only later that the more complicated Georgian form appeared. The latter demands a dative case ending for the real subject and the nominative case for the real object.

Vihman (1980) reports how Raivio, an Estonian-English bilingual child, omitted bound morphemes in Estonian but kept whole word functors, saying:

> Sina võid 'mängi minu 'värvid.
> (You can play with my crayons.)

instead of

> Sina võid 'mangi*da* minu 'värvid*ega.*

Estonian, a highly inflected language, has a complex morphology (fourteen case markers), and Raivio took more time in acquiring it than the relatively simple English morphology. Thus, because of linguistic differences between the two languages the child may seem to be dominant in one. (Slobin, 1973, has reviewed some of this research.)

However, the main reason for dominance in one language is that the child has had greater exposure to it and needs it more to communicate with people in the immediate environment. It is probably rare that both languages are needed throughout simultaneous language development and hence are developed to the same extent. As we saw in the previous section, more often than not the child will receive more input from one language than the other, because it is either the language of his or her principal caretaker or the language of the environment. Hildegard, Leopold's daughter, was dominant in English until the age of five, changed over to dominance in German during her stay in Germany, and reverted to dominance in English on her return to the States. This was also true for Burling's son Stephen, who throughout most of his stay in India was dominant in Garo.

The main effect of dominance is not only that the stronger language is more developed than the weaker one (more sounds are isolated, more words are learned, more grammatical rules are inferred), but also that the stronger language interferes with or influences the weaker one. In this sense, dominance retards differentiation by imposing aspects of the dominant language on the weaker one. Burling (1959) notes, for instance, that Stephen's phonemic system developed later in English than in Garo and that at first he used Garo phonemes instead of English ones when he spoke English. The two vowel systems finally became differentiated, but the consonantal systems never did, and Stephen used Garo consonants instead of English ones. Fantini (1979) also reports the interference of Spanish on his children's developing English phonology. Both Mario and Carla started acquiring English just after their second year (Spanish was their mother tongue), and their first English words were pronounced according to Spanish rules. They did not differentiate /b/ from /v/, they could not produce /θ/ and /ð/, and certain vowels were Spanish-like (Spanish /i/ for English /I/).

At the level of morphology, researchers have also noted the effect of one language on the other. Oksaar (1970) reports that a three-year-old Swedish-Estonian-speaking child attached Estonian endings to Swedish verb forms in Estonian sentences. And Fantini (1979) writes that although interference was reduced at this level, his children did transfer Spanish morphemes into English. For example: "Can you *desen*tie this?" instead of "Can you *un*tie this?"

At the level of syntax, Kinzel (1964) recounts how Anne, an English-French bilingual whose dominant language was English, would translate the English prepositions that are used with English verbs, then add them to French verbs, for example:

Je cherche *pour* le livre.

instead of:

Je cherche le livre.
(I'm looking *for* the book.)

She would also split the causative verb "faire" (to make) from the infinitive, as in English:

Tu fais ce pistolet marcher.

instead of:

Tu fais marcher ce pistolet.
(You make this gun work.)

And she would misplace the adverb, again following the English word order. Thus:

J'aime ça mieux.

instead of:

J'aime mieux ça.
(I like that better.)

In this same line, Swain (1974) reports on Michael's development of English, which was weaker than his French. His initial strategy for speaking English was to use English content words in otherwise French utterances, for example: "Toi tu *see*," where the French is "Toi tu vois." Then, as his English improved, he decreased the number of mixed utterances (that is, he used only English words), but his syntax remained influenced by French. For example: "It's what?" (from c'est quoi?) or "That's to me?" (from c'est à moi?).

It is important to view such interferences as the product of strategies employed by children to produce their weaker language. Feedback from the listener, occasional breakdowns in communication, and further language input will gradually help the child differentiate the two systems so that ultimately the languages will be maintained separate. As McLaughlin (1978) reports, interference is usually held to a minimum in bilingual children if the two languages are maintained in balance and their domains of use are clearly defined.

Successive Acquisition

Not all bilingual children acquire their two languages in a simultaneous or quasi-simultaneous manner. In fact, most are members of linguistic minorities who acquire their first language in the home and immediate community and their second language when they enter school. Some are given lessons in the second language, but most acquire it naturally by interacting with teachers, children, and other members of the majority language community. Some other children become bilingual because their parents move to another country and hence, like minority children, they find themselves speaking one language at home and the other outside it.

In this section we will briefly review how a child acquires a second language naturally, that is, by interacting with native speakers of that language. We will not consider the second-language learners who acquire their "foreign" language in the rather artificial and formal environment of the classroom. Such learning rarely results in functional and regular use of two languages (see Krashen, 1978, for instance, for a discussion of the difference between language acquisition and language learning).

AGE OF ONSET OF BILINGUALISM   Children can become bilingual at any age. In Box 4.1, the Russian-English bilingual spoke Russian at home in her early years and started to acquire English when she entered kindergarten. The Greek-English bilingual spoke only Greek until the age of twelve, when her family moved to the States and she became engulfed in an English-speaking environment: at school, in the community, on television, and so on. As adults, both are now active bilinguals in that they use their first and second languages in their everyday lives.

There exists a long-standing myth that the earlier a language is acquired, the more fluent a person will be in it. As both McLaughlin (1978) and Genesee (1978) report, this myth is based on a number of questionable assumptions. One of these is that young children acquire languages more quickly and with less effort than older children and adolescents. Another is linked to the notion of the critical period, as put forward by Lennenberg (1967) and others, which states that before the onset of puberty the brain is more malleable or "plastic" and hence is receptive to such tasks as language learning. In addition, they claim that the brain's hemispheric specialization for language (language lateralization) is not achieved until about the time of puberty; from then on language acquisition becomes harder and less optimal. And younger children are said to have fewer inhibitions, to be less embarrassed when they make mistakes, and hence to be better learners.

All these factors have come under considerable criticism in recent years (see Krashen, 1973; Seliger, 1978; Genesee, 1978; McLaughlin, 1978, among others). It has been shown that young children are rather unsophisticated and immature learners in that they have not yet fully acquired certain cognitive skills, such as the capacity to abstract, generalize, infer, and classify, that could help them in second-language acquisition. In addition, the notions of the critical period and of language lateralization have come under increasing attack. Krashen (1973), for example, believes that language lateralization occurs at four or five years of age and not at puberty. Seliger (1978) proposes the notion of different critical periods for different abilities, which in turn determine how completely one can acquire some aspects of language.

Finally, recent discussion has emphasized the psychosocial factors that lead to second-language acquisition. These, above all else, dictate the extent to which a second language will be acquired. Gardner and Lambert (1972) found that success in mastering a second language depends not so much on intellectual capacity or language aptitude as on the learner's attitude toward the other linguistic group and his or her willingness to identify with that group. To this should be added the motivation and, quite simply, the need, to communicate with members of the group. For example, an eight-year-old immigrant girl who has just been put into an all-English school will probably want and, in fact, need to communicate with the other children in order to survive in that environment, and this will encourage her to acquire the language. On the other hand, if she is surrounded by other children of her minority group, she may be less motivated to communicate with the English-speaking children (especially if their attitude toward her group is negative), but she may have no choice about whether or not to acquire English if it is the medium of instruction in the school. Thus the psychosocial factors that surround language acquisition are of primary importance in determining the extent of the child's bilingualism. Other factors, such as the critical period, language lateralization, language aptitude, and intelligence, play a lesser role. This is also true of age of onset of the second language, except that by late adolescence the acquisition of a native-like pronunciation does seem to become more difficult. (See Oyama, 1976, 1978, and Snow and Hoefnagel-Hohle, 1978, for the ongoing debate on the relationship between age of onset of second-language learning and degree of accent, level of sentence comprehension, and perception of phoneme boundaries.)

STRATEGIES IN SECOND-LANGUAGE ACQUISITION   There has been much debate on whether similar linguistic and cognitive strategies are employed in the acquisition of a first and of a second language. It was long thought that the knowledge of a first language affected the acquisition of a second and that many of the errors made in that language were due to the direct influence or interference of the first. The French accent of French youths learning English is an example of this kind of influence. This line of thought has been called the transfer position. More recently, however, other researchers have taken the position that acquisition of a second language parallels that of the first language, and that transfer (or interference) is of minor importance. This has been termed the developmental position. McLaughlin (1978), a supporter of this position, proposes that the child learning a second language recapitulates the learning process of a native speaker of that language. He writes: "There is a unity of process that characterizes all language acquisition, whether first or second language and . . . this unity of process reflects the use of similar strategies of language acquisition" (p. 206).

Most proponents of this position agree that there are important differences between the first and second language learner: the latter, because he or she is older, has a better knowledge of the world, a wider range of semantic concepts, a longer memory span, and a more developed cognitive system. Nevertheless, he or she will apply very similar linguistic strategies to the second language acquisition process. For instance, the child will use simple structures (subject-verb-object, for example) before more complex ones, overextend the meanings of words, disregard irregular past tenses, overgeneralize rules, and relate word order to word meaning. Ervin-Tripp (1974) observed that English-speaking children learning French in Geneva were not using word-for-word translations from English but instead were simplifying their French constructions and using first-language-learner structures, such as simple declarative sentences or uninverted questions. Milon (1974) observed that a seven-year-old Japanese child acquiring the English negation progressed through the same developmental stages as English-speaking children and did not transfer the Japanese negation system into English. And Dulay and Burt (1974) found that the vast majority of errors made by Spanish, Chinese, Japanese, and Norwegian-speaking children learning English were all similar to one another. Had the first languages been a factor in their second language acquisition, the errors would have been different from one group to another. Proponents of the developmental position expect to find, and often do find, more developmental errors involving simplifications and overgeneralizations than errors involving interference from the first language.

However, the picture is probably more complex than may at first appear. McLaughlin (1978) reports that Cancino, Rosansky, and Schumann (1974, 1975) examined the acquisition of yes/no questions and negations by six Spanish-speaking persons (both children and adults) and did not obtain the development pattern of English children. He also reports that Hakuta (1974) examined the acquisition of morphemes by a Japanese child learning English and found that the pattern did not correspond to that of children acquiring English as a mother tongue. And Mulford and Hecht (1979) report that the phonological development of English by Steinar, a six-year-old native speaker of Icelandic, could not be accounted for by either the transfer position or the developmental position alone; it was best explained by a systematic interaction between the two types. For instance, transfer best predicted the order of difficulty of English fricatives and affricates; the first sounds he mastered in English were those common to both languages: /f/, /s/, initial /θ/ and medial /ð/. Only later did the child master sounds not present in Icelandic—/z/, / ʃ /, /tʃ/, /dʒ/—and those involving some phonetic or allophonic adjustment of Icelandic phonemes, /v/ and /ð/, for instance. However, the developmental hypothesis best predicted the sound substitutions. For example, as Icelandic does not have an initial /ð/ sound, Steinar replaced the English initial /ð/ with substitutes of tighter closure (for example, /d/), as the developmental position would predict, and not with /θ/, as predicted by the transfer position. In addition, new English sounds were not always replaced by similar Icelandic sounds (as the transfer position would predict). The child quite often substituted English sounds, as in the case of / ʒ / replacing /dʒ/ in "engine," although neither sound occurs in Icelandic. Mulford and Hecht conclude that their subject's developing English phonology is best accounted for by both transfer and developmental factors.

Hakuta and Cancino (1977) review the twists and turns that the developmental and transfer positions have gone through in the last ten years. They show how interference can be seen as the result of active hypothesis testing by the second-language learner, how both interference and developmental errors appear and disappear at varying periods during the language acquisition process, and how acquisition is in fact an interplay between the native language and the target language. (See also "Speaking to a Monolingual" in Chapter 6). Hakuta and Cancino also review the work done on the acquisition of specific language patterns, such as negation and grammatical morphemes, which shows once again the complex interplay between the developmental and transfer strategies.

Researchers in second-language acquisition are now concentrating on isolating the social, cognitive, and linguistic strategies used. Fillmore (1976) proposes that there are three stages in the child's acquisition of a second language in a natural environment. In the first, the child establishes social relationships with the speakers of the second language; to do so, he or she engages in "interactional" rather than "informational" activities and relies heavily on fixed verbal formulas (You know what? I wanna do it, Guess what?) as well as nonverbal communication. In the second stage, the child concentrates on communicating with speakers of the language;

he or she thus moves away from socially useful intact formulas to new combinations of the words in the formulas. And in the third stage, the child makes sure that the form of the language is correct.

According to Fillmore, the second-language learner will use a number of cognitive and social strategies. The five cognitive strategies she uncovered are:

Assume that what people are saying is directly relevant to the situation at hand or to what they or you are experiencing. (Metastrategy: guess.)
Get some expressions you understand and start talking.
Look for recurring parts in the formulas you know.
Make the most of what you've got.
Work on big things; save the details for later.

And the three social strategies are:

Join a group and act as if you understand what is going on, even if you don't.
Give the impression, with a few well-chosen words, that you can speak the language.
Count on your friends for help.

Fillmore points to the fact that children at first use formulaic expressions which they acquire as wholes: Look it, Wait a minute, Whose turn is it? Once they have a number of these, they start analyzing them into constituents, which they use to create new sentences. Fillmore stresses that some children who acquire a second language quite rapidly make much use of such strategies, especially those pertaining to social relationships: they seek out children who speak the language being learned, they enjoy role-playing games, and they are uninhibited when speaking their second language. Further, the important thing for them is to communicate, even if they make mistakes doing so. And often the native-speaking children will help out by including the nonnative speakers in their play and by simplifying their speech for them.

Keller-Cohen (1980) reviews some of the cognitive and linguistic strategies used by the second-language learner. She holds to the view that "prior experience with language contributes to a child's second language learning by providing the child with heuristics for searching and organizing linguistic data and with knowledge about language (both general and specific)." Among the searching strategies that are used, Keller-Cohen mentions the following:

Pay attention to the order of linguistic elements.

Look for sequences: The first-language learner starts with one-word utterances and then, over time, increases the length of these utterances, whereas the second-language learner looks for larger units, such as full utterances.

Among the organizing strategies, she proposes the following:

Don't interrupt or rearrange sequences: This leads to a preference for uninverted forms (such as uninverted questions) over inverted forms.

Represent information simply: This entails using one grammatical form for diversity of meanings (for example, the infinitive form for all tense forms), starting with the dominant grammatical patterns (the most frequent word order)and limiting the number of constructions.

The child also brings to the learning process a knowledge of the properties of language. Keller-Cohen mentions the following properties known and used by the second-language learner:

Language is organized into sequences of units which are more or less long and complex and which contain sentence lengtheners such as introductory words or expressions, empty fillers, and slot fillers. Because of this kind of language, learners may produce quite long and quite complex utterances.

The order of linguistic elements is important.

Linguistic units can have multiple meanings and functions. This may lead to prolific overextensions of words and morphemes.

Language is often tied to the immediate context.

Finally, Keller-Cohen mentions particular features of the native language that will lead the learner to avoid certain types of constructions in the second language and to prefer types more similar to those found in the first language. Although the work on strategies in second-language acquisition is exciting, Hakuta and Cancino (1977) point out that it does not yet specify the process by which syntax is acquired. More information is still needed on the stages that the learner goes through in analyzing and decomposing the prefabricated forms that are first used.

The simultaneous use of linguistic, social, and cognitive strategies allows the learner to acquire the second language. At first this may be arduous, but if the motivation to interact with speakers of the second language and the need to do so are both present—as they often are in natural second-language acquisition—then progress will be rapid and the child will soon become bilingual.

Aspects of Bilingualism in the Child

In this section, I stress the following aspects of childhood bilingualism: the person–language bond, translating, language choice, code-switching, and playing with language.

The Person–Language Bond

Anyone who interacts for some time with a young bilingual child will notice the strong bond that exists between a person and a language. In the eyes of the child a person is tagged with a particular language, and if that person addresses the child in the other language, it may cause some distress. We saw this with Danny, when his mother, who usually spoke to him in English, asked him a question in German. Another example concerns Juliette, a two-and-a-half-year-old French-English bilingual, who was playing with Marc, a five-year-old English-speaking boy. Their usual language of communication was English, but to please and surprise her, Marc decided to speak to her in French. He asked his mother for the equivalent of "come" in French and then returned to Juliette and said, "Viens, viens." Much to his surprise, Juliette was far from pleased; instead of smiling, she said angrily, "Don't *do* that, Marc," and repeated this several times.

A number of observers have reported that children often pretend not to understand what parents or grown-ups tell them when they speak in the wrong language. Volterra and Taeschner (1978) mention two instances when Lisa, an Italian-German bilingual girl, reacted strongly to the violation of the person–language rule. In the first, an Italian friend started to talk to her in German, even though the usual language of interaction was Italian. Lisa became upset and started to cry. Her mother tried to calm her down and told her that the friend also spoke German, but this only made the situation worse, and Lisa slapped her mother. In the second instance, Lisa's father, who usually spoke to her in Italian, used a short German sentence. Lisa reacted immediately and said,

"No, non puoi."
(No, you can't.)

The father replied that he too could speak German, but this caused Lisa to be even more upset, and to repeat with more emphasis.

"No, tu non puoi!"
(No, *you* cannot!)

And Fantini (1978) reports that his Spanish-English bilingual children, Mario and Carla, are "guardians of the appropriate language use" and often remind their parents to speak Spanish when they are speaking English to one another.

Volterra and Taeschner (1978) propose that reactions of this type may result from the fact that the child is in the process of differentiating the two languages. One strategy used by the child is to determine which language is spoken with whom and to keep to that language. This makes the choice of words and rules simpler and reduces the effort needed. When the person–language bond is broken, the child is at a loss and becomes upset. This phenomenon continues well beyond the language differentiation stage, and even some seven- or eight-year-olds are not prepared to break the link.

As a consequence of the person–language bond, bilingual children are often ready to correct and help out the adult. For example, when Juliette's mother code-switches into English, Juliette will translate the switch into French, thus reestablishing the normal language pattern. Only when her mother really fails to understand something that Juliette is telling her in French will she agree to use English, but she switches back to French as soon as possible. Redlinger and Park (1980) give another example: Henrik, a French-German bilingual child, showed a reluctance to speak French in the presence of the investigator, whom he considered to be a monolingual German speaker. He would thus translate into German his mother's comments made in French and then proceed to respond to his mother in German—all for the sake of the investigator.

Translating

Henrik's translation for the supposedly monolingual German investigator leads to another interesting aspect of childhood bilingualism—translating skills. To illustrate this, Harris and Sherwood (1978) relate how BS, a young Italian girl, translated quite naturally into a number of languages. Her mother spoke only the Abruzzi dialect of Italian and her father spoke both the dialect and standard Italian. Before she was four, BS would translate from one dialect to the other to convey messages between her father and mother. When BS and her family moved to Venezuela and opened a grocery store, BS would greet customers in Spanish (a language she learned promptly) and translate messages from them to either parent. When she was eight, the family emigrated to Canada and BS quickly became quadrilingual. Harris and Sherwood write: "For ten years, until she left to go to the university, BS translated orally or in writing, phone calls, messages, conversations with visitors, mail, newspaper articles, etc. Indeed, she undertook almost all the written work that the family had to have carried out in English: filling out forms, composing business letters, etc" (p. 156). Another of her functions was to interpret TV programs at home and films at the cinema from English into Italian. This could take the form of successive interpretation, in which she would give the rough outline of the plot, or of simultaneous interpretation, a more trying form of translation.

Like many children of immigrant parents, BS found herself in the situation of liaison between her minority language environment and the majority language community. Her parents and her uncle's family turned to her not only for translations but also for explanations concerning the language and the culture. She tried to explain why things were done the way they were, both to her relatives from the viewpoint of the Canadians and to her native Canadian friends from the viewpoint of Italians. The differences in culture led to difficult situations in which BS would attenuate some of her father's statements. For example, when she interpreted for him at bargaining sessions with non-Italians, he would get worked up and become angry and upset; she would soften his outbursts in her translation, even at the risk of drawing some of her father's anger on herself. Harris and Sherwood report the following exchange:

Father to BS (in Italian): Tell him he's a nitwit.

BS to third party (in English): My father won't accept your offer.

Father angrily to BS (in Italian): Why didn't you tell him what I told you?

Some bilingual children have to interpret for their parents and relatives far more than others. This is especially true of the hearing children of Deaf parents, who communicate in sign language and are usually far from proficient in the dominant oral language, whereas the hearing child can both sign and speak. In Box 4.4 an American Sign Language–English bilingual relates how she first became an interpreter at the age of four and how she used her translating skills at the doctor's office and when making long distance phone calls for her parents.

BOX 4.4   BILINGUALS SPEAK

The Bilingual Child as Interpreter

An American Sign Language–English bilingual: There is nothing that stands out in my mind about being bilingual as a child with the possible exception of being an interpreter at four years of age. That was the main difference between myself and most other kids; I had to go home to interpret at the doctor's office for grandma or whoever it was that day.

One problem I did encounter many, many times was making long-distance calls. In those days, there was no dial-direct service, and trying to make an operator believe a four- to six-year-old who was trying to call Virginia from Boston was always a problem. Everyone wanted to speak to my "mommy." People who called the house and specifically asked for any member of my family never knew how to handle the situation when faced with having to discuss an adult problem with a nine-year-old.

Harris and Sherwood report that bilingual children may start translating quite early in life if the need is present. Ronjat's son, Louis, for instance, could translate single words and simple sentences at age two years and two months and acted as an interpreter for his French grandparents when they wanted to say something to the family cook, who was German. They also note that many young bilingual children consider translation a game (only later does it take on an important social role). When Hildegard finally realized that her German-speaking father also understood and spoke English, she went on translating into German for him as a game. Louis Ronjat realized when he was three that his parents were bilingual and could understand one another without his help, yet he went on translating between them at the table, even if they were addressing one another directly.

However, a bilingual child usually translates because he or she is asked to help in a particular situation or realizes that a person (adult or child) will be left out if he or she does not interpret. Harris and Sherwood (1978) relate how HB, a seven-year-old French-Bulgarian bilingual, was taken to visit a Bulgarian family that had recently arrived in Canada. He and the child of the family were left to watch a children's program in French. The authors write: "The other child, eleven years, did not speak French. Afterward HB told his mother he was tired because he had translated all the program into Bulgarian for his playmate" (p. 158).

Language Choice

As we saw in the preceding chapter, language choice is a highly complex subject, in which factors such as participant, situation, context, and function of discourse help the bilingual decide which language to use. A few studies address the question of language choice in childhood bilingualism. Fantini (1978) reports on the factors influencing language choice in his two children, Mario and Carla, and McClure (1977) examines language choice in Mexican American children aged three to fifteen. As might be expected from our discussion of the person–language bond, most studies state that the participant is the most important factor in language choice. Fantini reports that when his children knew the participant, they spoke to him or her in the appropriate language. The only problem occurred when they became intimate with an English-speaking person; they then had an inclination, almost a desire, to switch to Spanish, their language of intimacy. They did not go quite that far, but the habit of being intimate in Spanish led them to insert many Spanish words into their English. When Mario and Carla did not know the interlocutor or which language he or she spoke, other factors intervened. In a Spanish environment, the children would use Spanish; in an English environment, English would be used only after the children had discounted the possibility that the person spoke Spanish. If the person looked "Latin" they would use Spanish, but if he or she failed to respond in that language, they would continue in English. The other person's level of fluency was an important factor, and by age four both Mario and Carla could judge fluency. If they noticed that the person was speaking in his or her weaker language (Mexicans speaking to them in English, students of Spanish using Spanish), the children would inevitably choose to speak the interlocutor's stronger language. This confirms the theory that children are much less prepared to "play games" with the person–language bond than are bilingual adults, who will speak the interlocutor's weaker language to give the person practice in that language. As McClure (1977) writes, younger children seem to rely on a binary judgment of linguistic competence—a person either knows a language well or does not know it at all; relative fluency is not really taken into consideration at that age.

In her study, McClure reports that children rarely chose the inappropriate language with a monolingual. She notes that when they first entered school, some Mexican American children addressed the teacher in Spanish, but within a month they stopped doing so. They then resorted to one of two strategies: silence and passivity, or the use of nonverbal communication devices. McClure adds that children appeared to respect one another's language preference. A child who was fluent in English but preferred Spanish was addressed far more frequently in the latter language than were children who preferred to use English. McClure also stresses the importance of the child's social role in language choice. When taking care of younger siblings, children invariably used Spanish, as did their parents. If a younger child got hurt, he or she would be comforted in Spanish, even though immediately prior to the incident the two were speaking English. And when children played school, they did so in English even though their usual language of communication was Spanish.

The setting or situation appears to play an important role in language choice. As we saw above, both Mario and Carla were aware of the language of the milieu and used it with interlocutors unless other factors intervened. In Mexico or Bolivia they used Spanish outside the home, and in the United States they used English. Thus, they were surprised to hear Spanish in a Mexican restaurant in Austin, Texas; English should have been spoken in that setting, according to them. It is interesting to note that the telephone, the radio, and the television were an extension of the setting for them; a Spanish program on the radio in Vermont caused much surprise, Fantini reports. McClure also found that setting was an important, although not the only, factor in the language choice of her Mexican-American children; Spanish was used with greater frequency in the home, but English was also heard there; English was the language of the school, but the children also used Spanish among themselves; and in the community park and the mobile home project, either language was appropriate.

Finally, Fantini reports that when Mario and Carla had a special purpose in mind, such as to amuse, surprise, or shock, their language choice was often "marked" by being the opposite of what they would have used ordinarily. Thus, to amuse their parents they would speak English and to tease their grandparents they would use Spanish. They also used their languages to include and exclude participants. Fantini relates how Mario was in the kitchen with his English-speaking grandmother and his mother, to whom he customarily spoke Spanish. He started to speak English but was told to switch to Spanish, as it was the language of the home. He protested, however, and said that he wanted his grandmother to hear what he had to say!

Thus bilingual children quickly develop a complex language decision system. It is first tuned to the interlocutor (the person–language bond) but soon takes into consideration the situation and the function of the interaction (also see Redlinger, 1978). Other factors, such as the topic of the interaction and the age, status, and occupation of the interlocutor, become important later. Neither Fantini nor McClure found evidence of their role in the language choice of the children they studied, as the latter were probably still too young.

Code-Switching

The alternate use of two languages in the same utterance or conversation begins early in bilingual children. However, it is different from adult code-switching in a number of ways, and recent research has started to isolate these differences. For example, McClure (1977) notes that the Mexican American children she observed produced different kinds of code-switches depending on their age. Young bilinguals tended to code-mix more, that is, to insert single items from one language into the other. These tended to be nouns and, to a lesser degree, adjectives, and to be English words in a Spanish utterance. On the other hand, bilingual children over the age of nine code-changed, that is, switched languages for at least a phrase or a sentence, as often as they code mixed. Code-mixing represented 87 percent of the young bilinguals' code-switches but 46 percent of the older bilinguals' switches; code-changes represented 13 percent and 54 percent of the switches, respectively. It is interesting to note that although code-mixing mainly involved English words in Spanish, code-changing occurred as often in one language as in the other. Box 4.5 gives an example of code-switching involving what McClure calls code-mixing.

McClure examined the different factors that led to code-switching and how these developed over time. She found, for example, that switches aimed at resolving ambiguities or clarifying statements were used by children as young as three years old. For instance:

> *Girl:* You[r] dog.
> *Investigator:* You dog? My woof?
> *Girl:* You[r] dog! *Tu perro* (You dog).

Another early reason for switching is to attract or retain attention. These switches have the same function as raising the voice, touching the person, or making eye contact. For instance:

> Yo me voy a bajar, Teresa (I'm getting down, Teresa). *Look.*

BOX 4.5   **BILINGUALS SPEAK**

Code-Switching by a Bilingual Child

Translated extract from a telephone conversation in Russian between a five-year-old Russian-English bilingual and his bilingual aunt. Switches into English are italicized.

Nephew: You know what we did in *kindergarten* yesterday?
  Aunt: No, what?
Nephew: We went down to the water and we saw—uh, how do you say it in Russian?
  Aunt: It's okay, Lexy, tell me in English.
Nephew: Well, we saw this *fish* and we got a *stick* and *pushed* it and it was alive!

Slightly later, at about age six, McClure found instances of switches related to mode shift: shifting from narration to commentary or from soliloquy to questioning, for example. It is only at age eight or nine that switches for emphasis occurred. The most frequent of these involved commands of the type:

Stay here Roli. *Te quedas aquí* (you stay here).

McClure reasons that this kind of switch comes later because younger children do not use commands as often as the older ones, who frequently look after their younger siblings. Other late-occurring switches are those used for elaboration, as in:

Roli you stay here. *Tú quédate 'jito con Suzy* (you stay with Suzy, honey).

and those involving focus, such as topicalization. This is used to indicate a person's ethnic membership, as in:

Este Ernesto (this Ernest), he's cheating.

Other researchers, such as Genishi (1976), have also found that switching to mark ethnicity and group membership appear quite late in the child's code-switching repertoire.

Genesee (1980a) examined children's perceptions of code-switching. He was interested in the social and psychological interpretations that bilingual children make when different languages are used in face-to-face interaction. Genesee constructed a series of dialogues between a salesman and a customer and had each one switch to the other's language in a variety of combinations. The scene took place in Quebec, and the languages were English and French. The children were asked to listen to these dialogues and then give their impressions of the speakers' personal traits and their reactions to the situation and the verbal exchange. The eleven-year-old subjects (the other group was composed of high school seniors) were aware of a number of variables. The first concerned role-related social norms: they downgraded the salesman when he did not use the customer's language, and they considered the English Canadian customer happier, more comfortable, and less insulted when he received a reply in English. The children were also aware of the interpersonal language accommodation. For example, the English customer who replied in the salesman's native language, French, was thought to respect him significantly more than did the customer who replied in English. However, unlike the high school students, the younger children did not react to group membership and sociocultural status. The high schoolers showed a strong ingroup bias: the French Canadians, for instance, rated the French Canadian salesman more positively than did the English Canadians, irrespective of the language that the salesman used. The eleven-year-olds, on the other hand, seemed to favor the speaker who used their native language and were not influenced by his group membership.

Code-switching, therefore, occurs early in children but at first is used mainly to express a word or an expression that is not immediately accessible in the other language. With time it is used as a verbal or communicative strategy and ultimately as a marker of group membership.

Playing with Language

Just as monolingual children play with their language by making words rhyme, inventing new words, or using certain words in inappropriate contexts, so will bilingual children play with their two languages. They will mix languages because they think it is funny and as a way of shocking certain adults who are opposed to any form of code-switching. They will also speak to a person in the wrong language. Fantini (1978), for example, relates how Mario and Carla would tease their grandparents by speaking to them in Spanish instead of in English and surprise and amuse their parents by addressing them in English. Another game is to take a word from one language, give it a case ending of the other, and say the two words together. Gentilhomme (1980) gives an example of this. The Russian root for "to spank" is "šlopát"; if it is borrowed into French and given an infinitive "er" ending, the result (šloper) is quite amusing. Another example given by Gentilhomme involves the adaptation of the French word "assiette" (plate) into a Russian sentence by giving it an accusative case marker:

Daj mne asjetu
(Give me a plate)

For Russian-French bilinguals, who are often told not to mix languages, this type of word borrowing creates much amusement. A Russian-English bilingual reports how she and her friends would mix whole sentences by taking English content words and adding Russian endings to them as a way of making fun of adults who spoke in this way.

Another game consists of translating an idiomatic expression word for word into the other language and using that literal translation with a straight face. Gentilhomme (1980) states that calling someone "my little cabbage" in Russian (a direct translation of the French "mon petit chou," better translated by "my little lamb") made the children laugh a lot. Finally, one can always speak a language with the pronunciation of the other as a way of making fun of people who cannot speak that language fluently despite having lived in the country for what seems to children, an eternity.

Education and the Bilingual Child

As was discussed in the first section of this chapter, most bilingual children, many of whom belong to linguistic minorities, acquire their second language at school. Unless the minority has its own schools or has access to schools where its language is used as a medium of instruction, its children will enter a majority language school and will become bilingual, to some extent at least. In Chapter 1 we saw that the question of education of minority groups is very complex. Depending on the political aims of the authorities (national or regional), some minority groups are able to have their children taught in their own language, while others are not (Ferguson, Houghton and Wells, 1977). If the government's aim is to unify the country, assimilate minorities, or spread the national language, more often than not minority languages will not find their place in education. However, if the aim is to preserve ethnic identities, give equal status to all languages, deepen understanding among cultures, revive certain languages, or even render more efficient the learning of foreign languages, there will be more linguistic diversity in the educational process. The picture becomes even more complex when national and regional policies are contradictory and when other factors are taken into account, such as the number and importance of the languages in the country, their geographic concentration, their linguistic development, the social and religious structure of the population, the attitudes of the majority and minority groups, and the availability of teachers and materials.

Mackey (1972a) proposes a complex typology of educational programs, ranging from monolingual education in the minority language through bilingual education in both languages to monolingual education in the majority language. For the sake of simplicity, however, I will limit this discussion to two types: those programs that lead to linguistic and cultural assimilation, in which bilingualism is definitely not a goal in itself, and those that lead to linguistic and cultural diversification, in which the aim is to make and to maintain the child bilingual and to some extent bicultural.

Education Leading to Linguistic and Cultural Assimilation

MONOLINGUAL EDUCATION   The simplest and most widespread approach to assimilation is quite simply not to differentiate between majority and minority children and to put the latter into what is for them a "foreign" language classroom from the very start. This approach, called the "submersion" or "sink or swim" method, characterizes many educational programs throughout the world. It is the antithesis of what the school should be: a place where the child is made welcome and feels secure, where learning can be a constructive experience, and where teachers are supportive and expect the child to succeed.

Numerous problems surround this approach. If the child does not understand or speak the language used in the school, this slows down the learning of skills and of content and makes the child feel left out. The feelings of solitude and insecurity are amplified even further if the child is put in a class where most of the children already know the school language. Various means are used to stop the child from speaking his or her native language in school: grades are lowered, physical punishment is inflicted, and friends are separated. Box 4.6 presents three extracts by adults who still remember the discrimination they suffered in schools where the medium of instruction did not correspond to their mother tongue. The teachers are often not trained—or simply do not wish—to deal with minority children. For instance, Spolsky (1978) reports that the great majority of teachers in Navajo schools are Anglos (only 3 percent were

---

BOX 4.6   **BILINGUALS SPEAK**

Discrimination in the Monolingual School

A French-Alsatian bilingual: When I was in primary school, it was forbidden to speak Alsatian, both in and out of class. Children were punished if they were caught speaking Alsatian, and errors in spoken French were always corrected by the teacher.

An Arabic-Hebrew-English trilingual: In my boarding school the nuns forced us [the Arab students] to speak French with one another, even when we were playing. We had a special necklace that every violator of the rule had to wear. Whoever wore it watched out for the next student who spoke Arabic and put it around the new violator's neck.

A French-English bilingual: Although most of the English teachers knew some French, they would make absolutely no use of it [to help me]. They argued that the "hard way" was the only way to learn. My older sister and I were in the same boarding school. Her knowledge of English was far better than mine, but she was not allowed to help me, and we were forbidden to communicate in French.

Navajo in 1969). They come from outside the reservation and live in school compounds guarded by fences. They rarely learn to speak Navajo and hence cannot communicate easily with parents, and they take little interest in the Navajo way of life.

This type of school often creates a culture clash in the child between the values, attitudes, and lifestyle of the majority group and those of the home community. Learning may be conceived in different ways in the two groups: Ohannessian (1972) notes, for instance, that the American culture stresses learning by doing, whereas the Navajo culture relies on prolonged observation or "prelearning." He adds that coercion, often used in the Anglo society, may result in bewilderment, disgust, fear, or withdrawal in the Navajo child. If the minority language and culture are stigmatized in the school, this also leads to much suffering, anger, or withdrawal. In Box 4.7, a Sephardic Jew recalls his experiences in an Arab school in Cairo.

As the minority child grows up, there is the great danger that he or she may become divorced from the native language and culture, especially if he or she has to enter a boarding school. Hobart and Brant (1966) relate how Eskimo children on the western Canadian Arctic coast are airlifted from their small communities "with their warm, kinship-based, interpersonal environments, to the large, effi-

---

BOX 4.7   **BILINGUALS SPEAK**

Prejudice in School

A Sephardic Jew, native speaker of Italian, attending an Arab school in Cairo just after the Egyptian revolution: My first days in this school were a nightmare and the shock was tremendous. I knew but very little of the language and could barely decipher it . . . Since the approach to Arabic was fallacious from the very beginning, due to the fact that I was forced to learn it against my will, I came to hate this language with all my strength . . . The fact that I was periodically forced to write political themes against my people, against my race, and against my values, or blaspheme aloud during frequent oral examinations, aroused my anger to its paroxysm. As outburst[s] of violence and open revolt were not permitted to me for obvious reasons, this only added to my isolation and alienation from my environment. (In Andersson and Boyer, 1978, p. 101)

---

ciency-oriented, understaffed, strange, impersonal surroundings of the residential school hostels" (p. 61). Not only does this create a trauma of separation in both children and parents, but with time the children develop a marked distaste for the difficult conditions at home and become disobedient, disrespectful, and reluctant to undertake chores when they return in the summer:

Thus residential school children experience completely different worlds in their home communities and in the residential school. About the only tie between the two is an airplane ride. In the two worlds, they speak different languages, wear different clothes, eat different foods, live in different facilities, have different associates, follow different schedules, experience different disciplines, enjoy different recreations. The parents of children from outlying regions know nothing of the children's life in the school, and the school personnel know almost nothing of life in the camps from which the children come. (pp. 63–64)

The Eskimo children slowly dissociate themselves from parents and kinsmen as they adopt different values and the attitude that everything Eskimo is of little worth. Parents are looked down upon for not being able to provide the modern luxuries that the children come across during their stay in the residential schools. The consequence of all this can be quite dramatic. As Hobart and Brant write:

Where the effort is one of cultural replacement, there is always the possibility that the product may "fall between the two stools," may be unfitted to return to the traditional life of his father, having experienced a softer, "better" way, but may not acquire the motivations and internalized disciplines which are presumed in contemporary wage employment. Most Arctic settlements have examples of this wastage, drifters who are unable to adapt to the loneliness or the employment conditions of the town, but who despise traditional employments and live parasitically off the sharing patterns of the community. (p. 64)

Of course, many minority children do not end up as outcasts, especially if they are maintained in daily contact with a well-structured and supportive minority group. However, many fall behind in their school work and drop out of school before graduation (25 percent of Navajo students never finish high school, for example). This is due in part to the language and culture gap, but also to the "self-fulfilling prophecy syndrome": teachers and administrators have low expectations for the minority children, who adopt these low expectations for themselves.

One variant of totally monolingual education is the addition of specialized second-language classes (English as a second language, for example), where the minority children are taught in a rather formal way the language used as the medium of instruction in the school. Although these classes can help the children learn the language, many are too formal and can be an additional stigma: the child is pulled out of the regular classroom to attend such classes, and this widens the differences between him or her and the other children. In Box 4.8 a Portuguese-English bilingual recalls some of the problems she experienced in one of these classes.

A second variant is to teach the minority language as a subject.

BOX 4.8   **BILINGUALS SPEAK**

Formal Teaching of the Majority Language

A Portuguese-English bilingual: When I first went to school on arrival in the United States, I was put into an English as a Second Language class. This was where all the non- and limited-English-speaking students ended up. We were at least twenty of varying languages and ages. The teacher spoke only in English. She communicated her instructions to the new arrivals through the students who already understood English. Each language group would end up sitting together to be able to get the teacher's instructions and explanation via the students who were able to interpret. I don't think I learned to speak English in that class; what I learned was on the street from the children I played with.

BOX 4.9   **BILINGUALS SPEAK**

Being Taught One's Mother Tongue All Over Again

A Sign-English bilingual: My sign language class was taught by a nonnative signer, and he knew many formal signs that I didn't know ... I showed him the signs that I knew in ASL and he said they were wrong signs because he didn't know them. It really destroyed my self-image in terms of sign language. I got to the point where I would apologize to everyone about my signing skills ... I didn't have a very good feeling about sign language until recently.

A French-English bilingual: High school was where I had my first taste of ethnic prejudice, my first awakening that the world wasn't simply French and English ... the Irish students often made fun of the Francos, the Italians, and the Polish, so we "ethnics" hung around together. The most bizarre awakening for me consisted of two elements which I'd never encountered: Franco-Americans who spoke absolutely no French, and "Parisian French" itself. I was made to feel as if I had to learn [French] all over again ... because my Franco-American French was viewed by my teachers as not worthy of being spoken. I therefore had to spend hours on end in the language lab "unlearning" the French that I'd spoken all my life.

Again this may be useful, but often the language teacher is a member of the majority who learned the formal variety of the minority language. Hence, the children are confronted by a person who often has strict norms about the "real" minority language (it should be Castilian Spanish, not Mexican-American Spanish; Parisian French, not Canadian French) and who downgrades the children's native language. Box 4.9 presents two extracts from bilinguals who remained marked for some time by such negative attitudes; only as adults have they regained pride in their variety of the minority language.

In conclusion, I must stress once again that educating the minority child in the majority language can have many problems. Admittedly, many children do make it through the system, but at what cost! They often lose their native language and culture in the process. Many turn their backs on their minority group (they have gone "up and out") and assimilate themselves into the majority, often becoming the strongest proponents of the argument, "I made it through, why can't you?" But many other children are left by the wayside: they have fallen behind in school, have failed to master the majority language well, feel insecure, and often have negative attitudes toward both the majority group that rejects them and the minority group they have been taught to look down upon. It is in this sense that monolingual education is too costly.

TRANSITIONAL BILINGUAL PROGRAMS Because of the problems cited above, the revival of ethnicity, and other sociopolitical factors (see Chapter 1), educators and legislators in many countries have turned toward bilingual education, a label that means different things in different countries. Mackey (1972) writes:

Schools in the United Kingdom where half the school subjects are taught in English are called bilingual schools. Schools in Canada in which all subjects are taught in English to French-Canadian children are called bilingual schools. Schools in the Soviet Union in which all the subjects except Russian are taught in English are bilingual schools, as are schools in which some of the subjects are taught in Georgian and the rest in Russian. Schools in the United States where English is taught as a second language are called bilingual schools, as are parochial schools and even weekend ethnic schools . . . [Thus] the concept of "bilingual school" has been used without qualification to cover such a wide range of uses of two languages in education. (p. 414)

In this section we will discuss those programs that use two languages—the child's and the normal school language—to ease transition into the mainstream program. In a sense, these programs want to avoid "sinking" by teaching the child to "swim." Some programs go further than others in that they make the child literate in both languages, but all are characterized by their transitional nature: they aim to prepare the child as quickly as possible to pursue studies in the majority language, and there is no attempt to maintain the child's native language or enhance the minority culture. Instead of reviewing different types of programs and examining which subjects are taught in each language, how long the minority language is used, how many teachers there are, how children are chosen for the program, we will simply visit a bilingual class in a large American city in the Northeast. This class differs in many details from other such classes in this and other countries, but the transitional nature of the program is the same in all such classes.

The primary school we are visiting, in a brick building built at the turn of the century, contains a number of mainstream classes as well as a few bilingual classes: Greek-English, Vietnamese-English, and Haitian Creole-English. This latter is the class we will visit. When one enters the classroom, one is struck by the color: posters and photos of Haiti are pinned up, a history corner displays photos of Haitian leaders, and there are children's drawings all along the walls. About twenty children attend this class, ranging from grade one all the way to grade eight. At the time of our visit, the younger ones are playing football in the courtyard, shouting at each other in Haitian Creole, while the older ones are in music class. John, the teacher, is American, but he learned Creole in Haiti, where he worked for two years, and he speaks it quite fluently. In fact, the children's parents were quite surprised by this, as Creole is the informal language in Haiti, and native Haitians expect foreigners to speak French, the formal language (see Chapter 1).

When children enter first grade or when they arrive from Haiti, they are put into the bilingual class, where they spend three years. In the first year they do 90 percent of their course work with John in the bilingual class. The rest of the time is spent in an English-as-a-second-language class where all the minority children are regrouped from their bilingual classes. In the second year, they spend only half the school day in John's class; the children go to mainstream classes in math, English, and social sciences. In the third year, the bilingual classroom time is reduced to 10 percent. John teaches the children to read and write French (as they would in Haiti) and gives them the kind of reading, writing, and dictation exercises they would have back home. The older children study literature from books that contain poems, short stories, and extracts from French Caribbean literature. John also teaches the history and geography of Haiti, using Haitian textbooks. Although the books are in French, and the children learn to read and write French, John speaks to them in Creole, as would happen in Haiti (see the discussion of diglossia in Chapter 3).

John stresses several aspects of the program's strictly transitional nature. He notes that the school authorities want the children transferred to mainstream programs as soon as possible, preferably before the fourth year. He mentions that the children do not maintain their reading and writing skills in the minority language once they are in the mainstream program and that they no longer learn about their culture and their people. And he states that many mainstream teachers are openly opposed to bilingual education; they consider it expensive and a delay in mainstreaming the child. John also adds that parents are not always in favor of sending their children to the bilingual program; many feel that the children should learn English as quickly as possible, and they fail to understand at first how the use of French, and especially Creole, in the program, will help their children. Recognizing that his class is a "springboard" into the

English monolingual classroom, John feels that it is better than what existed before. For a few years, at least, the children can be in a transitory haven before being "swallowed up" by the regular system.

Despite problems such as lack of adequate personnel and materials, inadequate conceptualization, lack of support from school boards, and lack of critical evaluation, most bilingual programs similar to the one we visited do seem to ease the transition into the mainstream program. They do not do away with future discrimination that the child will suffer from certain children and teachers, but for awhile at least, the child is surrounded by others like him or her, is taught in the native language (which helps enhance the status of the language), learns English in an atmosphere that is not hostile, and above all, receives support and aid from the teacher.

To conclude, I will repeat that both the immediate submersion and slow integration approaches lead to linguistic and cultural assimilation. The children may remain bilingual and may even become bicultural if the minority has sufficient "force" to retain them (monolinguals in the community with whom to speak the language; social, religious, and educational organizations to help enculturate them), but many will either be totally assimilated into the dominant culture or feel estranged from both the majority and the minority groups. As Ray Castro writes in Box 3.1 (Chapter 3): "My capacity to use Spanish had dwindled to nothing. Identification with the dominant culture was no longer possible, but recreating my group sense seemed equally impossible without the help of Spanish, the language of my Chicano culture. I felt alone and lonely." It is cases such as these that mark the failure of assimilatory education.

Education Leading to Linguistic and Cultural Diversification

If a society wants to preserve ethnic identities, give equal status to all languages and cultures in the country, revive a language, teach a foreign language more efficiently, or make its citizens bilingual and bicultural, it will often develop educational programs that employ two languages and are based on two cultures. These programs also fall under the label of bilingual education, but they differ in many ways from transitional programs. Below we will discuss two such approaches: maintenance programs and immersion programs.

MAINTENANCE PROGRAMS These programs try to develop and maintain the minority child's cultural heritage as he or she is introduced to the majority culture and help the child become functionally bilingual in the two languages. They provide a linguistic and cultural continuity between the minority and the dominant group and prepare the child to live in a multilingual-multicultural society.

An example of this approach comes from Greenland. Hobart and Brant (1966) compare the education of Eskimos in the Canadian Arctic to those in Greenland. The Canadian Eskimo children are literally submerged in a totally different language and culture, and as a consequence, many become alienated from both the Eskimo culture and the white South Canadian culture. Eskimo children in Greenland, on the other hand, are taught to read and write in both Greenlandic and Danish; they study both Greenlandic and Western European geography, history, literature, art, and music; vocational training includes both modern industrial skills and traditional Greenlandic skills (such as kayak building and sealskin sewing); instruction takes place in both Danish and Greenlandic, and many of their teachers are Greenlandic themselves. The purpose of this education is to help people make their living where they are rather than force them to leave the region in search of a job. Hobart and Brant report that there are a few cottage-hostel residential schools for advanced grades, but the life there is thoroughly Greenlandic: the food is local, the discipline follows that of Eskimo parents, Greenlandic is the medium of communication, and the parents themselves are not far away. All this results in maintenance of group self-esteem and valuation of the traditional culture. As the authors write, Danes and things Danish are not accepted wholesale, mechanically, slavishly. Although a number of problems do exist in Greenlandic education—the high turnover rate of Danish teachers, the reduced prestige of the Greenlandic teacher, and increasingly Western qualifications for teachers of Eskimo background—Hobart and Brant conclude that education in Greenland seeks to make available to the student two identities, Greenlandic and Danish, and that it is doing so successfully.

Recently, in the United States a few maintenance programs have been established in the Native American and Hispanic communities. Pfeiffer (1975) reports that the bilingual/bicultural program at Rough Rock Demonstration School in northeastern Arizona was founded with two major premises in mind. First, the Navajo children should be educated to maintain their identity while learning to master the Anglo language and culture, so as to take their place in the Anglo world, if they desire; and second, the school should be administered by the Navajo people themselves. The program is thus bilingual and bicultural, and the children are brought up to respect their family, religion, societal rules, and protocol. A similar program is in effect at the Pine Hill Schools in the Ramah Navajo Reservation in northwestern New Mexico (Hale, 1978). Two objectives were set for the schools: to involve the community in the education of its children and to retain and reinforce Navajo cultural values, beliefs, and traditions. To meet these objectives, parents are involved in teaching children about Navajo traditions, culture, and arts and crafts, such as rug weaving, sandpainting, beading, and pottery. Also, science lessons explore Navajo beliefs and traditions, and math lessons include the Navajo method of counting and measurement; Navajo history, law, government, religion, economics, and the Navajo language are also taught. Programs such as these are making these children both bilingual and bicultural, members of their own community but also of the American nation. This is done by accepting both languages and cultures and by recognizing that one can be bilingual and bicultural without endangering the entity of the larger nation.

IMMERSION PROGRAMS   Another type of bilingual education has been referred to as the immersion approach. Children from a particular language and cultural background are first taught in a second language and then, little by little, their first language is introduced as a second medium of instruction. Although at first sight immersion programs resemble the monolingual submersion programs examined above, they differ on a number of important points (Ervin-Tripp, 1970). In the immersion program the children usually belong to the prestigious and dominant group; their home language is respected; all other children in the classroom are from the same language background; their parents are supportive of the program, and teachers have high expectations for the children's achievement. And finally, the mother tongue is brought in as a second medium of instruction during the course of the program.

The immersion programs in Canada are especially well known, although this type of education has existed for a long time. In the mid-1960s some English Canadian parents in St. Lambert, Quebec, realized that as members of a minority in a French-speaking majority, their children should become bilingual in English and French. They were dissatisfied with the traditional manner of teaching second languages in school, so they proposed that their children acquire French in a more natural manner, that is, as the language of teaching and interaction in the school. From this was born the St. Lambert project, which was monitored by psychologists and educators from McGill University (Lambert, Tucker, and others). The students, all English Canadian, were taught completely in French by a French teacher in kindergarten and grade one. In kindergarten they were allowed to speak English with one another, but in first grade this was discouraged. The teachers never spoke English to them or with one another, so as to create, as far as possible, a totally French-speaking environment. Starting in grade one the children were taught to read and write in French and were also taught math in that language. In grade two they started having English language classes for about an hour a day, but the rest of the program was in French. In the following grades, more English was brought in, so that by grade six a bit more than half of the teaching was in English.

The outcome of this approach has received much praise from those involved (Lambert and Tucker, 1972) and from others (McLaughlin, 1978, for instance). By grade six the children were in no way behind control groups in English skills and in content subjects (they had transferred their math concepts and reading skills from French to English), their level of intelligence was equivalent to that of the controls, and their knowledge of French was far better than that of other English Canadians their own age. Lambert (1980) summarizes the results of this and other projects:

The immersion pupils are taken along by *monolingual* teachers to a level of functional bilingualism that could not be duplicated in any other fashion short of living and being schooled in a foreign setting. Furthermore, pupils arrive at that level of competence without detriment to home language skill development, without falling behind in the all-important content subjects of education (the immersion experience does not take time from basic educational learning), without any form of mental confusion or loss of normal cognitive growth, and without a loss of identity or appreciation for their own ethnicity. (p. 2)

The success of the St. Lambert project led other schools throughout Canada and a few schools in the United States to employ the immersion approach. Variants were instituted, such as late immersion programs, starting in Grade seven, and partial programs, with one language as the medium of instruction in the morning and the other in the afternoon. Genesee (1978–79) reviews the results obtained from the various Canadian programs and reiterates that English language development, although slowed at first, is not affected by immersion education; below-average students are not handicapped by the approach; the acquisition of content is not impaired, and competence in the second language (in this case, French) is far better than is usually achieved by students in second-language courses.

One question that remains unanswered, according to Genesee, is: Are the language skills of the Canadian immersion program students adequate for interaction with their fellow French Canadians? Connors, Ménard, and Singh (1978) evaluated the functional competence of immersion students in French and reported that in free conversation the students had great difficulties interacting with French Canadians. They claim that the French tests (vocabulary tests, for example) used to measure linguistic competence in the program have very little to do with spontaneous give and take in real life. Most immersion students, after all, are English Canadians, and their life outside the school takes place in English. They do not have the French Canadian social and cultural contacts necessary to develop functional competence in the language. Even Genesee (1980) reports that although immersion students do use French outside the school when they have to (in stores, restaurants, and so on), they do not initiate conversations in French. One can also add that they probably do not interact much with French Canadians their own age. In a word, immersion education has given students the foundations to become bilingual, but because there is little systematic social use of French, they are not functionally bilingual.

When compared to bilingual education programs in the United States, immersion programs have always come away with flying colors. However, aside from the very different populations involved, the variables compared are just not the same. As Macnamara (1974) writes concerning California bilingual education programs and the St. Lambert project:

On looking more closely we find that what most depresses the Californian educators is the lasting difficulties which Chicano students have with English. What has most encouraged the Montreal educators is that the St. Lambert children have not harmed their English in learning French. These results are not comparable. The St. Lambert children have certainly learned a lot of French . . . but they are decidedly inferior to native speakers of French in all aspects of French. What we do not know is how the French of the St. Lambert children compared with the English of the Chicanos and the extent to which the differences are due to the programmes. (p. 96)

No simple conclusion can be proposed for this section on education and the bilingual child. We have seen that children often become bilingual in school, but more often than not, the educational system is not interested in maintaining this asset. Its principal aim is to "normalize" the child, to make him or her a member of the majority group. There may be some encouragement, however, in the recently developed forms of bilingual education leading to long-lasting bilingualism and biculturalism, including the immersion programs. Lambert (1980) writes:

To the extent that mainstream children are sensitized to and educated in another language and culture, the better the chances are of developing a fairer, more equitable society. The better too are the chances of improving the self-views of ethnolinguistic minority children who are heartened and complimented when they realize that mainstream children are making sincere gestures to learn about them, their ways of life, and their language. (pp. 2–3)

The Effects of Bilingualism on the Child

There has been, and still is, much debate among researchers and educators on the effects of bilingualism on the child. Some maintain that bilingualism has negative effects on language development, educational attainment, cognitive growth, and intelligence. Others argue that it has positive effects and that the child is not only ahead in school but has greater cognitive flexibility and creativity. I will attempt to summarize these positions and then explain why the results are so contradictory.

Apparent Negative Effects

Until recently, many researchers concurred with the famous linguist Otto Jespersen, who wrote in 1922:

It is, of course, an advantage for a child to be familiar with two languages: but without doubt the advantage may be, and generally is, purchased too dear. First of all the child in question hardly learns either of the two languages as perfectly as he would have done if he had limited himself to one. It may seem, on the surface, as if he talked just like a native, but he does not really command the fine points of the language . . . Secondly, the brain effort required to master two languages instead of one certainly diminishes the child's power of learning other things which might and ought to be learnt. (p. 148)

On the level of language development, observers found many problems, such as restricted vocabularies, limited grammatical structures, unusual word order, errors in morphology, hesitations, stuttering, and so on. For instance, in a vocabulary test administered by Tireman (1955), Spanish-English bilinguals were found to have mastered only 54 percent of the words supposed to be in their reading vocabulary. And in an English reading test administered in three Arizona schools, Kelley (1936) found that bilinguals had a handicap of 2.7 years. Observers in schools also noted that bilingual children showed a lack of interest and initiative, that they failed to adjust, and that they fell behind when compared to monolingual children. For instance, Macnamara (1966) tested Irish primary school children whose home language was English and whose school language was Irish, and found that they were eleven months behind monolingual children in problem arithmetic.

On the level of intelligence and cognitive development, numerous studies found bilingualism to be a handicap. Saer (1923), for example, found that Welsh-English bilingual children in rural areas had lower IQ scores than monolingual children, and this inferiority became greater with each year from age seven to age eleven. Darcy (1946) found that the mental ages of monolingual English-speaking children surpassed those of bilingual Italian-American children. And Jones and Stewart (1951) found that monolingual English children outperformed bilingual Welsh-English children in both verbal and nonverbal intelligence tests. Thus the great majority of studies done before 1960 found that bilingualism had a negative effect on the child's linguistic, cognitive, and educational development; only a few showed no effect or a positive effect.

Apparent Positive Effects

More recently, researchers have found that bilingualism is, after all, a great asset to the child. They note that the bilingual child has a better awareness of language differences and is better at learning new languages, and they report that in school he or she is more motivated and often ahead of other classmates. Especially in intelligence and cognitive growth, researchers stress the assets of bilingualism. In 1962 Peal and Lambert conducted a study that had great impact on the field. They took ten-year-old children from six French Canadian schools in Montreal and compared the French-English bilinguals to the French monolinguals on a battery of tests. The bilinguals scored higher both on verbal and nonverbal IQ tests. Subtests showed that bilinguals had a more diversified structure of intelligence and more flexibility in thought: greater cognitive flexibility, greater creativity, and greater divergent thought. In addition, bilinguals were ahead in content work at school, and their attitudes toward English Canadians were more favorable than those of their monolingual French counterparts. The authors conclude: "It is not possible to state from the present study whether the more intelligent child became bilingual or whether bilingualism aided his intellectual development, but there is no question about the fact that he is superior intellectually" (p. 20).

Another study that received much publicity was conducted by Ianco-Worrall (1972), who wished to investigate further Leopold's finding that for Hildegard the link between a phonetic word and its meaning was noticeably loose. Hildegard could tell a story quite easily in either German or English at a very early age; she accepted new names for objects in the other language. Ianco-Worrall therefore set about to test the notion that bilinguals separate word sounds from word meaning earlier than monolingual children. She used two groups of children—one bilingual in English and Afrikaans, and one monolingual—and involved them in a series of small experiments.

In the first, she told her subjects: "I have three words: cap, can, and hat. Which is more like cap, can or hat?" If the children chose "can," it indicated a phonetic preference; if they chose "hat" it indicated a semantic preference. In her younger group of subjects, more bilinguals chose the semantic response than did the monolinguals, and from this she concluded that bilinguals reach a stage in semantic development two or three years earlier than their monolingual peers.

In a second task, she said to her subjects, "Suppose you were making up names for things, could you then call a cow 'dog' and a dog 'cow'?" Again she found that bilinguals differed from the monolinguals. The majority of bilinguals answered "yes," whereas only a small minority of monolinguals did so.

This study has been followed by many others of the same kind. For example, Ben Zeev (1977) asked Hebrew-English bilinguals and monolingual English and Hebrew children the following question: "You know that in English this is named 'airplane.' In this game, its name is 'turtle.' Can the 'turtle' fly? How does the 'turtle' fly? [etc.]" She found, like Ianco-Worrall, that the bilingual children answered "yes" more often than did monolinguals, and she reasoned that this was because the link between the word and its meaning was less strong in bilinguals than in monolinguals. That is, bilinguals realize sooner the arbitrary nature of language. To test the divergent thinking capacity of bilinguals and monolinguals, Scott (1973) told his subjects to think of an object (a paper clip, for example) and then tell him all the things one could do with it. He found that bilinguals had substantially higher scores than monolinguals.

Swain and Cummins (1979) review most of the recent studies that show the positive effects of bilingualism. Among other things, these studies conclude that bilinguals are more sensitive to semantic relations between words, are more advanced in understanding the arbitrary assignment of names to referents, are better able to treat sentence structure analytically, are better at restructuring a perceptual situation, have greater social sensitivity and greater ability to react more flexibly to cognitive feedback, are better at rule discovery tasks, and have more divergent thinking. Lambert (1977) summarizes this research:

There is, then, an impressive array of evidence accumulating that argues plainly against the common sense notion that becoming bilingual, that is, having two strings to one's bow or two linguistic systems within one's brain, naturally divides a person's cognitive resources and reduces his efficiency of thought. Instead, one can now put forth a very persuasive argument that there is a definite cognitive advantage for bilingual over monolingual children in the domain of cognitive flexibility. (p. 30)

No Effects?

In the last few years, researchers have attempted to understand the reasons behind the overwhelming number of negative studies that appeared before 1960 and the majority of positive studies that have come out since then. Certain negative findings linked to language deficiencies have been accounted for quite straightforwardly by researchers like McLaughlin (1978), who writes: "It may be that the chief cause of the early difficulty for many children—especially children from minority ethnic groups—is not so much bilingualism per se as the fact that they are forced to learn a second language in the school" (p. 173). He adds that when children have equal exposure to the two languages, there is no evidence that they are behind in language skills. Skutnabb-Kangas and Toukomaa (1976) propose that there is a direct relationship between a child's competence in a first language and competence in a second. If the first language is poorly developed because, for instance, it is a minority language and there is not enough linguistic input from the environment (books, television, community), then exposure to a second language may well impede the continued development of skills in the first. And in turn, the poor development of skills in the first language will exert a limiting effect on the development of the second language, and hence lead to "semilingualism." This developmental interdependence hypothesis has led researchers to propose that linguistic minority children be given a good grounding in reading and writing in the first language before being introduced to a second. If this is done, bilingualism will not result in any negative effects.

Concerning educational attainment, McLaughlin (1978) argues that the critical factor is command of the second language. If the child has not yet mastered the language well and is tested on some content subject in that language, poor performance is predicted. "As the child's command [of the second language] improves, so will academic performance in subjects taught in that language" (p. 178). He also adds that before coming to any rapid conclusion, one should consider, for minority children, such factors as poor home environment, the parents' low socioeconomic status, negative attitudes of the majority group, conflicts in culture, and so on. When these factors are added to poor command of the second language, then progress in the majority language school may well be hindered.

The debate on the positive or negative effects of bilingualism has centered in recent times on the child's cognitive development. The early IQ studies were rife with problems and with factors unaccounted for: often they did not control for sex and age; they did not indicate how they chose their bilingual subjects (some did so on the basis of name); they did not control the socioeconomic background of the subjects; the tests they used were not adapted to the linguistic minority in question; and the studies did not control for the subjects' educational opportunities. It is no wonder that negative effects were found. As Lambert (1977) writes: "In general, the researchers in the early period expected to find all sorts of problems, and they usually did: bilingual children, relative to monolinguals, were behind in school, retarded in measured intelligence, and socially adrift. One trouble with most of the early studies was that little care was taken to check out the essentials before comparing monolingual and bilingual subjects" (p. 27).

More recent studies have taken greater care to control factors such as age, degree of bilingualism, and socioeconomic status, but some still fail to define what they are measuring (the dependent variable) and how their monolingual and bilingual subjects differ in educational background. In fact, one of the biggest problems with this kind of study is matching monolingual to bilingual groups. MacNab (1979) feels that they are usually matched on too few factors and that these are often the wrong ones. He gives the example of two families: one that sends its child to an immersion program and one that does not choose to do so. Even though their socioeconomic status is the same, and the children are the same age and sex, the fact that one family chooses an immersion program while the other does not may be of utmost importance: the former family may be more open to different cultures, more willing to try new experiences. Or maybe the child of the second family is "slower," and the family prefers to keep him or her in a regular program. MacNab writes: "In no case have children been randomly assigned to the groups *before* the bilingual training began and in no case have the subjects been tested *before* beginning the treatment" (p. 232, italics added).

A study that approaches this ideal situation was conducted by Barik and Swain (1976). They tested both immersion students and regular program students with the Otis-Lennon Mental Ability Test at regular intervals over a five-year period (they did not test them before they first went to school, however). When they adjusted scores for age and IQ at the beginning of the programs, they did not find any reliable difference between the two groups and they concluded: "These findings do not support the general trend of studies by other investigators who have found positive effects of bilingualism on cognitive growth" (p. 259).

Even the choice of a measure of bilingualism has come under attack. Early studies were not very careful in choosing their bilinguals, but later studies may have been too careful. MacNab (1979) reminds us that Peal and Lambert (1962) had a very strict criterion: their subjects had to be balanced bilinguals, as determined by four tests: word association, word embeddedness, word comprehension in the second language (English), and a self-rating of the four language skills. Subjects had to be equally good in the two languages to be chosen for the bilingual group. Thus, out of a population of 364 ten-year-olds, only 89 were considered balanced bilinguals, and 75 were classified as monolinguals.

As MacNab writes, over half of the otherwise eligible subjects were defined as neither bilingual nor monolingual. Based on this, he believes that the balanced bilinguals were probably more intelligent from the start and that the "rejects" or the monolinguals contained a greater proportion of duller children. He asks: "Will children who are 'slow' tend to be equally slow in the two languages or will they tend to 'specialize' in one, to concentrate their energy on one language and learn only as much of the other as necessary?" (p. 238). He believes that the latter possibility is more likely and concludes that Peal and Lambert obtained the positive results they did because their bilingual students were brighter from the onset.

Other problems arise when comparing the positive and the negative studies. As Swain and Cummins (1979) report, the positive findings are usually associated with majority language groups in immersion programs, where there is a high value attached to knowing two languages, where the second language is added to the first at no cost to the first, and where the parents are of relatively high socioeconomic status. (This situation corresponds to Lambert's additive form of bilingualism.) Negative findings, on the other hand, are found with submersion students who are surrounded by negative attitudes, who are forced to learn the majority language and are not encouraged to retain their first language, and who do not live in a social environment that induces learning (a subtractive form of bilingualism, according to Lambert). It is probably these psychosocial differences—and not bilingualism as such—that account for many of the contradictory results in the literature. Cummins (1978, 1980) proposes a "threshold hypothesis" to explain the apparently contradictory results of the many cognitive studies undertaken on bilingual children. He writes:

There may be threshold levels of linguistic proficiency which bilingual children must attain both in order to avoid cognitive deficits and allow the potentially beneficial aspects of becoming bilingual to influence cognitive growth. The threshold hypothesis assumes that those aspects of bilingualism which might positively influence cognitive growth are unlikely to come into effect until the child has attained a certain minimum or threshold level of proficiency in the second language. Similarly, if bilingual children attain only a very low level of proficiency in one or both of their languages, their interaction with the environment through these languages, both in terms of input and output, is likely to be impoverished. (1980, pp. 6–7)

Only further research will show whether the threshold hypothesis is correct.

At this point it is probably safer to propose that bilingualism as such has no major effect—either positive or negative—on the cognitive and intellectual development of children in general. As a student asked me one day: if half the world's population is bilingual and if many of these become bilingual as children, is it really true that they are different—brighter or duller, more creative or less so, more flexible cognitively or less so—from the other half who are monolingual? An increasing number of observers are of the opinion that bilingualism has no major effect—either positive or negative—on the development of children. McLaughlin (1978) summarizes this position very clearly:

In short, almost no general statements are warranted by research on the effects of bilingualism. It has not been demonstrated that bilingualism has positive or negative consequences for intelligence, linguistic skills, educational attainment, emotional adjustment, or cognitive functioning. In almost every case, the findings of research are either contradicted by other research or can be questioned on methodological grounds. The one statement that is supported by research findings is that command of a second language makes a difference if a child is tested in that language—a not very surprising finding. (p. 206)

5 The Bilingual Person

In 1928, Dr. Mieczyslaw Minkowski of Zurich, Switzerland, published a short paper entitled "Sur un cas d'aphasie chez un polyglotte" (The case of a multilingual aphasic). In it he described the recovery of languages in a trilingual patient of his who had become aphasic, that is, lost his ability to speak, after an apoplectic stroke. The case created quite a stir among linguists and neurologists at the time, and I will use it to introduce the subject of this chapter. Minkowski's patient was from the canton of Glarus in the German part of Switzerland. His mother tongue was Swiss German, a variety of German that is used for informal everyday purposes, and his second language was formal German, the variety learned at school and used for reading and writing and in business, education, and local government (see the discussion of diglossia in Chapter 3). He also learned a little French in school and spoke it from time to time with his father, who knew it well. At the age of nineteen, the man went to France, where he worked as a cook and waiter for six years. During his stay, French became his everyday means of communication and he quickly became fluent in it. When he was twenty-five, he returned to Switzerland, worked as a railroad conductor and then as a trader. He married a childhood friend from Glarus and they settled in Zurich. They had two children. Like other Swiss German families, they spoke Swiss German at home and with friends and acquaintances, and used standard German for more formal activities. The man no longer had the opportunity to speak French (his wife did not speak it) except when they went to the French part of Switzerland on vacation.

At the age of forty-four, nineteen years after his return from France, the man had an apoplectic stroke with loss of consciousness for several hours. On recovery, it was found that he was aphasic: he recovered comprehension of his three languages within a day or two, but his speech was altered more severely. Minkowski (1928, 1963) relates what happened when he did start to speak:

> The patient began to speak again two or three days after the fit, but to everyone's surprise he spoke in the beginning only French, first stammering out [a] few words, then successively more and more correctly. His wife did not understand him, and his children with their poor school French acted as translators between their parents. (p. 130)

His French improved quite quickly, and then he began to recover his second language, German, in which he made slow but increasing progress. As for Swiss German it did not reappear until four months after the stroke. Six months after the injury, his best language was still French; German was improving quite rapidly, but he spoke Swiss German in a very hesitant manner still. A few weeks later, during the Christmas vacation, another change took place. His Swiss German suddenly became almost fluent, as did his German, but his French started to regress. This continued, and in time he could no longer relate in French what he had just read in a French paper; he had to resort to Swiss German and German.

Minkowski uses psychosocial factors to explain the restitution of languages in the reverse order in which they were learned and most used. On questioning, the patient reported that the most beautiful years of his life had been those spent in France. His greatest love had been a French woman with whom he had lived in France for some time. After his return to Switzerland, he had remained a strong francophile, and his preferred language was French, even though he did not have occasion to use it much.

Minkowski's case study, which retains its fascination half a century later, serves as a useful introduction to the present chapter. In the first section I explain why the description of a person's bilingualism can be extremely complex. Minkowski's patient learned his three languages at different times during his life, his fluency in each was unequal, and he used two of them—Swiss German and German—for very different purposes. For six years of his life,

French was his most important language, but then it reverted to a more passive and occasional role. Also, he did not read and write the three languages equally well (Swiss German at that time was rarely written), and his attitude toward each was not the same: he loved French more than his other languages.

In the second section we will examine the psycholinguistics of bilingualism: the perception, production, and storage of languages. Did Minkowski's patient have three different internal dictionaries (lexicons) or only one? How did he keep his languages independent of one another when speaking to monolinguals, and how did he integrate them when code-switching with bilinguals? Did switching from one language to another slow him down in his perception and production of language? And how did his language processing differ from that of a monolingual?

In the third section, we will explore the bilingual brain by reviewing studies of bilingual aphasics as well as experimental studies that ask whether language is organized similarly in the monolingual brain and the bilingual brain. I will dwell on two aspects of this question: first, the recovery patterns in bilingual aphasics and the factors that account for normal parallel recovery but also for the rarer cases such as Minkowski's, and second, whether bilinguals use the right hemisphere of the brain to a greater extent than monolinguals in processing language.

In the last section we will discuss such topics as the bilingual's feelings about being bilingual, mental activities (thinking, dreaming, counting) as well as personality: does the bilingual change personality when changing language or does he or she quite simply adjust to the social environment which calls for a different language and a different behavior? We will also see that the bilingual rarely questions his or her bilingualism, and that it rarely interferes with everyday activities. The chapter ends with a quick survey of well-known people or were or are bilingual.

Describing a Person's Bilingualism

By adopting a functional definition of bilingualism (the regular use of two languages) I have avoided up to this point the very complex question of describing a person's bilingualism. Researchers in the area have proposed a variety of definitions of bilingualism, and lay people also have rather precise ideas about the subject. Fluency in two languages has often been proposed as the main criterion, and psycholinguists have used ingenious methods to test this. However, I will argue below that far too much weight has been put on fluency, to the detriment of other factors such as the regular use of two languages, their domains of use, and the bilingual's need to have certain skills (reading and writing, for instance) in one language but not in the other. A linguistic description of the bilingual that takes into account such factors is more complex than a simple index of fluency, but it is also more valid.

Fluency in Two Languages

To uncover the lay person's understanding of the term "bilingual," I asked a number of monolingual college students to answer this question: "If someone told you that X was bilingual in English and French, what would you understand by that?" The most frequent response (36 percent) was that X speaks both languages fluently, followed by X speaks English and French (21 percent), and by X understands and speaks English and French (18 percent). The same question asked of a group of bilinguals gave very similar results: speaking the two languages was the most frequent response (46 percent), followed by speaking the two languages fluently (31 percent).

Both groups were then asked to rate the importance of a number of factors that have been mentioned in definitions of bilingualism, such as using two languages on a regular basis, being fluent in two languages, belonging to two cultures, passing as a monolingual in two languages, and having both speaking and writing fluency in two languages. The ratings of these factors confirmed the answers to the open-ended question. The monolinguals gave a mean rating of 4.7 for "fluent in two languages" (1 was not important and 5 very important), and the bilinguals gave it a rating of 4.4. Speaking and writing fluency in two languages was given a rating of 4.0 by the monolinguals and 3.6 by bilinguals, and equal fluency in two languages was rated 3.7 and 4.1 by the two groups, respectively. Thus, both monolinguals and bilinguals feel that fluency in two languages is the most important factor in describing the bilingual person.

The importance of fluency is reflected in the definitions proposed by a number of linguists. Bloomfield (1933) writes:

In the extreme case of foreign language learning, the speaker becomes so proficient as to be indistinguishable from the native speakers round him ... In the cases where this perfect foreign-language learning is not accompanied by loss of the native language, it results in *bilingualism, [the] native-like control of two languages*. (pp. 55–56, italics added)

Thiery (1978), who studied the language background of international conference interpreters, writes:

A true bilingual is someone who is taken to be one of themselves by the members of two different linguistic communities, at roughly the same social and cultural level. (p. 146)

Bilinguals that fit the Bloomfield and Thiery definitions do exist, of course, but they are usually considered as rather special specimens by the people around them. A person will say, "X is perfectly bilingual," and they may add the wish that they too were bilingual. Thiery states that most of the "true" bilinguals he studied had learned their two languages before the age of fourteen, had spoken both languages at home, had moved from one language community to another during their school years, and had thus been taught in both languages. What is striking is that these bilinguals have no accent in either language, they are equally fluent in all skills in the two languages, and when talking to monolinguals they show absolutely no interference from another language.

Of course, if one were to count as bilingual only those people who pass as monolinguals in each language, one would be left with no label for the vast majority of people who use both languages regularly but do not have native-like fluency in each: they are not monolingual and yet, according to the definitions we have seen, they are not bilingual either! This paradox has led researchers to propose more realistic definitions. Haugen (1969), for instance, prefers to view fluency as a continuum:

Bilingualism ... may be of all degrees of accomplishment, but it is understood here to begin at the point where the speaker of one language can produce *complete, meaningful utterances* in the other language. From here it may proceed through all possible gradations up to the kind of skill that enables a person to pass as a native in more than one linguistic environment. (pp. 6, 7)

Macnamara (1967a) concurs with this notion of a continuum and adds that one should consider each of the four basic language skills: speaking, listening, reading, and writing. For him, a bilingual is a person who possesses at least one language skill even to a minimal degree in a second language, for example, a native speaker of Swahili who speaks English but who never learned to read and write it.

The notion of a fluency continuum in each language (and in each of the four skills) has led quite naturally to the measurement of bilingualism. Psychologists, especially, have been interested in isolating "balanced" bilinguals (those equally fluent in two languages) from "nonbalanced" bilinguals (those more fluent or dominant in one language). They tried using standard tests of language proficiency but often found, according to Macnamara (1969), that the tests did not apply to the language group under consideration (a Parisian French language test in Quebec, for instance), that they were unsuited to people with near-native command of the language, and that they did not evaluate the various styles of a language. Thus researchers developed more indirect tests that would be easy to administer and would reflect the person's degree of bilingualism.

Macnamara (1967a, 1969) groups these various tests into four categories: rating scales, fluency tests, flexibility tests, and dominance tests. The first set includes language background questionnaires, language usage rating scales, experimenter interviews, and self-rating scales. In self-rating, the bilingual rates his or her fluency on the four basic skills in each language. A balance score is then computed by subtracting the values of one language from those of the other. If the difference is zero or close to zero, the bilingual is considered to be equally fluent in the two languages. Self-ratings have repeatedly been reported to be highly related to independent assessments of language skills (by exterior judges) and to more direct tests of language proficiency.

In the category of fluency tests, one finds tasks like picture naming, word completion, oral reading, and following instructions. For example, Lambert (1955) developed a task in which subjects have to respond to instructions in each language. They put their fingers on a keyboard that has keys of different colors and are instructed in one language or the other to press specific keys. Their response time is used as an indication of whether they are balanced bilinguals or dominant in one language. Lambert writes: "The findings indicate that the differences between speeds of reaction in the two languages decrease as experience with a second language increases . . . If one were a perfect bilingual—equally facile in both languages—there should be no difference between the speeds of response in the two languages" (p. 198).

In the third group of tests are tasks in which bilinguals are asked for synonyms, associations, and word-frequency estimations in their two languages. Lambert, Havelka, and Gardner (1959), for instance, asked their subjects to identify as many English and French words as possible from the nonsense word *dansonodent*. If the person could detect as many English words (son, dent, on, ode, node) as French words (dans, son, de, on, dent) in a given time, he or she was considered to be a balanced bilingual.

In the fourth group, dominance tests, the bilingual is confronted with an ambiguous stimulus that could belong to either language and asked to pronounce or interpret it. The language most frequently used is the dominant one.

It is important to note that for all these types of tests, a balanced bilingual is one who does equally well in both languages. According to Lambert, Havelka, and Gardner (1959): "The closer an individual approaches bilingual balance, the more he will be able to perceive and read words in both languages with similar speeds, to associate in both languages with similar fluency, to make active use of his vocabularies in both languages, and to be set to verbalize in both languages" (p. 81).

Many researchers have accepted this assumption and have therefore used various combinations of these tests to screen their bilingual subjects: To choose the bilingual children for their well-known intelligence study (see preceding chapter), Peal and Lambert (1962) used a word association test, a word detection test, a vocabulary test, and a subjective self-rating. And Cummins and Gulutsan (1974) used a word association test, a self-rating, and a teacher rating of fluency to choose bilingual subjects for their cognitive development study.

This approach, however, has come under increasing attack on a number of grounds. First, Jakobovits (1969) and others have questioned whether it is valid to measure fluency by taking the difference between two language scores, especially in tests involving speed of response. Sociocultural factors may lead a subject to answer more slowly in one language than in the other; this would be reflected in the "balance score," and the subject would not be considered equally fluent, even if he or she is. A second and perhaps more important objection is that these laboratory tests just do not take into account the different domains in which the languages are used. As we saw in Chapter 3, language use depends on a number of psychosocial factors, such as situation, participant, and topic, and the bilingual rarely needs to use the two languages for similar purposes. This will affect, of course, any kind of test measuring fluency. Cooper (1971), for instance, found that Spanish-English bilinguals had had very different scores on word naming tasks depending on whether the domain proposed was family, neighborhood, school, or religion. In some domains they would have been considered balanced bilinguals, but in others they would not. Malherbe (1969) expresses his feelings about the measurement of bilingualism:

It is doubtful whether bilingualism *per se* can be measured apart from the situation in which it is to *function* in the social context in which a particular individual operates linguistically. The only practical line of approach ... is to assess bilingualism *in terms of certain social and occupational demands of a practical nature* in a particular society. Here again the criterion is to be "bilingualism for what." *Purpose and function* are the main determinants. (p. 50)

Most bilinguals use their languages for different purposes and in different situations, and hence "balanced" bilinguals, those who are equally fluent in both languages, are probably the exception and not the norm. A bilingual develops the four basic skills in each language (speaking, listening, reading, and writing) to the levels required by the environment, and it is rare that an identical level is needed for each skill. Thus, Minkowski's patient would probably not have been considered a "balanced" or "equally fluent" bilingual in a laboratory situation, as he had developed different skills in each of his three languages. But his language characteristics before his stroke were very similar to those of many other bilinguals.

In a survey of thirty bilinguals from eight different countries and involving thirteen language pairs (such as Portuguese-English, Japanese-English, Urdu-English, Farsi-English, American Sign Language–English), I found only seven (23 percent) who estimated that they were equally fluent in all four skills in both languages. Almost half felt they were equally fluent in speaking and listening but only eight (27 percent) felt they were equal in reading and writing. These percentages would probably have been even lower if the population surveyed was not college educated. As Fishman (1971) writes:

From the point of view of sociolinguistics any society that produces functionally balanced bilinguals (that is, bilinguals who use both their languages equally and equally well in all contexts) must soon cease to be bilingual because no society needs two languages for one and the same set of functions. (p. 560)

Thus, even though fluency in two languages may be the lay person's main criterion of bilingualism, it has been adopted by few researchers in their definitions of the phenomenon. Most have preferred to put the stress on the bilingual's *use* of two languages. Both Weinreich (1968) and Mackey (1968) define bilingualism as the alternate use of two (or more) languages, and in this book I have constantly stressed when and how a bilingual uses his or her languages, not fluency in these languages.

It is interesting to note that in my survey of lay persons, monolinguals differed most from bilinguals on the very question of language use. For monolinguals, the factor labeled "regular use of two languages" received a mean rating of 3 (that is, it was not considered an important factor); the bilinguals gave it a mean rating of 4.1, just below "fluency in two languages" (4.4). In the end, fluency in each of the four basic skills in the two languages is determined primarily by language use, and in turn, language use is determined by need. If a particular skill is not needed, it will not be developed or, if it has already been acquired, it will wither away.

The Complexity of a Person's Bilingualism

William Mackey (1968, 1976) has proposed a complex schema for the description of a person's bilingualism. First, he proposes that one determine the person's degree of bilingualism by testing for comprehension and expression in both the oral and written forms of each language. As we have just seen, a bilingual—a scholar or scientist, for example—may have reading and writing abilities in a language but not be able to speak and understand it; another may comprehend a language but not be able to speak, read, or write it. This "receptive bilingualism" characterizes many children of immigrant parents vis-à-vis the minority language as well as people who speak one of two related languages. Wald (1974) reports that speakers of the Miji Kenda languages in East Africa claim they can understand each others' languages but generally cannot speak them. They report using their own language with those who speak one of the other languages. A similar phenomenon takes place with speakers of Urdu and Hindi, and Danish and Norwegian (Haugen, 1966). Mackey also proposes that the bilingual's various linguistic levels (phonological/graphic, grammatical, lexical, semantic, and stylistic) be ascertained in each language. For instance, the bilingual may have a very strong accent in a language and yet behave like a native speaker at all other levels. (Joseph Conrad's mastery of spoken English was superlative, but he spoke it with a strong Polish accent.)

Second, Mackey (1968) suggests ascertaining the function of each language. He writes: "The degree of proficiency in each language depends on its function, that is, on the uses to which the bilingual puts the language and the conditions under which he has used it. These may be external or internal" (p. 557). The external functions are determined by the areas where the bilingual is in contact with the language and by the duration, frequency, and pressure of the contact. Thus, one will have to note the language used in the home, in the community, at school, at church, at work, in correspondence, and in the media. Mackey's internal functions include internal speech (counting, praying, cursing, dreaming) as well as the person's aptitude for learning and using a language, which, according to Mackey, is determined by sex, age, intelligence, memory, language attitude, and motivation.

Third, Mackey proposes that one describe the bilingual's ability to alternate between languages, the extent to which this is done, and the conditions under which it takes place. Finally, the description should consider interference (the use of features belonging to one language while speaking or writing another). Mackey would want to answer the following questions: How well does the bilingual keep his or her languages apart? To what extent does he or she fuse them? How does each language influence the use of the other?

To a description of the bilingual at a particular point in time, one may want to add some information concerning the person's language history, as this will often explain language use, attitudes, and fluency. The factors that lead to bilingualism are often important in this respect: some people learn two languages in the home and can speak both fluently, but they may be able to read and write in only one, others learn and use the second language in school and may have better reading and writing than speaking abilities. Immigrant workers usually pick up their second language at work and may never learn to read and write it, whereas diplomats and international businessmen are often required to be highly literate in both languages. This is also the case of the second-language teacher, except that he or she may have little use for the language outside the school. Immigration, marriage, education, trade, and commerce ensure the development of certain language skills but rarely all of them equally.

With time, the bilingual's level of fluency in each language skill reflects the need for that skill in that language. In Box 5.1, an English-French bilingual explains how moving to a different country about every ten years affected his fluency. He used both languages in all three countries, but after awhile the country's language became his stronger one, and his writing and even his speaking skills in the other language were affected.

Some people actually stop using one of their languages, either because of a conscious decision (as some German Jews stopped using German when they emigrated to the United States before World War II, and some Russian Jews drop their Russian when they emigrate to Israel) or because exterior events have made the language

---

BOX 5.1   BILINGUALS SPEAK

Changing Language Dominance

My first language was French, and it remained my only language until the age of eight. At that point I was put into an English school and I quickly learned to speak English. For the next ten years I lived in an English environment and became as fluent in the language as any native speaker. I even won a prize for my studies in English literature. I only had a few occasions to speak French, and thus my vocabulary was restricted, although I spoke the language without an accent. However, my writing skills in French were those of an English school boy. Although considered bilingual by my surroundings, I was really much more dominant in English.

At age eighteen, I left my English school and went to college in France and lived in that country for ten years. My French slowly overtook my English, first in speaking ability and then in writing skills, so that at the end of that period I was clearly dominant in French. I no longer spoke English very much (only with a few English friends), and I started making mistakes in my writing. French was now my dominant language in all four basic skills.

But one more change in dominance was to take place. At age twenty-eight I came to the United States, and after a few years here I feel that English, once again, is the stronger of the two languages. My English vocabulary has expanded dramatically, and I feel at ease when writing it. I still speak French every day, but I no longer write it, and when I have to write a letter to my relatives back home, I find myself hesitating and making mistakes I would never have made some years back. Thus, although bilingual since the age of eight, I have already changed language dominance three times.

---

unnecessary (the person moves, parents and relatives live far away or pass away). In this case, language forgetting occurs, a phenomenon that has received little attention and yet is probably as frequent as language learning in adults. Some of its characteristics are: language production becomes hesitant as the person searches for the appropriate words or expressions; code-switching is extensive, and the person borrows whole expressions from the dominant language, often without being aware of it; pronunciation is affected at the level of intonation and stress and also at the level of individual consonants; and writing skills suffer considerably unless the person maintains them. It is interesting that language comprehension suffers much less; apart from new terminology and new colloquialisms that the person may not know, he or she usually has no problems retaining a good understanding of the spoken language. Language forgetting is a slow process, but the person is usually quite aware of the change and may even apologize when talking to a native speaker. It is as if society allowed one to learn a language but not to forget it!

People undergoing this process can be termed "dormant bilinguals" in the sense that one of their languages is no longer used regularly. Galloway (1978a) presents a fine example of a person who had learned and used seven languages in his lifetime, although five had become more or less dormant. This person's native language was Hungarian, but at the age of four he moved to Poland, where he learned Polish and seemed to have forgotten Hungarian. When he was six he returned to Hungary, relearned Hungarian, and remained there until age ten, when he moved to Rumania. He lived in a multilingual town and learned Rumanian, which he used in school and with friends, and Yiddish, which he used socially. At age twelve he returned to Hungary, and Hungarian became once again his dominant language. In school he also learned German, English, and Hebrew. After a year in an Austrian concentration camp, where German was the dominant language, he spent six years in Germany, where he went to college: German was now his main language. Finally, at age twenty-five he left for the United States, where English became his preferred and primary language. Although his wife is Hungarian, the predominant language in the home is English. Thus, this heptalingual has two active languages, English and Hungarian, and five more or less dormant languages: German, Hebrew, Yiddish, Rumanian, and Polish, the latter two practically forgotten.

In the end, the description of a person's bilingualism may well have to be as complete as the one proposed by Mackey (1976) for a French-English Canadian bilingual. JRB was born in Gaspésie, Quebec, in 1900, and then moved to Moncton, New Brunswick, with his family. He used both English and French in his everyday life; through interviews and questionnaires, Mackey managed to estimate the amount of time JRB spent using each language up to age sixty-five. Mackey breaks his description down into the four basic skills of the two languages and the people who interacted with JRB: father, mother, siblings, grandparents, wife, children, friends, acquaintances, clients, neighbors, storekeepers, colleagues. The resulting description in number of hours per day, week, month, and year using either English or French is quite impressive and gives one a good idea of the complexity of bilingualism in JRB's life.

Describing a person's bilingualism is thus a difficult enterprise, which one should be careful not to simplify by using one or two tests of language fluency. The bilingual's language history and domains of language use are just as important as the fluency factor.

The Psycholinguistics of Bilingualism

In this section we will review some studies that have examined the bilingual's production, perception, and memorization of language. Many of these studies have emphasized the independence or dependence of the bilingual's languages—how does the bilingual keep the two languages separate? does the bilingual have one or two internal lexicons?—to the detriment of other questions such as: How does the bilingual process language as it is being heard? How does this differ from the monolingual's processing in terms of word recognition and parsing? Is a code-switched sentence processed any differently from a sentence in only one language? I will describe the research that has been done in the last twenty years and show how it has evolved toward the questions asked by current psycholinguistics.

The Coordinate-Compound-Subordinate Distinction

If there is one domain of research that has led to much debate, numerous experiments, and contradictory results, it is certainly that of the coordinate-compound-subordinate distinction. In his classic book *Languages in Contact,* which first appeared in 1953, Weinreich (1968) proposed in a rather theoretical way that there might be three types of bilingualism. In Type A, the coordinative type, the words of the two languages are kept totally separate, in that each word has its own very specific meaning. Thus the word "book" has its own meaning and the Russian equivalent "kniga" has its own, different meaning. In Type B, the compound type, the bilingual knows the words "book" and "kniga" but has one common meaning for both; that is, each word conjures up the same reality. In Type C, the subordinative type, the bilingual interprets words of the weaker language through the words of the stronger language. Thus, for example, if Russian is the bilingual's weaker or newly learned language, the word "kniga" may well evoke the word "book," which in turn refers to the meaning the person has for that word. In other words, the coordinate bilingual has two sets of meaning units and two modes of expression; the compound bilingual has one set of meaning units and two modes of expression, and the subordinate bilingual has the meaning units of the first language and two modes of expression: that of the first language and that of the second, learned by means of the first.

This rather theoretical distinction captured the interest of some psychologists, who adopted and modified it. Ervin and Osgood (1954) fused Weinreich's types B and C, which they termed compound, and put the emphasis on how the bilingual became either coordinate or compound. According to them, coordinate bilingualism is developed through experience in different contexts where the two languages are rarely interchanged (one language at home and the other at school, for example), and compound bilingualism is developed through experience in fused contexts, such as formal language learning in school or continual switching from one language to the other. Thus, from Weinreich's rather theoretical linguistic three-part distinction, a two-part distinction was proposed that was defined by learning and use. Also the stress was put on the lexicon, whereas Weinreich's distinction involved all aspects of language, including phonology, lexicon, and syntax.

Empirical evidence for this modified version was first obtained by Lambert, Havelka, and Crosby (1958). They reasoned that separate contexts of language acquisition would enhance the functional separation of the bilingual's two languages, while experience in fused contexts would reduce functional separation. To test their hypothesis, they isolated two groups of bilinguals. They chose as coordinate bilinguals those who had acquired their languages in separate contexts (one at home, the other outside the home), those who used different languages with their two parents, and those who had acquired their languages in distinct national or cultural settings. For their compound bilingual group, they chose subjects who used both languages indiscriminately with both parents, those who used both languages interchangeably inside and outside the home, and those who had learned the second language at school through vocabulary drills and translation. One of the tasks they asked of their subjects was to give the connotative meaning of a number of words; the subjects were given ten "semantic differential" scales (fast–slow, pleasant–unpleasant, good–bad) and told to indicate where each word fell along these scales. The authors expected that the coordinate bilinguals would show comparatively greater semantic differences between translation equivalents ("house" and "maison," "poor" and "pauvre") than would the compound bilinguals, as the former supposedly had different meanings for each member of the pair, whereas the latter did not.

The results showed that compound bilinguals differed in the expected way from coordinate bilinguals *only* when the latter had learned their two languages in different cultural settings. Interestingly, there was no difference between compound bilinguals and those coordinate bilinguals who had learned the two languages in the same cultural setting, as in the case of one language at home and the other outside, or one language with the father and the other with the mother. A second experiment, using translation equivalents, showed the expected difference between coordinate and compound bilinguals—all types of coordinate bilinguals differed from compound bilinguals—and Lambert, Havelka, and Crosby concluded their study with this claim: "The theory of coordinate and compound language systems has been given empirical support and the defining characteristics of these systems have been extended" (p. 243).

This conclusion was strengthened a few years later when Jakobovits and Lambert (1961) showed that a satiation task affected coordinate and compound bilinguals differently. If a subject is asked to repeat a word over and over again, the continuous repetition of the word decreases (or satiates) the connotative meaning given to the word on the semantic differential scales. The authors used this approach with bilinguals and expected that compound bilinguals who were satiated with a word in one language (house, for instance) would reflect this satiation effect when asked to rate its translation equivalent (maison). Coordinate bilinguals should show no cross-language satiation, as each word (house/maison) has a different meaning. The results they obtained confirmed this expectation: compound bilinguals showed cross-language satiation, that is, their semantic differential scales values were affected, whereas those of the coordinate bilinguals were not.

However, while some research was showing possible psychological evidence for Ervin and Osgood's coordinate-compound distinction, other research was showing negative evidence. Olton (1960), for instance, asked subjects to read a series of English and French words and to remember which words were accompanied by a small electric shock. Subjects were quick to learn that by quickly pressing a key after such a word, they could avoid the shock. Once these associations had been established, the subjects were given a new list of words, some of which were translations of the critical words. Olton's hypothesis was that compound bilinguals would press the key for the translation equivalents more quickly than coordinate bilinguals, since the former have the same meaning for both words. However, no difference was found between compound and coordinate bilinguals. Nor was a difference found in a word recognition task run by the same experimenter (Olton, 1960). Moreover, Kolers (1963) and Lambert and Moore (1966) undertook some word association studies of compound bilinguals and found considerable differences in the associational networks of the two languages, differences that would not exist if the meaning systems of the two languages were identical.

These contradictory results led researchers to reassess their hypotheses, and from its high point in the 1950s and early 1960s, the coordinate-compound distinction has now fallen into disfavor, at least among linguists and psycholinguists. Not only was the experimental evidence ambivalent, but the experiments themselves were criticized. Macnamara (1967a) writes: "Every study . . . deals with isolated words . . . yet no evidence derived from such materials is likely to describe adequately so complicated a process as the relating of language and meaning" (p. 66). To this I should add that many experiments, such as the ones using the semantic differential scales, did not in fact measure denotative meaning—the only aspect of meaning that Weinreich actually mentioned. As Segalowitz (1977) states, the denotative aspect of meaning is not amenable to semantic differential analysis. In addition, the choice of subjects for the experiments was questioned. In the original study by Lambert, Havelka, and Crosby (1958), for example, bilinguals who spoke a different language to each parent were put into the coordinate category along with subjects who had acquired their two languages in different cultural settings. But surely the father who says to his daughter "Donne-moi du pain" is referring to the same object as the mother who says "Give me some bread." In this case, the bilingual has one referent for two words—an instance of compound bilingualism.

On purely linguistic grounds, the problems with the distinction are numerous. Can there be a totally coordinate bilingual? As López (1977) points out, some words in the bilingual's two vocabularies have identical meanings, others have quite similar meanings, and still others have different meanings. Even totally different cultures have words that refer to similar concepts. If this were not the case, translating between languages would be well-nigh impossible. When one compares two languages, one invariably finds words that have overlapping meanings, as in the case of "rice" and Spanish "arroz." According to López, both are grains and both are white before cooking, but "rice" also has the attributes of boiled, bland, and served with roast beef and gravy, whereas "arroz" has the attributes of orangeish after cooking, spicy, fried, served with frijoles and tortillas. Some words share a great many attributes (table and Spanish mesa, for instance), whereas others, according to López, share relatively few attributes (mother and madre). Thus, it is probably the case that a bilingual can never be totally coordinate or totally compound, a point made by Weinreich himself.

Not only is a person's type of bilingualism a matter of degree, more coordinate in some domains and more compound in others, but within a bilingual's life there may be shifts along this continuum. As Macnamara (1970) writes: "The manner in which a person has learned his languages is unlikely to fix his semantic systems for life. Some may start with fused semantic systems but gradually sort them out; others may start out with separate systems but gradually permit them to merge" (p. 30). Diller (1970) and Paradis (1977) mention other problems with the distinction, such as the confounding of Weinreich's compound and subordinate types and the fact that Weinreich did not want to restrict his distinction to the semantic level; he felt that it could apply to other levels, such as phonology and syntax.

The consequence of misunderstanding Weinreich's original typology and modifying it to fit the context of language acquisition has had quite a dramatic impact in applied fields. López (1977) reports that Saville and Troike's *Handbook of Bilingual Education* (1971) states that the compound bilingual formulates his thoughts first in one language (usually his native language) and then goes through a high-speed translation process into the second language! He adds that in another publication, psychologists are said to be in agreement that the coordinate bilingual is probably less confused using two languages than is the compound bilingual! And some teachers have been overheard to say that bilingualism is confusing because one has to translate from one language into another! It is a pity that such a badly understood theoretical distinction with little evidence—a "vague and abstract" theory, according to Lambert (1978) himself—has survived for so long in the literature and has been used by educators to account for the bilingualism of their children. Some researchers (Lambert, 1978; Genesee, et al., 1978) have proposed replacing it with the early–late bilingual distinction, but there is as yet no strong evidence that bilinguals who acquire their second language in early childhood produce, perceive, or store it any differently from those who learn it as adolescents or as adults.

One or Two Lexicons?

A question that has received considerable attention from researchers in the last twenty years relates to the bilingual's internal dictionary or lexicon. It is well known that monolinguals have a rather extensive lexicon with "entries" for individual words. Each entry contains information about the word: its various meanings, syntactic class (noun or verb, for instance), pronunciation, orthography (if the language is written), and the constraints that control its use. But do bilinguals have two lexicons or one? More than sixty research papers have addressed this topic, and investigators are far from unanimous.

Proponents of the one-lexicon view (also referred to as language-independent storage, shared storage, interdependent storage, and common storage) state that linguistic information is stored in a single semantic system. Words from both languages are organized in one large lexicon, but each word is "tagged" to indicate the language it belongs to. Other researchers have claimed that bilinguals have two lexicons (also called independent storage or language-specific storage), and the information acquired in one language is available in the other only through a translation process.

The evidence that has been collected over the years for each of the hypotheses is quite impressive. For instance, in favor of the one-lexicon proposal, Kolers (1966a) showed that in recalling lists of unrelated words, subjects are influenced by the frequency of presentation of a word *even when* it is presented in the other language. If subjects are given a long list of words containing three random occurrences of the English word "fold" and an equal number of its French translation "pli," their recall increases linearly with the frequency of occurrence of the *meaning* of "pli" and "fold." That is, presenting each of the two words three times produces the same effect on the recall of either word as presenting either one six times. Clearly, this must indicate some kind of common lexical storage. Caramazza and Brones (1980) have come to the same conclusion with a different task. Spanish-English bilinguals were presented with words referring to semantic categories (furniture, for instance) and were then given instances of these categories (chair, table, sofa) as well as words that had nothing to do with the categories. Their task was to indicate as quickly as possible whether the word was a member of the category or not. Subjects were given instances of a category in both Spanish (silla) and English (chair). The authors found that the response time did not differ when the instance of the category was presented in the language of the category word or in the other language. They concluded from this that bilinguals have a single semantic representation for their two languages.

However, many studies have defended the two-lexicon hypothesis. For instance, Taylor (1971) asked English-French bilinguals to write down as many associations as they could to a given word in a given time. Some subjects were asked to give their responses in only one language, others were free to switch languages. Thus, for the word "roi" (king), a subject might write down: "reine" (queen), "palais" (palace), "kingdom," "England," "prince," and so on. Taylor found that although subjects switched quite freely, they preferred to stay within one language when giving their associations. That is, the intralanguage association links were stronger than the interlanguage links. She concluded that the words tend to be organized separately, in two separate lexicons. Tulving and Colotla (1970) also found evidence for a two-store hypothesis when they presented lists of words to trilingual subjects and asked them to recall the words verbatim. The lists were of varying lengths (twelve, eighteen, and twenty-four words) and contained words from one, two, or three languages. They found that subjects were better at recalling words from unilingual lists than from bilingual lists and better with bilingual lists than with trilingual lists. They concluded that this probably reflected the trilingual's separate storage of the three languages: the organization of lists of words into higher-order memory units is probably more difficult between different languages than within a single language.

What is interesting is that some other studies have found results that confirm neither hypothesis. For instance, Kolers (1963, 1968) asked bilinguals to give word associations to a number of stimulus words in a monolingual list (the task used by Taylor), and found that about one-fifth of the responses were the same in the subject's two languages; for instance, in English, "table" was associated with "chair," and likewise, in Spanish "mesa" (table) was associated with "silla" (chair). Kolers reasoned that this proportion was too large to support the separate-lexicon hypothesis. However, he also found that about one-quarter of the responses were specific to one language, and this led him to reject the single-store hypothesis.

Kolers' predicament is a good reflection of the general picture one gets from the many studies that have examined the bilingual's lexical organization. Paradis (1978), Kolers and Gonzalez (1980), and others have pointed out a number of problems underlying these studies. Researchers have confounded the basic question of one versus two lexicons with the task used to examine the question. Some have claimed that the way subjects perform on the recall of isolated word lists can tell us how the internal lexicon is organized (Cofer, 1965; Dalrymple-Alford and Aamiry, 1969). One assumption is that the organization of the best-recalled lists reflects the organization of the lexicon. A second assumption is that the way subjects reorganize lists during recall reflects the internal lexicon. Both assumptions have been criticized, however: short-term recall of random lists of words may tell us about the recall of word lists, but probably not about the way the lexicon is organized. To this we can add that different tasks tap different aspects and levels of the language system and thus give results that may appear to be ambivalent. Subjects concentrate on the form and the language of the words in some tasks (short-term recall of lists of words) and on the semantic characteristics of the word in other tasks (category-instance judgments and long-term memory tasks).

I should also add that the types of bilinguals involved in this research have rarely been described in detail. Even though I expressed reservations about the coordinate-compound-subordinate distinction, it is nevertheless true that bilinguals who learned their two languages in the same cultural setting will probably perform differently in certain word-related tasks than bilinguals who learned their two languages in very distinct settings. Finally, most studies of lexical storage in bilinguals, according to Paradis (1978), fail to make a distinction between a conceptual memory store independent of language (and hence of languages), and a linguistically constrained semantic store (or stores, for bilinguals). Evidence for this dichotomy comes in part from cases of aphasic disorders. Lecours and Joanette (1980), for instance, report on an interesting case of aphasia: the patient suffered from bouts of epileptic seizure during which he became totally aphasic but retained his general cognitive abilities, reflected by the fact that he could get off the train at the right station, register in a hotel, order a meal by pointing, and so on. Thus his conceptual store remained unimpaired, but his linguistic store was totally impaired, or at the very least, inaccessible. A similar phenomenon occurs with other aphasics.

Paradis (1978, 1980a, b) rejects the one-store hypothesis and proposes a model of the bilingual's lexical organization that explains many of the divergent results obtained by researchers:

To the extent that a bilingual speaks both languages like a native he cannot possess one single basic internal dictionary where words in both languages are pooled . . . Each aspect of a word is bound to be stored separately from the corresponding aspect in the other language, and only to the extent that the meanings of these words are connected to a sufficient number of the same non-linguistic conceptual features (that is, refer to similar mental representations) can they be considered equivalent. (1980b, p. 197)

In fact, Paradis proposes a three-store hypothesis. One store, corresponding to the bilingual's experiential and conceptual information, contains mental representations of things and events, properties, qualities, and functions of objects: in a word, what is known about the world. Then the bilingual has a language store for each of his two languages, each of which is differentially connected to the conceptual store. In the language stores the bilingual's conceptual features are grouped into units of meaning which can be said as words or expressions. Paradis writes:

Units of meaning in each language group together conceptual features in different ways. Thus the English unit of meaning "ball" is connected with conceptual features such as "spheric," "bouncy," "play," etc. ... The French unit of meaning that corresponds to "balle" shares these features, but it is also connected to "small." If it is too large to hold in one hand, it is no longer "une balle," but becomes "un ballon," a distinction which is irrelevant in English. A big ball is still a ball. Some units of meaning such as ball/balle share most of their features. Others share only a few. (1978, p. 2)

Thus the bilingual has one conceptual store that is differentially organized depending on which language is used to verbalize an idea, feeling, or experience. This explains why some words and expressions are difficult to translate into another language: they probably share few conceptual features, whereas other words and their translation equivalents share many features.

With this model, Paradis can account for some of the contradictory results obtained in the research literature. The greater the number of features shared by a word and its translation equivalent, the more they will tend to evoke the same response (one will be recalled for the other, one will be associated with the other). Studies using such words have led researchers to propose a one-lexicon hypothesis. But the more words diverge from one another in number of shared conceptual features, the greater the difference in response, leading other investigators to propose a two-lexicon hypothesis. Paradis also states that certain tests will access the conceptual store, thus leading to similar results for both languages, whereas other tasks will access only the linguistic stores, and hence give different results for each language. Although Paradis' model needs experimental validation, it is nonetheless an elegant and constructive way of resolving the rather complex problem of whether the bilingual has one or two lexicons.

Separation and Interaction of Languages

Psychologists, neurologists, and linguists have long been interested in the bilingual's ability to keep the two languages separate. As Macnamara (1967a) writes: "One of the most remarkable aspects of bilingual performance—so obvious in fact that it has scarcely been mentioned in the literature—is the bilingual's ability to keep his languages from getting mixed up. Many bilinguals know the entire phonological and syntactic systems of two languages and many thousand words in each, yet they manage to function in each language with very little interference from the other" (p. 66). Lambert (1972), who is also interested in the bilingual's ability to keep the two languages separate, asks: "How is it that the bilingual is able to 'gate out' or, in some fashion, set aside a whole integrated linguistic system while functioning with a second one, and a moment later, if the situation calls for it, switch the process, activating the previously inactive system and setting aside the previously active one?" (p. 300) These researchers and others set about to uncover the underlying psycholinguistic mechanism that allows the bilingual to speak either one language or the other and not a haphazard mixture. Their premise was that bilinguals usually keep their languages separate and that some special mechanism must allow them to switch from one language to another.

Penfield (1959), a well-known Canadian neurologist, proposed that bilinguals have an "effective automatic switch that allows each individual to turn from one language to another." This switching system would control which language was "on" and which language was "off" at any time. Psycholinguists were quick to point out that a one-switch model might not be adequate, because bilinguals can speak one language and listen to someone speaking another language. Thus the production system must be dissociated from the perception system, and a more complex switching model should be proposed.

This led Macnamara (1967a) to develop a model with both an output switch and an input switch. The output switch is under the speaker's control; he or she decides which language to speak and operates the switch consciously. The only time the speaker is not in conscious control is when overlearned or automatic sequences are involved, such as counting, swearing, or praying. In these cases the bilingual may use the other language without actually being aware of doing so.

Unlike the output switch, the input switch is automatic, controlled by the language signal coming in. If the language heard is French, the switch will automatically turn to French, and if the language is English it will switch over to English. This "data driven" aspect of the switch was proposed because bilinguals cannot ignore the language that is spoken to them, even though they may wish to do so. Experimental evidence for this comes from the bilingual stroop test, which has been used by a number of researchers (Preston and Lambert, 1969; Hamers and Lambert, 1972, among others). In this task, bilinguals are presented with color words printed in a color that sometimes does not correspond to the referent of the color word. For instance, the word "brown" might be printed in red, or the word "blue" in green. In the monolingual version of the task, the subject has to name the color that the word is printed in. It has been found repeatedly that the subject cannot gate out the color information given by the word itself and is thus slowed down and makes errors when the word and the color of the ink do not match, as when the word "green" is printed in red, and the subject has to say "red." The bilingual version of the test is similar except that sometimes the color must be named in the language of the word and sometimes in the other language. If the bilingual did have control over the input switch, it should be easier to gate out the written word when it is presented in the language that is not the response language (the word "green" printed in blue, which requires the French response "bleu," for instance). However, researchers have repeatedly found that bilinguals just cannot gate out the other language, and the interference is the same when the test word and the response are of the same or of different languages.

These results, among others, led Macnamara to propose an input switch that is under the control of the data and that operates as soon as it has received enough information. The bilingual makes a preliminary analysis of the signal by what Macnamara calls a "pre-attentive process," which indicates the language that should be switched on. One final aspect of the two-switch model is that each switch operates sequentially and independently of the other.

Researchers have also examined whether switching from one language to another takes time. Kolers (1966b) asked French-English bilinguals to read passages of varying linguistic makeup. Some passages were monolingual in English or French, others alternated languages, from sentence to sentence, and others had mixed sentences. Here the mixture of English and French was haphazard, with half the passages favoring the English word order and the other half the French order. For example:

His horse, followed *de deux bassets, faisait la terre résonner* (by two hounds, made the earth resound) under its even tread. *Des gouttes de verglas* (drops of ice) stuck to his *manteau* (coat). *Une violente bise* (a strong wind) was blowing. One side *de l'horizon* (of the horizon) lighted up and *dans la blancheur* (in the whiteness) of the early morning light, *il aperçut* (he saw) rabbits hopping at the *bord de leurs terriers* (edge of their burrows). (Kolers, 1966b, p. 359)

When asked to read these passages aloud and to answer questions testing their comprehension, subjects performed equally well on all three types of texts, showing that mixed passages were understood as well as monolingual passages. But when subjects were asked to read the texts aloud, the type of passage had a strong effect. For example, the French-dominant bilinguals read the monolingual French texts in an average time of 30 seconds, the alternating-sentence texts in 36 seconds, and the mixed texts in 45 seconds. Kolers computed that when subjects switched languages in oral reading, each switch took them between 0.3 and 0.5 second. He concluded that code-switching is inhibitory for production but irrelevant to comprehension.

Macnamara and his colleagues were interested in uncoupling the input switch time from the output switch time. They reasoned that in oral reading of a mixed text, both switches actually operate: the input switch is involved in the perception of mixed text, and the output switch is used to produce that text. Macnamara, Krauthammer, and Bolgar (1968) studied the output switch independently of the input switch by asking bilinguals to read numerals in one language or another. Numerals are linguistically neutral stimuli, and thus reading them in one or the other language only involves the output switch. They found that when bilinguals were forced to switch from one language to the other when reading a list of numerals aloud, it took them 0.2 second on the average, about half the global switching time found by Kolers. The authors conclude that language switching takes an observable amount of time, but that this is not usually reflected in natural discourse because the bilingual anticipates a switch before actually changing languages.

A few years later Macnamara and Kushnir (1971) studied the input switch by itself. First, they asked bilingual subjects to read Kolers' passages *silently* and measured the time it took. The subjects read mixed passages more slowly than monolingual passages, and the researchers computed that each switch took about 0.17 second (Kolers had found a switch time of 0.3 to 0.5 second but subjects were reading out loud and hence both the input and output switch had been involved). Second, they presented unilingual and mixed sentences to subjects and asked them whether their content was true or false. Examples of these sentences are:

A monkey can drink *eau* (water).
Turnips *sont* (are) vegetables.
Many cats *ont* (have) four *jambes* (legs).

The first sentence has one switch, the second two, and the third three. The authors found that as the number of switches increased, the reaction time to indicate whether the sentences were true or false also increased. Language switching took about 0.2 second. When added to the 0.2 second for the output switch, the resultant global switch time of 0.4 second corresponded well with the 0.3–0.5 second range proposed by Kolers (1966b). Macnamara and Kushnir conclude from these data that switching from one language to another—either as a listener or as a speaker—takes time, because switching runs counter to psychological "inertia." The bilingual's customary behavior is to stay within one language, and any deviation from this will take additional effort and time. They write: "We have certain expectations for strings of words and one such expectation is that all the words should be in a single language" (p. 485).

The code-switching results and the underlying assumptions on which they are based have come under increasing attack in recent years. Bilinguals speaking to other bilinguals often switch from one language to another, both between and within sentences (see Chapters 3 and 6), and in some situations code-switching is the norm, not the exception. Could switching really delay the processing of language, when its very purpose in everyday life is precisely to ease the communication flow between bilinguals? Researchers have scrutinized the experimental studies undertaken by Kolers and Macnamara and have criticized their choice of subjects, the tasks they used, and especially the setting of the experiments and the materials involved. As we saw in Chapter 3, code-switching takes place when bilinguals are together and switching is considered acceptable. It can be questioned whether such a situation existed in a laboratory environment where the subjects were dealing with a monolingual experimenter and were listening to artificial stimuli.

The second major criticism concerns the materials used by Kolers and Macnamara and his colleagues. Paradis (1980c) has shown that many of their sentences are in fact ungrammatical, both within a language and between languages. Within a language one finds grammatically incorrect sequences such as "dans le matin" (in French this would be "le matin"), or "I often think *d'un pays loin-*

tain" (this should be "à un pays lointain"). Apparently the experimenters were not themselves bilingual and did not ask native speakers of French to help them in the preparation of the materials. In addition, the mixed sentences are often impossible sequences. As we will see in the next chapter, switching is rule governed, and bilinguals do not switch from one language to another in a haphazard way. Thus a bilingual would never say a mixed sentence of the type:

Bien des singes *like* jouer.

because it violates a constraint that switching cannot take place between two verbs in a verb phrase containing an infinitive complement. The passages and sentences used by Kolers and others are replete with examples of this type.

It is interesting that when switches occur at constituent boundaries (between the noun phrase and verb phrase, for instance), the bilingual subjects process these sentences much better. This is because the constituent boundary is an important change-over point in natural code-switching. Thus Wakefield and colleagues (1975) found that bilinguals were faster at judging the truth value of sentences when the switch between languages occurred at the major syntactic boundary of a sentence than at minor boundaries within constituents. And Neufeld (1973) found no difference in the results of a truth-value-judging task when subjects were given either monolingual or switched sentences in which the switch occurred at the noun phrase–verb phrase break. One must therefore have great reservations about any statement concerning the amount of time involved in language switching. We now know that listening to a haphazard mixture of languages certainly takes time, but whether natural code-switching actually takes time and makes language processing more difficult remains an open question. Many believe that it does not.

Recent research on code-switching has shown that it occurs more frequently in bilingual conversations than was at first thought, and researchers now are asking how the languages interact during code-switching. It would seem that a one- or a two-switch model just cannot account for both the independence and the interaction of languages. Investigators have pointed out that certain aspects of a language may be "on" while others are "off," as shown by the fact that many bilinguals can speak one of their languages with the pronunciation of the other (a French-English bilingual, imitating Maurice Chevalier speaking English, for example).

There is also the problem of accounting for interferences, as when a bilingual said to an English speaker who knew no French: "Look at the *camion.*" The French word "camion" was pronounced in English, replacing inadvertently the correct English word "truck." How can a simple on–off switching system account for such interferences? There have also been questions concerning one-word switches. Is the underlying operation of switching for a single word the same as that involved for a phrase or sentence? And how does the listener decode these two types of switches? Obler and Albert (1978) criticize the data-driven aspect of the input switch. They cite Taylor (1976), who mentions that a bilingual may fail to comprehend what is being said for a few seconds because the language being spoken has been switched suddenly. Such a phenomenon cannot be explained in any simple way by a data-driven system. Instead of the input switch, Obler and Albert propose a flexible, continuously operating monitor system that channels the acoustic signal to the lexicon of one language or the other. To do this, it scans the data for linguistic cues signaling that one or the other language is being spoken, and also incorporates nonlinguistic environmental information such as the person speaking, the situation, and the topic. Thus, with the monitor, one language is never completely switched off as it would be with an on–off system.

Paradis (1977, 1980c), who has probably taken the strongest stance, believes that a bilingual switching mechanism has no neurological or psychological reality. He writes:

The decision to speak in English or in Russian is surely of the same order as the decision to speak at all or to remain silent, or the decision to wiggle one's little finger or to keep it still ... There is no need to postulate an anatomical localization or even a specific functional organization, other than that which every speaker already possesses and which allows him, among other things, to switch registers within the same language. (1977, p. 91)

Paradis proposes that a word in one language and a word from the other language are immediately perceived as words, just as two different words in the same language are. There is no need to postulate a particular switching mechanism to keep the two languages separate because they already *are* separated. Language choice is in no way different, at the psycholinguistic level, than choice of style or of variety within one language. Any delays involved in switching are of the same order as those involved in changing tasks or, for input, those occurring when the listener does not expect a particular change in style or language variety.

Paradis' position needs experimental evidence, and current psycholinguistic research is addressing some of his hypotheses. In the end, a psycholinguistic model will have to account for the bilingual's ability to maintain his or her two languages separate in certain situations and to integrate them in others. Sridhar and Sridhar (1980) address this latter aspect. They believe code-switching requires both language systems to be *on* at the same time, thus making less likely any strong version of a language switch mechanism. They propose an interactionist model to account for switching: an "assembly line" process in which individual components or constituents are put together separately and inserted into the appropriate slots in the syntactic frame of the base language being spoken. Whatever the final psycholinguistic account of language independence and language interaction, the models that will be proposed in the next few years and the data that will be obtained to confirm them will be of the utmost interest to the researcher on bilingualism.

Other Aspects

Several other domains of the psycholinguistics of bilingualism have also been examined, including the processing of language by non-balanced bilinguals, the comparison of monolinguals and bilinguals on various language tasks, and the translation abilities of bilinguals.

Dornic (1978, 1979) points out that a nonbalanced bilingual is probably much more typical than a balanced one. The fact that a person is not as fluent in one language as in the other may not be apparent at first if pronunciation of the weaker language is good and production is correct. But if the bilingual is put under stress, the underlying dominance pattern may become very clear. Dornic (1978) writes: "Information overload, environmental, emotional, or social stresses, fatigue, all these factors may unveil the hidden imbalance between the dominant and subordinate languages ... language dominance which under normal circumstances would not appear becomes evident under stress" (p. 259). Dornic shows how various tasks given to bilinguals in their nondominant language are influenced by environmental noise, mental fatigue, emotionally loaded events, and other external factors. The bilingual slows down, is less effective, and is even tempted to switch to his or her dominant language. This phenomenon has often been reported by bilinguals in their everyday experiences: some say they feel tired after speaking the nondominant language for a long time; others report how in particularly emotive situations they just cannot speak one of their languages. These reports illustrate once again that bilinguals use their two languages for different purposes and with different people, and very often one of the two languages will be their more familiar, more personal code. It seems quite reasonable that under stress they will be tempted to revert to the language with which they are more attuned.

Some researchers have compared bilinguals to monolinguals on various language tasks. Magiste (1979), for instance, compared a German-Swedish bilingual group, a trilingual group (in which German and Swedish were two of the three languages), and two groups of monolinguals, one Swedish and one German. All subjects were timed on two naming tasks (naming simple objects and naming numbers), a simple decoding task, and a reading-aloud task. She found that on all tasks bilinguals were slower than monolinguals even when they were strongly dominant in one language, and that trilinguals were slower than bilinguals. Magiste proposes two reasons for the longer reaction time: either bilinguals use each language less frequently than the respective monolinguals, or the two language systems interfere with one another. Although Magiste's basic finding is intriguing, one must nevertheless ask what reaction-time tasks tell us about the actual production and perception of language, either in monolinguals or bilinguals. Can one infer from these results that bilinguals are poorer or slower processors of language? It is my belief that the bilingual will be as fluent in a language as the psychosocial environment requires. Each language will be developed to the extent that it is needed; this may lead to total fluency in both languages for some bilinguals and limited fluency in one or both languages for others. To make any statement about the bilingual's efficiency or inefficiency as a communicator, as compared to the monolingual, one must take into account the overall, combined use of the two languages and not just the use of one or the other language.

A third aspect of the psycholinguistics of bilingualism concerns the ability to translate. To the uninformed monolingual, the bilingual is a born translator, who should have no problems mapping one language onto the other quickly and efficiently. And yet this is far from the truth. Many bilinguals report difficulties in translating, especially in writing. For instance, a young bilingual researcher wrote his Ph.D. dissertation in English but just could not translate it into French; his wife had to do it. Rosetti (1945) cites a Hungarian-Romanian bilingual in Transylvania who had been bilingual from infancy but who was quite incapable of translating from one language to the other. Lambert, Havelka, and Gardner (1959) found no correlation between their subjects' degree of bilingualism and the speed with which they translated lists of words, and a similar result was obtained by Macnamara (1967b). Such findings are explained in part by the fact that the bilingual usually uses each language for specific purposes, with certain people, and for certain topics. It is probably quite rare for a bilingual to use both languages in all domains of life.

In addition, translating is a complex skill that can be developed and trained. As Paradis (1980a) writes: "A given notion, evoked by a single word in one language, may require a cumbersome round-about circumlocution in another and will therefore be less easily evocable in that language. This is why a bilingual person who speaks both languages like a native might nevertheless encounter great difficulties in translating from one language into the other" (p. 421). In fact, Paradis (1980b) believes that the process underlying translation is quite different from those underlying speaking, understanding, reading, and writing two languages. He mentions cases of aphasic patients who lost the ability to speak one of their languages but who retained their ability to translate into that language when given the information in the other language. For example, on the days that a French-Arabic bilingual could not express herself at all in French, she was nevertheless quite capable of translating from Arabic into French when asked to do so. Thus, contrary to popular opinion, translation has little to do with fluency, and bilinguals range from being very poor to being very competent translators.

To conclude this section, I should stress that this research is still very much in its infancy. Over the last twenty years it has concentrated on certain aspects that are now seen as less important (the co-ordinate-compound-subordinate distinction, the one- or two-lexicon question), and it has put less stress on other aspects that are now popular (the underlying psycholinguistic operations in code-switching, for example). In addition, much of the research so far has used balanced bilinguals, who represent only a very small proportion of the bilingual population, and it has failed to study bilinguals in the contexts in which they actually use their languages. Future research will probably put more stress on the processing of language in bilinguals and will determine in what ways they (balanced and nonbalanced) are similar and in what way they are different from monolinguals in such operations as speech perception, word recognition, syntactic and semantic processing, memorization of continuous discourse, and so on. In addition, and perhaps more interestingly, researchers are starting to compare these operations when the two languages are kept separate and when they interact, as in code-switching and language interference (see, for example, Clyne, 1980).

The Bilingual Brain

Neurolinguists and psycholinguists have been interested in describing how language is organized in the "bilingual brain," as it has been called by Albert and Obler (1978), and how this organization differs from that of the monolingual. To study this difficult topic, one approach has been to observe and test bilingual aphasics in an attempt to answer questions such as: Which languages have been affected by the brain injury? Have the languages been affected to the same extent (at the various levels of the language as well as in production and perception)? Which factors can best account for the different patterns of recovery of the languages? The other approach has been to study normal bilinguals by means of experimental tasks such as dichotic listening and tachistoscopic presentation to ascertain whether language processing occurs mainly in the left hemisphere of the brain, as it appears to do in monolinguals, or in both hemispheres. These two complementary approaches are both aimed at describing language organization and processing in the brain of the bilingual.

Aphasia in Bilinguals

Aphasia is the disturbance of language and speech caused by brain damage. Such damage can be caused by a car or motorbike accident, for instance, by an object falling on the head, or by a stroke or brain tumor. A number of case studies of bilingual or multilingual aphasics have been published, and researchers such as Paradis (1977) and Albert and Obler (1978) have analyzed them carefully to isolate the major language recovery patterns of these aphasics, to determine the factors that led to recovery, and in general to learn more about language organization in the brain. Before mentioning some of the studies I should stress a number of points. First, the 140 or so published case studies may not be representative of the most common bilingual aphasics; researchers may well have put aside the normal cases in favor of the more spectacular ones. Second, some of the cases were reported second or third hand and hence are less reliable than first-hand accounts. Finally, one has no knowledge of how fluent the patients were in their two or more languages before injury, so it is difficult to determine which language has been affected the most. To this should be added the fact that in older studies, language testing was sometimes done by people who were not fluent in all the patient's languages. This resulted, as Paradis (1977) writes, in the examiner asking questions of the type: "Who are you born?" The look of puzzlement on the patient's face and the absence of an answer might well have led the interviewer to note that comprehension of English was impaired!

Despite these drawbacks, researchers have examined the bilingual aphasia case studies as a possible source of information on the workings of the bilingual brain. Paradis (1977), for instance, examined the recovery patterns of bilingual aphasics and the factors that allow certain languages to be recovered before others. The most frequent recovery pattern, accounting for about half the published aphasia cases, is the parallel restitution of the languages: similarly impaired languages are restored at the same rate. More interesting to the researcher are the patterns of nonparallel restitution. Among these the most frequent (about one-quarter of the cases) is selective recovery, in which the patient never regains one or more languages.

Such a case was reported by Minkowski in 1927. A Swiss German, who lived the first part of his life in Zurich, spoke Swiss German as his mother tongue and learned German at school, as well as French and some Italian. At the age of thirty, he moved to Neuchâtel, a French-speaking city, where he had accepted a position as professor of physics. French thus became his most-used language. At the age of forty-four he had an apoplectic stroke, which caused aphasia. Comprehension of his languages was restored rapidly, but he had to relearn how to speak. The first language he relearned was French. Standard German and some Italian followed, but Swiss German, his mother tongue, never returned, even though he spent the last five years of his life in Zurich.

Other types of recovery are even less frequent. Paradis (1977) reports eleven cases of differential recovery, in which the languages are differently impaired at the time of injury and are restored at the same or at different rates. Such a case was reported by Bychowski (1919). A Pole who spoke Polish (his mother tongue), German, and Russian was hit by a piece of shrapnel on the eastern front during World War I. He remained unconscious for three weeks and when he came to, his Russian was least impaired, his Polish was impaired but only in production (he understood it and replied in Russian), and German was the most impaired (he could only repeat phrases given to him). It is not reported how well he recovered his three languages, but we do know that his Russian was restored completely because of the Russian ambience in the hospital and the language exercises given him by a Russian nurse.

Successive restitution (eight cases reported by Paradis, 1977) occurs when one language does not begin to reappear until another has been restored. Such a case is reported by Minkowski (1927). A Swiss German mechanic who spoke Swiss German and German and who knew some French and Italian had a motorbike accident at the age of thirty-two. He became aphasic, and when language production was restored, he could speak only German. He spoke it to his landlady, who came to visit him frequently and who worked through German exercises with him. It was only five months after the accident, when German was almost completely restored, that the patient began to speak his first language, Swiss German. As for Italian and French, there was no recuperation for at least sixteen months.

An even rarer pattern of recovery has been termed antagonistic: one language regresses as the other progresses (six cases reported by Paradis, 1977). The case study at the beginning of this chapter is a fine example of antagonistic recovery. French was the first language the patient recovered; then, as German and Swiss German progressed, French started losing ground, so that at the end of the observation period the patient had lost almost all fluency in that language. Paradis (1980b) reports two interesting cases of alternate antagonism: one language is recovered but then disappears as the other language becomes available; this one in turn becomes unavailable and the first one reappears, and so on—a see-saw recovery pattern. In one case a forty-eight-year-old nun in Morocco, who was bilingual in French and dialectal Arabic, had a moped accident and became totally aphasic. Four days after her accident she was able to utter a few words in Arabic but could not speak French, although her comprehension of the language was quite good. However, two weeks later she spoke French quite fluently. One day later, much to the interviewer's surprise, her French was extremely poor, and her Arabic was once again quite fluent. The next day, the reverse was true: poor, dysfluent Arabic and good spontaneous French. To add to this complex recovery pattern, whenever she had difficulties speaking one language, she had no problems translating into it. However, she could not do the reverse, that is, translate into the language she spoke spontaneously! Thus, her translating ability was completely divorced from her speaking ability.

In a final type of recovery, called mixed, the bilingual's two languages are intermingled. Such a case was reported by L'Hermitte and colleagues (1966). A forty-six-year-old English businessman, who had lived and worked in France for sixteen years and who was very fluent in both languages, showed mixed recovery after becoming aphasic. His two languages interfered with one another in both writing and speaking. When asked to write in French, for example, he produced the following mixed passage that is quite incomprehensible (the interferences from English are italicized):

> J'es avec une massio*dial* a et *except* dans le cissuden. *W*ede main pour la pousse tard *being*ig *maid* mouche *was tr*iel mal.
> (*L'Hermitte et al., 1966, p. 326*)

Paradis and Lecours (1979) give a good example of mixed output by an English-French bilingual aphasic who was asked whether her father was English-speaking:

> Non, non, à la maison, c'était tout français.
> (No, No, at home, everything was in French.)
> A la maison, *my . . . my house,* c'est tout français.
> C'est tout français *everywhere . . .* Euh, *when . . .* (p. 605)

Researchers examining these various nonparallel recovery patterns have attempted to account for the order in which languages are restituted. Ribot (1881) proposed that the earliest learned language, that is, the mother tongue, would be the least damaged and therefore would be the first one to be recovered. This hypothesis, also called Ribot's rule or the primacy rule, is difficult to test, because in most cases the mother tongue is also the most familiar and the most used language before the injury. This fact led Pitres (1895) to propose that the language most in use immediately preceding the injury will be recovered first. In general, Pitres' rule (the habit strength rule) is a better predictor of the recovery pattern than Ribot's rule. Albert and Obler (1978), for instance, found twenty-five cases that followed Pitres' rule (and thirteen that did not), whereas twenty-six cases followed Ribot's rule but thirty did not.

The degree of use of a particular language just prior to brain injury is an important factor in language recovery, but so is the patient's psychological state before and after the injury. Minkowski (1963) explains the nonparallel language recovery of some of his patients by resorting to affective and emotional factors. For instance, the successive restitution pattern of the young mechanic was explained by the fact that he had a close relationship with his German-speaking landlady, who visited him every day in the hospital. In addition, Minkowski explains that the patient's relatives, who spoke Swiss German, had neglected him and that a young Swiss-German girl had disappointed him in love several years previously. These emotive factors—linked negatively to Swiss German and positively to German—may explain in part the patient's successive recovery. Minkowski examines two other cases in the same psychological light. The case of the professor of physics who recovered French first but never recovered his mother tongue, Swiss German is explained by the fact that French corresponded to his affectional and social needs at that time; the case of antagonistic recovery at the beginning of this chapter is accounted for by the fact that the Swiss German's six years in France had been the most beautiful years of his life, he had been in love with a French girl, and so on. Thus, Minkowski and others propose that psychological factors (anxiety, emotion, happiness) play an important role in the recovery pattern of certain bilingual aphasics.

The language used with an aphasic in therapy following the injury may also be important in accounting for language recovery. The Polish soldier who showed a differential recovery pattern managed to relearn Russian completely, perhaps in part because of the language exercises a Russian nurse had him do. The Swiss German mechanic's successive recovery resulted not only from psychological factors but also from the fact that his landlady helped him work on his German. More recently, Watamori and Sasanuma (1978) have reported two cases of Japanese-English bilinguals who showed much more progress in the language that was used for therapy than in their other language.

A language that a bilingual reads and writes may have a better chance of recovery than a language that is only spoken. Paradis (1977) states that when the neurological correlates of reading and writing are not affected, the *visual* element of language may facilitate restitution of other elements of the language. It is interesting to note that besides the other factors mentioned, Minkowski's Swiss German mechanic made greater progress in German, a written language, than in Swiss German, which was rarely written at the time.

Many other factors appear to play a role in language recovery. The patient's age when injured may be a factor: Obler and Albert (1977), for instance, found that if the bilingual is elderly, one cannot predict that the most recently used language will recover first, whereas if he or she is young or middle-aged, the prediction is possible. The severity of the injury may also play a role: Paradis (1977) writes that when the cortical structures connected with linguistic structure are severely damaged, the patient may concentrate on only one language. Other factors which have been proposed are: how well a language is known; the last language used by the patient before injury and the first language used with the patient after the injury; the affective value attached to a language; and the context and mode of usage of a language.

From this it can be seen that no one factor, but a combination, accounts for the nonparallel recovery of languages. In fact, the whole picture of bilingual aphasia is probably even more complex than may at first appear. Modern testing procedures are showing interesting but complex language patterns in bilingual aphasics. Albert and Obler (1975) report on the case of a thirty-five-year-old woman who spoke Hungarian, French, English, and Hebrew. After an operation to remove a tumor, she showed different types of aphasia in her four languages: her Hebrew was produced with great effort and in a telegraphic manner, but her comprehension of it was good (an example of Broca's aphasia); her English was fluent but made little sense, and she had problems understanding it (an instance of Wernicke's aphasia), and her Hungarian and French shared elements of these two types of aphasia. Thus a single lesion caused two distinctly different clinical varieties of aphasia at the same time. If we add alternate, antagonistic, and mixed recovery patterns, we see that the study of bilingual aphasics can be extremely problematic.

Although the study of bilingual aphasia is still in its infancy, it does seem to show that when languages are not recovered, they are only inhibited and not lost. Paradis (1977) proposes that selective impairment is not caused by damage to the stored language itself but by an incapacity to retrieve what is stored. The evidence for this comes from bilingual aphasics who may still understand a language but may no longer be able to speak it, and from the many cases of aphasics who finally recover their languages. In addition, cases of alternate antagonism, where languages "come and go," show that the underlying competence for a language is still present. Paradis (1977) concludes: "When one language does not return, it is not because the language as such has been forgotten but because it has been temporarily or permanently inhibited" (p. 89).

Language Lateralization

It is a well-known fact in neurolinguistics that the left hemisphere of the brain is dominant for language; some even say that it contains the language center. The evidence for this dominance is strong, at least for right-handed males: if the right hemisphere is surgically removed, no permanent aphasia will result, whereas removal of the left hemisphere usually produces permanent aphasia; speech comprehension and production are practically impossible when the left hemisphere is anesthetized with sodium amytal but is hardly impaired when the right hemisphere is anesthetized; only 2 percent of monolingual aphasics have a right hemisphere lesion as compared to 98 percent with a left hemisphere lesion (Galloway, 1980); and countless experimental tasks have shown the superiorty of the left hemisphere in language processing.

The question now is whether bilinguals also show strong left-hemisphere dominance for language. Until recently, many researchers felt that bilinguals use the right hemisphere in language processing more than monolinguals. They pointed out that case studies of bilingual aphasics showed more right-hemisphere lesions. Galloway (1980) reports, for instance, that whereas only 2 percent of right-handed monolingual aphasics have a right hemisphere lesion, 15 percent of bilingual aphasics have such a lesion. In addition, a number of experimental studies with normal bilinguals have shown some right-hemisphere involvement. Genesee and colleagues (1978), in a study of the relationship between age of onset of bilingualism and hemispheric involvement, used three groups of adult subjects: bilinguals who acquired their two languages (English and French) simultaneously in infancy; those who had acquired their second language between the ages of four and six; and those who had acquired their second language after age twelve. They presented English and French words individually to these subjects and asked them to indicate as quickly as possible which language it belonged to. During this task they monitored the subjects' brain waves (their EEG). They found that infant and childhood bilinguals showed shorter wave peak latencies in the left hemisphere, whereas adolescent bilinguals showed shorter latencies in the right hemisphere. From this they concluded that late bilinguals used a more right-hemisphere-based, holistic strategy to categorize the words as French or English, whereas the earlier bilinguals (infant and childhood bilinguals) used a left-hemisphere-based, possibly semantic strategy of analysis.

Other factors in bilingualism have been proposed as involving the right hemisphere. The stage hypothesis (Obler, Albert, and Gordon, 1975; Galloway, 1978b) states that right-hemisphere processing is more evident in the initial stages of second language acquisition; as the bilingual becomes more fluent in the second language, the left hemisphere takes over and the right is no longer involved. Others have proposed that informal acquisition of a language involves the right hemisphere more, whereas formal, classroom language learning involves the left hemisphere to a greater extent. Finally, language-specific factors such as type of language (appositional versus propositional, direction of the script, vowel characteristics, and tonality) have also been proposed as factors in right-hemisphere involvement (see Vaid and Genesee, 1980, for a complete review of this literature).

In the last few years, however, there has been increasing evidence that monolinguals and bilinguals may not differ at all in hemispheric involvement during language processing. Some researchers have pointed out that the Galloway (1980) finding of more right hemisphere lesions in bilingual than in monolingual aphasics should be interpreted with caution, as there has been a tendency to report only the interesting case studies. Other researchers have enumerated the problems with the past experimental studies: some, for instance, did not control for the sex of their subjects, and yet it is an important factor, because females may be less language-lateralized than males (note that the study by Genesee et al., 1978, did not control for sex). Other studies did not control for handedness, another important factor correlated with hemispheric lateralization. Others did not ascertain the language proficiency of their bilinguals, did not run a monolingual control group, and ran too few bilingual subjects.

A study by Soares and Grosjean (1981) attempted to control for each of these factors. They asked a group of monolingual English subjects and a group of Portuguese-English bilinguals who had learned English after the age of twelve to read a set of individually presented English and Portuguese words presented to the right or to the left visual field by means of a tachistoscope. As expected, the monolinguals responded faster to words presented in the right visual field, which is connected directly to the left hemisphere. The question asked by Soares and Grosjean was: would the adolescent bilinguals behave like the monolinguals or would they be faster with words presented in the left visual field, as predicted by the Genesee et al. study? The authors found that the bilinguals behaved exactly like the monolinguals. Both groups gave shorter reaction times when words were presented to the left hemisphere, and both groups showed similar asymmetry patterns (eight out of ten subjects in each group showed left-hemisphere dominance). The authors concluded that when relevant variables such as sex and handedness are controlled, left hemisphere dominance in language processing is similar in monolinguals and bilinguals. In addition, they propose that the age of onset of bilingualism is not a factor in the greater level of right-hemisphere involvement.

Other recent studies have confirmed this conclusion. Galloway (1980) reports that adult Mexicans just beginning to acquire English show no evidence of greater right-hemisphere involvement for English, thus rejecting the stage hypothesis she had proposed a few years earlier. Gordon and Zatorre (1981) report that Spanish-English bilingual children show a left-hemisphere advantage for both Spanish and English words, and they thus do not support the hypothesis that the right hemisphere plays a more prominent role in the acquisition of a second language before puberty. And Gordon (1980) has found left-hemisphere advantage in Hebrew-English bilinguals regardless of when the second language was learned, how long it has been used, and how well it is known. Hence, it appears that, contrary to what some researchers have thought, bilinguals and monolinguals both process language in the left hemisphere to the same extent.

Language Organization in the Bilingual Brain

What do the aphasia case studies and language lateralization studies tell us about language organization in the bilingual brain? Most researchers would probably agree that the bilingual's languages are *not* stored in completely different locations. But from that point, views on language organization diverge somewhat, as Paradis (1981) notes. Proponents of what Paradis calls the "extended-system hypothesis" state that there is, as it were, one large language stock made up of elements from each language. When a second language is learned, the new sounds (phonemes) are treated as allophones (variants of existing phonemes) and are supported by the neural mechanism that underlies all phonemes. Evidence for this position comes from the ease with which bilinguals can speak one language with the accent of the other language, and from the fact that many bilingual aphasics are at first impaired in all their languages. On the other hand, proponents of the "dual system hypothesis," according to Paradis, state that within the same general language area, there are different networks of neural connections underlying each level of the language (sounds, words, grammar). The two language systems are thus separately represented in the brain. Evidence for this hypothesis, according to Paradis, comes from the aphasic studies: selective, successive, and antagonistic restitution of languages show selective inhibition and hence the neural independence of the languages, at least at some level.

It is interesting that electrical stimulation of certain areas of the bilingual brain (Ojemann and Whitaker, 1978) does not provide evidence that allows us to choose between the two hypotheses. The authors electrically stimulated a number of sites in the brains of two bilingual patients who were being treated for intractable epilepsy. During the stimulation the subjects were shown slides of common objects and were asked to name them in a particular language. Ojemann and Whitaker were interested in the locations where stimulation affected naming in one language or in both languages. Their results are of great interest. In their first subject they found six cortical sites where both languages were disturbed by the stimulation and seven sites where one language was disturbed more than the other. They concluded that within the language area, there are sites common to both languages (evidence for the extended-system hypothesis) and sites specific for each language (evidence for the dual-system hypothesis). What is interesting is that each patient's second language seemed to be represented in a wider area of the brain than the first language. This suggested to them that during the initial stage of second-language acquisition, a wider area of the brain is needed, at least for naming objects, and that as proficiency in the language progresses, or with continued use, the area becomes smaller.

Paradis (1981) proposes a compromise solution to the two hypotheses stated above. He agrees that both languages may be stored in identical ways in a single extended system, but he also thinks that the elements of each language, because they normally appear in different contexts, probably form separate networks, subsystems within the larger system. Paradis writes: "According to this hypothesis (the subset hypothesis) bilinguals have two subsets of neural connections, one for each language (and each can be activated or inhibited independently because of the strong associations between the elements) while at the same time they possess one larger set from which they are able to draw elements of either language at anytime" (p. 7). Each subset can be impaired individually, thus accounting for the various types of nonparallel recovery, or the entire set may be inhibited. In addition, bilinguals may stay within a subsystem when speaking or bring in elements from the other subsystem—in effect, code-switching.

To conclude, the bilingual brain is still very much terra incognita. Only further clinical and experimental research will tell us how similar it is to the monolingual brain and in what ways it may be different.

The Bilingual as a Person

In this section we will discuss the attitudes and feelings bilinguals have toward bilingualism: the inconveniences and the advantages of being bilingual and the differences some see between themselves and monolinguals. We will also examine the attitudes of monolinguals toward bilingualism. Second, we will discuss some mental activities, such as counting, praying, thinking, and dreaming, as well as the interaction of language and emotion, stress and fatigue. Third, we will attempt to answer a question often asked by monolinguals: does the bilingual have two personalities or one? Finally, we will discuss some bilinguals who are well known for their contributions to humanity and not for their bilingualism. This will enable us to understand that for the bilingual individual, bilingualism is a fact of life, as normal as sleeping and eating.

Attitudes and Feelings about Bilingualism

Most of the attitudes toward bilingualism that one reads about have been expressed by educators, linguists, psychologists, and sociologists, who are usually monolingual. In this section, bilinguals express their own attitudes and feelings. It is important to note that the data on bilinguals' attitudes, obtained in a survey by Vildomec (1971) and in my own survey, are probably not representative of all bilinguals. Vildomec questioned forty European multilinguals, most of whom were teachers, lecturers, students, researchers, and civil servants. In my survey I polled thirty bilinguals and fourteen trilinguals from seventeen different countries, including the United States, Iran, Venezuela, Burma, Uganda, Haiti, Thailand, and Lebanon. They represented thirteen language dyads and ten language triads, but like Vildomec's multilinguals, they were all students or college-educated members of the middle class. The attitudes obtained from these two surveys may not, therefore, reflect those of bilinguals with a different educational level and socioeconomic status or those from other countries.

One of the questions in my survey concerned the inconveniences of being bilingual. For the majority of bilinguals (52 percent) and trilinguals (67 percent), the reply was a simple "No inconvenience." This is in marked contrast with a prevailing monolingual attitude

---

BOX 5.2   **BILINGUALS SPEAK**

What Are the Inconveniences of Being Bilingual?

Luganda-English bilingual: It sometimes inconveniences me when I have to act as a translator.

Arabic-French-English trilingual: There is the tendency to mix the languages within the same sentence.

English-German bilingual: Some adjustment as a child.

American Sign Language–English bilingual: One inconvenience is having to act as an interpreter in social situations; the two worlds [Deaf and hearing] rarely mesh well together.

Greek-English bilingual: Sometimes it is hard to express yourself in both languages concerning a particular subject.

Arabic-English bilingual: Biculturalism can be a problem at times.

Spanish-English bilingual: At times I feel that I don't know either Spanish or English.

English-American Sign Language bilingual: Possible source of conflict.

French-English bilingual: Not belonging to one specific cultural group.

---

that bilingualism is a hindrance. For some bilinguals the inconvenience was related to the weaker language and to the fact that it often led to code-switching and language mixing. Some disliked having to act as interpreters; others felt they did not belong to any cultural group or that belonging to two cultures was a source of conflict. Box 5.2 gives some of the responses to this question.

Vildomec also asked his multilinguals about the disadvantages of using two or more languages on a regular basis. Many mentioned the ever-present problem of one language interfering with another, especially when they are tired, angry, nervous, or worried. This also occurs when the person travels and one language suddenly becomes more important or when the domain of a language is extended unexpectedly, as when a person is asked to talk about his or her work in the wrong language. Other inconveniences mentioned in Vildomec's survey were the impact of multilingualism on memory and language independence (some subjects reported difficulties in keeping their languages separate as they grew older) and the fact that some were poor translators. A few subjects also reported momentary

---

BOX 5.3   **BILINGUALS SPEAK**

The Effect of Bilingualism on the Dominant Language

A French-Alsatian bilingual: Since the age of thirty, I have had the feeling that being bilingual is having a negative effect on my French. My vocabulary is more limited, I keep away from technical terms, new words are assimilated more slowly, and I use a French dictionary more often to check on French words. The older I get the more this impression is strengthened, so that I am now starting to have complexes. I find consolation in reasoning that knowing and using two languages quite well is as useful as knowing and using only one language.

---

difficulties in choosing the appropriate language, particularly if they were surrounded by people of different nationalities. Finally, Vildomec cites a multilingual who had a very negative experience during World War II. The Germans had occupied his country, and he and other people in his city were being questioned by the occupying forces. Those who reported speaking German (that is, who were bilingual) were separated from monolinguals and sent to a concentration camp. They were probably considered potential spies and hence dealt with more harshly.

In Box 5.3, a university professor, who is bilingual in Alsatian and French, reports how her French appears to be more limited as time goes by; she believes this is because of her bilingualism. One final inconvenience that has been reported is the negative effect an accent may have on others, especially if people look down on the bilingual's minority group. Bossard (1945) writes: "Benjamin . . . has been a travelling salesman. He was reared in a Yiddish speaking home, and he speaks English today with a remarked Yiddish accent. Benjamin says that this fact handicaps him in selling, particularly in certain areas of the country" (p. 705).

It would be wrong to conclude from the above that all bilinguals have negative feelings about their bilingualism. Apart from the few inconveniences that we have reported, the dominant picture that emerges from my survey and Vildomec's is that bilinguals are quite positive about their bilingualism. A majority of subjects in my survey answered that there was "no inconvenience," whereas not a single subject felt there were no advantages. Box 5.4 presents some of the answers to the question on the advantages of being bilingual.

BOX 5.4   **BILINGUALS SPEAK**

What Are the Advantages of Being Bilingual?

Burmese-English bilingual: I can speak to my Burmese friends in Burmese if I don't want the people around me to know what we are saying.

Armenian-Arabic-English trilingual: You feel at home wherever you are.

Spanish-English-French trilingual: It broadens your scope. It means you have two worlds instead of one (friends, cultural aspects, job possibilities).

Haitian Creole-French-English trilingual: It gives me the ability to communicate with different types of people.

Marathi-Hindi-English trilingual: There are plenty of advantages: being able to discover the beauty of various languages; reading literature in its original language; talking to people; understanding how each language has a different logic, a whole different manner and means of expression.

German-French-English trilingual: There is the advantage of being able to read a greater variety of books, of traveling, and of conversing with people directly.

Dutch-English bilingual: It is primarily the fact that you are able to communicate with people in different countries.

English-German bilingual: Communication with people of another culture breeds open-mindedness.

American Sign Language-English bilingual: Bilingualism gives you a double perspective on the world.

Greek-English bilingual: The ability to help others who only know Greek and need an interpreter.

Spanish-English bilingual: Understanding what others don't.

Greek-English bilingual: Communication with two cultures.

Russian-English bilingual: A bond with other bilingual people.

Spanish-English bilingual: More jobs; able to communicate with more people.

English–American Sign Language bilingual: Social mobility; increased awareness of social interaction.

BOX 5.5   BILINGUALS SPEAK

Positive Feelings

German-French-English trilingual: Being a trilingual has helped me in various ways. I have achieved greater stature in my work environment; I have developed my lingual capacities; I have become more open-minded toward minorities and more aware of their linguistic problems; I have enjoyed various forms of literature and felt a certain amount of pride in being able to read in three different languages ... Life never becomes boring, because there is more than just one language available. Being trilingual has been a guide to understanding and helping others.

Most bilinguals appreciate being able to communicate with people from different cultures. Others feel that bilingualism gives two perspectives on life, that it fosters open-mindedness, gives more job opportunities, and allows one to read literature in the original text.

A Ugandan student, bilingual in Luganda and English, puts the emphasis on education: "I strongly believe that bilingual people are blessed. I can't imagine what I would be or where I would be if I were monolingual. I am very fortunate that I have learned a second language that is used almost universally." An English-German bilingual stresses biculturalism: "In my opinion, bilingualism breeds biculturalism, and biculturalism breeds open-mindedness toward other languages and cultures. It helps to eliminate cultural ignorance. Being bilingual is a horizon-broadening experience." In Box 5.5, a German-French-English multilingual expresses the many advantages she has found in being bilingual.

Being bilingual may even have the ultimate advantage of preserving one's life. A Bengali-Urdu-English trilingual in Bengladesh reports that his knowledge of the occupiers' language, Urdu, during the war of independence was a vital asset. He writes: "When the Pakistani Punjabi/Urdu-speaking army was marauding my country [Bengladesh], I was arrested by a platoon one day. Fortunately, I escaped unhurt because I showed them that I could speak Urdu and that I could recite a few verses of the Koran in Arabic." He later explained to me over the phone that many Bengalis who could not speak Urdu had been shot on the spot! Many other bilinguals in other countries and at other times have probably lived through similar episodes.

Vildomec asked his subjects what positive influence multilingual-

BOX 5.6   BILINGUALS SPEAK

Do You Feel That You Are Different from a Monolingual?

A Burmese-English bilingual: I do not feel I am any different from monolinguals.

An Armenian-Arabic-English-trilingual: The only difference is that I can speak with different kinds of people, read and understand foreign writing and see foreign movies.

A Bengali-Urdu-English trilingual: I don't feel much different from monolinguals.

An Arabic-English-French trilingual: I am different from monolinguals in the sense that I can communicate with other people better. I think I am more open. I can understand other people because I know their language.

A Farsi-English bilingual: I don't really think it is a big deal speaking two languages . . . I don't feel I'm different [from monolinguals].

ism had on their elocution and style and on their mental operations. Some reported greater clarity in speaking their languages and richer vocabulary and grammar. Others said that multilingualism had helped them learn other languages and had improved their mental discipline and alertness. Some mentioned a greater awareness of the relativity of things and a more critical approach to life.

In my survey I asked bilinguals if they felt any different from monolinguals. As can be seen in Box 5.6, bilinguals generally do not consider themselves different, except that they can communicate with more people. Many bilinguals feel that the apparent difference between them and monolinguals is a figment of the imagination of monolinguals.

It is interesting to compare the attitudes and feelings of bilinguals and monolinguals toward bilingualism. As Haugen (1972) remarks, the attitudes of monolinguals are extremely varied, ranging from very positive to very negative: "Bilingualism is a term that evokes mixed reactions nearly everywhere. On the one hand, some people (especially academics) will say: 'How wonderful to be bilingual!' On the other, they warn parents, 'Don't make your child bilingual' " (p. 308). If the bilingual is college educated, a member of the middle or upper class, and speaks both languages without an accent, monolinguals are impressed by the ability to speak two languages and by the

---

BOX 5.7   **BILINGUALS SPEAK**

The Apparent Dangers of Bilingualism

I have been a bilingual as far back as I can remember, but it was not until I began reading the literature on the subject that I realized what this meant. Without knowing it, I had been exposed to untold dangers of retardation, intellectual impoverishment, schizophrenia, anomie, and alienation, most of which I had apparently escaped, if only by a hair's breadth. If my parents knew about these dangers, they firmly dismissed them and made me bilingual willy-nilly. They took the position that I would learn all the English I needed from my playmates and my teachers, and that only by learning and using Norwegian in the home could I maintain a fruitful contact with them and their friends and their culture. In the literature I found little mention of this aspect. What I found was a long parade of intelligence tests proving bilinguals to be intellectually and scholastically handicapped . . . My own happy experience with bilingualism, which enabled me to play roles in two worlds rather than one, was apparently not duplicated by most of those whom the researchers had studied. (Haugen, 1972, p. 307)

---

ease with which the person switches from one to the other. But if the bilingual is an immigrant worker who speaks the dominant language with a strong accent or is a child adapting slowly to a totally monolingual school, then monolinguals refer to "semilingualism" and to the apparent dangers of bilingualism. Haugen (1972), as a researcher in this field and as a Norwegian-English bilingual himself, has witnessed the latter attitude, which is prevalent in the United States, as shown in Box 5.7.

It is interesting to see how bilinguals are described in popular works, as this often reflects the lay person's point of view. In *Tinker, Tailor, Soldier, Spy,* (1980), John Le Carré describes Toby Esterhase, a spy working for British intelligence in the following way: "Tiny Toby spoke no known language perfectly, but he spoke them all. In Switzerland, Guillam had heard his French and it had a German accent; his German had a Slav accent and his English was full of stray flaws and stops and false vowel sounds" (p. 93). In the eyes of the author, Toby reflects the cosmopolitan, the person who has moved from one country to another and who has no home base. Although some bilinguals fit this stereotype, the great majority have roots in a particular linguistic community, and their dominant language and culture are those of the community.

Another view of the bilingual is reflected in Jack Higgins' *The*

Eagle Has Landed (1976), a fictitious story of a German attempt to kidnap Churchill during World War II. Before being decimated by an American force, a troop of elite parachutists land in Norfolk and approach within a few miles of the house where Churchill is staying. The leader of the German group, Kurt Steiner, is totally bilingual and bicultural. His father is a major general in the German army, his mother was American, and he was brought up in both England and Germany. At several places in the book the author refers to his bicultural upbringing. Steiner tells an English priest that although he is German, his mother was American and he went to school in London. He continues: "In fact, [I] lived there for many years. Now what does that mixture signify?" (p. 285). In the final scene, after harrowing escapes, Steiner is face to face with Churchill and ready to shoot. Churchill tells him to do his duty but he hesitates, and this proves fatal as Kane, an American officer, rushes out and shoots Steiner first. The dialogue between Churchill and Kane continues: " 'Strange,' the Prime Minister said. 'With his finger on the trigger, he hesitated. I wonder why?' 'Perhaps that was his American half speaking, sir,' Harry Kane said" (p. 356). Although this is only fiction, the author's treatment of Steiner indicates how some monolinguals view bilinguals. Some even go so far as to state that bilinguals must have split personalities and split minds. In general, the more monolingual a group is, the more difficult it is for them to understand that bilinguals are just like everyone else. In those African and Asian nations where almost everyone is at least bilingual, negative attitudes toward bilingualism are almost completely absent.

Mental Activities, Emotion, and Stress

Little is known about the languages used by bilinguals in their mental activities or when under stress or in an emotional situation. It does seem to be true that many mental operations are language specific. To the question, "Which language do you count in?" 62 percent of the bilinguals in my survey said their first language. Kolers (1978) reports that the bilinguals he interviewed tended to do mathematics in the language they learned it in. If they had learned arithmetic in one language, they would continue using that language, and if they had learned calculus in another, they would switch to that language whenever they do calculus. An Arabic-English-French trilingual writes: "There is one type of activity that I find I always use French for, and that is mental arithmetic. I learned arithmetic in French, and I find that I remember multiplication tables best in that language and have continued using it for that purpose." An Alsatian-French bilingual reports: "I do not know how to count in Alsatian very well. I have to think about numbers above twenty and especially about dates."

This language specificity of certain overlearned operations is found in such activities as praying. Many a bilingual can recite the Lord's Prayer or a verse from the Koran in one language, but to do so in the other language would require a slow and painstaking translation. The language one uses when talking to oneself often depends on the imagined situation or the topic being thought about. Some people even report using both languages on such occasions. Rabel-Heymann (1978), a German-English bilingual living in Canada, reports having heard herself say, as she was preparing a meal: "Salad . . . mit einem Ei . . . Why not?" When looking at houses for sale in the newspaper, she said to herself: 'Hundertneunundzwanzig tausend Dollar—for a three bedroom bungalow?"

When one asks a bilingual which language he or she thinks in, the most common reply is "both" (70 percent in my survey). What this means is that when thought (which usually is independent of language) is subvocalized, the bilingual will choose one or the other language depending (as we saw in Chapter 3) on the person, the topic, or the situation being thought about. When asked about dreams, bilinguals respond that when they do speak in a dream, it may be in either language (64 percent of respondents in my survey). Again, the people involved in the dream and the situation appear to trigger the language. A French-English bilingual in the United States reported dreaming about a little village in the French part of Switzerland that he knew well but had not returned to for several years. In the dream he met an inhabitant of the village and spoke French to him.

It is interesting to note that persons who do not speak a language very well may find themselves speaking it fluently in their dreams; they wake up wishing that the dream could become real! Vildomec (1971) reports how a multilingual who spoke some Russian dreamed that he was speaking fluent Russian. The only word he remembered from the dream was "majka," supposedly meaning "cat." However, he quickly realized that it was in fact a Czech word, his first language, for an insect, and that a similar word in Slovak (macka) meant cat. He thus concluded that his whole dream had not taken place in fluent Russian after all but in a sort of "Pan-Slavonic gibberish"! Another example from Vildomec shows that code-switching and interference also occur during dreams. A Czech multilingual found himself saying in his dream the Czech sentence:

Tak toje falšij ček.
(So it is a forged check.)

On awakening he realized that "ček" was an interference from the English "check" (in Czech it is šek) and that "falšij" was an interference from Russian (in Czech it is falešný). Vildomec reports that this amount of interference surpassed anything that the multilingual had ever experienced when awake.

It is interesting to listen to bilinguals talk about their use of languages when they are under stress or in an emotional state. Box 5.8 presents three personal accounts. In the first an English native

---

BOX 5.8   **BILINGUALS SPEAK**

Expressing Emotions

An English-French bilingual: It is often liberating to speak a language that is not one's mother tongue because it is easier to speak of taboo subjects. I find it easier to speak of anything connected with the emotions in French, whereas in an emotional situation in English I am rather tongue-tied, the affective content of the words is so much greater. I can also swear much more easily in French and have a wider range of "vulgar" vocabulary ... I am finding that gradually the way I use French is influencing the way I use English—I can now say "shit" and "fuck off." Perhaps one day I'll even manage "I love you."

An American Sign Language–English bilingual: There are times when I'm more comfortable using sign ... If I get really frightened, am under a lot of stress, or I've become very emotional, I find that I can't speak. There's a nightmare that I have: I'm teaching a class and I want to say something, so I open my mouth but nothing comes out. One time I was in a very emotional situation and I was unable to speak, but the people with me could sign. They also were bilingual, so I signed and we communicated using sign language. Sometimes I get to a point where speaking becomes a real problem.

A Portuguese-English bilingual: I express certain feelings in Portuguese or in English differently. In English I can be more direct, especially if I am feeling either very happy or really "down." For example, I find it hard to say in Portuguese and in a Portuguese context (unless I am with someone very close to me) something like "I am feeling so sad and depressed today"; in Portuguese I would say that indirectly. I also think that I am more polite in English. However, if there is something that makes me angry and if I allow some of my anger to come out, there is no doubt that I will use Portuguese, no matter the context or the situation.

speaker who settled in France at the age of twenty-one and married a French person reports that it is easier for her to express her emotions in French, her second language, than in English, her mother tongue. The reason she gives is that the affective content of words is just not the same for her in the two languages. She can swear in French but has problems doing so in English. Other bilinguals have reported similar trends: swearing in one language is easier than in the other, either because it is the bilinguals' first language or because—as in this case—the bilingual feels freer to do so in that language. In the second account, an American Sign Language–English bilingual reports how in a very emotional situation she just could not speak and had to sign. This person is perfectly fluent in English, and a person who does not know her would never think that she was bilingual. And in the third account, a Portuguese-English bilingual relates how certain feelings are better expressed in one language: extreme happiness, for instance, in English, but anger in Portuguese.

Bilinguals also report switching from one language to the other when they are very tired, angry, or excited. They may revert to their mother tongue or to whatever language they usually express their emotions in. Stress may also cause more interference, problems in finding the appropriate words, and unintentional switching. A French-English bilingual was once bitten by a sting ray while bathing in shallow waters in California. This is extremely painful and can result in momentary paralysis of the leg. He was with a group of English-speaking persons, but his utterances were a mixture of English and French: short English phrases about getting to a doctor as quickly as possible and French interjections to help relieve the pain. Along the same lines, an interesting phenomenon occurred during Reinhold Messner's amazing solo ascent of Mt. Everest in 1980. Messner, who lives in what is now part of the Italian Tyrol, is a native speaker of German but is also fluent in Italian and English. He reports (Messner, 1981) that at 7,800 meters it seemed as if someone was next to him (this has been reported by other climbers at those heights) and that, much to his surprise, he spoke out loud only in Italian, and not in German, his mother tongue. He does not explain this phenomenon, but it could be that his "companion" was Italian speaking or that the lack of oxygen had made him partly aphasic in German. Finally, I should note that some bilinguals wish the person closest to them (friend, wife, husband, companion) were also bilingual. Gentilhomme (1980) writes that not being able to speak about love in both languages may leave a bilingual feeling frustrated and insufficient.

Personality and Bilingualism

Do bilinguals have one or two personalities? As Box 5.9 shows, some bilinguals report that when they change language they feel they are changing their attitudes and behaviors. Both the French-English and Greek-English bilinguals in Box 5.9 are more aggressive and more tense in French or Greek than they are in English, and the Russian-English bilingual is more reserved and more gentle in Russian.

What these three bilinguals experience when they change language has been alluded to quite frequently in the literature. Haugen

---

BOX 5.9   **BILINGUALS SPEAK**

Two Personalities?

A French-English bilingual: I am deeply convinced and fully aware that I switch personality when I switch language. I know that I am more aggressive, more caustic, when I speak French. I am also more rigid and more narrow-minded in defending my assertions.

A Kurdish-Arabic bilingual: I feel that my personality does change when I change languages.

A Greek-English bilingual: In English my speech is very polite, with a relaxed tone, always saying "please" and "excuse me." When I speak Greek, I start talking more rapidly, with a tone of anxiety and in a kind of rude way, without using any English speech characteristics.

A Russian-English bilingual: I definitely feel as though I have two personalities . . . For example, my Russian-American "self" wears jeans to school, but my Russian-Slavic "self" disdains slacks on women and wears dresses and skirts . . . Recently I was visiting the Russian Orthodox Theological Seminary in upstate New York. I was sitting at a table with six of my Yugoslav friends and one American. The American and I started discussing language acquisition. I felt I knew what I was talking about and I boldly stated my point—raising my voice to be heard above the other conversations. As I noticed that my friends stopped to listen to our conversation, I became embarrassed and stopped talking. I felt uncomfortable about being so loud. So I simply sat and listened to the general conversation. Had I been with my American friends I would have been as loud as I wanted, fighting to get my point across, but here I sat serenely, not interfering with the men's conversation . . . I find when I'm speaking Russian I feel like a much more gentle, "softer" person. In English I feel more "harsh," "businesslike."

(1956), for instance, reports that Julian Green, a French-born American writer, just could not translate one of his books from French into English: "It was as if, writing in English, I had become another person." Green finally had to sit down and write an entirely new book. Di Pietro (1977) observes that in an Italian American store in Washington, D.C., the butcher's style differs with the language being spoken. In English he is rather matter-of-fact and formal, whereas in Italian he often carries on a light banter of jokes, and if the customer is a young, attractive woman, he will engage in mild flirtations.

Mkilifi (1978) observes similar behavior among bilinguals in Tanzania. He writes: "When discussing such notions as agnosticism and democracy a bilingual might hold slightly varying views depending on whether the discussion is in English or Swahili" (p. 146). Gallagher (1968) reports that in North Africa when an Arabic-French bilingual is enjoying himself with French friends, his attitude, indeed his whole character, is quite distinct from that expressed by his more robust joking in Arabic. He adds that the North African's authoritarian attitude toward his wife and children at home in Arabic changes publicly in more Western settings such as the *salon de thé* where French is used. And his attitudes toward women change drastically with the language: he will ignore a high official's secretary until he realizes that she speaks fluent French.

Ervin (1964) showed experimentally that bilinguals tell different stories in each language when asked to relate what they see on TAT cards (cards showing pictures with ambiguous content). When subjects describe these cards they are presumed to be projecting their feelings, attitudes, motives, in a word, their personalities. Ervin's subjects were French adults who had lived in the United States for an average of twelve years. Forty of the sixty-four were or had been married to Americans, and all spoke both English and French fluently. Each subject took part in two sessions six weeks apart. They were asked to describe nine TAT pictures in one language at the first session and in the other language at the second. Ervin reports that three variables showed significant language effects: verbal aggression to peers, withdrawal–anatomy, and achievement. To illustrate this, she gives a twenty-seven-year-old Frenchwoman's responses in French and English to one TAT card. This woman spoke English with her American husband and child. Most of her friends were American, and in her work as a full-time clerk she used English most of the time.

French version: She seems to beg him, to plead with him. I don't know if he wants to leave her for another woman or what . . . I think he wants to leave her because he's found another woman he loves more . . . I don't know whose fault it is but they certainly seem angry. Unless it's in his work, and he wants to go see someone and he wants to get in a fight with someone, and she holds him back and doesn't like him to get angry.

English version: In the past, well I think it was a married couple, average, and he got out of the Army and got himself a job or something like that or has decided he would go to college. He's decided to get a good education . . . he keeps on working and going to college at night some of the time . . . He'd have to give something up, and he's very discouraged and his wife tries to cheer him up . . . He'll probably keep on working his way through and finally get his diploma and get a better job and they will be much happier and . . . well, his wife will have helped him along. (p. 504)

Ervin observes that in French the picture elicited a variety of themes of aggression and striving for autonomy, whereas in English the heroine supports her husband in his achievement strivings.

Ervin-Tripp (1968) reports on how some Japanese American women reacted to sentence completion tests. These women were married to Americans and were generally isolated from the American Japanese minority group. They used Japanese in three situations only: on visits to Japan, during their jobs in Japanese restaurants (for some, at least), and when they talked to bilingual friends. When they were given sentences to complete (each sentence was given in English and Japanese), Ervin-Tripp found that they proposed very different endings. She gives the following three examples:

When my wishes conflict with my family . . .
Japanese: it is a time of great unhappiness.
English: I do what I want.

I will probably become . . .
Japanese: a housewife.
English: a teacher.

Real friends should . . .
Japanese: help each other.
English: be very frank.

Ervin-Tripp (1973) also tested a twenty-seven-year-old Japanese American who was born in the United States but who lived in Japan between the ages of eight and fourteen. He was thus fully bilingual and bicultural. She showed him a picture of a boy lying down with someone bending over him, and he provided the following descriptions in Japanese and English:

Japanese: A son comes home ill and dies before his mother, who goes mad with grief.

English: A young man was invited in off the highway when he was lost by a hypnotist, who robbed him.

Another picture showed a figure sitting on the floor, faced away, with the head resting on a couch or bench:

Japanese: A woman weeps over her lost fiancé and thinks of suicide.

English: A girl tries to complete a sewing project for class.

Ervin-Tripp observes that there is much more emotion in the Japanese responses; these involve members of the family and deal with love, unfaithfulness, and loss of loved ones. In the English responses the relationships are formal, the people abstract and cold.

Is it possible to conclude from all this evidence, both personal and experimental, that there is some truth to the Czech proverb, "Learn a new language and get a new soul"? Some would answer in the affirmative and go so far as to say that the bilingual has a split mind. Adler (1977) writes: "Often [bilinguals] have split minds ... all the particularities which language conveys, historical, geographical, cultural, are re-embodied in the bilingual twice: he is neither here nor there; he is a marginal man" (p. 38). About the bilingual child, he writes: "His standards are split, he becomes more inarticulate than one would expect of one who can express himself in two languages, his emotions are more instinctive, in short, bilingualism can lead to a split personality and, at worst, to schizophrenia" (p. 40). Later Adler reports that an English-Afrikaans bilingual psychiatric patient appeared sane in one language and mad in the other. And a person suffering from schizophrenia heard voices in only one language; when asked about these voices in the other language, the person would deny having heard them.

Such cases should be treated with extreme care, as they are often reported second hand, and one has no information concerning the patient's medical and personal history. It may be true, as Haugen (1961) writes, that "in the case of people who for other reasons are maladjusted, bilingualism can become a factor in the situation leading to disturbance. This is most likely to be true where the linguistic difference is strongly associated with social status" (p. 406). But to my knowledge, bilinguals are no more likely to become psychotic than monolinguals.

Leaving aside the rare medical cases of split minds in bilinguals, what can we say about the one- or two-personality question, the fact

---

BOX 5.10   BILINGUALS SPEAK

One Personality in Different Situations

A French-English bilingual: Many times I have experienced a feeling of "not being the same person" when I express myself in English, since my native language is French. When I try to analyze these situations, I realize that it is more a matter of context. I obviously tend to associate one language with its context and therefore feel quite awkward when using one specific language in the wrong setting.

A Swiss German-French-English trilingual: One may argue that by changing languages one switches to a different behavior only partially, so as to adapt to certain situations. For example, when talking English, French, or German to my sister, my personality does not change. However, depending on where we are, both our behaviors may adapt to certain situations we find ourselves in.

A French-Flemish-English trilingual: I don't really know if my personality changes when I change language. The main reason for this uncertainty is that I use the two languages in different situations and therefore I would act differently even if it was in the same language.

---

that some bilinguals feel they change personality when they change language? I propose that what is seen as a change in personality is simply a shift in attitudes and behaviors corresponding to a shift in situation or context, independent of language. As Ervin (1964) writes: "It is possible that a shift in language is associated with a shift in social roles and emotional attitudes. Since each language is learned and usually employed with different persons and in a different context, the use of each language may come to be associated with shift in a large array of behavior" (p. 506).

As we saw in Chapter 3, bilinguals will choose a language according to the situation, the interlocutor, the topic, and the intent of the conversation. These factors trigger different attitudes, impressions, and behaviors, and what is seen as a personality change due to language shift may really be a shift in situation and interlocutor. Box 5.10 presents extracts from three bilinguals on this topic: the third expresses the argument I am proposing very clearly: "I use the two languages in different situations and therefore I would act differently even if it was in the same language." And the second bilingual speaks English, French, or German to her sister, depending on the topic, the situation, and other people present, but this change in language never modifies her attitude and behavior toward her sister. In a word, it is the environment and the culture as a whole that cause the bilingual to change languages, along with attitudes, feelings, and behaviors—and not language as such.

Some Well-known Persons Who Were or Are Bilingual

Bilingualism is such a natural aspect of life that few of the people mentioned below are known for their bilingualism. It was part of their everyday life and in no way hindered them from contributing to the advancement of humanity. Box 5.11 lists some of these well-known persons along with the languages they spoke on a regular basis. The data may not always be complete, as biographies rarely mention the languages a person knows or uses. Many well-known politicians are bilingual, especially the leaders of African and Asian nations, (such as Julius Nyerere of Tanzania, and Indira Gandhi of India). And even in the Western Hemisphere a number of leaders use two or more languages on a regular basis. Pierre Trudeau of Canada is such a case, as was Marshall Tito of Yugoslavia. By the age of twenty-four, Tito knew five languages, almost all of which he used regularly as leader of a multilingual country.

Henry Kissinger, Secretary of State during the Nixon administration, was born Heinz Alfred Kissinger and lived in Furth, Germany, until the age of fifteen, when his family fled the Jewish persecutions. Kissinger and his family settled in Washington Heights, New York, and after learning English (in a sink-or-swim environment!) he went on to Harvard and to his work in American diplomacy. Kurt Waldheim, former Secretary General of the United Nations, is bilingual, as were his predecessors: Dag Hammarskjöld, a native speaker of Swedish, spoke French, English, and German fluently, and U Thant spoke English and Burmese fluently.

In philosophy and religion we also find some well-known persons using two or more languages on a daily basis. Mahatma Gandhi spoke at least three languages, as did Albert Schweitzer, a well-known theologian, musician, and missionary. Martin Luther spoke to his students in Latin when dealing with theology and the church and in German when discussing other topics. They code-switched constantly between the two languages. Erasmus, the Dutch humanist and scholar and the first editor of the New Testament, spoke five languages. His mother tongue was Dutch but he used Latin not only for diplomacy and theology but also in everyday conversations. He lived in England, France, and Switzerland and thus learned and

BOX 5.11

Some Well-Known Persons Who Were or Are Bilingual

Politics

Indira Gandhi: Hindi, English
Kurt Waldheim: German, English
Henry Kissinger: German, English
Marshall Tito: Serbo-Croatian, German, Slovenian, Czech, Russian
Menachem Begin: Polish, Hebrew, English
Pierre Elliott Trudeau: French, English
King Hussein: Arabic, English
Julius Nyerere: Swahili, English

Philosophy and Religion

Mahatma Gandhi: Gujarathi, Hindi, English
Martin Luther: German, Latin
Pope John Paul II: Polish, Latin, Italian, English, German
Jesus Christ: Aramaic, Hebrew, Latin?, Greek?
Desiderius Erasmus: Dutch, Latin, French, Italian, English
Albert Schweitzer: Alsatian, German, French

Fine Arts and Cinema

Pablo Picasso: Spanish, French
Salvador Dali: Spanish, English
Ingrid Bergman: Swedish, English, Italian
Sophia Loren: Italian, French, English
Maurice Chevalier: French, English
Greta Garbo: Swedish, English

Science and Social Science

Marie Curie: Polish, French
Guglielmo Marconi: Italian, English
Enrico Fermi: Italian, German, English
Georg von Békésy: Hungarian, English
Bruno Bettelheim: German, English
Roman Jakobson: Russian, French, English, German, Czech

Literature

Joseph Conrad: Polish, French, English
Samuel Beckett: English, French
Miguel Angel Asturias: Spanish, French
Rabindranath Tagore: Bengali, English
Czeslaw Milosz: Russian, Polish, English
John Milton: Latin, English
Isaac B. Singer: Yiddish, Polish, Hebrew, English

Music

George Frederick Handel: German, English
Frédéric Chopin: French, Polish
Arthur Rubinstein: Polish, German, French, English
Pablo Casals: Spanish, French

used English, French, and Italian. On his deathbed, his last prayer was in Latin, but his last words were in Dutch, "Lieve God" (dear God). Pope John Paul II is reported to speak twelve languages, some of which he probably uses daily (such as Polish, Latin, Italian, and English). Every morning before starting work he reads papers in five different languages.

Perhaps the most surprising bilingual in this domain is Jesus Christ, who may even have been trilingual. He was probably a native speaker of Aramaic, the most-used language in Palestine at that time, but in his rabbinical training he learned Hebrew, which was still spoken in certain parts of Palestine at that time. He must have used Hebrew when talking to the Pharisees and on solemn occasions such as the Last Supper. He may also have known Greek and Latin, both of which were spoken in Palestine but to a lesser extent. Greek was a commercial language used by the upper classes and by the Romans themselves. Latin, the language of the occupying forces, was used in the law courts and in trading. It is interesting to wonder what language Jesus used with Pontius Pilate: Latin or Greek? Or did Jesus speak Aramaic or Hebrew and Pilate answer in Latin or Greek, through an interpreter?

There are a number of bilingual scientists. Marie Curie, one of the few people to be awarded the Nobel Prize on two occasions, was born Maria Skłodowska, a citizen of Poland. She attended a Russian school in Warsaw, then went to Paris. She was probably trilingual, although French became her dominant language. The Italian Guglielmo Marconi, who invented the radio, did much of his research in Great Britain and hence was bilingual in Italian and English. The nuclear physicist Enrico Fermi was Italian but did his doctoral studies in Göttingen, Germany, and emigrated to the United States at the age of thirty-seven. Quite a few Nobel Prizes have been awarded to naturalized citizens of the United States who came to this country either because of political oppression in their home countries—Fermi in Italy, Békésy in Hungary—or because of research conditions—Roger Guillemin of France, for instance, who works at the Salk Institute in San Diego, and who won the Nobel Prize for Medicine in 1977.

In music and the fine arts, Handel, a Prussian, settled in England; Chopin was born in Poland, but his father was French and later he settled in Paris; Arthur Rubinstein was also born in Poland, where he lived before moving to Berlin and then to France, England, and the United States; both Salvador Dali and Pablo Picasso were born in Spain but fled the country when Fascism was installed. Well-known bilingual actors include Greta Garbo with her marked Swedish accent in English, Maurice Chevalier with his French accent in English (some say he could speak without an accent!), and Ingrid Bergman, who is fluent in Swedish, her native language; English, her work language; and Italian, her family language.

It is in the domain of literature that the question of bilingualism becomes interesting. Some writers write only in their first language. Isaac B. Singer, for instance, speaks a number of languages but writes in Yiddish, his native language. He tried to write in Hebrew, but nothing he created in that language satisfied him. Czeslaw Milosz, 1980 Nobel Prize laureate for literature, speaks Polish, Russian, English, Latvian, and French, but writes only in Polish and has translated Shakespeare, Milton, Baudelaire, and Eliot into Polish.

Other bilingual writers write only in their second or third language, the most famous being Joseph Conrad, who was born Teodor Józef Konrad Korzeniowski in Poland, where he lived until the age of sixteen. He learned some French in school, then lived in France between the ages of sixteen and twenty. At the end of his stay, Conrad was completely bilingual in Polish and French. He then joined the English merchant navy and learned to speak and write English. When he ended his sailing career at the age of thirty-five, he had already written some prose in English, and after that he became a full-time novelist. What is especially interesting is that he did not write his books in Polish, his first language, or in French, a language he wrote fluently, but in English, his *third* language. Karl (1979) informs us that Conrad's refusal to write in Polish was his way of separating himself from his father and his culture and country. He had to defend himself constantly against attacks from both the English and the Poles. As Karl writes: "Ironically, this attack from the English that he was a Pole in disguise was matched by attacks from Poles that he was an Englishman in disguise. He had to defend himself for not bringing up his sons to speak Polish: they were English" (p. 650). Conrad's English prose was superlative and required almost no editing, but in speaking he did retain a strong accent, which prevented him from lecturing publicly. Karl reports the following exchange between Conrad and a Belgian critic twenty years after Conrad had settled in England:

My pronunciation [in English] is rather defective to this day. Having unluckily no ear, my accentuation is uncertain, especially when in the course of a conversation I become self-conscious. In writing I wrestle painfully with that language which I feel I do not possess but which possesses me—alas. (p. 697)

Conrad retained complete fluency in Polish and French, and at home he would often carry on conversations in all three languages. He also gave advice to translators who were translating his books into French and Polish.

Finally, a few writers write in two languages. Samuel Beckett is one of these. Born in Ireland, a native speaker of English, he learned French at school and obtained a bachelor's degree in French and Italian. He never really used French in his daily life, however, until he became an instructor at the Ecole Normale Supérieure in Paris when he was twenty-two. His first works—tales and poems—were in English. In 1937, at the age of thirty-one, he moved to Paris permanently but continued to write in English; *Murphy,* for instance, was published in 1938. During World War II he fought in the Resistance and then went into hiding in the Vaucluse. In 1951 his first French novel, *Molloy,* appeared, and from then on he wrote in both French and English. Beckett obtained the Nobel Prize for Literature in 1969 for his contribution to the literature of two languages.

Another exception among bilingual writers is Vladimir Nabokov, who was born in St. Petersburg, Russia, in 1899 and was brought up bilingual in Russian and French. He learned English as an adolescent and studied at Trinity College, Cambridge. Nabokov became very well known as an emigré writer in Russian, publishing such works as *Mashenka, The Exploit, The Gift,* and *The Eye* in that language. But later he wrote in English and became famous in the English-speaking world for such novels as *Ada, Bend Sinister,* and *Lolita.* Nabokov also translated Russian writers into English and English writers into Russian. Thus Beckett and Nabokov are the proof that one person can write literature in two different languages.

⑥ Bilingual Speech and Language

Depending on the topic, situation, interlocutor, and intent, a bilingual may speak one language or the other, borrow elements of one language when speaking the other, or switch from one to the other. In addition the bilingual's languages may deviate from those of monolinguals either because of lack of fluency or because the two languages have had a permanent influence on one another. This very interesting, but highly complex language situation has been the subject of considerable research and of much debate among researchers. In his book *Languages in Contact,* Weinreich (1968) uses the term "interference" to refer to any difference that may exist between the speech of a monolingual and that of a bilingual. Haugen (1956, 1969) prefers a three-part distinction: switching, that is, the alternate use of two languages (see Chapter 3); interference, the overlapping of two languages, and integration, the use of words or phrases from one language that have become so much a part of the other that it cannot be called either switching or overlapping except in a historical sense. Subsequent researchers have given interference a lesser role; Clyne (1967, 1972), for instance, prefers the term transference, which has a less negative connotation and more recently other researchers have put the stress on code-switching. This has led to a new flurry of distinctions such as code-mixing, code-changing, and language-mixing and to on-going research on the constraints that govern the alternate use of two languages in the same conversation and on the existence of bilingual language varieties that have their own norms.

It is not my intent in this chapter to give a historical overview of the numerous studies of bilingual speech and language, nor will I attempt to resolve the controversies concerning interference, language mixing, and language norms. Instead I will limit the discussion to bilingual speech in two very distinct environments: first, the bilingual speaking to a *monolingual* in a *monolingual* environment and second, the bilingual speaking to a *bilingual* in a *bilingual* environment. I will also discuss the long-term effects that bilingualism may have on a language, especially on its vocabulary.

To illustrate, I have put together three short monologues based on real language data. In the first, a French-English bilingual is talking to an English-speaking friend who knows no French. The bilingual tells how he and his friend John stopped next to a farm to stretch their legs on their way to a meeting:

> We looked at the sheeps grazing in the field for ten minutes and then we went back to the car. John, who liked very much the countryside, wished we could stay a bit longer, but it was getting late and so we hurried up. There was a horse next to the car, but we didn't have time to pat it. We climbed in and drove off.

Although French is his stronger language, we note that he is quite fluent in English and has no problems communicating with his friend. We also note two deviations from standard English. The first is pluralizing "sheep" by adding an "s." He has overgeneralized the pluralization rule of English based on such regular patterns as pet/pets and light/lights. The second deviation, "liked very much the countryside" instead of "liked the countryside very much" is probably a literal translation of the French "aimait beaucoup la campagne." In the first section of this chapter we will study such deviations that occur when bilinguals are speaking to monolinguals. We will first examine within-language deviations, then concentrate on interferences, the involuntary influence of one language on the other. It is rare that a bilingual can lock out one language completely when speaking the other, especially when he or she is tired or under stress.

To illustrate the second section of this chapter, we return to our French-English bilingual, who is now speaking to a bilingual friend. He tells her about a hike he went on in the Blue Hills. The base language is French, code-switches and lexical borrowings are italicized.

Hier on est allé faire une *hike* de *six miles* dans les *Blue Hills.* On a fait trois sommets, *up and down,* et ensuite on a pris un *trail* qui nous a amené près de *Clear Pond.* Les *guys* étaient en forme mais *Helen* avait l'air *tired.* A la fin on s'est tous entassés dans la *station wagon* de *Bob* et on est allé *bruncher* chez moi.

(Yesterday we went on a six-mile hike in the Blue Hills. We climbed three hills, up and down, and then we followed a trail that took us to Clear Pond. The guys were doing fine, but Helen looked tired. Afterward we all squeezed into Bob's station wagon and came home for brunch.)

This monologue is a good example of what some have called code-mixing and others have described as massive interference or semi-lingualism. In fact, and quite clearly, our bilingual is simply using the resources of his two languages to speak to his bilingual friend. Had a monolingual French- or English-speaking person been present, he would have said the same thing in one language with no mixing. Some researchers have unfortunately used the term "interference" to describe the conscious code-switching and borrowing that takes place among bilinguals, who follow strict linguistic constraints. In this extract there are *no* interferences; the French and the English segments are perfectly correct and could have been uttered by a monolingual.

The second section of this chapter will cover the two strategies open to the bilingual when speaking to another bilingual: switching completely to the other language for a word, phrase, or sentence (code-switching) or borrowing a word from the other language and adapting it to the base language. The monologue above has numerous instances of code-switching (hike, six miles, up and down) and one instance of borrowing: the English verb "brunch" has been adapted to French phonology and morphology to give "bruncher." We will review the reasons that lead bilinguals to borrow, then examine different types of loans and how they are adapted. We will discuss the different types of code-switches and the grammatical constraints that govern them. And we will end by examining how regular code-switching and borrowing in a stable bilingual community can lead to a new language variety.

The third section is concerned with the effect of bilingualism on language. To illustrate, let us return to our French-English bilingual. Here he is telling a monolingual French person who knows no English about a possible film scenario involving a person named Jean-Marie:

Jean-Marie écoute son transistor, un verre de Scotch à la main. Après le flash d'information et l'interview d'un chanteur de rock, il enfile ses jeans tout neufs et descend au parking du building. Le traffic du weekend étant impossible, il décide de prendre sa Harley-Davidson pour aller au match de rugby.

(Jean-Marie is listening to his transistor radio, a glass of whiskey in his hand. After the newsbreak and an interview of a rock singer, he puts on his new jeans and goes down to the parking lot of the building. As the weekend traffic is very heavy, he decides to go to the rugby game on his Harley-Davidson.)

I did not italicize the many English words for the simple reason that "transistor," "Scotch," "flash," "interview," and "rock" are now integral parts of the French language. They are pronounced in the French way and are used by monolinguals who know no English. Thus, our French-English bilingual is speaking only one language, and surprising as it may seem, he is not code-switching or borrowing from English. Although bilingualism can lead to language convergence and pidginization (see Chapter 1), the third section of the chapter stresses language borrowing. We will attempt to distinguish between borrowing at the individual level (bruncher), which I will call *speech* borrowing, and borrowing at the community or national language level (jeans, rock), which I will call *language* borrowing. We will then discuss the reasons that lead to language borrowing and the resistance to it, both linguistic and psychosocial. This latter type, spearheaded by language conservatives, has been present since the beginnings of language contact. Although it has been effective on some occasions, as in the case of Latin loans in German, it has more often than not failed to stop the foreign terms from entering the language. These loans are often the sole survivors of periods of language contact; they live on long after the bilingualism that brought them into the language has passed away. It is a fitting tribute to bilingualism that we should end this book by examining its legacy to language.

Speaking to a Monolingual

In the preceding chapter I noted that most bilinguals are less fluent in one language than in the other, although dominance may also depend on the skill (speaking, writing, and so on), the situation, or the topic of conversation. And even if a bilingual has the language competence of a monolingual in both languages, he or she will seldom be able to keep the two languages completely separate when talking to a monolingual; from time to time they will influence one another, even if only momentarily. As Haugen (1969) writes:

Is it possible to keep the patterns of two (or more) languages absolutely pure, so that a bilingual in effect becomes two monolinguals, each speaking one language perfectly but also perfectly understanding the other and able to reproduce in one the meaning of the other without at any point violating the usages of either language? On the face of it one is inclined to say no. Hypothetically it is possible, just as a perfectly straight line or perfect beauty or perfect bliss are theoretically possible, but in practice it is necessary to settle for less. (p. 8)

The deviations when a bilingual speaks to a monolingual may be due to a lack of fluency in the language or to interference of the other language, despite the bilingual's wish to keep the languages separate. I will not discuss slips of the tongue and malapropisms, as these are common to both monolinguals and bilinguals, but I will note three points before continuing the discussion. First, some bilinguals are more prone to deviations than others because of such factors as the manner of learning, mastery, and use of the language as well as the attitudes of the bilingual and of the community toward such deviations. Second, fatigue, stress, topic of conversation, situation, and the interlocutor will affect the frequency of deviations. Age also seems to be a factor: Clyne (1978) reports that elderly German immigrants in Australia employ such German words as "ob," "und," and "weil" in their English without being aware of them. And third, deviations rarely cause a breakdown in communication except when a person is in the process of learning a second language. When the bilingual has achieved a stable level of fluency, breakdowns are much less frequent. This discussion will concentrate more on the stable bilingual than on the second-language learner.

Interlanguage

Recent studies have analyzed the errors made by language learners. Some researchers, including Corder, Selinker, Nemser, and Richards, have proposed that as the learner acquires a second language, he or she passes through various language stages or systems before acquiring the system of the native speaker of that language. Corder (1967) talks of "transitional competence," Nemser (1971) uses the expression "approximative system," and Selinker (1972) proposes the term "interlanguage," which he defines as a separate language system based on the observable output which results from a learner's attempted production of a target language norm.

The evidence for such an interlanguage (or series of interlanguages) comes from the errors made by the learner; not all can be attributed to the first language or to the language being learned—some seem to find their source in an intermediate system. Once the second language has been learned, the "learner" has a language system similar to that of a native speaker; in a word, the person has become a "true" bilingual with two native-like language systems. Often, however, the learner stops learning after reaching a certain level of fluency, and as a consequence the interlanguage becomes "fossilized" (Selinker, 1972). Box 6.1 presents an extract taken from Kegl (1975) of English as a fossilized interlanguage. The person speaking is a seventy-six year-old Slovenian American who arrived in the United States when she was twenty-five and has never returned to Slovenia. She is bilingual in that she uses her two languages on a regular basis: Slovene to some of her friends and at the Slovenian club, both Slovene and English to her daughter and other friends, and English to her granddaughter and with people outside the Slovenian American community. Her English is quite understandable, but it is replete with deviations; many are due to the influence of Slovene (interferences), and others can be accounted for by her English interlanguage.

Why do some people never reach total fluency in their second language? Researchers seem to agree that a primary reason is linked

---

BOX 6.1   **BILINGUALS SPEAK**

A Fossilized Interlanguage

This is not my story but this is story my grandpa told me. Everybody go in a war. My father was forty-two year old. He had to go. He was captured—in a prison—what the call it—he was captured. And then he was transferred to the Siberia. That's true story. He was transferred to Siberia. That a true story, ja. And there he was five years. He watch ninety pigs . . . he gotta control ninety pigs . . . There was not house like this. It was like big shack. It was made from mud and tree branches. There was branches all around and they make it from the mud that it keep it together. They got only mud and the mud keep together—there was home like. But they was all live together—mother, father, workers, pigs, cows, kids. They was all in one room, but it was a big room. But they got no wooden floor no nothing. They got mud floor—clay, but they got no floor. He come home my mother no even know. (Kegl,1975) to the level of fluency needed for everyday communication. Selinker (1972) writes that an entirely fossilized interlanguage competence is a result of the speaker's realization that he or she knows the language well enough to communicate. When this stage is reached, the person stops learning.

Richards (1972) reports on various groups that never develop total fluency in their second language. Among the factors that lead to fossilization in immigrants, for instance, are the area and pattern of settlement, the group's numerical strength, educational level, and cultural cohesiveness. An important factor is integration into the majority group. If the attitudes and behaviors of the immigrant group and of the majority group do not favor assimilation, the immigrants will learn the majority language only to a level adequate for communication in the workplace, stores, and public administration. If, on the other hand, integration and upward mobility are favored, fluency in the majority language will be greatly enhanced. Haugen (1956) writes aptly: "Mere *communication* may be satisfied by a relatively modest mastery of the second language; *social identification* with a dominant group may require something approaching native command" (pp. 96–97).

Gardner and Lambert (1972) have studied the underlying attitudes and motivations of second-language learners and have isolated two types. One type needs to know a language for purely utilitarian reasons and therefore has an instrumental orientation to learning it; the second wishes to be integrated, at least in part, into the other language group and not be rejected by that group. These learners, who have an integrative orientation to language learning, usually attain a much higher level of fluency than the first type.

Both Selinker (1972) and Richards (1972) point out that a fossilized interlanguage can become the recognized language variety of a group of people. Selinker writes: "Not only can entire interlingual competences be fossilized in individual learners performing in their own interlingual situation, but also in whole groups of individuals, resulting in the emergence of a new dialect . . . where fossilized interlanguage competences may be the normal situation" (p. 217). Such varieties can be found within established immigrant groups: Clyne (1967, 1972) refers to the English spoken by German immigrants in Australia as German English, and Haugen (1953) refers to Norwegian spoken by immigrants and their children in America as American Norwegian. New varieties of a language may also be found in once-colonized countries. In India, Indian English has stable characteristics different from British and American English. Richards (1972) mentions that "this all" instead of "all this" is now part of the code of Indian English, and John (1980) reports that the "th" sound in such words as "thin" and "thistle" is systematically replaced by a "t" sound. Other varieties of English are found in Nigeria and the Philippines. (A more recent study of interlanguage can be found in Klein and Dittmar, 1979.)

Our discussion of deviations will be concerned only with those of individual bilinguals who do not belong to a stable language group that has its own fossilized interlanguage norms. Thus, we will not call something a deviation that is in fact perfectly acceptable in the group's interlanguage. Any deviation will be compared to the speech of the monolingual speakers of that language. We will study two types of deviations: within-language deviations caused by simplification, overgeneralization, and hypercorrection, and between-language deviations (interferences) caused by influence of the other language. I should point out right away that many deviations are the result of both within- and between-language influences and hence are difficult to classify. Dommergues and Lane (1976) give two examples from French-English bilinguals in which the source of the deviation is unclear. In the first, the deviation "to catch up" in

I wasn't fast enough to catch up the runners.

may be influenced by the French "pour rattraper" (to catch up) or be based on the English pattern

I wasn't fast enough to look up the numbers.

or may be due to a simple failure to insert "with." In the second example, the deviation "how it is called" in the sentence

I don't know how it is called.

could be due to the influence of French:

Je ne sais pas comment cela s'appelle.

or to an analogy with the English pattern

I don't know how it is done.

Although I will attempt to give unambiguous examples, it is important to remember that many deviations have a dual origin.

Within-Language Deviations

One type of deviation that is quite common in the bilingual's weaker language is overgeneralization, also called false analogy and under-learning. Just as the child learning his or her first language will overgeneralize the past-tense rule of verbs, as in

I taked the bus with Mommy.

so too, the nonfluent bilingual will overgeneralize certain patterns. But unlike the child, who will learn the exceptions to the past tense rule, the bilingual may never do so. Selinker (1972) reports that a Hebrew-English bilingual who was very fluent in English said

What did he intended to say.

probably based on a pattern like:

What he intended to say.

not realizing that an auxiliary preceding the verb carries the tense marker. Similar examples are reported by Frith (1978):

She must goes to school every day.
(based on: She goes to school every day.)

She did not found it.
(based on: She found it.)

Overgeneralization may occur in phonology and morphology as well as syntax and semantics. Selinker reports having heard an Indian speaker of English extend the meaning of "drive" to all vehicles, which led to "driving a bicycle" instead of "riding a bicycle."

A second common type of deviation is the result of simplification. The demands of communication—conveying a message in what may be a constraining situation—force the speaker to concentrate on the meaning and simplify the form by dropping pluralization and tense markers, omitting the function words, simplifying the syntax, dropping the auxiliaries and using only one tense. Coulter (1968) gives three examples from the discourse of two elderly Russian speakers of English:

It was nice, nice trailer, big one.
I have many hundred carpenter my own.
I was in Frankfurt when I fill application.

In the first sentence the articles are omitted, in the second the "of" and the plural marker in "carpenter" are omitted, and in the third, "out," "the," and the tense marker in "fill" are left out. Veronique (1980) reports that North Africans in the south of France often simplify the French pronouns "il" and "elle" to /i/ and that "qui" and "que" become /k/. And many an English or American person who has lived in France for a number of years and who is otherwise fluent in French maintains a simplified or neutral form of "un" (a) which allows him or her to leave the gender of the noun unspecified, neither "un" nor "une". Meisel, Clahsen, and Pienemann (1979) report that Luigina, a young Italian girl in Germany, would drop the verb in her German sentences so that she would not have to choose the verb and mark it appropriately. She would say:

Ich mädchen.
(I girl.)

Other deviations result from hypercorrection and spelling pronunciation as well as the avoidance of certain words, expressions, and grammatical rules that may be especially difficult for the speaker.

There is some controversy among researchers as to the relative importance of these within-language deviations. It has been proposed that in the speech of second-language learners, such deviations are at least as frequent as interferences, but that in the speech of bilinguals with stable or native-like fossilized language systems they are much less important. The little data that is available appears to support this: Mougeon and Hébrard (1975) report that 70 percent of the errors made by French-English Canadian bilingual children were due to interference from French and not to overgeneralization, simplification, or other within-language strategies; Sheen (1980) reports that 74 percent of all the errors he found in the speech of nine bilingual adults were due to interference. This appears to show that during second-language learning, intralanguage deviations may be more important than interferences but that when the second language has reached a high level of fluency, the remaining deviations are mostly due to the influence of the other language. This is supported informally by remarks bilinguals make to one another when they are conscious of their language production; they are of the type "That's another calque you just made," or "That's a Gallicism," not "You've dropped the verb" or "You've forgotten to mark the past tense."

Interference

Most researchers on bilingualism have proposed very similar definitions of interference: Weinreich (1968) defines it as "those instances of deviation from the norms of either language which occur in the speech of bilinguals as a result of their familiarity with more than one language"; Haugen (1956) refers to it as "the overlapping of two languages"; Mackey (1968) defines it as "the use of features belonging to one language while speaking or writing another"; and Clyne (1972) calls transference "the adoption of any elements or features from the other language."

As I noted earlier, these definitions do not distinguish the controlled and more or less conscious use of code-switching and speech borrowing from the involuntary or accidental use of elements from the wrong language when speaking to a monolingual. This confusion has led certain researchers such as Fishman to reject the term "interference" because it carries pejorative and disruptive connotations, and has led others to stress the positive aspects of interference in a bilingual environment. Haugen (1972) writes: "We need to get away from the notion of 'interference' as somehow noxious and harmful to the languages. The bilingual finds that in communicating he is aided by the overlap between languages and he gets his message across by whatever devices are available to him at the moment of speaking" (p. 322).

In this section I refer to interference as the involuntary influence of one language on the other. This type of influence becomes quite apparent when a bilingual is speaking to a monolingual. In this situation the bilingual realizes that code-switching and borrowing might impede communication. If, despite this, one language is influenced by the other, one can then talk of interference. I should stress again that we will consider only the bilingual who masters two standard monolingual language varieties, not the bilingual who speaks an immigrant language variety that has borrowed heavily and permanently from the majority language (as in the case of American Norwegian, for example). When that person speaks to a monolingual from the home country (in this case, Norway) it can be argued that the two are no longer using the same language variety (Haugen, 1977).

Before examining different types of interference, we should note several points. First, interference in language production has received much more attention than interference in language perception. We know very little about the influence of one language on the other when the bilingual is listening to someone speak. Second, interferences seldom affect communication; bilinguals usually develop enough skills in their weaker language to communicate satisfactorily with monolinguals, and the latter quickly grow accustomed to a foreign accent, a stilted syntax, and words with slightly different meanings. Language conservatives magnify the significance of interferences, which are usually of small import to the persons communicating. Third, the occurrence of certain syntactic and lexical interferences seems to depend on factors such as fatigue, stress, interlocutor, last language spoken, and so on. The "true" bilingual, that is, the person equally fluent in two languages, could be characterized as having no permanent interference. From time to time, however, the other language will make itself felt by a slight shift in intonation or by the strange use of a word or of an expression, but only a conscious observer will be aware of this. Finally, in fluent or near-fluent bilinguals, interferences are often two way, with each language influencing the other (at least at the lexical level). This often leads a bilingual who is otherwise perfectly fluent in both languages to remark that he or she speaks neither language well. What the bilingual forgets is that despite a few unimportant interferences, the meaning is conveyed almost perfectly.

Interferences can occur at all levels of language production in both speaking and writing. Below we discuss interferences in four domains: pronunciation, words and idiomatic expressions, syntax, and spelling.

PRONUNCIATION   A "foreign accent" is often a direct reflection of the interference of another language at the level of pronunciation, that is, at the level of phonology and prosody. And unlike other aspects of a second language, it usually cannot be eradicated after the age of fifteen or sixteen. Joseph Conrad started to learn English at the age of twenty and soon mastered it to a level rarely attained by native speakers of that language, and yet he spoke it with a strong Polish accent.

Weinreich (1968) proposes the following definition for interference at the phonological level: "Interference arises when a bilingual identifies a phoneme of the secondary system with one in the primary system and, in reproducing it, subjects it to the phonetic rules of the primary language" (p. 14). For example, when the weaker, or secondary, language has two phonemes, and the stronger, or primary, language has only one, the bilingual may fail to distinguish the two phonemes and may use a sound from the stronger language to replace both. Thus, French has only one /i/ sound as in "petit," whereas English has two: /i/ as in "seat" and "leave" and /I/ as in "sit" and "live." This may lead the French-English bilingual to underdifferentiate between the two sounds and replace both with the French /i/, producing phrases such as

Heet the nail
(instead of hit)

The reem of the glass
(instead of rim)

Haugen (1956) reports that there is no "z" sound in Norwegian, so Norwegian Americans say "rossess" instead of "roses." In Portuguese there is no "ch" sound (as in church) and so many Portugese Americans replace the sound with "sh," a sound that does exist in Portuguese. This gives "shicken" instead of "chicken", "sheck" instead of "check", and so on. French does not have a "th" sound, so nonfluent bilinguals replace it with a "z", a "t" or a "d", depending on the context. Thus Maurice Chevalier in *Gigi* sings

Sank evven for leetle girls.
(instead of: Thank heaven for little girls.)

Other, less serious interferences occur when the two languages have different pronunciations for a single sound (the French "r" as opposed to the English "r"); the substitution of one for the other is quite apparent but does not impede understanding.

Interferences may also occur at the level of prosody. French people speaking English often tend to give equal stress to all the syllables in the word, as is done in French, whereas English polysyllabic words have one primary stress, sometimes a secondary stress, and a number of unstressed syllables. Thus the word "library" will be stressed LI-BRA-RY by the French person instead of LI-brary. A more serious interference occurs when the French person, knowing that every English word receives a primary stress places the stress on the wrong syllable and weakens the others, thereby rendering the word unintelligible when it is said out of context. As an example, when a rather fluent French-English bilingual told an English friend that she had visited Edinburgh, she stressed the second syllable and reduced the first to a schwa, giving "e DIN burgh" /ə'dinbrə/, making the name totally unintelligible. Only repeated and altered pronunciations of the word finally made it comprehensible to the listener.

Finally, an interference in intonation may occur where a particular pattern means one thing in one language but something different in the other language. This is the case with the expression of doubt and of certainty in English and French, for instance.

WORDS AND IDIOMATIC EXPRESSIONS   Interferences at the word level are very similar to the various types of lexical borrowings made by bilinguals when speaking to one another. However, word interferences are involuntary, and the monolingual listener may misunderstand what is being said. One type of word interference is caused by importing a word from the other language and adapting it phonologically and morphologically to the language being spoken. Thus, a French-English bilingual once said to her English-speaking nephew, "Marc, you're BAVING!" She pronounced "baving," based on the French "baver" (to dribble), like "patting." The boy looked at his aunt with puzzled eyes, and she quickly corrected herself. Another example involves the involuntary borrowing of an English word in French. In

> Une fois qu'on a EXTENDU son visa.
> (As soon as you have extended your visa.)

the English "extend" has been adapted phonologically and morphologically to the French sentence. (The correct French word is prolongé.) The monolingual listener looked surprised but understood what was being said by reference to the French "extension," which shares some of the meanings of "prolongement." A third example of this type of interference can be found in the sentence:

> Look at the CAMION!

Here the French word "camion" (truck) is pronounced as if it were an English word (it is made to rhyme with canyon). Finally, in

> Il est beaucoup plus MATURE.
> (He is much more mature.)

the English word "mature" is pronounced like the French "nature", replacing the French word "mûr." In all of these examples a bilingual was speaking to a monolingual and was unaware of the borrowing.

A second and probably more frequent type of interference consists in extending the meaning of words that already exist in the language being spoken. This is especially likely to occur when words in the two languages resemble one another phonetically and orthographically but have different meanings. For instance, a French-English bilingual once said to his English-speaking child at the zoo

> Look at the CORNS on that animal.

The word "corn" was based on the French "corne," meaning "horn," among other things, and this meaning was erroneously attached to the English word.

Sheen (1980) gives examples of similar interferences in the speech of French-English bilinguals:

And Julia is MUTILATED; she broke her legs.

Here "mutilated" is given one of the meanings of "mutilé," that of "badly hurt."

But where my father went it was not an EXPERIENCE.

Here "experience" is given one of the meanings of "expérience," that of "experiment." In the sentence

If you wanted to be A RESPONSIBLE for an exchange group.

"a responsible" is based on "un responsable," a person in charge of something. In

I love NATURE here.

"nature" is given one of the meanings of French "nature," that of countryside.

Of course, the interference and its source do not have to resemble one another phonetically. For instance:

Don't move the NEEDLES of the clock.

is based on the French "aiguilles (needles) d'une montre"; the correct English term would be "hands."

So we TAKE an apéritif and go to the dining room.
(Sheen, 1980)

Here "take" is influenced by "prendre (take) un apéritif"; the correct English word would be "have." The phrase

It was very well PLAYED ...   *(Sheen, 1980)*

is based on French "joué" (played); "acted" would have been preferable.

Haugen (1969) notes that such interferences can be quite amusing, at least to the perceiver. He reports that a Norwegian American who was working with a thrashing crew, hearing a loud crack in the thrashing rig, said:

I tink I hear someting SMELLING.

based on Norwegian "smelle" (to crack)! He also recounts that when asked by a stranger where his father was, a boy answered

Oh, he's in the STOVE.

Here the interference comes from the Norwegian "stova," meaning living room.

Interference occurs at the level of idiomatic expressions when such expressions are translated literally (or calqued) into the other language. Sheen (1980) reports that a French-English bilingual said

I'm telling myself stories.
(instead of: I'm kidding myself.)

because he translated the French expression ("Je me raconte des histoires") literally into English. Mackey (1976) gives similar examples:

Il parle à travers son chapeau.

This is based on "he's talking through his hat"; the French expression is "Il parle pour ne rien dire."

Winter is before the door.

is based on the German expression "Winter steht vor der Tür"; the English expression is "Winter is around the corner."

He was laughing in his fist.

is a translation of "Er hat sich ins Fäustchen gelacht"; the English idiom is "He was laughing up his sleeve."

Depending on the context, interferences involving words and idioms will affect communication to a greater or lesser degree. Very often the monolingual interlocutor understands what is being said because of the context. When a breakdown does occur, the interlocutor will usually tell the bilingual, and the latter will make a correction or use a paraphrase. Mackey (1976) notes that some bilinguals avoid loan words (such as "weekend" in French) because they are not sure whether these words are truly loanwords or interferences. These cautious bilinguals adopt the strategy of avoiding loanwords—a safe way of not falling into the interference trap.

SYNTAX   Several types of interference can occur at the level of syntax. For instance, using the word order pattern of one language in the other can given ungrammatical, although quite often understandable, sentences. Thus a French-English bilingual may order adjectives and adverbs according to the French pattern when speaking English. Sheen (1980) gives several examples:

But we had very soon a governess.
But he knew well French.
I started only to learn Russian grammar in high school.

The position of the verb may also be influenced by the other language. Thus:

C'est fou ce que les noix ont.
(instead of: C'est fou ce qu'ont les noix.)

is based on "It's incredible what walnuts have." A similar pattern is found in

Là où l'accent tonique est.

based on "The place where the stress is." The French version would be "Là où est l'accent tonique."

Another type of interference involves the presence or absence of determiners. Mackey (1976) gives the phrase spoken by a French-English bilingual:

On the page five.

This is based on the French "Sur la page cinq," which uses the determiner "la," but in English, no determiner is required. Clyne (1967) reports that German-English bilinguals quite often fail to insert a definite article in certain German phrases because the equivalent phrase in English does not require one, for example

in Juni

based on "in June" instead of "im Juni," or

in Winter

based on "in winter" instead of "im Winter."

One also finds prepositions misused because of the influence of the other language. For example, Clyne (1967) reports that a German-English bilingual said

in diesem Bild

based on "in this picture," instead of "auf diesem Bild," and

in meiner Ansicht

based on "in my opinion," instead of "nach meiner Ansicht." Mougeon, Bélanger, and Canale (1978) have found misuses of prepositions by English-French bilinguals in Ontario:

J'ai vu ça sur la télévision.

based on "I saw that on TV." In standard French it would be "J'ai vu ça à la télévision." These same bilinguals produced sentences of the type

We're going at Montreal.

based on "Nous allons à Montréal."

Among other syntactic interferences we should note the wrong use of tense and aspect. Two examples taken from Sheen (1980) will illustrate this. In

> But now since I am teaching

the use of the present continuous tense is based on the French "depuis que j'enseigne," whereas in English the verb should be in the present perfect continuous: "But (now) since I have been teaching." In the sentence

> He was dancing well, but as an actor he was not good.

the tense is based on the French imperfect ("Il dansait bien") instead of on the English past tense.

Weinreich (1968) classifies interferences of grammatical relations into three categories. In the first are the most serious, those that produce an unintended meaning. He cites a sentence spoken by a German-English bilingual: "This woman loves the man," based on "diese Frau liebt der Mann." The person wanted to communicate "The man loves this woman," but in fact produced the opposite meaning. A similar case may be found in the situation where an English-French bilingual tells a close friend that he misses him (the close friend) very much. If he says "Je te manque," based on "I miss you," he actually conveys the opposite meaning: "You miss me." The correct French would be "Tu me manques."

In Weinrich's second category we find interferences that produce a meaning that is understandable by implication. He cites the German-English bilingual who says, "Yesterday came he," based on the German "gestern kam er." The sentence in English is ungrammatical but perfectly understandable.

Weinreich's third category contains interference patterns that are possible in the language being spoken but not required by its grammar. Thus the English-Russian bilingual who maintains a subject-verb-object order in Russian, based on English word order, produces a perfectly good Russian sentence with an unnecessarily strict word order. And likewise, the English-Greek bilingual who inserts a pronoun before the verb in Greek often produces an acceptable sentence although the pronoun is not needed as the verb carries pronominal information.

SPELLING   Kegl (1975) reports that a Slovenian American informant used to write letters to her in an English orthography that was so different from the norm that she had to read the letters aloud to understand them. The beginning of one letter ran:

Daer Judi,
Ha var ju? Is veri kolt der?
(How are you? Is it very cold there?)

Not only did Slovenian syntax interfere with the informant's English, but her spelling was also influenced by that of her native language. Bilinguals who have learned to write in their two languages do not usually reach the level of interference attained by Kegl's informant, but they may still be subject to the influence of one language on the other. Clyne (1972) gave a dictation to thirty German-English bilingual children in Australia and found substantial interference from English in the German spelling. Many had problems with the capitalization of nouns: "Hauser" was written with a lowercase "h" (as in English) and "stadt" with a lowercase "s" by many subjects. Many also had doubts about compounds, such as "Ostbäume," which was written as two words by about two-thirds of the bilinguals. In addition, the students dropped letters— the "h" as a lengthening device in "Stühlen," for instance—and replaced German consonant clusters by English clusters—"sch" replaced by "sh," for instance.

Words that are spelled similarly in two languages are often a source of interference for the bilingual writer, however fluent he or she may be. Thus French-English bilinguals often write "development" with two "p's" (based on the French développement), "rhythm" with only one "h" (French rythme), "address" with one "d" (French adresse) and "apartment" with two "p's" (French appartement). Unfortunately for the bilingual, English and French share many such words, and it is often necessary to check a dictionary (or ask a monolingual) for the spelling of these words. Such interferences are often bidirectional, affecting the spelling of both languages.

To conclude this section, I will stress once more that a bilingual will develop his or her languages to the level of fluency that is needed for communication. For some this is near perfect and equal fluency in both languages; others do not need to be as fluent in one language as in the other. Once the bilingual has attained a stable level of fluency (and is no longer learning one or the other language), he or she may well continue to produce deviations when speaking, but these rarely interfere with communication. Deviations in bilingual speech, like slips of the tongue, rarely affect the interchange of meaning.

Speaking to a Bilingual

A bilingual speaking to a monolingual usually stays within one language without difficulty. When the bilingual addresses another bilingual, however, the situation is quite different. Although, as we saw in Chapter 3, any two bilinguals usually have an agreed-upon language of communication, they will resort to the other language if they need to and the psychosocial environment permits it. Two main approaches are open to them: they can either switch to the other language, or they can borrow a word and adapt (integrate) it into the language they are speaking. Thus, a French-English bilingual can say:

Ca m'étonnerait qu'on ait *code-switched* autant que ça.

or

Ca m'étonnerait qu'on ait CODE-SWITCHÉ autant que ça.

Both mean: "I can't believe that we code-switched as often as that." I refer to the first approach as code-switching and to the second as borrowing. In this second approach the bilingual can also extend the meaning of a word from the language he or she is speaking under the influence of the other language.

Unlike earlier research, which often examined code-switching at the level of *speech* in the bilingual and borrowing at the level of *language* in the language group, more recent studies have examined both code-switching and borrowing in everyday speech. However, not all researchers agree on how to define the two. Reyes (1974) believes that borrowing involves only single words that may be either morphologically adapted (incorporated borrowings) or not adapted (spontaneous borrowings); switching takes place at clearly discernible syntactic junctures. Pfaff (1979) uses the term "language mixing" to include single lexical items that may or may not be morphologically adapted as well as longer sequences corresponding to code-switches. Haugen (1956) and Hasselmo (1970), on the other hand, stress whether the item, however large, has been adapted to the phonological and/or morphological pattern of the language being spoken. If so, it is an integration (borrowing), and if not it is a code-switch. My distinction is similar to the one proposed by Haugen and Hasselmo: a code-switch can be of any length (a word, a phrase, a sentence) and is a complete shift to the other language, whereas a borrowing is a word or short expression that is adapted phonologically and morphologically to the language being spoken.

Before going further, I will make several comments about code-switching and borrowing. First, Hasselmo (1970) has pointed out that switches are not always clean, in that the shift to another language is not always perfect. This may raise the question of whether one is dealing with a "ragged switch" (as it is called by Hasselmo) or a borrowing, at least at the level of the word. Take for example a Portuguese-English bilingual who speaks English with a strong Portuguese accent. When the person brings an English word into a Portuguese sentence (and the word does not need to be marked morphologically), is this a switch or a borrowing? The phonology is clearly Portuguese, which may lead us to classify the word as a borrowing, yet the speaker may have intended to switch to English and not to integrate that word into Portuguese. Should the word be classified as a switch even though phonetically it sounds like a borrowing? This is an intriguing problem that needs further clarification. In most of the following examples a clear-cut case can be made for putting the item into the code-switching or borrowing category, but keep in mind that this is not always true.

A second comment concerns language borrowing as opposed to speech borrowing. The question of when a particular loan passes into the language of the community so that even monolinguals use it is an interesting one. To illustrate, here are two sentences uttered by a French-English bilingual:

Je passe le weekend à la maison.
(I'm spending the weekend at home.)

Ça a POPPÉ.
(It popped.)

In the first sentence, "weekend" is now part of the French language and is considered as such by the bilingual. In the second sentence, however, the bilingual borrows the verb "pop" from English and adapts it to French. But the resulting word "popper" is not, and probably never will be, a part of the French language. In this discussion we will deal only with the latter type, which I will term "speech borrowing." Elements borrowed at the level of language ("language borrowings") are discussed in the third section of this chapter.

A third comment concerns the reasons why bilinguals either code-switch or borrow. In the discussion below, I consider the pragmatic and semantic factors that lead bilinguals to resort to elements of the other language. But a question that remains unanswered, at the word level at least, is why a bilingual adapts some words into the base language (borrows) but maintains other words in their original configuration (code-switches). And why do some bilinguals prefer to borrow and others prefer to code-switch? Some researchers have proposed that nonfluent bilinguals borrow words from their weaker language but code-switch into their stronger language, whereas fluent bilinguals code-switch in both languages. Others have maintained that in the presence of language conservatives, bilinguals prefer to code-switch to show that they are conscious of using elements from the other language, but in an environment that is conducive to language mixing they will do more borrowing. A third possibility is that bilinguals bring in a word from the other language by code-switching and then, as that word is used repeatedly, they slowly adapt it to the phonology and morphology of the base language. It is certainly true that some bilinguals prefer to code-switch while others prefer to borrow and that some words are better switched than borrowed; the reasons will have to await further study.

A final comment has to do with bilinguals' awareness of code-switching and of borrowing. As we saw in Chapter 3, monolinguals often look down upon both activities as the ungrammatical mixing of languages, an attitude that may lead some bilinguals never to code-switch or borrow, even when they are with bilinguals they know well. But most code-switch and borrow among themselves, and they usually accept this behavior, especially if it is widespread in the community. We will see in the third part of this section that code-switching and borrowing are the norm in certain bilingual communities; the person who fails to do so is considered distant and affected. Jokes and puns are even based on code-switching and borrowing. Haugen (1969), for instance, records a joke told among Norwegian-Americans. The master tells his servant:

Tag grisen, John, og sæt i vognen.
(Take the grease, John, and put it in the wagon.)

The servant, after looking wonderingly at his master, goes away and comes back with a pig in his arms! The humor of the joke rests on the word "grisen." In Norwegian "gris" is a pig, but in Norwegian American it has also taken on the meaning of the English word "grease." Hence the bewilderment of John, who could not tell if he had to bring the grease or the pig!

Bilinguals are aware in a general sense that they borrow and code-switch, but they would probably be hard put to state how often they do so. Like monolinguals, bilinguals concentrate on what is being said and not on how it is said. Making a bilingual aware of code-switches or borrowings is very similar to making a person conscious of hesitation phenomena. For a short while the person tries not to hesitate, and the bilingual tries not to code-switch, but as the conversation starts up again and content becomes paramount, the person no longer hears the hesitations and the bilingual is no longer aware of each code-switch or borrowing.

Speech Borrowing

REASONS FOR BORROWING   In Chapter 3 we discussed the reasons that lead bilinguals to code-switch. Although the emphasis was on verbal and communicative strategies, I also gave some purely linguistic or semantic reasons for code-switching. These are almost identical to the reasons for word borrowing: the bilingual cannot find a particular word in one language and thus resorts to the other; the language being spoken does not have a particular word or the bilingual has not learned it; the words in the two languages are not equally familiar and the bilingual chooses the one that is best known; and the "most available word" phenomenon leads the bilingual to borrow from the other language, especially when he or she is tired, lazy, or under stress.

Instead of discussing each of these reasons in greater detail, I would like to examine the case of the person who settles in a country or region that has a different language. Overnight the person finds new realities and new distinctions in such domains as work, housing, schooling, fauna and flora, food, and sports. Very often the vocabulary of the first language is just not adequate to express these new realities: there may be no words for certain concepts or necessary distinctions. Hence the immigrant will often resort to using words of the other language. As Weinreich (1968) writes: "Lexical borrowings [to designate new things] can be described as a result of the fact that using ready-made designations is more economical than describing things afresh. Few users of language are poets" (p. 57).

Clyne (1967) illustrates how the German immigrant in Australia who wants to buy a home needs new terms: "When the migrant decides to buy his home, he gets to know the difference between brick, brick veneer, and weatherboard houses and between double-, single-, and triple-fronted ones. These words have no equivalent for him in German, for in Germany houses are usually rented, single-fronted, and mostly built of stone" (p. 73). Clyne says the German immigrant quickly borrows Australian farming terms (drover, stockman, creek, paddock) and English words that allow finer distinctions: "breakfast" is more specific than the German "Frühstück," which refers to a continental breakfast; "lunch" is preferred to "Mittagessen," which means a hot meal.

Haugen (1969), who has studied the language of Norwegian Americans extensively, gives examples of domains where the English words just could not be replaced by Norwegian words as these often did not exist:

> By filing a KLEIM (claim) they were entitled to a HOMSTEDD if they would SETTLA on the land for a prescribed period and till it. The SETTLAR then acquired a DID (deed) to the homestead which became the HEIMFARM or HEIMPLASS (homeplace) because it had been DIDA (deeded) to the owner by GÅVVEMENTE (the government). (p. 76)

Also:

> [The immigrant] took a TRIPP, if he could afford it, and he might STOPPA or STÅ (stay) with relatives. He no longer carried his baggage in a kista or a koffert but in a TRONK and a SUTKEIS. (p. 87).

Loanwords allowed the immigrant to label all sorts of new objects and concepts. Haugen (1969) reports that Norwegian Americans even borrowed English words as common as "river," "field," "fence," "barn," "cousin," and "pail." Although the immigrants knew the Norwegian counterparts to these words, they came to use the English terms more and more. Haugen makes the distinction between necessary loanwords that fill lexical gaps and "unnecessary" loanwords, which are condemned by purists as reflecting laziness and the law of least effort. However, Haugen remarks that in addition to following the tendency to give an object the name used in the new culture, Norwegian Americans (like other immigrant groups) were under strong pressure to adapt their language to the new economic and social environment. As he writes: "The immigrant was forced to create an instrument of communication which would express the significant distinctions of American society in all those fields where he participated in the activities of that society. This was true even while he still spoke his native tongue, and hence the loans which he was forced to make" (p. 374). It is interesting to note that in more personal domains, such as religion, clothing, and parts of the body, the immigrants used fewer English words, whereas in the areas linked to American life they borrowed quite extensively from English.

Haugen (1969) states that some loanwords allowed one to make finer distinctions. For instance, "øl" was used by Norwegian Americans for home-brewed beer but "beer" for the beer bought at the store; "høna" referred to the live chicken but "chicken" to the meat. With time, however, these distinctions disappeared. Clyne (1967) also reports that in time German is used in fewer and fewer domains in Australia, and the bilingual often uses English loanwords to avoid making decisions about the appropriate word in German. Thus, to avoid having to choose between "belebt" and "beschäftigt," the bilingual will use "busy"; to avoid choosing between "Abfall" and "Unsinn," he or she will use "rubbish."

In certain immigrant groups, word borrowing is also a reflection of the immigrant's wish to acculturate into the majority group, especially if the group and its language are considered more prestigious. Higa (1979) reports that in the Japanese community in Hawaii, the borrowing of English words, including pronouns (me, you), expressions of time (last year, one month), kinship terms (papa, mama, brother, sister), and expressions of quantity (thirty, some, too much) reflects group identity and demonstrates a certain degree of acculturation into the American society. Those who wish to acculturate faster will be more prone to borrow than those who wish to maintain their identity as members of a different linguistic and cultural group.

LOANWORDS AND LOANSHIFTS Haugen (1956, 1969) distinguishes between two main types of borrowing: the loanword imported in part or whole from the other language and adapted phonetically and morphologically into the base language (such as czar, croissant, pizza, and chili in English) and the loanshift, in which the meaning of a word or group of words in the base language is extended to cover a new concept. Thus, the French word "réaliser" not only has its original meaning of bringing into concrete existence (making real) but now has taken on the English meaning of being aware of something.

According to Haugen (1969), loanwords can be further divided into pure loanwords and loanblends. In the latter, one part is borrowed and the other belongs to the base language. For instance, in Australian German "GUMBAUM" (gumtree) is a blend of English "gum" and German "baum" (tree). Other examples, taken from Clyne (1967), are COUNTRYPLATZ, PETROLPUMPE, SIDECAFÉ, REDBRICKHAUS, and GRÜNGROCER. In Pennsylvania German one finds BOCKABUCK (pocketbook) and JULEKARD (Christmas card). This discussion, however, will concentrate on pure loanwords and say no more about the hybrid category of loanblends.

Loanwords are integrated phonologically and morphologically into the borrowing or base language. An interesting question concerns the integration process. Haugen (1969) proposes a three-stage process of phonological adaptation. First, a bilingual introduces a new word in a phonetic form as close as possible to that of the model. If he repeats it, or if other speakers start using it, a further substitution of native elements will take place. Finally, when the monolingual learns it, there is a total or practically total phonetic substitution. Of course, if the original borrower is not a fluent bilingual, the word will not be perfectly replicated and will immediately undergo considerable phonetic adaptation. Before a word is finally adopted by a language group, it often goes through a period of uncertain linguistic status. Haugen (1956) reports that in Yaqui the Spanish word "dios" (God) appeared as "díos" or "líos," and in American Polish the English word "society" appeared as "sosajda," "susajda," and "sosajta."

The main process in phonological adaptation is substitution of base language phonemes for the phonemes in the original word. Thus English /w/ becomes German /v/ when an English word is brought into German; English /I/ becomes French /i/, and English /r/ becomes French /r/ when the French-English bilingual borrows an English word, and so on. In addition, the word is adapted to the stress and phonological rules of the language. Hence, when an English word containing a consonant cluster is borrowed into Japanese, it is modified substantially, because in Japanese every consonant must be followed by a vowel. Thus "strike" has become "sutoraiki" (union strike) and "sutoraiku" (baseball strike), and "jacket" has become "jaketo" (Battison, 1978). By the time the word is finally integrated, when it has left the sphere of bilingual speech and entered that of the language (that is, when it is used by monolinguals), its form may be extremely different from the original. Weinreich (1968) mentions the following three English words borrowed into American Italian: "Brooklyn" has been integrated as /broko'lino/, "husband" as /'osbiru/ and "box" as /'bokisa/.

Not only are loanwords adapted to the phonology of the base language, they are also usually integrated into its morphology. In many languages nouns have to be marked for gender, and a number of studies have reported on how gender assignments are made for loanwords. Clyne (1967) mentions three factors that play a role in assigning gender to English nouns in Australian German. In most cases the word is given the gender of the German equivalent. Thus COLLIE DOG is given the masculine gender (der) because "Hund" (dog) is masculine; BREAKFAST is given the neuter gender (das) because "Frühstück" is neuter; and LIBRARY is given the feminine gender (die) because "Bibliothek" is feminine. In other cases, an English word that resembles its German counterpart receives the same gender. Thus, German "der Hydrant" leads to "der FIRE HYDRANT." Or the suffix of the word may determine its gender: words that end in "er" in German are masculine, and hence "settler," "squatter," and "inspector," are also given the masculine gender. But Clyne notes, as do other researchers, that a few words always fluctuate: "scoreboard" is given any one of the three genders, and "building" is feminine for some and neuter for others.

An analysis of several loan situations shows that bilinguals give the words their natural gender when possible: masculine for males, feminine for females. This gives "el TRAINER," "un BOXER," "la MAID," and "esa GIRL" in the loans of Spanish-English bilinguals (Pfaff, 1979), and "a NORSA" (a nurse) among Portuguese-English bilinguals. Also, depending on the language pairs in question, the form of the word is important: if the ending resembles a feminine ending in the base language, the word will be feminine, and the same is true of masculine endings. Pfaff reports that English nouns ending in "er" and "ity" are given feminine genders by Spanish-English bilinguals because these endings resemble "a" and "idad" feminine endings in Spanish. Hence "la JIRA" (the heater), "la LIABILITY," "la RESPONSIBILITY," and so on. In addition, Weinreich (1968) reports that base language nouns quite often give their gender to the loan words that replace them. Hence, German Americans gave "boiler" a masculine gender because it replaced masculine "kesel." Weinreich also notes that speakers of different base languages may have a preferred gender for loan words: masculine in American Norwegian, American Lithuanian, and American Portuguese, but feminine in American German, for instance. Poplack and Pousada (1981) have undertaken an extensive study of the gender assignments of English words in Montreal French and in Puerto Rican Spanish. They show clearly that no single factor can possibly account for the totality of gender assignments. Rather, a number of different factors do so; some, such as the phonological shape of the word, are more important than others, such as the suffix of the word. Also, certain factors are more important in one language than in another. Thus the phonological shape of the loanword is more important in Puerto Rican Spanish than in Montreal French whereas assigning the unmarked gender to a loan is more frequent in Montreal French than in Puerto Rican Spanish.

Pluralization usually follows the rules of the base language. Some languages have specific pluralization rules for foreign words, but most do not. Clyne (1967) reports that in Australian German, English and other foreign nouns take an "s" in the plural form. However, loans ending in "er" are not inflected for plural because German words with that suffix are invariant. Hence the German-English bilingual will often say "two builder" or "two carpenter."

Borrowed verbs are often put into the largest, most common verb class of the base language. For Portuguese-English bilinguals "to jump" becomes "jampar" and "to change" becomes "chinjar" (Pap, 1949), and Spanish-English bilinguals also appear to put loanwords into that class, although many verbs also take the "ear" ending: "to flirt" becomes "flirtear," "to check" becomes "checkear," and so on (Lawton, 1979). In addition, Pfaff (1979) has found that English verbs in Spanish contexts are subject to the following constraint:

An English verb not morphologically adapted to Spanish is permitted only in sentences in which tense/mood/aspect and subject are otherwise marked.

Thus, Pfaff found examples such as

Estaba TRAINING para pelear.
(He was training to fight.)

Va a CHARTER un camión.
(It's going to charter a bus.)

"Training" and "charter" are not adapted to Spanish morphology, but Pfaff found only a very few examples where the main verb was not inflected. In nineteen out of twenty-four cases, the main verb was adapted, as in

Los hombres me TRUSTEARON.
(The men trusted me.)

To end this section on loanwords, it is important to repeat that as long as the loan is part of bilingual speech and is not recognized and accepted by the monolingual language community, it remains open to phonological and morphological fluctuation. Haugen (1956) expresses this most aptly:

Borrowed items tend to remain in an uncertain linguistic status for some time after their first adoption. Bilinguals show their awareness of the origin of such items by vacillating in the degree of substitution. Before a particular form of the loan has met general social acceptance, each borrower may achieve his own compromise replica, with more or less fidelity to the model according to his wishes or his ability. (p. 55)

Only when monolinguals adopt the loan does it receive, in time, its final form.

A second type of borrowing, called a loanshift, consists in either taking a word in the base language and extending its meaning to correspond to that of a word in the other language or of rearranging words in the base language along a pattern provided by the other language and thus creating a new meaning (Haugen, 1956, 1969). In either case the influence from the other language is purely semantic and not phonetic as in the case of loanwords. The question of why the bilingual chooses a loanshift in preference to a loanword is a complex one, but Haugen (1969) proposes this reason: "If a native word is similar in sound to a desired foreign word, it is often given the meanings of the foreign word; if not, it is more common to borrow the foreign word" (p. 380). A loanshift may be used instead of a loanword also because the community has a policy of language purity. Borrowing a word outright from the other language may be frowned upon, even by other bilinguals, so the bilingual changes the base language so that it can express the concept. It is interesting to note that a major type of lexical interference is precisely the semantic extension of words (see the preceding section); when a bilingual speaks to a monolingual, this approach may be the only way to convey a finer distinction or a concept that is better expressed in the other language, although this may create a misunderstanding if the shift is too great. However, when speaking to another bilingual, he or she can borrow a word outright or code-switch to the other language. Why a loanshift is sometimes chosen in preference to the other two routes has not yet been fully explained.

Haugen (1956, 1969) distinguishes between two types of loanshifts: extensions and creations. Extensions, which have also been termed semantic loans (Pap, 1949), usually consist in extending the meaning of a word in the base language so that it resembles the meaning of a word in the other language. Quite often the words in the two languages resemble one another phonetically. Thus, Portuguese-English bilinguals in the United States have taken the Portuguese word "humoroso" (meaning capricious) and have extended its meaning to cover that of the English word "humorous." They have also taken "grosseria" (meaning a rude remark) and have extended its meaning to "grocery." German-English bilinguals in Australia have taken the German word "magasin" meaning storeroom and have extended its meaning to that of the English word "magazine" (Clyne, 1967). And Spanish-English bilinguals in Puerto Rico have extended the meaning of "soportar" (to endure) to take on one of the meanings of the English word "support," that of supporting an action. It is interesting to note that bilinguals in Puerto Rico also extend the meaning of English words. Thus, Lawton (1979) reports the following code-switch:

> Maria *don't assist* la clase.
> (Mary doesn't attend class.)

Here, the English word "assist" has taken on the meaning of the Spanish "asistir a," which means to attend. I should note that the words in the two languages do not necessarily have to resemble one another phonetically. Portuguese-English bilinguals took the Portuguese word "frio" (cold spell) and extended its meaning to infection, under the influence of the English "cold." But as Haugen stated, loanshifts are often similar in sound to their counterparts in the other language.

For a while bilinguals will keep in mind the two meanings of a loanshift (the original meaning and the borrowed meaning), but with time they may forget the original meaning. Weinreich (1968) mentions the American Italian word "fattoria" which originally meant a farm but then took on, under the influence of English, the meaning of factory. Because of the urban life of Italian Americans, the original meaning was rarely used, and it slowly disappeared from usage.

The second type of loanshift, which Haugen terms "creation," involves rearranging words (or morphemes) in the base language so that they correspond to the pattern of the other language. These creations, also called calques or loan translations, are found at the level of compounds and of idiomatic expressions. For instance, the English word "skyscraper" has been borrowed into various languages, not as a loan but as a rearrangement of native morphemes. This gave French "gratteciel," Spanish "rascacielos," German "Wolkenkratzer," Russian "nebroskrjób" and so on. Some bilinguals in the appropriate environment actually go a step further and coin new words. Weinreich (1968) cites the case of Yiddish "mitkind" (literally "fellow child"), created to match the English "sibling." In this case we are one step removed from the calque or loan translation. Diebold (1961) mentions the coined Huave Indian word "òmāl-màncik" (literally "tip of metal"), corresponding to the English "bullet."

Many bilinguals speaking to other bilinguals borrow idiomatic expressions by translating them literally into the language they are speaking. Below are listed a few loanshift creations reported by various researchers: German-English bilinguals in Australia (Clyne, 1967):

für schlechter oder besser.
(for better or worse.)
Wie meinen Sie?
(How do you mean?)

Spanish-English bilinguals (Redlinger, 1976):

I put myself to think about it.
(Me puse a pensarlo.)

Spanish-English bilinguals in Florida (Lozano, 1980):

cambiar de mente.
(to change one's mind.)
instead of: cambiar de opinión.
tener buen tiempo.
(to have a good time.)
instead of: divertirse.

Portuguese-English bilinguals (Pap, 1949):

responder para tràs.
(to talk back.)
correr para mayor.
(run for mayor.)

Creations, like extensions, may slowly replace the original expression, and after a while the bilingual may believe that the loanshift is in fact the norm and not the exception.

In the third section of this chapter we will examine how borrowings are integrated into the language. It is important to note, however, that only a small percentage of speech borrowings produced by bilinguals ever move up to the level of becoming part of the monolingual's language.

Code-Switching

Various aspects of code switching have already been discussed. In Chapter 3 we reviewed the reasons that lead to code-switching; in Chapter 4 we discussed briefly code-switching by children and the development of various communicative strategies; and in Chapter 5 we reviewed early experiments that seemed to show that code-switching takes time both for the listener and for the speaker. We noted that these experiments were not in fact studying code-switching but instead were examining the perception and production of arbitrary language mixing, something that bilinguals do not usually produce.

Here we will concentrate on the linguistic aspects of code-switching, discussing first whether one can always determine the base language being spoken. We will then examine the linguistic categories that may be involved in switches as well as the category preferences of certain types of bilinguals. We will also discuss the linguistic constraints governing code-switching; why, for example, a switch cannot occur at one word boundary but can at another. And we will end by asking a much-debated question among linguists: Does code-switching necessitate a special grammar or can it be explained by the appropriate use of the two monolingual grammars? The point I hope to highlight is the linguistic complexity of code-switching. As Poplack (1979) writes: "Code-switching is a verbal skill requiring a large degree of competence in more than one language, rather than a defect arising from insufficient knowledge of one or the other" (p. 72).

BASE LANGUAGE   Weinreich (1968) was of the opinion that when code-switching takes place, the speaker and the listener are usually quite capable of stating which base language they are using. They might say to the interested listener, "We were speaking Arabic but we switched over to English for words or expressions" or "Basically we were speaking Arabic to one another." And the linguist analyzing their conversation can often determine the base language by examining which language is spoken more and especially by looking at the determiners, the verbs, and the word order. The task is simpler when the linguist is dealing with bilinguals who only code-switch from their less fluent language to their dominant language but never the other way around or with bilinguals who only code-switch for words or short phrases.

But the situation is not always quite so simple. As we saw in Chapter 3, a change of topic, the approach of a third person, or a rapid change of situation may well lead bilinguals to switch languages within the same utterance. Kegl (1975) reports how a Slovene-English bilingual adult speaking to her mother on the phone would switch languages, even after each sentence, when the topic changed. Things to do with the Slovenian neighborhood where the mother lived (food, friends, acquaintances) would be said in Slovene; things to do with the suburb where the daughter lived would be said in English. For example:

> Not from the bottle ... no ... no ... *domač* (homemade), you know, *sam ... sam da machne pokus ... ne da, taku se rdeče* (only ... only a strong taste of it ... not that, that is red), you know, *pa peča* (and burns). Judy is doing homework and Tony is ... uh ... watching TV. (pp. 130–131)

In this type of rapid switching the situation and topic affect language choice; the bilingual is in fact changing languages at well-defined points in the conversation. However, this is not always the case: bilinguals also switch back and forth between languages within *one* semantic domain. This has led Sankoff and Poplack (1980) to express doubts concerning the postulate that every sentence spoken by a bilingual can be assigned to a base language, especially in communities where code-switching is extremely frequent and practically a norm (as among Puerto Ricans in East Harlem). These researchers believe that in such cases the language of the determiners and of the verbs cannot reliably determine the base language of the utterances. Of the bilinguals they studied in East Harlem, the more fluent produced the most intrasentence switches, and in many cases the researchers found it impossible to determine the base language. Spanish-dominant speakers, on the other hand, almost always switched into English from an unambiguous Spanish base and preferred tag switches. Thus, determining the base language being used is far from easy, except in the most straightforward cases, such as tag switches or single-noun switches. Questioning the bilinguals and examining their speech is not always sufficient. Future studies may examine how often and in which communities it is impossible to determine the base language.

LINGUISTIC CATEGORIES   When one examines examples of code-switches published by researchers, one quickly realizes that certain linguistic categories are preferred, and frequency counts tend to confirm this impression. For instance, Pfaff (1979) found that 84 percent of all the code-mixes in the utterances of Spanish-English bilinguals in the Southwest involved single lexical items (74 percent nouns, 6 percent verbs, and 4 percent adjectives), 10 percent involved phrases (6 percent noun phrases), and 6 percent involved whole clauses. Poplack (1979) did a frequency count of code-

---

BOX 6.2   BILINGUALS SPEAK

One-Word or Two-Word Switches

Noun

Hindi-English: (Vaid, 1980)	*Idea* bura nahĩ hai. (It's not a bad idea.)
French-English:	Il commence à y avoir un *pattern*. (There's starting to be a pattern). J'apprend le *slang* en ce moment. (I am now learning slang.)
Russian-French: (Timm, 1978)	Dva *valets*. (Two/footmen.)
Spanish-English: (Poplack, 1979)	Leo un *magazine*. (I read a magazine.)

Adjective

Hindi-English: (Vaid, 1980)	Dekho, tum *young* admi ho. (Look, you're a young man.)
French-English:	Je suis pas assez *quick*. (I'm not quick enough.) On peut devenir complètement *fluent*. (One can become completely fluent.)

Adjective and Noun

French-English:	Le *last name* est———. (the last name is———.) Des *wild guys* à cheval. (some wild guys on horseback.)
Russian-French: (Timm, 1978)	Odna *petite personne*. (a / little person.)

Verb

Hindi-English: (Vaid, 1980)	To ap *practice* kar sakte haĩ. (So you can practice.)
French-English:	Il y a la prise qui *shows*. (The outlet is showing.) L'information que tu *convey*. (The information that you convey.)

switches in the utterances of Spanish-English bilinguals in New York but did not include in her count habitualized lexical borrowings, which she feels may or may not be phonologically integrated into the base language, nor did she include food names, place names, proper names, explanations, or comments about the language. Hence her linguistic categories are similar to Pfaff's but her percentages are different. Poplack's results are as follows: tag switch, 22.5 percent; sentence switch, 20.3 percent; phrase switch, 18.7 percent; noun switch, 9.5 percent; clause switch, 8.4 percent; interjection switch, 6.3 percent; and other switches (quotation, conjunction, idiomatic expression), 14.4 percent.

Boxes 6.2 and 6.3 present examples of switches taken from various studies. Box 6.2 gives examples of one- or two-word switches. These involve content words, such as nouns, adjectives, and verbs, rather than function or grammatical words, such as determiners, prepositions, and conjunctions. One reason for this is that content words carry most of the semantic and pragmatic information, so these are the words bilinguals want to insert into their utterances. Box 6.3 presents longer switches: those involving a whole phrase or clause as well as idiomatic expressions, discourse markers, and fillers.

Poplack (1979) presents some interesting reasons why some of the Spanish-English bilinguals she studied prefer phrase and clause switches, whereas others prefer one- or two-word switches (nouns and tags). According to her, one group is fluent in both languages and can thus make more within-sentence switches: these require a good knowledge of the two languages, because they must conform to precise syntactic rules. Another group favors single noun switches and tag switches. They are usually Spanish-dominant speakers who use switching for metaphorical or stylistic reasons at specific points during a conversation. The categories they use (some nouns but mainly tags) can be inserted quite freely into the sentence and do not have to obey syntactic constraints. Poplack's finding is an interesting one and needs to be replicated with other bilingual groups. But more work is needed on the reasons that lead some bilinguals to favor short switches and others to favor phrase and clause switches.

LINGUISTIC CONSTRAINTS   It is only in the last ten years or so that linguists have started to recognize that code-switching is linguistically constrained and not haphazard. Before, many people thought that any word or series of words from the other language could

---

BOX 6.3   **BILINGUALS SPEAK**

Longer Switches

Noun or verb phrase

Russian-French: Imela *une femme de chambre.*
(Timm, 1978)   (She had / a chambermaid.)

Spanish-English: Todos los Mexicanos *were riled up.*
(Pfaff, 1979)   (All the Mexicans were riled up.)
                             No van a *bring it up in the meeting.*
                             (They're not going to bring it up in the
                                 meeting.)

Prepositional phrase

English-Spanish: But I wanted to fight her *con los*
(Poplack, 1979)   *puños,* you know.
                             (But I wanted to fight her with my
                                 fists, you know.)

Clause

Hindi-English: Maine bahut bardaš kiya hai *but now*
(Vaid, 1980)   *it's getting too much.*
                             (I have withstood a lot but . . .)

English-Spanish: So you *todavía* haven't decided *lo que*
(Sankoff and Poplack, 1980) *vas a hacer* next week.
                             (So you still haven't decided what
                                 you're going to do next week.)

Russian-French: Chustvovali, chto *le vin est tiré et qu'il*
(Timm, 1978)   *faut le boire.*
                             (They felt that / the wine is uncorked
                                 and it should be drunk.)

---

be brought into the base language at any point, with no restrictions. However, when linguists such as Gingras, Timm, Gumperz, Lipski, Poplack, Pfaff, and others started examining closely the patterns of code-switching, they soon realized that it is governed by very strict linguistic constraints.

Poplack (1979) proposes two general constraints that, according to her, account for the grammatical aspect of code-switching. The first, called the free-morpheme constraint, states that a switch cannot take place between the stem of a word and its affix (bound mor-

---

BOX 6.3 continued

Discourse markers, fillers

Spanish-English: (Sankoff and Poplack, 1980)	Yo estaba aburrecido, muriéndome, *you know.* (I was dying of boredom, you know.)
(Lance, 1975)	*Pues,* yeah I want to go. (Well, yeah I want to go.)
(Lance, 1975)	*I mean,* si hay una persona . . . (I mean, if there is a person . . .)
(Redlinger, 1976)	Como dos años, *I guess.* (About two years, I guess.)

Idiomatic expressions

French-English:	Pour l'instant il faut prendre *one step at a time.* (For the time being one must take one step at a time.) Et le travail, *there's nothing to it.* (And as for work, there's nothing to it.) J'ai l'impression d'être *back in the country.* (I have the feeling of being back in the country.)
Spanish-English (Espinosa, 1975)	Vamos a ir al *football game* y despues al baile a tener *the time of our lives.* (Let's go to the football game and then to the dance to have the time of our lives.)

---

pheme) unless the stem has been phonologically integrated into the language of the affix. Thus, one cannot have run*eando* (running) or eat*iendo* (eating), because the stems (run, eat) are in English phonology and the affixes (-eando, -iendo) are in Spanish phonology. According to Poplack, this constraint applies not only to affixes but also to idiomatic expressions such as

Si Dios quiere y la Virgen.
(God and the Virgin willing.)

as well as to set phrases (greetings, excuses) and discourse elements (you know, I mean), all of which appear to function as affixes. In an analysis of 1,835 switches, Poplack found no examples of switches between the stem and its bound morpheme, and less than 1 percent of switches within idiomatic expressions. One exception she found to the free-morpheme constraint was

> Estamos como marido y *woman.*
> (We are like man and wife.)

instead of

> Estamos como marido y mujer, *or*
> Estamos como *man and wife.*

The second constraint Poplack puts forward, the equivalence constraint, was developed independently by Poplack (1978) and by Lipski (1978). It states that the word order immediately before and immediately after a switch point must be possible in both languages; if this is not so, a switch cannot occur. An example taken from Poplack (1979) will clarify this constraint:

English: I   / told him / that / so that / he   / would bring it / fast.
Spanish: (Yo) / le dije   / eso / pa'que / (él) / la trajera   / ligero.
Code-
   switch: I   told him   that *pa'que*   *la trajera*   *ligero.*

The boundaries indicated by slashes are permissible switch points, and as we see, a switch did take place at one of these boundaries. Switching could also have occurred after "I," after "him," or after "that." However, because the English segment "told him" is different from the Spanish segment "le dije," a code-switch cannot occur after "told." This is also the case for "would bring it," where the equivalence constraint rules out a switch after "would" and after "bring." A code-switched sentence taken from Lipski (1978) shows the same constraint at work:

> No sé, porque *I never used it.*

The switch between "porque" and "I" is possible because the English and Spanish syntactic structures are similar on either side of that point:

> Spanish: No sé, / porque / nunca lo usé.
> English: I don't know, / because / I never used it.

Code-switching at other word boundaries (except after sé) would violate the equivalence constraint.

The equivalence constraint applies to languages that do not share the same adjective placement rules in the noun phrase. Thus the French-English bilingual can say:

J'ai acheté *an American car.*
(I have bought an American car.)

but not

*J'ai acheté *an American* voiture.

as the object noun phrases in this case are not similar in the two languages:

English order: Article-Adjective-Noun (an American car).
French order: Article-Noun-Adjective (une voiture americaine).

However, a sentence of the type:

J'ai acheté une voiture qui est *American.*
(I have bought a car that is American.)

can occur, because French and English have predicate adjectives that occupy the same syntactic position.

Poplack (1979) found that less than 1 percent of code-switches in the corpus she studied violated the equivalence constraint, showing that the constraint is very much at work. And Sankoff and Poplack (1980) found that the syntactic boundaries where switching occurred also corroborated the constraint. Spanish-English bilinguals favored switching before or after a tag, before a predicate adjective, and between clauses, because none of these boundaries violate the equivalence constraint. However, they found no instances of switching between a clitic (an unstressed pronoun, for instance) and the verb, or between a negative and the verb, as clitics and negatives are positioned and marked differently in the two languages.

Many of the constraints found by other researchers (Gumperz, 1976b; Timm, 1975, 1978) can be regrouped under Poplack's two constraints. It is interesting, however, that both Gumperz and Timm indicate that switching cannot take place between a subject pronoun and the verb, as in

Yo (I) *went to the store.*
Je (I) *saw the large tree.*

although such a switch does not appear to violate the equivalence constraint. One could argue, however, that an unstressed subject pronoun really behaves like a bound morpheme in that it is bound to the following verb; hence, this switch would be governed by Poplack's first constraint. As Gumperz suggests, the longer the noun phrase, the more natural the switch before the verb phrase.

Another very infrequent switching location mentioned by Timm is between the verb and the infinitive complement. For instance

They want *a venir* (to come).
Quieren (they want) *to come.*

This switch does not violate the equivalence constraint, and yet it is very infrequent. Here the reason could be the tight semantic or prosodic bond between the two verbs. Thus, the two constraints proposed by Poplack may need to take into account such factors as the length of the phrase (in the case of subject or object pronouns) and the semantic or pragmatic unity of the segments.

IS THERE A CODE-SWITCHING GRAMMAR? The question of whether there is a code-switching grammar is much debated. As Sankoff and Poplack (1980) write: "There has been some debate over whether discourse containing code-switches is generated by the alternate use of the two monolingual grammars or whether a single code-switching grammar exists, combining elements of the two monolingual grammars" (pp. 10–11). It is their belief that bilinguals probably do have a code-switching grammar. They feel that intrasentential switching involves the juxtaposition of constituents that are too intimately related to be generated separately by rules from two distinct grammars. They add that because code-switching takes place quickly and fluently (switches are rarely marked by a pause or a break), switches must be generated by a single grammar. Sankoff and Poplack postulate the existence of three grammars: two monolingual grammars and a code-switching grammar. This latter grammar is made up of the combined lexicons of the two languages as well as the grammatical categories of the two monolingual grammars, limited by the bound morpheme constraint and the equivalence constraint. These constraints are incorporated into the code-switching grammar by the use of superscripts attached to rewrite rules in the code-switching grammar. These superscripts carry enough information to prevent any violation of the code-switching constraints.

For instance, the rewrite rule of a noun phrase (NP) in the three grammars would be:

Spanish: NP→ Det N Adj
English: NP→ Det Adj N
Code-switching: NP→ Det $N^{sp:n}$ $Adj^{sp:adj}$

This means that, in the Spanish example, the noun phrase can be expressed as a determiner (Det) followed by a noun (N) followed by an adjective (Adj). When the symbols are replaced by words in the code-switched phrase, the determiner can be either Spanish or English, but the noun and the adjective will be in Spanish, as indicated by the superscripts ($N^{sp:n}$ means that the noun must be in Spanish). This rewrite rule precludes:

*the *casa* white
(the white house)

as the superscripts indicate that both the N and the Adj should be lexicalized as Spanish words, to give

the *casa blanca.*

Woolford (1981) does not believe that a grammar specific to code-switching is necessary. In her proposal, the two monolingual grammars overlap at the level of phrase-structure rules. When constructing a sentence frame (a phrase-structure tree) the speaker draws from the phrase-structure rules of either language: when those rules are the same in both languages, then the nodes (or categories, such as NP, VP, Adj, N, Vb) may be filled freely from either lexicon. However, when the nodes are created by a rule that exists in only one of the languages, they must be filled from the lexicon of that language. It is important to note that the two lexicons remain separate, as do the word formation components, thus accounting for the bound morpheme constraint.

Let us take the rewrite rule of the NP to illustrate Woolford's grammar. First, Woolford does not agree that NP is rewritten

Det Adj N (English)
Det N Adj (Spanish)

Instead, both languages share the first part of the rewrite rule:

NP → Det $\overline{N}$,

($\overline{N}$ stands for a noun and its modifiers, such as adjectives) but differ on the second part:

English: $\overline{N}$ → Adj N
Spanish: $\overline{N}$ → N Adj

Thus, the grammar predicts that the determiner can be in English or Spanish but that the $\overline{N}$ must be totally in one language or the other.

If the Spanish $\overline{N}$ is rewritten, giving N Adj, then the final nodes *must* be filled from the Spanish lexicon. Hence

*the *casa* white

is precluded from Woolford's grammar also.

It is too early to say which of the two formal explanations of code-switching is the most parsimonious and the most adequate, but both show clearly one direction taken by code-switching research. Other studies are now examining the distinction between one-word switches and lexical borrowings; the difference between code-switching in bilinguals and style shifting in monolinguals; and the acquisition of code-switching in bilingual children and in adults who learn a second language in a natural environment.

Norms and Varieties in Bilingual Communities

Lexical borrowing and code-switching at the bilingual community level are an integral part of the language varieties developed by these communities. Monolingual speakers who enter bilingual communities are surprised and often shocked to hear the amount of borrowing and switching that takes place. As Haugen (1977) writes:

They hold that such infringements on the rhetorical norm, as they conceive it to be, are due either to laziness, a moral defect, or to ignorance, an intellectual defect, or to snobbery, a social defect. One critic of midwestern Norwegian, a visitor from Norway, wrote: "Strictly speaking, it is no language whatever, but a gruesome mixture of Norwegian and English, and often one does not know whether to take it humorously or seriously" (p. 94).

What monolinguals fail to understand is that lexical borrowing and code-switching are quite simply the result of the bilinguals' need to communicate with one another. These phenomena may lead, over a long period of time, to a breakdown in communication with one or the other monolingual group (especially if one is overseas), but they enhance communication within the bilingual group. As Haugen (1969) writes, an apparent confusion of tongues must in no way be equated with a confusion of communication; the speech of bilinguals that is replete with borrowings and code-switches is as effective as monolingual speech.

In fact, with time, a bilingual community will develop several varieties of language, each with its own domains of use and norms of correctness. Hasselmo (1970) refers to three modes of speaking among Swedish Americans: an English mode for communicating with some, but not necessarily only, English monolinguals; a Swedish American mode with English as the base language for communication between bilinguals; and finally an American Swedish mode with Swedish as the base language, used among bilinguals. This last contains integrated features from English as well as code-switching at the level of content words and discourse markers. Among German Australians, Clyne (1972) has found four language varieties: English; German Australian in which German patterns are transferred into English; German, which is disappearing quite quickly as there are few German monolinguals to maintain it; and Australian German, the primary form of communication among bilinguals, involving lexical borrowing and code-switching.

In the American Southwest we find a similar pattern of language varieties. In a study of Spanish-English bilinguals in Austin, Texas, Eliás-Olivares (1976) refers to a continuum ranging all the way from standard Spanish to standard English. In between are Popular Spanish, Español Mixtureado, Caló (Pachuco), and Chicano English. Español Mixtureado (also called Pocho or Tex-Mex) uses a Spanish base with many English borrowings and code-switches. It is spoken primarily by the young, especially high school students, who are competent in English and is not only a means of communication but also an ideological statement. (See the discussion of language attitudes in Chapter 3.)

All of the varieties within each group have their own norms. The monolingual norms need little mention, as they are defended by the monolingual communities. As for the so-called "mixed varieties," such as Australian German, American Swedish, Español Mixtureado, they too have their own norms. Gumperz (1970, 1971) writes that members of stable bilingual communities interact largely with other bilinguals and that such interaction generates its own norms of correctness. Haugen (1977) mentions several principles that govern the use of the immigrant language and of English in the Norwegian American and Swedish American communities. First, function words are seldom borrowed; second, cognates are rarely borrowed as phonetic entities (that is, as loanwords); instead they induce semantic transfer (loanshifts); third, compounds such as "state church" and "Swedish made" are either borrowed as units or retained as Swedish originals; and finally, lexical borrowing rarely runs higher than 5–10 percent of the words produced in an utterance. Any violations of these principles, such as the borrowing of

function words or overborrowing, would be contrary to well-estab-
lished norms and constraints, just as borrowing and switching are
seen as violating the monolingual norm.

It takes time for a bilingual community to develop its own norms.
As Haugen (1977) writes of the Norwegian American community,
its members were at first torn between the "pure" version of the
home language and the dominant presence of the majority language:

> Even though they admired the book norms exhibited by clergymen, they
> did not approve of people from their own group who tried to speak a
> "pure" Norwegian like that of the ministers. On the other hand, they
> poked fun at those who adopted excessive numbers of English words,
> calling them "yankeefied" and holding them to be "proud," "trying to be
> big shots," and the like. Most people steered a middle course between
> these extremes, and while professing a low opinion of their own dialects,
> an attitude reflecting their low status in the homeland, they went right on
> using them into the second and third generation. In doing so they created
> quite unconsciously a communicative norm which anyone who has
> known their society will immediately recognize as genuine" (p. 98).

Elías-Olivares, in her study of the Spanish and English varieties
in Austin, has found a very similar situation. If a speaker uses only
Spanish with a Chicano audience, and the situation is informal, the
audience will think that the speaker is trying to show off. Speaking
only in English, however, will be perceived as an indication that the
speaker wishes to acculturate to the Anglo majority and break the
ties with the bilingual community.

Thus, lexical borrowing and code-switching are not only a reflection of the linguistic needs of individual speakers, they also characterize bilingual communities and their sociolinguistic norms. Observers who study bilingual communities through monolingual eyes
too often overlook the importance of such language norms.

The Legacy of Bilingualism

Bilingualism not only affects the speech of the individual, as in interference, lexical borrowing, and code-switching, it also affects language. And when bilingualism no longer exists within a community,
its passage often leaves a permanent trace in the language that has
survived, just as the passage of civilizations can be seen in existing
cultures. Bilingualism leaves its mark in a number of ways. Gumperz (1970, 1971), has suggested that some languages spoken within

bilingual communities may tend to converge over time. For instance, Kannada-Marathi bilingualism has existed for over a thousand years in certain parts of the state of Maharashtra, India, and has led to an almost complete convergence of the grammars and phonologies of the two language varieties used by bilinguals. They only need to learn two sets of terms for objects and grammatical relationships; switching languages simply means substituting words in a sentence. Gumperz notes that such language convergence takes place only over a long period of time in a stable bilingual community with favorable social conditions. Another effect of bilingualism is the emergence of a new language, a pidgin, that differs significantly from the source languages that were originally in contact. With time, the pidgin may become a creole by being elaborated into a full language by children aquiring it as a native language.

In this section we will concentrate on an effect of bilingualism that is less dramatic than language convergence and pidginization—language borrowing. Rare is the language that has not borrowed from another language, be it at the level of sounds and grammar, or more frequently, at the word level. English has borrowed words from Latin, Old Norse, French, German, Greek, and Italian and has itself influenced numerous languages. Whenever borrowing takes place, bilingualism is at its source—either individual bilingualism or group bilingualism. As Haugen (1969) writes: "It would seem that one of the most widespread effects of bilingualism is the deposit it leaves on the languages involved . . . It is an axiom of linguistic study that wherever such influences of one language upon another can be traced (which is everywhere), bilinguals have been its medium" (p. 4).

We will first distinguish between speech and language borrowing, then examine the reasons that lead to language borrowing and the resistance to it. Finally, we will examine the impact of borrowing on language: the importation of new words to cover new concepts and distinctions but also the specialization or rejection of old words.

From Speech to Language Borrowing

The process that leads to language borrowing is complex and still poorly understood. At one point in time, a word is part of one language but not of another. At another point in time, that same word is used by monolingual speakers of two languages. What has happened to the word between those two points in time? Most linguists agree that at first a word is borrowed by one or more bilinguals. This is at the level of speech borrowing: the phonological and morpho-logical status of the word is vague; the word is often used in parallel with the equivalent monolingual word (if such a word exists), and not all bilinguals use the borrowing in their everyday speech. Many borrowings never go beyond this stage.

However, if the word starts being used by monolinguals and the media, for instance, and if it can survive the resistance of language conservatives, its chances of finally being accepted into the language are great. Of course, this process is most complex and has a number of variants: some words are borrowed almost overnight, others go through a long intermediary stage; some words are brought in by one bilingual, others are slowly accepted by a large bilingual community before being transferred to the monolingual group. Weinreich (1968) uses the analogy that speech borrowing is like sand being carried by a stream; language borrowing, on the other hand, is like the sand that is deposited at the bottom of a lake. Whether the sand keeps moving with the stream or is deposited depends on many factors, and the transformation of a speech borrow-ing into a language borrowing also depends on a host of linguistic, social, cultural, and economic variables.

According to Mackey (1970), we cannot say at what particular point a word leaves the domain of speech borrowing, which he terms "interference," and enters the domain of language borrowing, termed "integration." As he writes: "The question of whether or not a given element belongs to both codes or only to one does not take a yes/no answer. It is also a matter of degree" (p. 201). Several ap-proaches have been put forward by researchers to determine where a word is on the speech borrowing–language borrowing continuum. Hasselmo (1969) proposes a measure of word acceptability in which speakers of the borrowing language are asked to indicate on a 4-point scale how acceptable the word is. As an example, take the words "croissant," "nation," "page," and "clocher" and give them a 1–4 rating, with 1 standing for not acceptable in English and 4 for very acceptable in English. All four words are French, but "nation" and "page" are totally integrated into English (they would receive a rating of 4), "croissant" is beginning to be accepted by certain speakers of English (rating of 2 or 3), but "clocher" (steeple) is un-acceptable as an English word to most people, and would thus re-ceive a rating of 1.

A second approach proposed by Hasselmo (1969) is to determine the translatability of a word. If a person, usually a bilingual, is un-able to supply a suitable monolingual equivalent to the borrowed word, it may be that the word has become part of the language, replacing the word formerly used for that concept. Finally, Mackey (1970) has measured the integration of loanwords by determining their availability. In New Brunswick, Canada, he asked young French-English bilinguals to list English and French words in sixteen different semantic domains. By comparing the frequency of occurrence of an English word to that of its French equivalent, he determined the word's integration coefficient. He found, for instance, that body parts retained their French labels (brain was rarely preferred to cerveau, jaw was rarely preferred to mâchoire) but that in the domain of housing and cooking many French words were being replaced by English. Thus "sink" had a coefficient of 0.47 (lavabo is the French term), "plug" had a coefficient of 0.64 (replacing prise de courant), and "pickle" had a coefficient of 0.72 (replacing cornichon). Other high coefficients were: "map" (0.75), replacing "carte," and "office" (0.79), replacing "bureau"; words such as "flashlight," "manager," and "mixer" were totally integrated into New Brunswick French.

It is interesting to note that during the transition between speech and language borrowing, a loanword is often treated in a special way by monolinguals. They may precede its use by a phrase like "the French term is . . ." or may attempt to pronounce it in its original form. When writing the word, they may italicize it or put it in quotation marks. In Japanese, a distinct form of writing, called katakana, is used for foreign words, except for those of Chinese origin, and hence loans become extremely conspicuous in Japanese papers and books (Higa, 1979). A loanword is finally accepted when it is no longer treated differently from other words in the language and when dictionaries, national academies, and influential writers accept it. It is then a loanword only in the historical sense.

Why Languages Borrow

Weinreich (1968) proposes three reasons why languages borrow from one another. First, there are internal linguistic factors such as word frequency and homonymy. Words that are used less frequently, according to Weinreich, are less stable and more subject to replacement. Also, a language may borrow a word to replace one of a pair of homonyms, so as to resolve the clash that results from words pronounced alike with different meanings. A second reason, according to Weinreich, is that languages have a constant need for synonyms in domains such as emotions, food, and communication.

The old words lose their "power," and borrowings are gladly accepted.

However, these are minor reasons compared to Weinreich's third reason: the need to designate new things, new places, and new concepts. When one culture is influenced politically, technologically, economically, and/or culturally by another, its language will soon reflect that influence. Of course, words or expressions can be coined to express new distinctions and new realities, but very often words are borrowed from the language of the influencing group. This has happened throughout history and with most languages. Thus the spread of Christianity and hence of Latin resulted in the borrowing of numerous Latin words into European languages, as did the influence of the Roman Empire earlier. The Norman invasion of Great Britain and the spread of Norman French culture resulted in numerous French words being adopted into the English language in the domains of law, religion, politics, art, and literature. The age of French chivalry and courtly love at the time of the Crusades led to the borrowing of French words into Italian and other European languages; later the Italian Renaissance spread Italian throughout Europe, and several European languages borrowed from Italian. In the nineteenth century, French, the language of diplomacy, had an impact on other languages, and today the spread of American culture and technology can be seen in the many American words being borrowed into the languages of the world.

An interesting combination of Weinreich's second and third reasons explains the borrowing of "boyfriend" and "girlfriend" into French. The language has near synonyms to these words, such as "fiancé(e)," "compagnon/compagne," "concubin/concubine," and "amant/maitresse," but to young French people these words are either too formal or too old-fashioned to express the modern relationship between young men and women, which has been influenced in part by American culture. "Boyfriend" and "girlfriend" better reflect this relationship and are therefore used by many young French people.

The prestige of the other language group and/or the positive feelings that a people may have toward it are important factors in language borrowing. For instance, much to the displeasure of the older generations, many young people in Europe are influenced by American music, dress, leisure, food, and so on. As a consequence, their speech is replete with American terms. Prestige, a very powerful factor underlying the direction and extent of language borrowing, is not just a recent phenomenon. Concerning the influence of

French on English in the twelfth century, Jespersen (1923) writes: "As John of Salisbury .... says expressly .... it was the fashion to interlard one's speech with French words; they were thought modish" (p. 91).

Finally, different varieties of a language will borrow different words. Thus Canadian French has borrowed words from English that are not found in Parisian French and vice versa. In the former variety but not in the latter, one finds "sweater," "scarf," "jello," and "truck;" in Parisian French but rarely in Canadian French one finds "rugby," "pullover," "catch," and "scooter" (Mackey, 1976). These words reflect, of course, the different aspects of the Anglo-American culture that have influenced the two groups of French speakers. A similar difference is probably also found in the varieties of dialectal Arabic: Algerian Arabic has been influenced somewhat by French, whereas Egyptian Arabic has been influenced to some degree by English. And the language variety of immigrants will naturally contain many more borrowings than the variety spoken in the home country, as in the case of English loans in southwestern American Spanish.

Resistance to Borrowing

Only a small percentage of the borrowings in the speech of bilinguals are ever integrated into a language. The reasons for this rather high "mortality rate" are primarily structural and sociocultural (Haugen, 1969; Weinreich, 1968). First, the language is usually a stable system with its own adequate and firmly implanted phonology, morphology, and syntax. Haugen states that the danger of destroying the morphological system of Icelandic has been advanced as a reason for the lack of loanword importation in that language. The major domain that accepts loans, therefore, is vocabulary, but here too the language may be adequate for the monolingual. In addition, new loans may create a confusion in usage or a state of homonymy and hence will not be integrated into the language. Secondly, sociocultural factors play a large role in the resistance to borrowing. If the recipient language is prestigious (such as Spanish, French, English, Russian) and is the object of much loyalty, then borrowing will be reduced. The French, for instance, are very proud of their language and feel that it can express certain ideas and concepts that other languages cannot verbalize as well. Such positive feelings lead many French people to reject borrowings and to use the appropriate French term.

BOX 6.4

Franglais (Franglish)

Tout dans le living room paraissait confortable; le shaker sur le bar, le fauteuil club à côté du cosy-corner. Simone, très sexy dans son blue jeans et son twin set de cashmere fully fashioned, se remit du compact sur le bout du nez avant d'enfiler ses snow-boots et son duffle-coat. (Etiemble, 1964, p. 304)

French version, as proposed by Etiemble: Tout dans le vivoir paraissait confortable; le secoueur . . . sur le bar, le fauteuil cleube à coté du divan d'angle. Simone, glaciale . . . dans son pantalon de treillis bleu et son deux pièces de cachemire entièrement diminué, prit son pain de poudre pour se retoucher le bout du nez avant d'enfiler ses bottillons et sa capuche de molleton. (Etiemble, 1964, p. 305)

Puristic attitudes toward a language will also minimize borrowing. A number of French intellectuals complain of the vassalage of French to English. According to them, the French government has resigned itself to the domination of Anglo-American culture in France and to the "elimination of the French language." Etiemble (1964), a well-known French intellectual, wrote a book entitled *Parlez-vous Franglais?* in which he reacts to the mixture of English and French that he terms "Atlantic Pidgin." Box 6.4 presents a text of Franglais cited by Etiemble and beneath it the "correct" French version proposed by the author, which according to many French people, sounds less natural than the Franglais version. This is a sure sign that many of the loans used by Etiemble are now an integral part of French.

Reactions like Etiemble's are not new. In 1300 Robert de Gloucester wrote about the domination of French over English: "If a man knows no French, people will think little of him . . . I imagine there are in all the world no countries that do not keep their own language except England alone" (From Jespersen, 1923, p. 94). Who would have thought that some 650 years later the situation would be reversed, with English as the dominant language! The opinions of such influential persons as Robert de Gloucester in his time and of Etiemble today are heeded by many people, who then attempt to clear their language of foreign elements, usually to little avail.

Some countries have an official policy of language preservation. This can entail discouraging, or even forbidding, the use of loans in official meetings and documents, establishing an official language policy task force that coins new words, and encouraging the spread of the country's language outside of the national borders. France is well known for its official language policies: the Académie Française oversees the evolution of the French language by its work on the dictionary; the government has committees proposing French words in place of foreign words, and laws prohibit the use of foreign terms in official documents and even in advertising. It is difficult to assess the impact of sociocultural and official resistance to borrowing. In the end, it is the majority of the speakers who "makes the law," and despite official pressure to use a native word, speakers may well continue to use the foreign term because they are accustomed to using it and no longer consider it foreign. Hence, the official French word "bouteur" will probably never replace the loan "bulldozer," nor will "oléoduc" replace "pipeline."

Such seemingly unimportant factors as word length have been found to play a role in whether the native word is kept or the foreign word is adopted. Higa (1979) reports that when a foreign word and its newly coined equivalent are introduced into Japanese, the shorter of the two is usually adopted. For instance, when "department store" was translated into Japanese as "hyakkaten," it was preferred to the English term; then, when the English was shortened to "depaato," it completely replaced the Japanese term.

Some languages do manage to keep out or eliminate foreign terms, whether the reason is structural or sociocultural. German is well known for having eliminated many borrowings from Latin, and some Native American languages have managed to reduce loanwords to a very small number. Casagrande (reported in Haugen, 1956) studied Comanche and found that the acculturation vocabulary from contact with Spanish and then American settlers was made up almost completely of loanshifts and coined words. For instance, the meaning of "arrow" was extended to include "bullet," the concept for "pump" was expressed by a word that meant "raise water forcefully with the hands," and the concept for "bicycle" became "makes one's self go with the feet."

The Impact of Borrowing on Language

Throughout this discussion I have stressed lexical borrowing as the main result of language contact, but it is not the only linguistic domain that is affected. The phonology, morphology, and grammar of languages also reflect the impact of bilingualism. Weinreich (1968) notes that sounds can be imported into languages, and new patterns of sounds can develop. The English / ʒ / as in "rouge" comes from French; the final cluster /ng/ in French comes from English; Huave, an American Indian language, acquired a sixth vowel, /u/, through contact with Spanish (Diebold, 1961) as well as a new phoneme, /f/ as in "fótò." In addition, through bilingualism, languages acquire new distinctions and patterns: /g/ as distinct from /k/ in Czech; /o/ as distinct from /uo/ in Lettish (Weinreich, 1968); and /b/, /d/, and /g/ as word initial consonants in Huave (Diebold, 1961). At the level of morphology, languages also influence one another: thus, the Latin-French suffixes "ible" and "able" have been borrowed into English (as in terrible, excusable) and have been extended to forms like "bearable" and "eatable," in which the underlying verb is Anglo-Saxon (Bloomfield, 1933). In grammar, Weinreich reports that the influence of Middle Greek caused the disappearance of the infinitive in Balkan languages and that the influence of German led to the development of a passive voice in Estonian, Serbian, and Slovenian. In American Sign Language, English has influenced word order: the subject-verb-object order is now much more frequent than it used to be.

However, it is in the domain of vocabulary that the long-term effect of bilingualism is felt the most. Bloomfield (1933) reports that in the case of Albanian, the repeated domination by outside groups so swamped the language that it now contains only a few hundred native words; all the rest are loans from Latin, Roman, Greek, Slavic, and Turkish. Higa (1979) writes that only 37 percent of current Japanese words are of Japanese origin; a full 47 percent are of Chinese origin, 10 percent from other languages (mainly English), and 6 percent are hybrids, that is, made up of elements from different languages. Borrowings may be loanshifts or loanwords that have been totally integrated into the language. In English it is a simple matter to write a text in which every third or fourth word is a borrowing from another language, in this case French:

> The *poet* lived in the *duke's manor*. That day, he *painted*, played *music* and wrote *poems* with his *companions*. In the evening, they sat around a large *table* to a *dinner* of *soup, veal* in *sauce, carrots,* and *fruit*.

The importation of a loanword may at first create a confusion in usage, but the final result will either be specialization of the old and new words or the elimination of the old. Thus, in English, the Old English "calf" refers to the animal and the Norman French loan "veal" to the meat; the same is true of "ox" and "beef," "swine" and "pork." In addition, many Old English words have been replaced by French counterparts that originally came from Latin: "snell" was replaced by "active," "rūn" was replaced by "secret," "lot" by "glory," "gram" by "cruel," and so on. And what is true of rather stable languages such as English and French is even more true of immigrant languages such as Australian German (Clyne, 1967) and American Norwegian (Haugen, 1953), where native words are rapidly replaced.

Thus bilingualism is at the source of language borrowing. As long as languages continue to come into contact with one another, through individual bilinguals and in bilingual communities, they will not fail to influence one another. Language borrowing is the legacy of those who live with two languages.

References

Adler, M. 1977. *Collective and individual bilingualism.* Hamburg: Helmut Buske Verlag.

Aellen, C., and W. Lambert. 1969. Ethnic identification and personality adjustment of Canadian adolescents of mixed English-French parentage. *Canadian Journal of Behavioral Science* 1:69–86.

Albert, M., and L. Obler. 1975. Neuropsychological aspects of bilingualism in mixed polyglot aphasia. Unpublished manuscript.

——— 1978. *The bilingual brain.* New York: Academic Press.

Andersson, R. 1977. Philosophical perspectives on bilingual education. In *Frontiers of bilingual education,* eds. B. Spolsky and R. Cooper. Rowley, Mass.: Newbury House.

Andersson, T., and M. Boyer. 1978. *Bilingual schooling in the United States.* Austin, Texas: National Educational Laboratory Publishers.

Anisfeld, E., and W. Lambert. 1964. Evaluational reactions of bilingual and monolingual children to spoken languages. *Journal of Abnormal and Social Psychology* 69:89–97.

Apte, M. 1976. Multilingualism in India and its socio-political implications: An overview. In *Language and politics,* eds. W. O'Barr and J. O'Barr. The Hague: Mouton.

Arnberg, L. 1979. Language strategies in mixed nationality families. *Scandinavian Journal of Psychology* 20:105–112.

Ayer directory of publications. 1979. Philadelphia: Ayer Press.

Bain, B. and A. Yu. 1980. Cognitive consequences of raising children bilingually: "One parent, one language." *Canadian Journal of Psychology/Revue Canadienne de Psychologie* 34:304–313.

Barber, C. 1973. Trilingualism in an Arizona Yaqui village. In *Bilingualism in the Southwest,* ed. P. Turner. Tucson: University of Arizona Press.

Barik, H., and M. Swain. 1976. A longitudinal study of bilingual and cognitive development. *International Journal of Psychology* 11:251–263.

Barker, G. 1975. Social functions of language in a Mexican-American community. In *El lenguaje de los Chicanos: regional and social characteristics used by Mexican Americans.* eds. E. Hernández-Chavez, A. Cohen, and A. Beltramo. Arlington, Va.: Center for Applied Linguistics.

Battison, R. 1978. *Lexical borrowing in American Sign Language.* Silver Spring, Md.: Linstok Press.

Ben-Zeev, S. 1977. The influence of bilingualism on cognitive strategy and cognitive development. *Child Development* 48:1009–1018.

Bergman, C. 1976. Interference vs. independent development in infant bilingualism. In *Bilingualism in the bicentennial and beyond,* ed. G. Keller, R. Teschner, and S. Viera. New York: Bilingual Press/Editorial Bilingüe.

Berke, L. 1980. Attitudes of deaf high school students towards American Sign Language. In *Proceedings of the Second National Symposium on Sign Language Research and Teaching,* eds. F. Caccamise and D. Hicks. Silver Spring, Md.: National Association of the Deaf.

Berry, J. 1971. The Madina project, Ghana. In *Language use and social change,* ed. W. Whiteley. London: Oxford University Press.

Bilingual Education Act. 1981. Amendment to Title VII of the Elementary and Secondary Education Act of 1965. In *A compilation of federal education laws.* Washington, D.C.: U.S. Government Printing Office.

Blanco, G. 1978. The implementation of bilingual/bicultural education programs in the United States. In *Case studies in bilingual education,* ed. B. Spolsky and R. Cooper. Rowley, Mass.: Newbury House.

Bloomfield, L. 1933. *Language.* New York: Holt, Rinehart and Winston.

Blum, D. and S. Steptoe. 1980. The immigrants. *Wall Street Journal,* Sept. 17.

Bossard, J. 1945. The bilingual as a person: linguistic identification with status. *American Sociological Review* 10:699–709.

Bright, W. 1973. North American Indian language contact. In *Current trends in linguistics,* vol. 10, ed. T. Sebeok. The Hague: Mouton.

Bright, W., and J. Sherzer. 1976. Areal features in North American Indian languages. In *Variation and change in language,* ed. A. Dil. Stanford: Stanford University Press.

Brosnahan, L. 1963. Some historical cases of language imposition. In *Language in Africa,* ed. J. Spencer. Cambridge: Cambridge University Press.

Burling, R. 1978. Language development of a Garo and English speaking child. In *Second language acquisition,* ed. E. Hatch. Rowley, Mass.: Newbury House.

Bychowski, Z. 1919. Über die Restitution der nach einem Schädelschuss verlorenen Umgangssprache bei einem Polyglotten. *Monatschrift für Psychologie und Neurologie* 45:183–201.

Cancino, H., E. Rosansky, and J. Schumann. 1974. Testing hypothesis about second language acquisition: the copula and the negative in three subjects. *Working Papers in Bilingualism* 3:80–96.

———— 1975. The acquisition of the English auxiliary by native Spanish speakers. *TESOL Quarterly* 9:421–430.

Caramazza. A., and I. Brones. 1979. Lexical access in bilinguals. *Bulletin of the Psychonomic Society* 13:212–214.

Castro, R. 1976. Shifting the burden of bilingualism: the case for monolingual communities. *The Bilingual Review/La Revista Bilingüe* 3:3–28.

Celce-Murcia, M. 1978. The simultaneous acquisition of English and French in a two-year-old child. In *Second language acquisition,* ed. E. Hatch. Rowley, Mass.: Newbury House.

Child, I. 1943. *Italian or American? The second generation in conflict.* New Haven: Yale University Press.

Clyne, M. 1967. *Transference and triggering.* The Hague: Marinus Nijhoff.

———— 1972. *Perspectives on language contact.* Melbourne: Hawthorne Press.

———— 1978. Some (German-English) language contact phenomena at the discourse level. In *Advances in the study of societal multilingualism,* ed. J. Fishman. The Hague: Mouton.

———— 1980. Triggering and language processing. *Canadian Journal of Psychology/Revue Canadienne de Psychologie* 34:400–406.

Cofer, C. 1965. On some factors in the organizational characteristics of free recall. *American Psychologist* 20:261–272.

Comrie, B. 1979. Russian. In *Languages and their status,* ed. T. Shopen. Cambridge, Mass.: Winthrop.

Connors, K., N. Ménard, and R. Singh. 1978. Testing linguistic and functional competence in immersion programs. In *Aspects of bilingualism,* ed. M. Paradis. Columbia, S.C.: Hornbeam Press.

Cooper, R. 1971. Degree of bilingualism. In *Bilingualism in the barrio,* ed. J. Fishman, R. Cooper, and R. Ma. Bloomington: Indiana University Press.

———— 1978. The spread of Amharic in Ethiopia. In *Advances in the study of societal multilingualism,* ed. J. Fishman. The Hague: Mouton.

Corder, S. 1967. The significance of learners' errors. *International Review of Applied Linguistics* 5:161–170.

Coulter, K. 1968. Linguistic error-analysis of the spoken English of two native Russians. Master's thesis, University of Washington.

Covington, V. 1980. Problems of acculturation into the deaf community. *Sign Language Studies* 28:267–285.

Cummins, J. 1978. The cognitive development of children in immersion programs. *Canadian Modern Language Review* 34:855–883.

———— 1980. Theoretical underpinnings of French immersion. Paper presented to the Immersion '80 Conference, Fredericton, New Brunswick, Canada.

Cummins, J., and M. Gulutsan. 1974. Some effects of bilingualism on cognitive functioning. In *Bilingualism, biculturalism and education,* ed. S. Carey. Edmonton: University of Alberta Printing Department.

Curtiss, S. 1977. *Genie: a psycholinguistic study of a modern-day "wild child."* New York: Academic Press.

Dalrymple-Alford, E., and A. Aamiry. 1969. Language and category clustering in bilingual free recall. *Journal of Verbal Learning and Verbal Behavior* 8:762–768.

Danoff, M. 1978. *Evaluation of the impact of ESEA Title VII Spanish/English bilingual education programs.* Palo Alto: American Institutes for Research.

Darcy, N. 1946. The effect of bilingualism upon the measurement of the intelligence of children of preschool age. *Journal of Educational Psychology* 37:21–44.

Development Associates. 1977. *A study of state programs in bilingual education.* Washington, D.C.

Diebold, A. 1961. Incipient bilingualism. *Language* 37:97–112.

Diller, K. 1970. "Compound" and "coordinate" bilingualism: a conceptual artifact. *Word* 26:254–261.

Di Pietro. R. 1977. Code-switching as a verbal strategy among bilinguals. In *Current themes in linguistics: bilingualism, experimental linguistics and language typologies*, ed. F. Eckman. Washington, D.C.: Hemisphere Publishing.

Dommergues, J. Y., and H. Lane. 1976. On two independent sources of error in learning the syntax of a second language. *Language Learning* 26:111–123.

Dornic, S. 1978. The bilingual's performance: language dominance, stress and individual differences. In *Language interpretation and communication*, ed. D. Gerver and H. Sinaiko. New York: Plenum Press.

——— 1979. Information processing in bilinguals: some selected issues. *Psychological Research* 40:329–348.

Doyle, A., M. Champagne, and N. Segalowitz. 1978. Some issues in the assessment of linguistic consequences of early bilingualism. In *Aspects of bilingualism*, ed. M. Paradis. Columbia, S.C.: Hornbeam Press.

Dulay, H., and M. Burt. 1974. Errors and strategies in child second language acquisition. *TESOL Quarterly* 8:129–138.

——— 1979. Bilingual education: a close look at its effects. *NCBE Focus* 1:1–4.

Eisenstein, M. 1980. Childhood bilingualism and adult language learning aptitude. *International Review of Applied Psychology* 29:159–172.

Eliás-Olivares, L. 1976. Ways of speaking in a Chicano community: a sociolinguistic approach. Ph.D. dissertation, University of Texas.

Epstein, I. 1915. *La pensée et la polyglossie.* Lausanne: Payot.

Ervin, S. 1964. Language and TAT content in bilinguals. *Journal of Abnormal and Social Psychology* 68:500–507.

Ervin, S., and C. Osgood. 1954. Second language learning and bilingualism. *Journal of Abnormal and Social Psychology* 49 (suppl.):139–146.

Ervin-Tripp, S. 1968. An analysis of the interaction of language, topic and listener. In *Readings in the sociology of language*, ed. J. Fishman. The Hague: Mouton.

——— 1970. Structure and process in language acquisition. *Monograph Series on Language and Linguistics* 23:313–344.

——— 1973. Identification and bilingualism. In *Language acquisition and communicative choice*, ed. A. Dil. Stanford: Stanford University Press.

——— 1974. Is second language learning like the first? *TESOL Quarterly* 8:111–127.

Espinosa, A. 1975. Speech mixture in New Mexico: the influence of the English language on New Mexican Spanish. In *El lenguaje de los Chicanos*, ed. E. Hernandez-Chavez, A. Cohen, and A. Beltramo. Arlington, Va.: Center for Applied Linguistics.

Etiemble. 1964. *Parlez-vous franglais?* Paris: Gallimard.

Fantini, A. 1978. Bilingual behavior and social cues: case studies of two bilingual children. In *Aspects of bilingualism*, ed. M. Paradis. Columbia, S.C.: Hornbeam Press, 1978.

——— 1979. Transference in child speech: a sociolinguistic phenomenon. Paper presented at the Delaware Symposium on Language Studies, University of Delaware, Newark, Del.

Ferguson, C. 1971. Diglossia. In *Language structure and language use*, ed. A. Dil. Stanford: Stanford University Press.

Ferguson, C., C. Houghton, and M. Wells. 1977. Bilingual education: an international perspective. In *Frontiers of bilingual education,* ed. B. Spolsky and R. Cooper. Rowley, Mass.: Newbury House.

Fillmore, L. 1976. The second time around: cognitive and social strategies in second-language acquisition. Ph.D. dissertation, Stanford University.

Fishman, J. 1965a. Who speaks what language to whom and when? *Linguistique* 2:67-88.

―――― 1965b. The status and prospects of bilingualism in the United States. *Modern Language Journal* 49:143-155.

―――― 1966. *Language loyalty in the United States.* The Hague: Mouton.

―――― 1971. Sociolinguistic perspective on the study of bilingualism. In *Bilingualism in the barrio,* ed. J. Fishman, R. Cooper, and R. Ma. Bloomington: Indiana University Press.

―――― 1972a. Language maintenance in a supra-ethnic age. In *Language in sociocultural change,* ed. A. Dil. Stanford: Stanford University Press.

―――― 1972b. *Language and nationalism.* Rowley, Mass.: Newbury House.

―――― 1980. Language maintenance. In *Harvard encyclopedia of American ethnic groups,* ed. S. Thernstrom. Cambridge, Mass.: Harvard University Press.

―――― 1981. Language maintenance, the "ethnic revival" and diglossia in the U.S.A. *La Linguistique,* in press.

Fishman, J., R. Cooper, and R. Ma. 1971. *Bilingualism in the barrio.* Bloomington: Indiana University Press.

Fishman, J., and J. Hofman. 1966. Mother tongue and nativity in the American population. In *Language loyalty in the United States,* ed. J. Fishman. The Hague: Mouton.

Fishman, J., and V. Nahirny. 1966. The ethnic group school and mother tongue maintenance. In *Language loyalty in the United States,* ed. J. Fishman. The Hague: Mouton.

Forum. 1979. Study finds 3.6 million school age children are limited English proficient. *Forum* 2(6):1-2.

Frith, M. 1978. Interlanguage theory: implications for the classroom. *McGill Journal of Education* 13:155-165.

Gaarder, A. 1977. Language maintenance or language shift. In *Bilingualism in early childhood,* ed. W. Mackey and T. Andersson. Rowley, Mass.: Newbury House.

Gal, S. 1979. *Language shift: social determinants of linguistic change in bilingual Austria.* New York: Academic Press.

Gallagher, C. 1968. North African problems and prospects: language and identity. In *Language problems in developing nations,* eds. J. Fishman, C. Ferguson, and J. Das Gupta. New York: Wiley.

Galloway, L. 1978a. Language impairment and recovery in polyglot aphasia: a case study of a hepta-lingual. In *Aspects of bilingualism,* ed. M. Paradis. Columbia, S.C.: Hornbeam Press.

―――― 1978b. Cerebral organization in bilingualism and second language. Paper presented to the Second Language Research Forum, University of Southern California.

―――― 1980. The cerebral organization of language in bilinguals and second language learners. Ph.D. dissertation, University of California at Los Angeles.

Gardner, R., and W. Lambert. 1972. *Attitudes and motivation in second language learning.* Rowley, Mass.: Newbury House.

Genesee, F. 1978. Is there an optimal age for starting second language instruction? *McGill Journal of Education* 13:145–154.

———— 1978–79. Scholastic effects of French immersion: an overview after ten years. *Interchange* 9:20–29.

———— 1980a. The social psychological significance of code-switching for children. Unpublished manuscript, Department of Psychology, McGill University.

———— 1980b. Social psychological consequences of bilingualism. Unpublished manuscript, Department of Psychology, McGill University.

Genesee, F., and R. Bourhis. 1981. Language variation in social interaction: the importance of situational and interactional context. Unpublished manuscript, Department of Psychology, McGill University.

Genesee, F., J. Hamers, W. Lambert, L. Mononen, M. Seitz, and R. Starck. 1978. Language processing in bilinguals. *Brain and Language* 5:1–12.

Genishi, C. 1976. Rules for code-switching in young Spanish-English speakers: an exploratory study of language socialization. Ph.D. dissertation, University of California, Berkeley.

Gentilhomme, Y. 1980. Expérience autobiographique d'un sujet bilingue Russe-Français: prolégomènes théoriques. Paper presented to the Third International Conference on Languages in Contact. Justus-Liebig-Universität, Giessen, West Germany.

Giles, H., D. Taylor, and R. Bourhis. 1973. Toward a theory of interpersonal accommodation through language: Some Canadian data. *Language in Society* 2:117–192.

Giles, H., R. Bourhis, and D. Taylor. 1977. Towards a theory of language in ethnic group relations. In *Language, ethnicity and intergroup relations,* ed. H. Giles. London: Academic Press.

Gingràs, R. 1974. Problems in the description of Spanish-English intrasentential code-switching. In *Southwest areal linguistics,* ed. G. Bills. San Diego: Institute for Cultural Pluralism.

Glazer, N. 1966. The process and problems of language maintenance: an integrative review. In *Language loyalty in the United States,* ed. J. Fishman. The Hague: Mouton.

Goldberg, M. 1941. A qualification of the marginal man theory. *American Sociological Review* 6:52–58.

Gordon, D. and R. Zatorre. 1981. A right-ear advantage for dichotic listening in bilingual children. *Brain and Language* 13:389–396.

Gordon, H. 1980. Cerebral organization in bilinguals. I. Lateralization. *Brain and Language* 9:255–268.

Gray, T. 1978. The AIR report: another view. *Forum* 1:1–2.

Gumperz, J. 1970. Verbal strategies in multilingual communication. In *Bilingualism and language contact,* ed. J. Alatis. Washington: Georgetown University Press.

———— 1971. *Language in social groups.* Stanford: Stanford University Press.

———— 1976a. Social network and language shift. Unpublished manuscript, University of California, Berkeley.

———— 1976b. The sociolinguistic significance of conversational code-switching. In *Papers on language and context,* ed. J. Cook-Gumperz and J. Gumperz. Working papers of the language behavior research laboratory, University of California, Berkeley.

Gumperz, J., and E. Hernández-Chavez. 1970. Cognitive aspects of bilingual education. In *Language use and social change,* ed. W. Whitely. London: Oxford University Press.

Gumperz, J. and E. Hernández-Chavez. 1978. Bilingualism, bidialectalism and classroom interaction. In *A pluralistic nation,* ed. M. Lourie and N. Conklin. Rowley, Mass.: Newbury House.

Hakuta, K. 1974. Prefabricated patterns and the emergence of structure in second language acquisition. *Language Learning* 24:287–297.

Hakuta, K., and H. Cancino. 1977. Trends in second language acquisition research. *Harvard Educational Review* 47:294–316.

Hale, B. 1978. Spotlight on a Navajo bilingual bicultural education program. *Forum* 1:3.

Hamers, J., and W. Lambert. 1972. Bilingual interdependencies in auditory perception. *Journal of Verbal Learning and Verbal Behavior* 11:303–310.

Han, M. 1978. Desirability of bilingual education in the Japanese-American community. In *Bilingual schooling in the United States,* ed. T. Andersson and M. Boyer. Austin, Texas: National Educational Laboratory Publishers.

Harris, B., and B. Sherwood. 1978. Translating as an innate skill. In *Language interpretation and communication,* ed. D. Gerver and H. Sinaiko. New York: Plenum Press.

Harvard encyclopedia of American ethnic groups. 1980. Ed. S. Thernstrom. Cambridge, Mass.: Harvard University Press.

Hasselmo, N. 1969. How can we measure the effects which one language may have on the other in the speech of bilinguals? In *Description and measurement of bilingualism,* ed. L. Kelly. Toronto: University of Toronto Press.

———— 1970. Code-switching and modes of speaking. In *Texas studies in bilingualism,* ed. G. Gilbert. Berlin: Walter de Gruyter.

Haugen, E. 1956. *Bilingualism in the Americas: a bibliography and research guide.* Alabama: University of Alabama Press.

———— 1961. The bilingual individual. In *Psycholinguistics,* ed. S. Saporta. New York: Holt, Rinehart and Winston.

———— 1966. Semi-communication: the language gap in Scandinavia. *Sociological Enquiry* 36:280–297.

———— 1969. *The Norwegian language in America: a study in bilingual behavior.* Bloomington: Indiana University Press.

———— 1972. The stigmata of bilingualism. In *The ecology of language,* ed. A. Dil. Stanford: Stanford University Press.

———— 1973a. Bilingualism, language contact and immigrant languages in the United States: A research report 1956–1970. In *Current trends in linguistics,* vol. 10, ed. T. Sebeok. The Hague: Mouton.

———— 1973b. The curse of Babel. *Daedalus* 102:47–57.

———— 1977. Norm and deviation in bilingual communities. In *Bilingualism,* ed. P. Hornby. New York: Academic Press.

Heye, J. 1975. *A sociolinguistic investigation of multilingualism in the canton of Ticino, Switzerland.* The Hague: Mouton.

———— 1979. Bilingualism and language maintenance in two communities in Santa Catarina, Brazil. In *Language and society,* ed. W. McCormack and S. Wurm. The Hague: Mouton.

Higa, M. 1979. Sociolinguistic aspects of word-borrowing. In *Sociolinguistic studies in language contact,* ed. W. Mackey and J. Ornstein. The Hague: Mouton.

Higgins, J. 1976. *The eagle has landed.* New York: Bantam.

Hobart, C., and C. Brant. 1966. Eskimo education, Danish and Canadian: a comparison. *Canadian Review of Sociology and Anthropology* 3:47–66.

Hoffman, G. 1971. Puerto Ricans in New York: a language-related ethnographic summary. In *Bilingualism in the barrio,* ed. J. Fishman, R. Cooper, and R. Ma. Bloomington: Indiana University Press.

Ianco-Worrall, A. 1972. Bilingualism and cognitive development. *Child Development* 43:1390–1400.

Imedadze, N., and D. Uznadze. 1978. On the psychological nature of child speech formation under condition of exposure of two languages. In *Second language acquisition,* ed. E. Hatch. Rowley, Mass.: Newbury House.

Jakobovits, L. 1969. Commentary on "How can one measure the extent of a person's bilingual proficiency?" In *Description and measurement of bilingualism,* ed. L. Kelly. Toronto: University of Toronto Press.

Jakobovits, L., and W. Lambert. 1961. Semantic satiation among bilinguals. *Journal of Experimental Psychology* 62:576–582.

Jespersen, O. 1922. *Language.* London: George Allen and Unwin.

———— 1923. *Growth and structure of the English language.* New York: Appleton-Century.

John, A. 1980. "Approximative languages" and language learning situations. *International Review of Applied Linguistics* 18:209–216.

Jones, W., and W. Stewart. 1951. Bilingualism and verbal intelligence. *British Journal of Psychology* 4:3–8.

Kahane, H., and Kahane, R. 1979. Decline and survival of Western prestige languages. *Language* 55:183–198.

Karl, F. 1979. *Joseph Conrad.* New York: Farrar, Straus and Giroux.

Kegl, J. 1975. Some observations on bilingualism: a look at some data from Slovene-English bilinguals. Master's thesis, Brown University.

Keller-Cohen, D. 1980. A view of child second language learning: using experience with language to learn language. Paper presented to the Fifth Annual Conference on Language Development, Boston University.

Kelley, V. 1936. Reading abilities of Spanish and English speaking pupils. *Journal of Educational Research* 29:209–211.

Khubchandani, L. 1978. Distribution of contact languages in India. In *Advances in the study of societal multilingualism,* ed. J. Fishman. The Hague: Mouton.

Kinzel, P. 1964. *Lexical and grammatical interference in the speech of a bilingual child.* Seattle: University of Washington Press.

Kjolseth, R. 1972. Bilingual education programs in the United States: for assimilation or pluralism? In *The language education of minority children,* ed. B. Spolsky. Rowley, Mass.: Newbury House.

Klein, W. and N. Dittmar. 1979. *Developing grammars: the acquisition of German syntax by foreign workers.* Berlin: Springer-Verlag.

Klima, E., and U. Bellugi. 1980. *The signs of language.* Cambridge, Mass.: Harvard University Press.

Kloss, H. 1966. German-American language maintenance efforts. In *Language loyalty in the United States,* ed. J. Fishman. The Hague: Mouton.

———— 1967. Bilingualism and nationalism. *Journal of Social Issues* 23:39–47.

———— 1968. Notes concerning a language-nation typology. In *Language problems in developing nations,* ed. J. Fishman, C. Ferguson, and J. Das Gupta. New York: Wiley.

———— 1977. *The American bilingual tradition*. Rowley, Mass.: Newbury House.

Kolers, P. 1963. Interlingual word associations. *Journal of Verbal Learning and Verbal Behavior* 2:291–300.

———— 1966a. Interlingual facilitation of short-term memory. *Journal of Verbal Learning and Verbal Behavior* 5:314–319.

———— 1966b. Reading and talking bilingually. *American Journal of Psychology* 3:357–376.

———— 1968. Bilingualism and information processing. *Scientific American* 218:78–89.

———— 1978. On the representations of experience. In *Language interpretation and communication*, ed. D. Gerver and H. Sinaiko. New York: Plenum Press.

Kolers, P., and E. Gonzalez. 1980. Memory for words, synonyms and translations. *Journal of Experimental Psychology: Human Learning and Memory* 6:53–65.

Krashen, S. 1973. Lateralization, language learning and the critical period: some new evidence. *Language Learning* 23:63–74.

———— 1978. The monitor model for second language acquisition. In *Second language acquisition and foreign language teaching*, ed. R. Gingras. Arlington, Va.: Center for Applied Linguistics.

Lambert, W. 1955. Measurement of the linguistic dominance of bilinguals. *Journal of Abnormal and Social Psychology* 50:197–200.

———— 1972. Psychological studies of the interdependencies of the bilingual's two languages. In *Language, psychology and culture: Essays by W. E. Lambert*, ed. A. Dil. Stanford: Stanford University Press.

———— 1977. Culture and language as factors in learning and education. In *Current themes in linguistics: bilingualism, experimental linguistics and language typologies*, ed. F. Eckman. Washington, D.C.: Hemisphere Publishing.

———— 1978. Psychological approaches to bilingualism, translation and interpretation. In *Language interpretation and communication*, ed. D. Gerver and H. Sinaiko. New York: Plenum Press.

———— 1980. The two faces of bilingual education. *Focus* 3:1–4.

Lambert, W., H. Frankel, and G. Tucker. 1966. Judging personality through speech: a French-Canadian example. *Journal of Communication* 16:30–321.

Lambert, W., J. Hamers, and N. Frasure-Smith. 1979. *Child rearing values: a cross-national study*. New York: Praeger Publications.

Lambert, W., J. Havelka, and C. Crosby. 1958. The influence of language acquisition contexts on bilingualism. *Journal of Abnormal and Social Psychology* 56:239–244.

Lambert, W., J. Havelka, and R. Gardner. 1959. Linguistic manifestations of bilingualism. *American Journal of Psychology* 72:77–82.

Lambert, W., R. Hodgson, R. Gardner, and S. Fillenbaum. 1960. Evaluational reactions to spoken languages. *Journal of Abnormal and Social Psychology* 60:44–51.

Lambert, W., and N. Moore. 1966. Word-association responses: comparison of American and French monolinguals with Canadian monolinguals and bilinguals. *Journal of Personality and Social Psychology* 3:313–320.

Lambert, W., and G. Tucker. 1972. *Bilingual education of children: the St. Lambert experiment*. Rowley, Mass.: Newbury House.

Lance, D. 1975. Spanish-English code switching. In *El lenguaje de los Chicanos: regional and social characteristics used by Mexican Americans,* ed. E. Hernandez-Chavez, A. Cohen, and A. Bertramo. Arlington, Va.: Center for Applied Linguistics.

———— 1979. Spanish-English bilingualism in the American Southwest. In *Sociolinguistic studies in language contact,* ed. W. Mackey and J. Ornstein. The Hague: Mouton.

Lane, H. 1976. *The wild boy of Aveyron.* Cambridge, Mass.: Harvard University Press.

———— 1980. A chronology of the oppression of sign language in France and the United States. In *Recent perspectives on American Sign Language,* ed. H. Lane and F. Grosjean. Hillsdale, N.J.: Lawrence Erlbaum Associates.

Lane, H., and F. Grosjean. 1980. *Recent perspectives on American Sign Language.* Hillsdale, N.J.: Lawrence Erlbaum Associates.

Lawton, D. 1979. Code-shifting in Puerto Rican Spanish/English. *Linguistics* 17:257–265.

Le Carré, J. 1980. *Tinker, tailor, soldier, spy.* New York: Bantam.

Lecours, A., and Y. Joanette. 1980. Linguistic and other psychological aspects of paroxysmal aphasia. *Brain and Language* 10:1–23.

Lemaire, H. 1966. Franco-American effort on behalf of the French language in New England. In *Language loyalty in the United States,* ed. J. Fishman. The Hague: Mouton.

Lenneberg, E. 1967. *Biological foundations of language.* New York: Wiley.

Leopold, W. 1970. *Speech development of a bilingual child,* vols. 1–4. New York: AMS Press.

———— 1978. A child's learning of two languages. In *Second language acquisition,* ed. E. Hatch. Rowley, Mass.: Newbury House.

Levy, J. 1975. *Cesar Chavez.* New York: W. W. Norton.

Lewis, E. G. 1972. *Multilingualism in the Soviet Union.* The Hague: Mouton.

———— 1976. Bilingualism and bilingual education: the ancient world to the renaissance. In *Bilingual education: an international sociological perspective,* ed. J. Fishman. Rowley, Mass.: Newbury House.

———— 1978a. Bilingual education and social change in the Soviet Union. In *Case studies in bilingual education,* ed. B. Spolsky and R. Cooper. Rowley, Mass.: Newbury House.

———— 1978b. Bilingualism in education in Wales. In *Case studies in bilingual education,* ed. B. Spolsky and R. Cooper. Rowley, Mass.: Newbury House.

———— 1979. A comparative study of language contact: the influence of demographic factors in Wales and the Soviet Union. In *Language and society,* ed. W. McCormack and S. Wurm. The Hague: Mouton.

Lewis, R. 1974. Yatong Ok'shi' Have a happy day. Opening conference address. In *1973 Proceedings of the National Indian Bilingual Education Conference.* Albuquerque, N.M.: U.S. Government Printing Office.

L'Hermitte, R., H. Hécaen, J. Dubois, A. Culioli, and A. Tabouret-Keller. 1966. Le problème de l'aphasie des polyglottes: remarques sur quelques observations. *Neuropsychologia* 4:315–329.

Lipski, J. 1978. Code-switching and the problem of bilingual competence. In *Aspects of bilingualism,* ed. M. Paradis. Columbia, S.C.: Hornbeam Press.

López, M. 1977. Bilingual memory research: implications for bilingual education. In *Chicano psychology,* ed. J. Martinez. New York: Academic Press.

Lorwin, V. 1972. Linguistic pluralism and political tension in modern Belgium. In *Advances in the sociology of language*, vol. 2, ed. J. Fishman. The Hague: Mouton.

Lozano, A. 1980. Tracing the Spanish language. *Agenda* 10:32–38.

Ma, R., and E. Herasimchuk. 1971. The linguistic dimensions of a bilingual neighborhood. In *Bilingualism in the barrio*, ed. J. Fishman, R. Cooper, and R. Ma. Bloomington: Indiana University Press.

Mackey, W. 1967. *Bilingualism as a world problem*. Montreal: Harvest House.

—— 1968. The description of bilingualism. In *Readings in the sociology of language*, ed. J. Fishman. The Hague: Mouton.

—— 1970. Interference, integration and the synchronic fallacy. In *Bilingualism and language contact*, ed. J. Alatis. Washington, D.C.: Georgetown University Press.

—— 1972a. A typology of bilingual education. In *Advances in the sociology of language*, vol. 2, ed. J. Fishman. The Hague: Mouton.

—— 1972b. Dialinguistic identification. In *Studies for Einar Haugen*, ed. E. Firchow, K. Grimstad, and W. O'Neil. The Hague: Mouton.

—— 1976. *Bilinguisme et contact des langues*. Paris: Editions Klincksiek.

—— 1977. The evaluation of bilingual education. In *Frontiers of bilingual education*, ed. B. Spolsky and R. Cooper. Rowley, Mass.: Newbury House.

Mackey, W., and V. Beebe. 1977. *Bilingual schools for a bicultural community: Miami's adaptation to the Cuban refugees*. Rowley, Mass.: Newbury House.

MacNab, G. 1979. Cognition and bilingualism: a reanalysis of studies. *Linguistics* 17:231–255.

Macnamara, J. 1966. *Bilingualism and primary education*. Edinburgh: Edinburgh University Press.

—— 1967a. The bilingual's linguistic performance: a psychological overview. *Journal of Social Issues* 23:59–77.

—— 1967b. The linguistic independence of bilinguals. *Journal of Verbal Learning and Verbal Behavior* 6:729–736.

—— 1969. How can one measure the extent of a person's bilingual proficiency? In *Description and measurement of bilingualism*, ed. L. Kelly. Toronto: University of Toronto Press.

—— 1970. Bilingualism and thought. In *Bilingualism and language contact*, ed. J. Alatis. Washington, D.C.: Georgetown University Press.

—— 1974. The generalizability of results of studies of bilingual education. In *Bilingualism, biculturalism and education*, ed. S. Carey. Edmonton: University of Alberta Printing Department.

Macnamara, J., M. Krauthammer, and M. Bolgar. 1968. Language switching in bilinguals as a function of stimulus and response uncertainty. *Journal of Experimental Psychology* 78:208–215.

Macnamara, J., and S. Kushnir. 1971. Linguistic independence of bilinguals: the input switch. *Journal of Verbal Learning and Verbal Behavior* 10:480–487.

Mägiste, E. 1979. The competing language systems of the multilingual: a developmental study of decoding and encoding processes. *Journal of Verbal Learning and Verbal Behavior* 18:79–89.

Makkai, V. 1978. Bilingual phonology: systematic or autonomous? In *Aspects of bilingualism*, ed. M. Paradis. Columbia, S.C.: Hornbeam Press.

Malherbe, E. 1969. Comments on "How and when do persons become bilingual?" In *Description and measurement of bilingualism*, ed. L. Kelly. Toronto: University of Toronto Press.

MacLaughlin, B. 1978. *Second-language acquisition in childhood.* Hillsdale, N.J.: Lawrence Erlbaum Associates.

McClure, E. 1977. Aspects of code-switching in the discourse of bilingual Mexican-American children. Technical report no. 44. Center for the Study of Reading, University of Illinois at Urbana-Champaign.

Meisel, J., H. Clahsen, and M. Pienemann. 1979. On determining developmental stages in natural second language acquisition. *Wüppertaler Arbeitspapiere zur Sprachwissenschaft* 2:1–53.

Messner, R. 1981. I climbed Everest alone . . . at my limit. *National Geographic* 160:552–566.

Mikeš, R. 1967. Acquisition des catégories grammaticales dans le langage de l'enfant. *Enfance* 20:289–298.

Milon, J. 1974. The development of negation in English by a second language learner. *TESOL Quarterly* 8:137–143.

Minkowski, M. 1927. Klinischer Beitrag zur Aphasie bei Polyglotten, Speziell im Hinblick aufs Schweizerdeutsche. *Schweizer Archiv für Neurologie und Psychiatrie* 21:43–72.

———— 1928. Sur un cas d'aphasie chez un polyglotte. *Revue Neurologique* 49:361–366.

———— 1963. On aphasia in polyglots. In *Problems of dynamic neurology*, ed. L. Halpern. Jerusalem: Department of Nervous Diseases, Rothschild Hadassah University Hospital and Hebrew University Hadassah Medical School.

Mkilifi, M. 1978. Triglossia and Swahili-English bilingualism in Tanzania. In *Advances in the study of societal multilingualism*, ed. J. Fishman. The Hague: Mouton.

Morales-Carrión, A. 1980. Reflecting on common Hispanic roots. *Agenda* 10:28–31.

Mougeon, R., M. Bélanger, and M. Canale. 1978. Le rôle de l'interférence dans l'emploi des prépositions en français et en anglais par des jeunes Franco-Ontariens bilingues. In *Aspects of bilingualism*, ed. M. Paradis. Columbia, S.C.: Hornbeam Press.

Mougeon, R., and R. Hébrard. 1975. Acquisition et maîtrise de l'anglais par les jeunes bilingues de Welland. Franco-Ontarian Section, Oise, Working Paper.

Mulford, R., and B. Hecht. 1979. Learning to speak without an accent: acquisition of a second language phonology. Paper presented to the Fourth Annual Conference on Language Development, Boston University.

Muthiani, J. 1979. Sociopsychological bases of language choice and use: the case of Swahili vernaculars and English in Kenya. In *Language and society*, ed. W. McCormack and S. Wurm. The Hague: Mouton.

Myers Scotton, C. 1978. Language in East Africa: linguistic patterns and political ideologies. In *Advances in the study of societal multilingualism*, ed. J. Fishman. The Hague: Mouton.

Namias, J. 1978. *First generation.* Boston: Beacon Press.

National Center for Education Statistics, 1978a. Geographic distribution, nativity and age distribution of language minorities in the United States: Spring 1976. U.S. Department of Health, Education and Welfare, 78 B-5.

———— 1978b. Place of birth and language characteristics of persons of Hispanic origin in the United States: Spring 1976. U.S. Department of Health, Education and Welfare, 78 B-6.

———— 1979. Birthplace and language characteristics of persons of Chinese, Japanese, Korean, Pilipino and Vietnamese origin in the United States. U.S. Department of Health, Education and Welfare, 79 B-12.

Nemser, W. 1971. Approximative systems of foreign language learners. *International Review of Applied Linguistics* 9:115–123.

Neufeld, G. 1973. The bilingual's lexical store. *Working Papers on Bilingualism* 1:35–65.

O'Barr, W. 1976. Language use and language policy in Tanzania: an overview. In *Language and politics,* ed. W. O'Barr and J. O'Barr. The Hague: Mouton.

Obler, L., and M. Albert, 1977. Influence of aging on recovery from aphasia in polyglots. *Brain and Language* 4:460–463.

———— 1978. A monitor system for bilingual language processing. In *Aspects of bilingualism,* ed. M. Paradis. Columbia, S.C.: Hornbeam Press.

Obler, L., M. Albert, and H. Gordon. 1975. Asymmetry of cerebral dominance in Hebrew-English bilinguals. Paper presented to the thirteenth annual meeting of the Academy of Aphasia, Victoria, British Columbia.

Ohannessian, S. 1972. The language problems of American Indian children. In *The language education of minority children,* ed. B. Spolsky. Rowley, Mass.: Newbury House.

Ojemann, G., and H. Whitaker. 1978. The bilingual brain. *Archives of Neurology* 35:409–412.

Oksaar, E. 1970. Zum Spracherwerb des Kindes in Zweisprachiger Umgebung. *Folia Linguistica* 4:330–358.

Olton, R. 1960. Semantic generalization between languages. Master's thesis, McGill University.

Oyama, S. 1976. A sensitive period for the acquisition of a non-native phonological system. *Journal of Psycholinguistic Research* 5:261–285.

Oyama, S. 1978. The sensitive period and comprehension of speech. *Working Papers on Bilingualism* 16:1–17.

Padilla, A. 1977. Bilingual schools: gateways to integration or roads to separation. *The Bilingual Review/La Revista Bilingüe* 4:52–67.

Padilla, A., and E. Liebman. 1975. Language acquisition in the bilingual child. *The Bilingual Review/La Revista Bilingüe* 1–2:34–55.

Pandit, P. 1975. The linguistic survey of India-perspectives on language use. In *Language surveys in developing nations,* ed. O. Ohannessian, C. Ferguson, and E. Polomé. Arlington, Va.: Center for Applied Linguistics.

Pap, L. 1949. *Portuguese-American speech: an outline of speech conditions among Portuguese immigrants in New England and elsewhere in the United States.* New York: King's Crown Press.

———— 1979. Language attitudes and minority status. In *Sociolinguistic studies in language contact,* ed. W. Mackey and J. Ornstein. The Hague: Mouton.

Paradis, M. 1977. Bilingualism and aphasia. In *Studies in neurolinguistics,* vol. 3, ed. H. Whitaker and H. Whitaker. New York: Academic Press.

———— 1978. Bilingual linguistic memory: neurolinguistic considerations. Paper presented to the Linguistic Society of America, Boston.

———— 1980a. Language and thought in bilinguals. In *The sixth LACUS forum.* Columbia, S.C.: Hornbeam Press.

―――― 1980b. Contributions of neurolinguistics to the theory of bilingualism. In *Applications of linguistic theory in the human sciences.* Department of Linguistics, Michigan State University.

―――― 1980c. The language switch in bilinguals: psycholinguistic and neurolinguistic perspectives. In *Languages in contact and conflict,* ed. P. Nelde. Wiesbaden: Franz Steiner Verlag.

―――― 1981. Neurolinguistic organization of a bilingual's two languages. In *The seventh LACUS forum,* ed. J. Copeland. Columbia, S.C.: Hornbeam Press.

Paradis, M., M.-C. Goldblum, and R. Abidi. 1981. Alternate antagonism with paradoxical translation behavior in two bilingual aphasic patients. *Brain and Language,* in press.

Paradis, M., and A. Lecours. 1979. L' Aphasie chez les bilingues et les polyglottes. In *L'Aphasie,* ed. A. Lecours and F. L'Hermitte. Paris: Flammarion.

Pascasio, E., and A. Hidalgo. 1979. How role relationships, domains and speech situations affect language use among bilinguals. In *Language and society,* ed. W. McCormack and S. Wurm. The Hague: Mouton.

Pavlovitch, M. 1920. *Le langage enfantin: acquisition du serbe et du français par un enfant serbe.* Paris: Champion.

Peal, E., and W. Lambert. 1962. The relation of bilingualism to intelligence. *Psychological Monographs* 76: Whole Number 546.

Penfield, W. 1959. The learning of languages. In *Speech and brain-mechanisms,* ed. W. Penfield and L. Roberts. Princeton: Princeton University Press.

Perreault, R. B. 1976. *One piece in the great American mosaic: the Franco-Americans of New England.* Lakeport, N.H.: André Paquette Associates.

Pfaff, C. 1979. Constraints on language mixing: intrasentential code-switching and borrowing in Spanish/English. *Language* 55:291–318.

Pfeiffer, A. 1975. Designing a bilingual curriculum. In *Proceedings of the first inter-American conference on bilingual education,* ed. R. Troike and N. Modiano. Arlington, Va.: Center for Applied Linguistics.

Pifer, A. 1979. *Bilingual education and the Hispanic challenge.* Reprinted from the 1979 Annual Report, Carnegie Corporation of New York.

Pitres, A. 1895. Etude sur l'aphasie chez les polyglottes. *Revue de Médecine* 15:873–899.

Poplack, S. 1978. Syntactic structure and social function of code-switching. *Centro de Estudios Puertorriqueños* Working Papers 2:1–32.

―――― 1979. "Sometimes I'll start a sentence in Spanish Y TERMINO EN ESPAÑOL": toward a typology of code-switching. *Centro de Estudios Puertorriqueños* Working Papers, 4:1–79.

Poplack, S. and A. Pousada. 1981. A comparative study of gender assignment to borrowed nouns. *Centro de Estudios Puertorriqueños Working Papers* 10:1–43.

President's commission on foreign language and international studies. 1979. *Strength through wisdom: a critique of U.S. capability.* Washington, D.C.: U.S. Government Printing Office.

Preston, M., and W. Lambert. 1969. Interlingual interference in a bilingual version of the Stroop color word task. *Journal of Verbal Learning and Verbal Behavior* 8:295–301.

Prinz, P., and E. Prinz. 1979. Simultaneous acquisition of ASL and spoken English (in a hearing child of a deaf mother and hearing father). *Sign Language Studies* 25:283–296.

Rabel-Heymann, L. 1978. But how does a bilingual feel? Reflections on linguistic attitudes of immigrant academics. In *Aspects of bilingualism*, ed. M. Paradis. Columbia, S.C.: Hornbeam Press.

Redlinger, W. 1976. A description of transference and code-switchng in Mexican-American English and Spanish. In *Bilingualism in the bicentennial and beyond*, ed. G. Keller, R. Teschner, and S. Viera. New York: Bilingual Press/Editorial Bilingüe.

Redlinger, W. 1978. Mothers' speech to children in bilingual Mexican American homes. *International Journal of the Sociology of Language* 17:73–82.

Redlinger, W., and T. Park. 1980. Language mixing in young bilinguals. *Journal of Child Language* 7:337–352.

Reyes, R. 1974. Studies in Chicano Spanish. Ph.D. dissertation, Harvard University.

Rhodes, N. 1980. Attitudes toward Guaraní and Spanish: a survey. *Linguistic Reporter* 22:4–5.

Ribot, T. 1881. *Les maladies de la mémoire*. Paris: G. Baillère.

Richards, J. 1972. Social factors, interlanguage and language learning. *Language Learning* 22:159–188.

Ronjat, J. 1913. *Le développement du langage observé chez un enfant bilingue*. Paris: Champion.

Rosen, L., and K. Gorwitz. 1980. New attention to American Indians. *American Demographics* 2:18–26.

Rosetti, A. 1945. Langue mixte et mélange des langues. *Acta Linguistica* 49:73–79.

Rubin, J. 1968. *National bilingualism in Paraguay*. The Hague: Mouton.

Saer, D. 1923. The effect of bilingualism on intelligence. *British Journal of Psychology* 14:25–38.

Saint-Jacques, B. 1976. *Aspects sociolinguistiques du bilinguisme Canadien*. Quebec: Centre International de Recherche sur le Bilinguisme.

Sankoff, D., and S. Poplack. 1980. A formal grammar for code-switching. *Centro de Estudios Puertorriqueños Working Papers* 8:1–55.

Saville, M., and R. Troike. 1971. *A handbook of bilingual education*. Washington: D.C.: T.E.S.O.L.

Sawyer, J. 1978. Passive and covert bilinguals: a hidden asset for a pluralistic society. In *The bilingual in a pluralistic society*, ed. H. Key, G. McCullough, and J. Sawyer. Long Beach: California State University.

Schmidt-Mackey, I. 1977. Language strategies of the bilingual family. In *Bilingualism in early childhood*, ed. W. Mackey and T. Andersson. Rowley, Mass.: Newbury House.

Schneider, S. 1976. *Revolution, reaction or reform*. New York: Las Americas.

Schumann, J. 1978. The acculturation model for second-language acquisition. In *Second language acquisition and foreign language teaching*, ed. R. Gingras. Arlington, Va.: Center for Applied Linguistics.

Schweda, N. 1980. Bilingual education and code-switching in Maine. *Linguistic Reporter* 23:12–13.

Scott, S. 1973. The relation of divergent thinking to bilingualism: cause or effect. Unpublished manuscript, Department of Psychology, McGill University.

Scotton, C. 1979. Codeswitching as a "safe choice" in choosing a lingua franca. In *Language and society*, ed. W. McCormack and S. Wurm. The Hague: Mouton.

Scotton, C., and W. Ury. 1977. Bilingual strategies: the social functions of code-switching. *Linguistics* 193:5–20.

Segalowitz, N. 1977. Psychological perspectives on bilingual education. In *Frontiers of bilingual education,* ed. B. Spolsky and R. Cooper. Rowley, Mass.: Newbury House.

Seliger, H. 1978. Implications of a multiple critical periods hypothesis for second language learning. In *Second language acquisition research,* ed. W. Ritchie. New York: Halsted Press.

Selinker, L. 1972. Interlanguage. *International Review of Applied Linguistics* 10:209–231.

Sheen, R. 1980. The importance of negative transfer in the speech of near bilinguals. *International Review of Applied Linguistics* 18:105–119.

Simon, W. 1969. Multilingualism: a comparative study. In *Studies in multilingualism,* ed. N. Anderson. Leiden: E. Brill.

Skutnabb-Kangas, T. 1981. Guest worker or immigrant—different ways of reproducing an underclass. *Journal of Multilingual and Multicultural Development* 2:89–115.

Skutnabb-Kangas, T., and P. Toukomaa. 1976. *Teaching migrant children's mother tongue and learning the language of the host country in the context of the socio-cultural situation of the migrant family.* Helsinki: Finnish National Commission for UNESCO.

Slobin, D. 1973. Cognitive prerequisites for the development of grammar. In *Studies of child language development,* ed. C. Ferguson and D. Slobin. New York: Holt, Rinehart and Winston.

Snow, C., and M. Hoefnagel-Hohle. 1978. The critical period for language acquisition: evidence from second language learning. *Child Development* 49:1114–1128.

Soares, C., and F. Grosjean. 1981. Left hemisphere language lateralization in bilinguals and monolinguals. *Perception and Psychophysics* 29:599–604.

Sorensen, A. 1967. Multilingualism in the North West Amazon. *American Anthropologist* 69:670–684.

Spolsky, B., ed. 1972. *The language education of minority children.* Rowley, Mass.: Newbury House.

———— 1978. American Indian bilingual education. In *Case studies in bilingual education,* ed. B. Spolsky and R. Cooper. Rowley, Mass.: Newbury House.

Sridhar, S., and K. Sridhar. 1980. The syntax and psycholinguistics of bilingual code-mixing. *Canadian Journal of Psychology/Revue Canadienne de Psychologie* 34:407–416.

Stokoe, W. 1978. *Sign language structure.* Silver Spring, Md.: Linstok Press.

Swain, M. 1972. Bilingualism as a first language. Ph.D. dissertation, University of California at Irvine.

———— 1974. Child bilingual language learning and linguistic interdependence. In *Bilingualism, biculturalism and education,* ed. S. Carey. Edmonton: University of Alberta Printing Department.

Swain, M., and J. Cummins. 1979. Bilingualism, cognitive functioning and education. *Language Teaching and Linguistics: Abstracts* 12:4–18.

Taylor, I. 1971. How are words from two languages organized in bilinguals' memory? *Canadian Journal of Psychology/Revue Canadienne de Psychologie* 25:228–240.

——— 1976. *Introduction to psycholinguistics.* New York: Holt, Rinehart and Winston.

Thiery, C. 1978. True bilingualism and second language learning. In *Language interpretation and communication,* ed. D. Gerver and H. Sinaiko. New York: Plenum Press.

Timm, L. 1975. Spanish-English code-switching: el porque y how-not-to. *Romance Philology* 28:473–482.

——— 1978. Code-switching in *War and Peace.* In *Aspects of bilingualism,* ed. M. Paradis. Columbia, S.C.: Hornbeam Press.

——— 1980. Bilingualism, diglossia and language shift in Brittany. *International Journal of the Sociology of Language* 25:29–41.

Tireman, L. 1955. Bilingual child and his reading vocabulary. *Elementary English* 32:33–35.

Troike, R. Research evidence for the effectiveness of bilingual education. *NABE Journal* 3:13–24.

Troike, R., and E. Perez. 1978. At the crossroads. In *Bilingual education: current perspectives. Synthesis.* Arlington, Va.: Center for Applied Linguistics.

Tulving, E., and V. Colotla. 1970. Free recall of trilingual lists. *Cognitive Psychology* 1:86–98.

Vaid, J. 1980. The form and functions of code-mixing in Indian films: the case of Hindi and English. *Indian Linguistics* 41:37–44.

Vaid, J., and F. Genesee. 1980. Neuropsychological approaches to bilingualism: a critical review. *Canadian Journal of Psychology/Revue Canadienne de Psychologie* 34:417–445.

Valdés Fallis, G. 1976. Social interaction and code-switching patterns: a case study of Spanish/English alternation. In *Bilingualism in the bicentennial and beyond,* ed. G. Keller, R. Teschner, and S. Viera. New York: Bilingual Press/Editorial Bilingüe.

Van der Plank, P. 1978. The assimilation and non-assimilation of European linguistic minorities: a sociological retrospection. In *Advances in the study of societal multilingualism,* ed. J. Fishman. The Hague: Mouton.

Veltman, C. 1979. *The assimilation of American language minorities: structure, pace and extent.* Washington: National Center for Education Statistics.

Véronique, D. 1980. La variabilité dans le français des travailleurs migrants maghrébins. *Champs Educatifs* 1:17–24.

Vihman, M. 1980. The acquisition of morphology by a bilingual child: a whole-word approach. Paper presented at the Fifth Annual Conference on Language Development, Boston University.

Vildomec, V. 1971. *Multilingualism.* Leyden: A. W. Sythoff.

Volterra, V., and R. Taeschner. 1978. The acquisition and development of language by bilingual children. *Journal of Child Language* 5:311–326.

Waggoner, D. 1980. European language minorities other than Spanish in the United States. Paper presented to the Ninth Annual International Bilingual-Bicultural Education Conference, Anaheim, Calif.

Wakefield, J., P. Bradley, B. Yom, and B. Doughtie. 1975. Language switching and constituent structure. *Language and Speech* 18:14–19.

Wald, B. 1974. Bilingualism. In *Annual Review of Anthropology,* ed. B. Siegel, A. Beals, and S. Tyler, 3:301–321.

Watamori, T., and S. Sasanuma. 1978. The recovery processes of two English-Japanese bilingual aphasics. *Brain and Language* 6:127–140.

Weinreich, U. 1968. *Languages in contact.* The Hague: Mouton.

Wilbur, R. 1979. *American Sign Language and sign systems.* Baltimore: University Park Press.

Woodward, J. 1980. Some sociolinguistic aspects of French and American Sign Languages. In *Recent perspectives on American Sign Language,* ed. H. Lane and F. Grosjean. Hillsdale, N.J.: Lawrence Erlbaum Associates.

Woolford, E. 1981. A formal model of bilingual code-switching. Unpublished manuscript, Department of Linguistics, Massachusetts Institute of Technology.

Zierer, E. 1977. Experiences in the bilingual education of a child of pre-school age. *International Review of Applied Linguistics* 15:144–149.

Acknowledgments

The author wishes to thank the following for permission to reproduce material in this book:

Beacon Press for excerpts from June Namias, *First Generation* (Boston: Beacon Press), 1978, copyright © 1978 by June Namias.

Bilingual Press/Editorial Bilingüe for excerpts from Ray Castro, "Shifting the Burden of Bilingualism: The Case for Monolingual Communities," *The Bilingual Review/La Revista Bilingüe* 3 (1976): 3–28; and for the poem by Pedro Ortiz Vasquez, "Quienes Somos," *The Bilingual Review/La Revista Bilingüe* 2 (1975): 293–294.

Editions Gallimard for excerpts from Etiemble, *Parlez-Vous Franglais?* copyright © 1964 Editions Gallimard.

Einar Haugen for excerpts from Haugen, *The Norwegian Language in America: A Study in Bilingual Behavior* (Bloomington, Ind.: Indiana University Press), 1969; and for excerpts from "The Stigmata of Bilingualism" in *The Ecology of Language*, ed. Anwar Dil (Stanford: Stanford University Press), 1972.

Judy Kegl for excerpts from "Some Observations on Bilingualism: A Look at Some Data from Slovene-English Bilinguals," master's thesis, Brown University, 1975.

Governor Robert Lewis for excerpts from "Yatong ok'shi! Have a Happy Day," conference address, in *1973 Proceedings of the National Indian Bilingual Education Conference* (Washington: U.S. Government Printing Office), 1974.

Lawrence Erlbaum Associates and the author for excerpts from Barry McLaughlin, *Second-Language Acquisition in Childhood* (Hillsdale, N.J.: Lawrence Erlbaum Associates), 1978.

Mouton Publishers for excerpts from Joshua Fishman, "The Historical and Social Contexts of an Inquiry into Language Maintenance Efforts" in *Language Loyalty in the United States*, ed. Joshua Fishman (The Hague: Mouton), 1966; and for the reproduction of chart 1 in Joan Rubin, *National Bilingualism in Paraguay* (The Hague: Mouton), 1968.

Robert B. Perreault for excerpts from Perrault, *One Piece in the Great American Mosaic: The Franco-Americans of New England* (Manchester, N.H.: L'Association Canado-Américaine), 1976.

National Clearinghouse for Bilingual Education (InterAmerica Research Associates) for excerpts from Wallace Lambert, "The Two Faces of Bilingual Education," *FOCUS* 3 (1980):1–4.

National Council of La Raza and the author for excerpts from Arturo Morales-Carrión, "Reflecting on Common Hispanic Roots," *Agenda* 10(2), 1980:28–31.

National Educational Laboratory Publishers for excerpts from "From Egypt to America: A Multilingual's Story" and from Mieko Han, "Desirability of Bilingual Education in the Japanese-American Community," both in *Bilingual Schooling in the United States*, ed. T. Andersson and M. Boyer (Austin, Tex.: National Educational Laboratory Publishers), 1978.

Newbury House Publishers (54 Warehouse Lane, Rowley, Mass., 01969) for excerpts from Theodore Andersson, "Philosophical Perspectives on Bilingual Education" in *Frontiers of Bilingual Education*, ed. Bernard Spolsky and Robert Cooper, 1977; and for excerpts from Rolf Kjolseth, "Bilingual Education Programs in the United States: For Assimilation or Pluralism?" in *The Language Education of Minority Children*, ed. Bernard Spolsky, 1972.

W. W. Norton and Co. for an excerpt from Jacques Levy, *Cesar Chavez* (New York: W. W. Norton), 1975.

University of Wisconsin Press for excerpts from Joshua Fishman, "The Status and Prospects of Bilingualism in the United States," *Modern Language Journal* (1965): 143–155.

Index

Accent, *see* Interference

Acculturation: of adult immigrants, 158–162; of children, 164, 209–211

Acquisition of two languages, simultaneous, 180–191; case study, 180–181; interference, 180, 187, 190–191; awareness of languages, 180, 187–188; patterns, 181; mixed-language stage, 181–184; compared with monolingual acquisition, 181–182; separation of two languages, 182–188; blends and compounds, 184; confusion and avoidance of words, 184–185. *See also* Childhood bilingualism; Language dominance; Language-person bond in children

Acquisition of two languages, successive, 192–198; age of, 192–193; psychosocial factors, 192–193; compared to first-language acquisition, 193–195; developmental and transfer positions, 193–195. *See also* Second-language acquisition, strategies in

Age, *see* Acquisition of two languages, successive; Childhood bilingualism

Ainu, 5

Albert, M.: bilingual brain, 258; recovery patterns in bilingual aphasics, 261–262; stage hypothesis, 264

Aphasia in bilinguals, 228–229, 258–263; case studies, 228–229, 258–261; recovery patterns, 259–261; right- and left-hemisphere lesions, 264

Assimilation, *see* Education, bilingual; Language maintenance and shift in United States; Language policy; Language shift; Minority languages

Attitudes: toward bilingualism in United States, 65–67; within and between language groups in Quebec, 118–120; toward languages, 120–123; evolution, 122–123; of monolinguals toward bilinguals, 274–275. *See also* Feelings about being bilingual; Language attitudes, consequences of

Barber, C.: on attitudes to speaking Yaqui, 127; language choice in Pascua, Ariz. 130, 134–135, 138, 141, 142; bilingual children, 176

Beckett, Samuel, 288

Belgium, 3, 13–15, 37–38; language groups, 13; language strife, 14–15

Bergman, C., on simultaneous language acquisition, 182–183

Biculturalism, 157–166; definition, 157; and bilingualism, 157–158; in adults, 158–162; level attained, 160–161; and